How to Transfer Computer Data and Settings

Other Computer Titles

by

Robert Penfold

BP470	Linux for Windows users
BP484	Easy PC Troubleshooting
BP495	Easy Windows Troubleshooting
BP503	Using Dreamweaver 4
BP504	Using Flash 5
BP507	Easy Internet Troubleshooting
BP518	Easy PC Peripherals Troubleshooting
BP521	Easy Windows XP Troubleshooting
BP523	Easy PC Interfacing
BP527	Using Flash MX
BP530	Using Dreamweaver MX
BP531	Easy PC Upgrading
BP534	Build Your Own PC
BP536	Using Photoshop 7
BP537	Digital Photography with your Computer
BP539	Easy PC Web Site Construction
BP540	Easy PC Security and Safety
BP541	Boost Your PC's Performance
BP542	Easy PC Case Modding
BP549	Easy PC Wi-Fi Networking
BP552	Build Your Own Media PC

How to Transfer Computer Data and Settings

Robert Penfold

Bernard Babani (publishing) Ltd
The Grampians
Shepherds Bush Road
London W6 7NF
England
www.babanibooks.com

Please note

Although every care has been taken with the production of this book to ensure that any projects, designs, modifications, and/or programs, etc., contained herewith, operate in a correct and safe manner and also that any components specified are normally available in Great Britain, the Publisher and Author do not accept responsibility in any way for the failure (including fault in design) of any projects, design, modification, or program to work correctly or to cause damage to any equipment that it may be connected to or used in conjunction with, or in respect of any other damage or injury that may be caused, nor do the Publishers accept responsibility in any way for the failure to obtain specified components.

Notice is also given that if any equipment that is still under warranty is modified in any way or used or connected with home-built equipment then that warranty may be void.

© 2005 BERNARD BABANI (publishing) LTD

First Published - April 2005

British Library Cataloguing in Publication Data

A catalogue record for this book is available from the British Library

ISBN 0 85934 556 4

Cover Design by Gregor Arthur

Printed and bound in Great Britain by Cox and Wyman

Preface

Life was much simpler in the early days of computing with a PC. Data and the operating system itself were usually stored on floppy discs, and moving data from one PC to another was simple. You simply used the data discs with whatever PC you happened to be using at the time. Sending data to someone usually meant sending them a copy of the relevant disc or discs. However, even in the early days of PC computing, some pioneering users managed to swap data via modems and ordinary telephone lines. Unfortunately, the reliability provided by these early modems was usually quite poor. Long and expensive telephone calls often produced unusable results.

Setting up a new PC to make it ready for use was also relatively simple. You booted the PC with one floppy disc, ran whatever application program you happened to need at the time from another disc. Even when hard discs became popular, installing the operating system and applications on to the hard disc usually took a matter of minutes. The time spent customising the PC to meet your exact requirements was not an issue, because little customisation was possible. If you did not like the way something worked it was just too bad!

Technology has moved on, and these advances have certainly provided PC users with real benefits. Computers are faster, easier to use, and most software is to some extent customisable. Advances in computing have produced some problems though. Being able to gradually customise your PC over a period of a year or two until it "fits like a glove" is clearly a big step forward from the old days. On the other hand, when you buy a new PC there is the problem of setting up the new computer to operate just like the old one. You might have made hundreds of changes since buying the old PC. The chances of remembering in detail all the changes and additions are probably quite slim. So are the chances of remembering how to implement every piece of customisation.

Swapping data between modern computers is quite simple in principle, but in practice it is often complicated by the sheer quantities of data involved. When I go out on a photographic trip I frequently come back with a gigabyte or two of data. While working on this book I will probably generate about 500 megabytes of data. The humble 1.55 megabyte floppy disc is of limited use in modern computing.

Fortunately, there are ways of transferring settings from one PC to another, and it is even be possible to transfer the entire system from an old PC to a new one. This minimises the need to manually set up a new PC, and can even eliminate this task altogether. Transferring large amounts of data to another PC is not too difficult provided you set about the task in the right way. The existing facilities of your PC system might be all that you need. This book tells you how to tackle the transfer of practically any PC settings or data.

Robert Penfold

Trademarks

Microsoft, Windows, Windows XP, Windows Me, Windows 98 and Windows 95 are either registered trademarks or trademarks of Microsoft Corporation.

All other brand and product names used in this book are recognised trademarks, or registered trademarks of their respective companies. There is no intent to use any trademarks generically and readers should investigate ownership of a trademark before using it for any purpose.

Contents

1
Basic data transfers 1

Size matters 1
Flash memory 2
Card reader 6
Speed 9
External drives 11
USB drives 12
Hard drives 13
External CD-RW 14
Making selections 15
Copy and Paste 22
XP and CD-Rs 25
CD burning software 30
Existing multisession 32
UDF reader 36
Points to remember 39

2
Networks and direct connection ... 41

Missing link 41
USB 42
Too many chiefs 42
Serial transfer 44
Parallel 45
Software 45
Naming 50
Properties 53
Ports 57
The BIOS 58
BIOS changes 60
Modes 61
Points to remember 63

3

Setting up a LAN 65

- **Proper networking** 65
- **Adding ports** 67
- **Blanking plate** 69
- **Alignment** 71
- **Shocking truth** 73
- **Wristbands** 74
- **Basic network** 76
- **Shared resources** 79
- **Internet sharing** 81
- **Microfilter** 83
- **Compatibility** 86
- **Network risks** 88
- **Security Center** 92
- **Points to remember** 93

4

Going wi-fi 95

- **Why wi-fi?** 95
- **Drawbacks** 96
- **Security** 98
- **Interference** 99
- **Standards** 100
- **Table 1** 101
- **Channels** 102
- **Wi-fi Alliance** 103
- **Bluetooth** 104
- **Piconet** 105
- **Channels** 106
- **Getting connected** 107
- **Speed** 109
- **PCI adapter** 111

Ad hoc 113
Extending range 115
Directional 116
Accelerators 117
Points to remember 119

5

Installation and security 121

Installation 121
Reading matters 122
Firmware 123
Setting up 124
Standalone 125
Settings 126
Security 128
WEP 130
WPA 132
802.11i 134
Other settings 135
Adapter installation 136
Control program 137
Sharing 142
Disc sharing 144
Naming 145
Network Setup Wizard 146
Sharing folders 149
Network Places 154
Printer sharing 161
Operating system 163
Printer installation 164
Default printer 169
Firmware upgrades 172
Points to remember 179

6

Transferring settings 181

- The easy way 181
- Transfer Wizard 182
- Outlook Express 183
- Getting started 184
- Decisions 191
- Making the transfer 194
- Address backup 198
- Finally 203
- Points to remember 205

7

Hard disc cloning 207

- Back to basics 207
- Hardware differences 208
- Copying methods 209
- Windows Backup 211
- Backup Wizard 212
- Restoring 217
- Advanced mode 226
- Alternatives 229
- Restoring 234
- Tidying up 241
- Driver installation 243
- Video settings 245
- Direct cloning 251
- Jumpers 254
- Minimalist cases 256
- Points to remember 259

8

Internet file swapping 261

FTP method 261
Up and down 262
FTP program 262
Downloading 265
Email transfer 268
Large inboxes 269
Filtering 269
Sending 271
Archiving 274
Attachment too large 277
Size matters 278
Reconstruction 280
Photo albums 281
Making an album 283
Resolution 285
Encryption 291
Simple text 294
Points to remember 297

Index 299

1

Basic data transfers

Size matters

In the early days of personal computing there were few difficulties if some files had to be transferred from one PC to another. Every PC was equipped with a floppy disc drive, and it was just a matter of copying the files to a floppy on one PC, and then copying the files from the floppy onto the hard disc of the second PC. Actually, in the very early days it was unusual for a PC to have a hard disc drive. Files were stored on numerous floppy discs, and any of these discs could be used in whatever computer you were using at the time. No copying was required unless you wished to have a separate copy for each PC.

The floppy discs originally used with PCs had a capacity of 360 kilobytes, or 0.36 megabytes. This may seem laughable by today's standards, but you have to bear in mind that most files in that era were simple text types or something similarly basic. A large file would be perhaps 100 kilobytes or so and would easily fit onto a floppy disc. As new applications were found for computers, the data files tended to become more complex and much bigger. Later versions of the floppy disc had capacities of 720 kilobytes, 1.2 megabytes, and 1.44 megabytes, the latter being the size still in common use today.

Unfortunately, floppy disc technology did not keep pace with computing in general, and the 1.44 megabyte discs soon became inadequate for many applications. There were various attempts to introduce high capacity floppy discs, such as the 2.88 megabyte type that was designed to replace the 1.44 megabyte discs. However, the "super-floppies" were not commercial successes and are now obsolete. The cost of the discs tended to be disproportionately high, there were reliability issues in some cases, and the capacities offered were quite low in comparison to the amount of data generated by a typical PC. With one or two hundred

1 Basic data transfers

megabytes of data to copy it did not matter whether you used 1.44 or 2.88 megabyte discs. It was not a practical proposition either way!

Despite their size limitation, it would be wrong to totally dismiss floppy discs as a means of swapping data between two PCs. Admittedly, if you need to transfer a 30-megabyte PDF file or two hundred image files at 4 megabytes each, floppy discs are not the solution. It is actually possible to spread large files across a number of discs using some compression programs, so large amounts of data can be transferred using numerous floppy discs. This is not very practical though, as it would take a long time to produce the discs, and then a similar amount of time would be needed in order to copy and reconstruct the files at the destination PC.

Using data compression can reduce the number of discs required, but the reduction obtained is often quite small. There is no guarantee that any reduction will be obtained. Many files have built-in file compression and can not be compressed any further. Practically all audio and image files have built-in data compression. Most programs that produce large files will have built-in compression in an attempt to keep file sizes within reason. Simple text and straightforward bitmap image files usually compress quite well, with a reduction of about 60 to 70 percent being typical.

Of course, not all files are huge, and you might need to transfer only a few at a time. The low capacity and relatively slow transfer rate of floppy discs is then of little importance, and they should do the job perfectly well. If you need to transfer a few megabytes of data, placing it on several floppy discs is not the easiest way of doing things but it is a practical approach. Beyond a few megabytes of data it is probably better to find an alternative method.

Flash memory

These days there are plenty of alternatives to floppy discs, and they all offer far higher capacities. In some cases the capacities on offer are equivalent to hundreds or even thousands of 1.44-megabyte floppy discs. Probably the most popular of these alternatives at present is Flash memory, which is sometimes in the form of a so-called "pen drive". This is a gadget that looks rather like a large pen, but removing the top reveals a USB connector (Figure 1.1).

It is not really a drive in the conventional sense, since the data is not stored on some form of disc or tape. There are no moving parts, and a device of this type is purely electronic. These devices are also known as

Basic data transfers 1

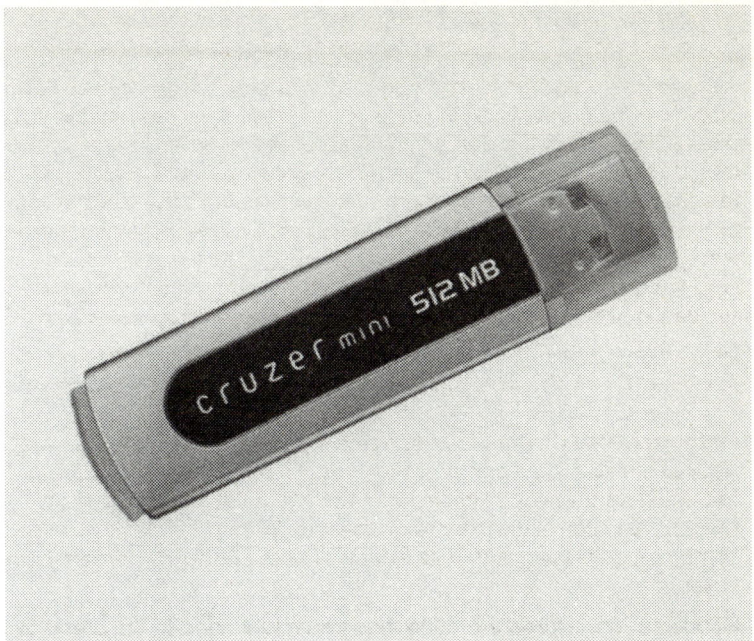

Fig.1.1 This USB Flash drive contains 512 megabytes of memory

"Flash drives", which is a bit more accurate but is still a little misleading. The "drive" part of these names is derived from the fact that the gadget is accessed as a drive in the operating system and when using application software.

The data is stored on Flash memory, which is the same type of memory that is used in digital cameras and various portable electronic devices. Unlike the main memory of a PC, Flash memory does not get a severe case of amnesia when the power is switched off. You may sometimes encounter references to "non-volatile" or just "NV" memory, and this name is used to describe any form of memory that retains its contents when the power is switched off. Flash memory is of the non-volatile variety, which makes is suitable for transferring data from one PC to another.

In addition to the Flash memory itself, a pen drive includes a USB interface and some electronics. Together with the driver software built into modern versions of Windows, this makes the unit appear as a normal drive to the

1 Basic data transfers

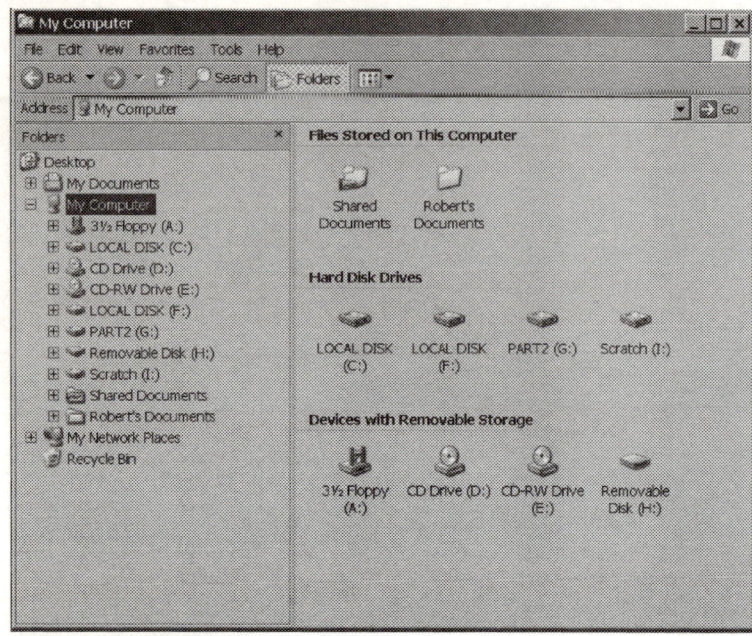

Fig.1.2 Windows lists the newly added Flash device as Drive H

operating system. Note that versions of Windows prior to XP and ME will require suitable drivers to be installed in order to make a pen drive usable. The necessary software is normally supplied with the drive, but it is advisable to check this point if you are not using a current version of Windows. The Plug and Play feature of Windows ME and XP will recognise a pen drive and automatically install the software to support it. However, with Windows ME you might need the Windows installation disc in order to complete the installation.

The pen drive will normally be added to the end of the existing series of drive letters. For example, if the PC already has drives from A to F, the newly added pen drive will be drive G. In the example of Figure 1.2, Windows Explorer has found the Flash drive and it is listed as drive H. Windows usually refers to Flash drive as a "Removable Disk", which means that it is effectively an outsize floppy disc as far as the operating system is concerned. The practical importance of this is that removing the drive will not have dire consequences for the smooth operation of the PC.

Basic data transfers   1

Fig.1.3 The extension lead for a Flash drive is a form of A to A cable

Note though, that it might be necessary to switch off the drive via software control before it is removed. In fact this will almost certainly be necessary. There is otherwise a risk of an error message being produced, and the operating system could become confused. The deactivation process usually requires little more than operating a button in the Windows taskbar. The instructions provided with the drive should explain how to switch the drive on and off.

Pen drives are mainly used as a means of swapping data between a portable PC of some kind and a desktop computer. Any reasonably modern laptop or notebook PC will have a USB port, as will anything but the oldest of desktop computers. One slight problem with older PCs is that they do not often have any front panel USB ports. Fitting and removing a pen drive from a port at the rear of the PC will usually be awkward, but there is a simple solution.

It is merely necessary to add a short USB extension cable to the port, and then connect the drive to the cable rather than direct to the port. Some drives are supplied complete with a short cable for this purpose. Note that the required cable is not the usual A to B type that is used for scanners, printers, etc. It is a form of A to A cable that has the larger type of USB plug at one end, and a matching socket at the other end (Figure 1.3).

1 Basic data transfers

The capacities of early pen drives were often quite low, with something in the region of 16 to 32 megabytes being typical. This is equivalent to about one or two dozen floppy discs, and is sufficient for many purposes. Flash memory technology has moved on quite fast in recent years, resulting in much higher capacities and massive price reductions. Capacities of around 128 to 512 megabytes are now commonplace, making it possible to transfer large amounts of data via these drives. Real-world pen drives often incorporate other features, such as MP3 players or some form of wireless adapter. Of course, the extra features substantially increase the cost, so it is better to opt for a basic drive unless you really need the extra facilities.

Card reader

Pen drives are useful gadgets, but they have an obvious limitation in that it is not possible to change the "disc". In other words, you really have something more like an external hard disc drive than a floppy disc drive. You can unplug one drive and fit another, but it is not possible to leave the drive in place and change the "disc". For many purposes it would be better if the drive could be left connected, with some interchangeable Flash memory cards being used rather like very high capacity floppy discs. Provided all your PCs were equipped with a suitable drive, data could be written to a memory card on one PC and then read on any of the others.

A big advantage of this method is that it would not involve switching off a drive before removing the "disc". Unplugging a memory card would leave the drive connected to the USB port, so there would be no vanishing hardware to confuse the operating system. The "discs" would appear and disappear as they were moved from one PC to another, but Windows is not fazed by simple disc changing of this type. The memory cards could therefore be freely exchanged between PCs, just like floppy discs.

There is a device called a "card reader" that is the flash memory equivalent of a floppy disc drive. The card reader connects to a USB port, and like a pen-drive, and it is used by the operating system as a "Removable Disk". The difference is that there is no built-in memory. Some card readers are designed for use with a single type of memory card, such as the one shown in Figure 1.4. This accepts type 1 Compact Flash cards. Other card readers can be used with half a dozen or more different types of memory card. Some printers have a built-in card reader (Figure 1.5), and these usually have slots for all the popular types of memory card. Some PCs have a built-in card reader, but this feature is still something

Basic data transfers   1

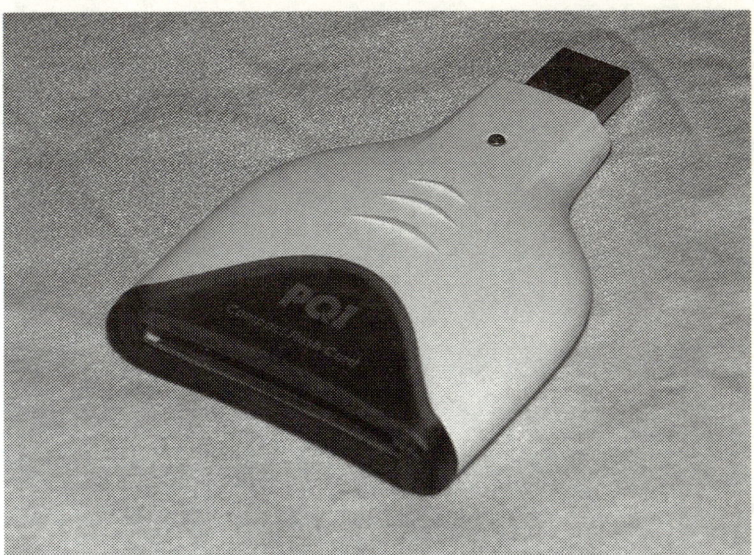

Fig.1.4 This USB card reader can only be used with Compact Flash cards

of a rarity for anything other than media PCs. Whatever "flavour" cards the reader accepts, they are the equivalent of the floppy discs. One card can be removed and another one can be fitted in its place.

Swapping discs other than the floppy variety has sometimes caused problems in the past. The usual snag was that on changing the disc the operating system refused to acknowledge that a change had been made. It still showed the contents of the original disc in file browsers, and attempts to access any of these files obviously failed and produced an error message. Fortunately, this does not happen with card readers, which are treated by the operating system as a truly removable disc drive. If you remove one card and fit another, file browsers should show the files on the second card, and there should be no difficulty in accessing them.

Although the cards are used like high-capacity floppy discs, they are formatted more like hard disc drives. They are mostly formatted using the old FAT16 system, but with large cards the more recent FAT32 system is sometimes used. In fact the very high capacity cards must use FAT32 formatting, since the FAT16 system can not handle capacities of more than two gigabytes.

1 Basic data transfers

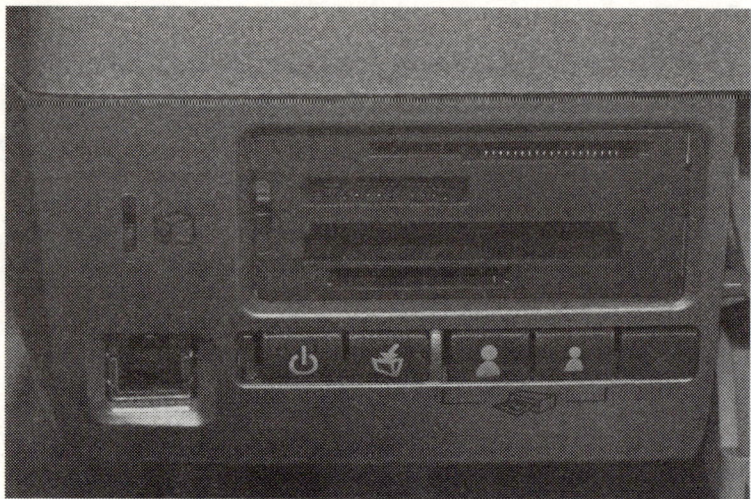

Fig.1.5 This printer has slots for various types of Flash card

FAT16 and FAT32 drives can be read by any version of Windows, including Windows 2000 and XP systems where the hard disc drive uses the NTFS file system. Consequently, there should be no difficulty in reading a card produced using a PC running Windows ME even if the card reader is connected to a PC running Windows 2000 or XP. A transfer in the opposite direction should be equally successful. In fact many gadgets that use memory cards also use the FAT16 or FAT32 file systems. Memory cards from many digital cameras, for instance, can be read on a PC that is equipped with a suitable card reader. Note though, that some devices use their own system of formatting, and that cards from older digital cameras are often unreadable via an ordinary card reader.

Several different types of memory card are available, but it is a good idea to use one of the most popular types unless there is a good reason to do otherwise. The more popular types of card are available in high capacity versions and are relatively cheap. The maximum capacities of the less common types are sometimes quite low, and they can easily cost more than twice as much as an equivalent card in a more popular format. The two most popular types of Flash card are Type 1 Compact Flash (CF) and Secure Digital (SD) cards. Type 1 Compact Flash cards are the most widely used, and almost certainly represent the best choice for PC data transfer and storage. Compact Flash cards having capacities

Basic data transfers 1

Fig.1.6 This Compact Flash card contains 256 megabytes of memory

of up to a few gigabytes are now readily available. Figure 1.6 shows a Compact Flash card that has a capacity of 256 megabytes.

Speed

The "Flash" name tends to give the impression that this type of memory is extremely fast. Unfortunately, the name refers to the process used when writing data to the card, and it is not meant to imply super-fast operation. The reading and writing speeds of Flash memory are actually quite slow by current standards, and they are not even very fast when compared to various types of true disc storage. Most Flash memory manufacturers use a speed rating that is essentially the same as the one used for CD-ROM drives. There is a slight difference in that the rating used for a CD-ROM drive is the maximum it can achieve, and the actual speed obtained near the middle of the disc is usually much lower. There is no Flash memory equivalent to this, and the quoted speed should be obtained when writing to any part of the disc.

A speed rating of X1 is equivalent to about 150k per second. Most memory cards are not actually marked with a speed rating, although this information is usually included in the manufacturer's data. A card that has no marked rating usually has a speed of about X4 to X12, and can

1 Basic data transfers

read or write data at about one megabyte or so per second. Note that there is no point in using a faster card with a reader that is connected to a USB 1.1 port. A "bog standard" memory card can transfer data at a rate that is about double that of a single device on a USB 1.1 port.

At the time or writing this it is possible to obtain memory cards that have speed ratings of up to about X80, although it seems likely that significantly faster cards will be developed. These cards are mainly intended for use with electronic gadgets that handle large amounts of data, such as digital video cameras and the more upmarket digital cameras. However, they also offer the potential for moving large amounts of data from one PC to another in a reasonably short time. A card having a rating of X60 for example, can read and write data at up to nine megabytes per second. In theory at any rate, a gigabyte of data could written to the card in less than two minutes, and then copied onto another PC in a similar amount of time.

Of course, transfer speeds of this order can not be achieved using a USB 1.1 interface. In order to fully utilise the speed of a fast Flash card it is essential to use a reader that supports a high speed interface such as USB 2.0 or Firewire. Using either type of interface and a matching card reader should enable data to be read and written at something very close to the maximum speed rating of the card. Where high-speed operation is needed it is important to check that a USB card reader is a genuine USB 2.0 type. Some are described as "USB 2.0 compatible", which means that they are actually USB 1.1 devices that can operate at USB 1.1 speeds with a USB 2.0 interface.

Note that some manufacturers do not use speed ratings such as X20 and X40. Instead they simply state the maximum rate at which data can be read from and written to the card. In order to compare the speeds of various cards it might be necessary to do a conversion from one type of speed rating to the other. I have a SanDisk Ultra II card that has quoted read and write rates of 9 and 10 megabytes per second respectively. Dividing these figures by 0.15 gives their equivalent ratings in the Xn system.

This gives read and write speeds of X60 and X67 respectively. The read speed of a Flash card is usually a little faster than the write speed. In the Xn system it is the slower rate that is used, so my SanDisk Ultra II card is an X60 type and not an X67 card. To convert an Xn rating into its equivalent in megabytes per second, multiply its speed rating by 0.15. An X80 card, for example, can transfer data at up to 12 megabytes per second.

External drives

Flash storage is fine if you do not need to transfer very large amounts of data. The cost of the equipment is low, and compared to most of the alternatives it is physically tiny. A Compact Flash card containing a gigabyte of data will easily fit into a purse or wallet, and is easily transported from one location to another. The only slight problem is that most Flash cards are so small that they are easily mislaid, so it pays not to get careless when dealing with them. Pen drives and card readers are also very small and portable. As the cost of Flash memory cards gradually comes down, their potential uses increase. However, as things stand, they are not a good choice when very large amounts of data must be transferred.

The alternative is to use some form of disc storage device, and there are several options. We will start with external disc drives, and there are several types to choose from. In the past the ZIP drives were very popular, and the parallel port variety was probably the most popular type due to its relatively low cost. Other types of drive that use a PC's parallel port have been produced. Most of these drives are now obsolete, and although they are sometimes available at quite low prices, they are probably not a worthwhile option. The serial and parallel ports of PCs are due to be phased out in the not too distant future, so any form of drive that uses a parallel interface could have a limited operating life.

Another consideration is the speed limitation of a parallel port. In theory it is possible to read or write data at up to about two megabytes per second using a parallel port in a high-speed mode. Unfortunately, parallel port drives often fall far short of this rate in practice. In my experience the maximum rate is often about 10 to 20 percent of the theoretical maximum, and in some cases was more like five percent. Some drives seem to perform much better under MS/DOS than under Windows, which suggests that their driver software for Windows is not as efficient as it could be.

Another problem with many parallel port drives is that the operating system tended to lose track of them. With some drives it can be difficult to get the operating system to acknowledge the existence of the device in the first place. An external drive is unusable unless the operating system can be persuaded to give the device a drive letter.

In my experience, this problem becomes much worse if a drive is moved from one PC to another and back again. The main advantage of an external drive is that it can be moved easily from one PC to another,

1 Basic data transfers

making it unnecessary to have a separate drive for each PC. Unfortunately, moving parallel port drives from one PC to another can get the operating system confused, making it time consuming and awkward to complete what should have been straightforward data transfers. Anyway, these days there is probably no point in using any form of external disc drive that uses a parallel interface. Much better alternatives are available.

USB drives

The USB interface made it possible to produce external disc drives that were not particularly fast, but were much more consistent than many of the parallel port alternatives. Also, with USB operation it is much easier to move a drive from one PC to another. When using a parallel port drive it is usually necessary to switch off the PC before connecting or disconnecting the drive. When using a USB interface it is possible to connect and disconnect the drive while the PC is still operating. There is often a facility to switch off the drive under software control, which also removes it from the operating system. This enables the drive to be disconnected safely, although there will not necessarily be any dire consequences if the drive is unplugged without deactivating it first.

Although USB 1.1 ports are in many ways ideal for external drives, the relatively slow transfer rates obtained are a major drawback if large amounts of data have to be transferred. Another problem with USB 1.1 ports is that they can provide only a limited amount power. The power line of a USB 1.1 port provides 5 volts at 0.5 amps, or just 2.5 watts. This is not enough to power most drives, which therefore require a mains adapter to act as the power source. Admittedly this is not a huge problem, but yet another mains lead is something most computer users could do without.

USB 2.0 supports transfer rates of up to 480 kilobits per second, which equates to something in the region of 50 megabytes of data per second. In practice it would probably not be possible to achieve speeds quite as high as this, but using a USB 2.0 interface it is unlikely that the interface itself will be the limiting factor. The maximum transfer rate is likely to be limited by the drive, the PC, or a combination of the two. It also provides a higher supply current of 2 amps. This gives a maximum of just 10 watts to power each USB 2.0 peripheral, but this is adequate for some drives.

Basic data transfers 1

Fig.1.7 An external hard disc drive from Belkin

Hard drives

Most of the popular external drives of a few years ago are no longer made, having been squeezed out by Flash memory devices, CD-RW drives, and external hard disc drives. There is a high-capacity (750-megabyte) version of the popular ZIP drive, but that is about it. A wide selection of obsolete drives is available on the second-hand market, but it is unlikely that any of these units represent a worthwhile proposition any more. They mostly sell at very low prices, which accurately reflect their worth.

These days the choice is between an external hard disc drive or an optical storage (CD/DVD) drive. External hard disc drives, such as the Belkin device shown in Figure 1.7, are increasingly popular, and they have some major advantages. Provided they are used with a USB 2.0 or Firewire interface, an external hard disc drive should offer a level of performance that is similar to a typical internal unit. Even with several gigabytes of data to transfer, it should only take a few minutes to store it on the drive and then copy it onto another PC.

External hard disc drives can seem rather expensive when compared to the alternatives, but bear in mind that the performance is likely to be much higher, and that a hard drive does not require you to buy any

1   Basic data transfers

storage media. It comes complete with what will typically be about 40 to 160 gigabytes of rewritable storage media. A low cost external hard disc is likely to be the best option if you need to transfer or backup large amounts of data. Even if it does cost a little more than the alternatives, the time saved by the faster transfers will almost certainly justify the additional cost.

It is possible to obtain a gadget that converts an ordinary internal (ATA) hard disc drive into an external USB type. Basically it is just a matter of connecting the hard drive into the adapter unit and bolting it in place. Power is supplied to the drive and interface unit by a mains adapter, and with this connected you have what is effectively an ordinary external hard drive.

While you could by an ATA hard disc and one of these adapters, and then fit them together in order to produce an external drive, this is not really the idea. If you upgrade your (say) 40-gigabyte hard disc to a 120-megabyte type, you are left with a spare 40-gigabyte drive. One option is to leave the drive in the computer and use it as a second internal drive. The old drive could be used to provide an additional 40 gigabytes of storage, or it could be used to backup important files. Alternatively, using the old drive in an external adapter would give a very useful drive for data transfers, backing up data, or whatever. Since you would already have the drive and would only need to buy the adaptor, this should be a very inexpensive means of providing a portable drive.

External CD-RW

Most desktop PCs are supplied with a CD-RW or DVD-RW drive of some sort. This makes one or other of these drives the obvious choice when transferring large amounts of data from one PC to another. With the drives already installed in the PCs, the only expense involved is the cost of the discs. The cost of rewritable discs is much higher than the non-rewritable equivalents, but the cost per gigabyte is still well within reason. Do not overlook the possibility of using CD-R discs for transferring data. Although they can not be reused, the cost per disc can be as little as a few pence, and the discs could be useful as backup copies of your data.

Probably the main shortcoming of rewritable discs is that they are not particularly fast. Most of these discs permit write speeds that are, at best, comparable to a "bog standard" Flash card. Of course, the read speeds are much higher, and with a modern drive should be several megabytes per second. Modern CD-RW drives support relatively high write speeds, but it can be difficult to find discs that will work reliably at these speeds with your particular make and model of drive. Anyway, even without resorting to the latest high speed discs and drives, CD-RW discs are adequate for most purposes, as are the various types of DVD-RW discs.

With so many PCs having built-in CD-RW or DVD-RW drives, external versions might appear to be of little practical value. If you need to add an optical drive to a PC that lacks a built-in drive of this type, fitting an internal unit is likely to be far cheaper than using an external equivalent. However, if you do not feel like delving into the interior of your PC to fit an internal drive, an external unit is probably worth the additional expense. Bear in mind though, that the cost of having your local computer shop install an internal drive might be less than that of purchasing an external drive.

Most people that buy external optical drives probably use them with portable PCs. These days it is quite common for notebook and laptop PCs to be fitted with some form of optical drive, but by no means all of them are equipped with an optical read/write drive. Having an external drive back at base enables data to be backed up or transferred easily to another PC. Since there will normally be no need to take the drive out and about with the PC, it does not make it any less portable.

In terms of performance, an external optical drive should not be at any disadvantage compared to an internal unit provided it uses a USB 2.0 or Firewire interface. These both support transfer rates that are far higher than the read or write rates of the drives. Performance when using a USB 1.1 interface will be severely limited by the relatively low speed of this interface. Also, not all optical drives are compatible with a USB 1.1 interface, so check this point carefully before buying an optical drive for use with this type of port.

Making selections

These days many forms of internal and external drive can be used without the need for special file writing software. Most drives appear in Windows Explorer as a standard Windows drives that can use the normal Copy and Paste functions to copy files or folders from one drive to another. There are exceptions though, and with anything prior to Windows XP it is not possible to write data to a CD-RW drive without additional software. However, data can be read from this type of drive, which is effectively an ordinary CD-ROM drive as far as the operating system is concerned.

1 Basic data transfers

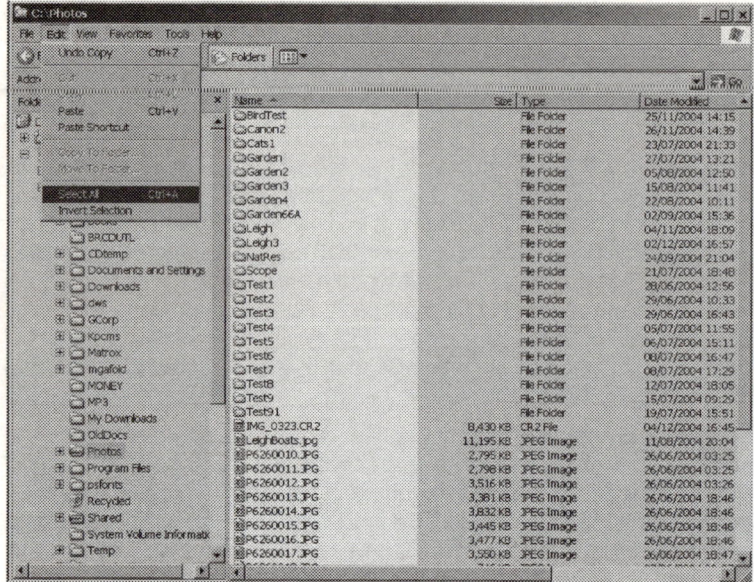

Fig.1.8 The Select All option in the Edit menu can be very useful

There is a similar situation when using a DVD writer with any form of Windows.

Reading from the drive should not be a problem provided the driver software is installed correctly, but writing to it requires a suitable application program. With internal or external hard disc drives and Flash drives it should be possible to use them as standard Windows drives. Reading or writing to the drives can be achieved using Windows Explorer or any normal application program.

Reading and writing folders and files under Windows is very much easier than using a text based operating system such as MS-DOS. One of the main reasons for the success of GUIs (Graphical User Interfaces) is the ease with which files and folders can be moved, copied, and deleted. The "drag and drop" method is popular with many users, but you do need to be very careful when using this method. It is very easy for a slip of the finger to result in unwanted copies being produced, files being deposited in the wrong place, and so on. It is not usually too difficult to sort out any careless errors, but it can be time consuming to clean up the mess when things go awry with a large number of files.

Basic data transfers 1

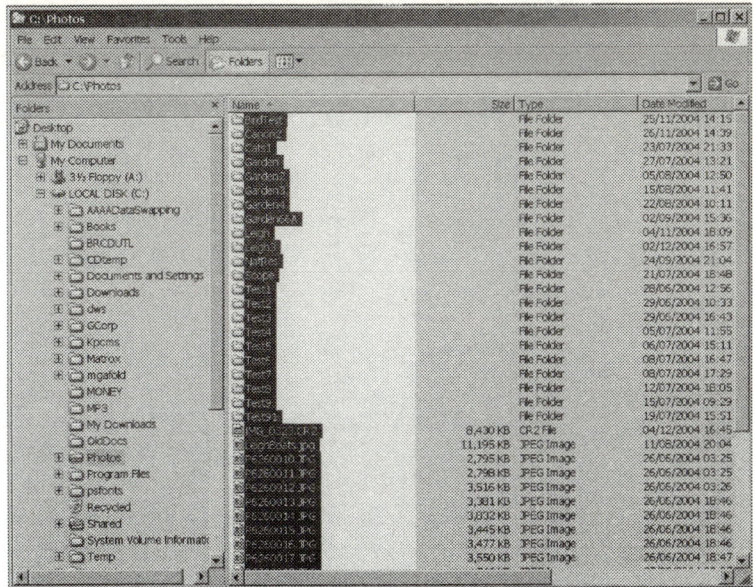

Fig.1.9 Windows Explorer highlights the selected files

My preferred method of copying files is to use the pop-up menus that are available from Windows itself and most applications programs. The first step is to select the files or folders that you wish to manipulate, and there are some useful Windows tricks that make it easy to select large number of files. One of the most useful of these is the Select All option that can be found in the Edit menu of Windows Explorer (Figure 1.8). This simply selects all the files and folders in the currently selected drive or folder within that drive. The selected files in Windows Explorer and other file browsers are usually shown highlighted in inverse video (Figure 1.9).

Of course, in many cases it will only be necessary to select certain files or folders. It is possible to add selections one at a time by holding down the Control key and then left-clicking each file or folder that you wish to select. As usual, each item that is selected will be highlighted. Another useful ploy enables a block of entries to be selected. Start by selecting the first entry in the usual way. Next, left-click on the final entry in the block while holding down the Shift key, and the whole block should then be highlighted (Figure 1.10). Note that this system works just as well if

1 Basic data transfers

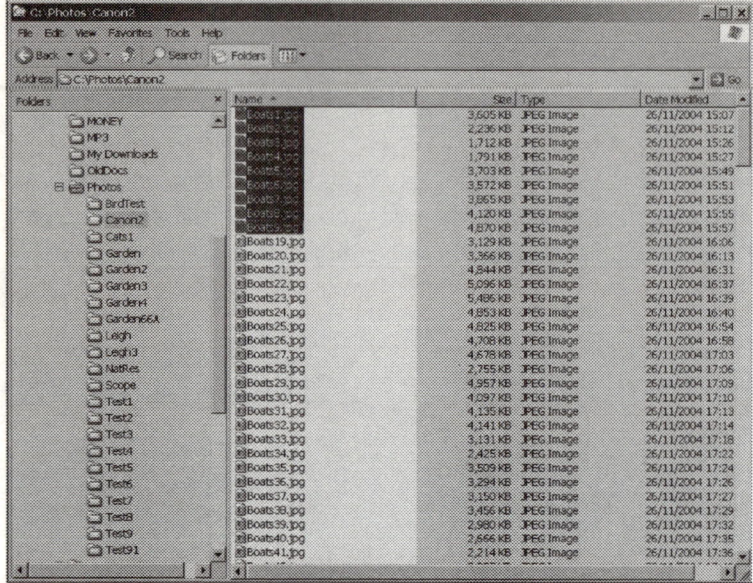

Fig.1.10 The Shift key has been used to select a block of files

you select the bottom entry first, and then left-click the upper entry while holding down the Shift key.

It is possible to select another block without deselecting the first one. Having selected the initial block, hold down the Control key and select an entry at one end of the second block. Then hold down both the Shift and Control keys while selecting the entry at the opposite end of the second block. Both blocks should then appear highlighted to confirm that they have been selected (Figure 1.11). Further blocks can be selected using the same method, and individual entries can be added by holding down the Control key and left-clicking their entries.

Sometimes you might need to select practically everything, but perhaps one or two items are not required. One way of handling this is to first select everything using the Select All option in the Edit menu. Then hold down the Control key and left-click the entries for any items that are not required. There is an alternative method, which is to first select the items that you do not wish to include in the final selection. Next, the Invert Selection option is selected from the Edit menu (Figure 1.12). This results in the original selections being deselected, and everything else being selected (Figure 1.13).

Basic data transfers   1

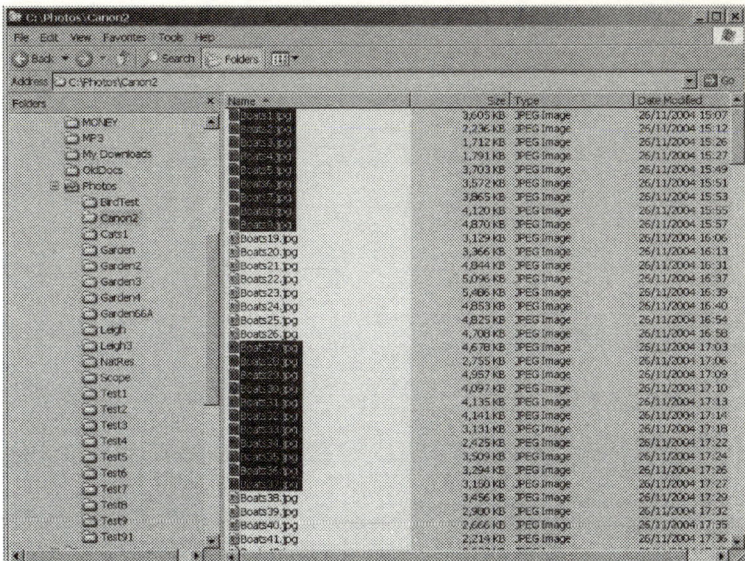

Fig.1.11   The Control key enables another block to be selected

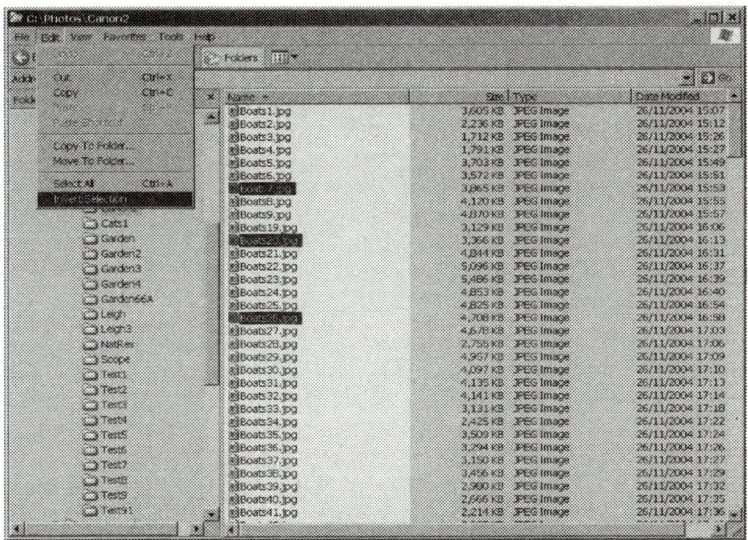

Fig.1.12   Invert Selection is available from the Edit menu

1 Basic data transfers

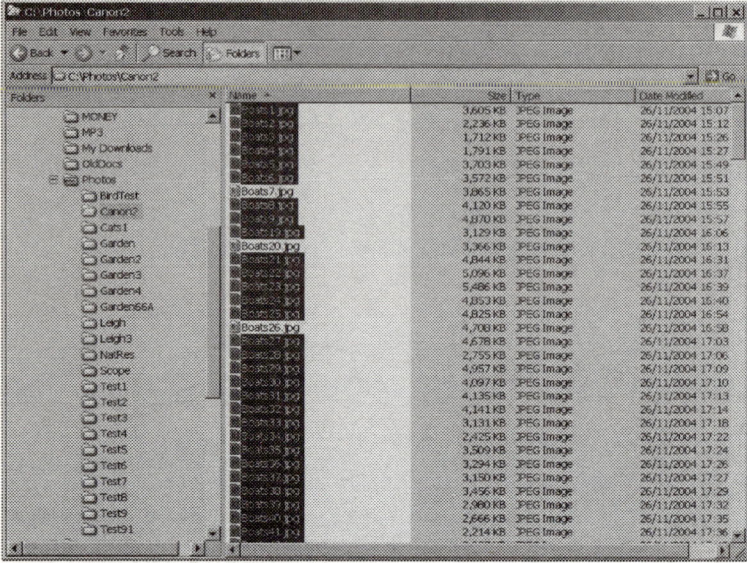

Fig.1.13 Everything but the original selections are now selected

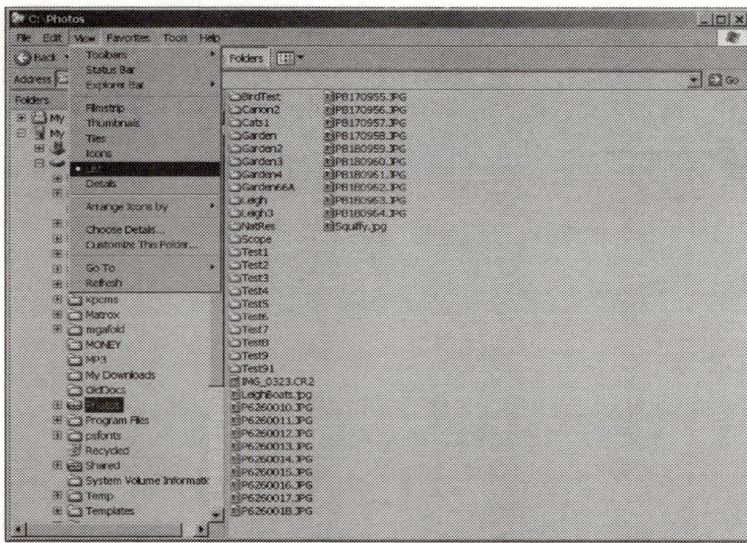

Fig.1.14 The List option is available from the View menu

Basic data transfers 1

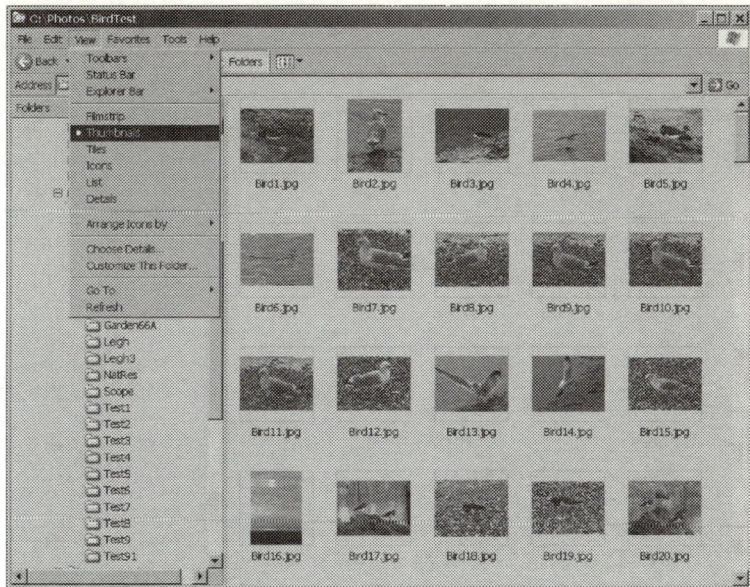

Fig.1.15 Some types of image file can be shown as thumbnails

In the examples shown here, the entries in Windows Explorer are shown as simple text entries. When copying large numbers of files it is generally better to have the program operate in this mode, because it allows a relatively large number of entries to be displayed on the screen. This minimises the amount of scrolling required and makes it easy to keep track of what you have selected. I mainly use the Details option in the View menu of Windows Explorer, which gives the name of each file or folder, plus other information such as the last date the object was modified.

In order to get as many entries as possible onto each screen-full it is better to use the List option in the View menu (Figure 1.14). This only provides the name, with no other information about the file or folder being provided. However, this is usually the only information needed when copying files. When selectively copying image files it can be useful to use the Thumbnails option (Figure 1.15). This shows a small "thumbnail" version of each image, provided the file type is a common one such as Jpeg. This makes it easy to select the required files, but has the disadvantage of providing relatively few entries per screen.

1 Basic data transfers

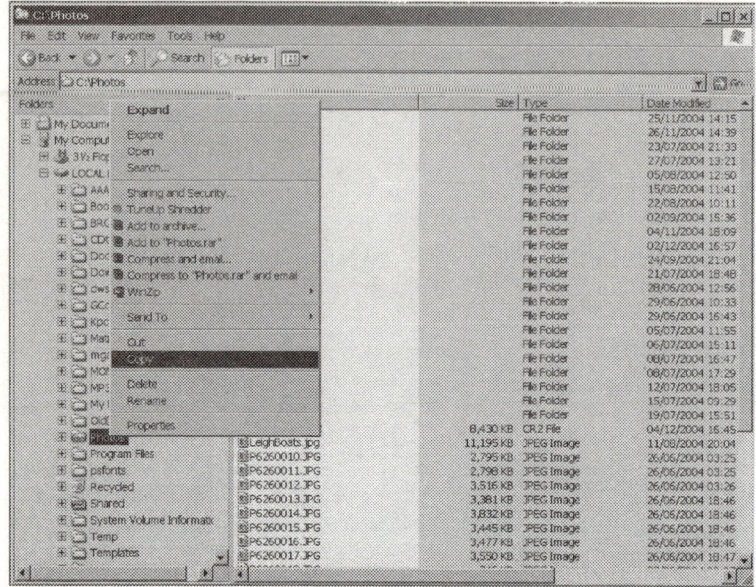

Fig.1.16 Right-clicking an entry produces a pop-up menu that includes a Copy option

Copy and Paste

Having selected the appropriate files and/or folders they can then be copied to the new location. For this example, a folder contain a large number of files will be copied from the main hard disc drive (drive C) to a backup hard disc (drive F). Right-clicking on a file or folder produces a small pop-up menu (Figure 1.16), and the Copy option is then selected. Where a multiple selection is to be copied, complete the selection process first, and then right-click on any selected object to produce the pop-up menu.

The menu also has the usual Cut option. The difference between Cut and Copy is that the former deletes the copied material, whereas the latter leaves it in place. Both of these options are available from the Edit menu once a selection has been made, but the right-clicking method is quicker. Note that the Cut option does not delete the original files and folders until the copies are in place. Therefore, if the cut files and folders are not copied, the originals will be left untouched.

Basic data transfers 1

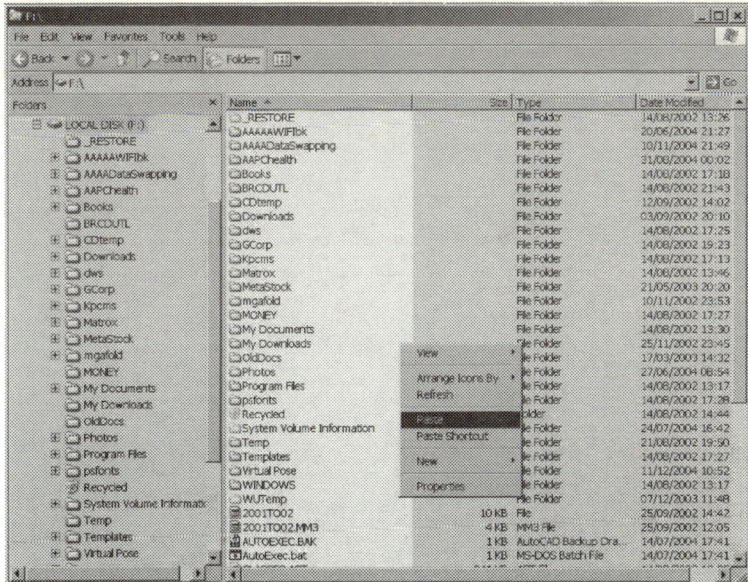

Fig.1.17 The Paste option is selected from the pop-up menu

Having issued the Cut or Copy command, the next step is to navigate Windows Explorer to the destination for the material. In this example I am copying the folder to drive F, and I have the contents of this folder displayed in the right-hand section of the window (Figure 1.17). Right-clicking on a blank area in this section produces a pop-up menu, where the Paste option is selected. The folder and its contents are then copied to the destination drive. A bargraph will be displayed if the copying process will take more than a few seconds. In addition to showing how far the copying has progressed, it will also give an estimate of how much longer the copying will take. This is only a very rough estimate though, and it will often be well wide of the mark.

Windows will give a warning message if you try to overwrite existing files on the destination drive (Figure 1.18). The Yes and No buttons enable you to individually select whether each object will be overwritten with the copied version. In most cases it is the Yes to All button that gives the desired result. With this option selected, existing files will always be overwritten by a copied file of the same name. The purpose of copying numerous files is usually that an up-to-date backup of the files is required. You therefore need any old files on the destination drive to be overwritten

1 Basic data transfers

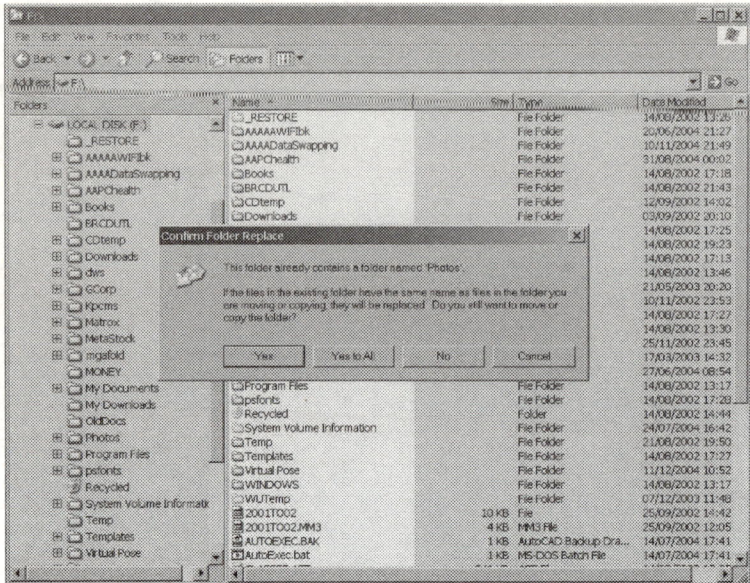

Fig.1.18 A warning is given if you try to overwrite existing files

by more recent versions on the source drive. If you wish to have the old and the new versions, the two versions must be stored in separate folders on the destination disc, or perhaps on separate discs in the case of a CD-RW or DVD-RW drive.

One slight problem in using the Copy command to backup numerous files is that many of the overwritten files will actually be the same as the ones copied from the source disc. It is only the files that have been changed since the last backup that need to be copied to the destination drive. When writing the backup to a hard disc drive this is unlikely to be of any great importance. Even copying a few hundred megabytes of data should take no more than a few seconds.

It is a bigger drawback when writing the backup to a slower disc such as a CD-RW type, or if very large amounts of data are involved. In either case it would probably be better to use a proper backup program. Many of these can keep track of which files have been added or altered since the last backup was made, and only these files will be copied.

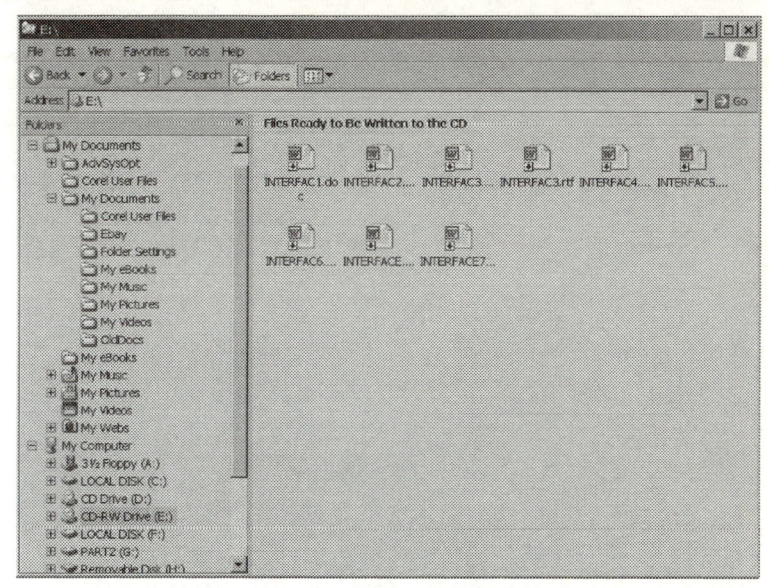

Fig.1.19 At first glance it looks as though the files have been copied to the CD, but nothing has been copied at this stage

XP and CD-Rs

With versions of Windows prior to Windows XP there is no built-in facility for using a CD writer. Of course, it is possible to use one of these drives with any reasonably recent version of Windows, but only with the aid of suitable software. Most CD/RW drives are supplied complete with CD writing software, as are most computers that have a built-in drive of this type. The most popular bundled CD writing software is Nero, although you are unlikely to get the most up-to-date and comprehensive version of this program as a freebie. However, even one of the older versions is more than adequate for copying some files to a disc.

The built-in CD writing facilities of Windows XP are rather limited, but they are adequate for simple file copying. It is probably best to settle for the integral facilities if you do not require the additional features of a CD writing program. It makes sense not to burden your PC with any software that you do not really need. The CD writing facility of Windows XP can be a bit confusing, since it does not operate in quite the same way as writing files to other drives. In the example of Figure 1.19 I have copied

1 Basic data transfers

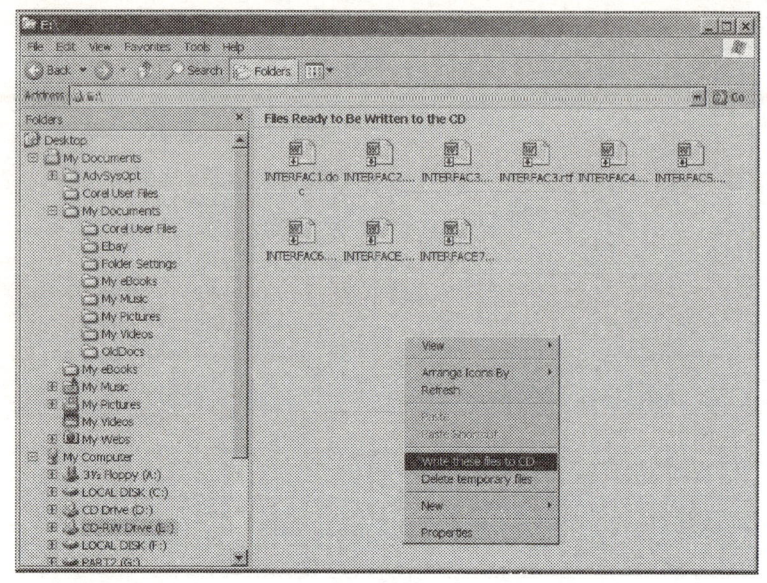

Fig.1.20 This pop-up menu has an option to write the files to the CD

some files from the hard disc drive to the CD writer (drive E). On the face of it, the files have been successfully copied to the CD-R disc.

Although Windows Explorer shows the files as being present on drive E, this is not actually the case. In actual fact there is no disc in drive E, so it could not possibly contain the files. As explained in the text that appears immediately above the icons for the files, the files are ready to be copied to drive E. At this point in the proceedings, Windows has simply made a note of the files that you wish to copy to drive E, but it has not copied anything. Incidentally, it does not matter if the PC is shut down at this stage. The next time it is switched on, Windows will remember that these files are ready to be copied to drive E.

On the face of it, life would be much easier if the files were simply written to the disc when the Paste command was issued. CD/RW drives and PCs with this type of drive are often supplied with a program that runs in the background and permits the Copy and Paste functions to operate normally. The Nero program is usually supplied with a program called InCD, which permits easy copying of this type. There are other utilities of this type that are supplied with other CD writing programs. A CD

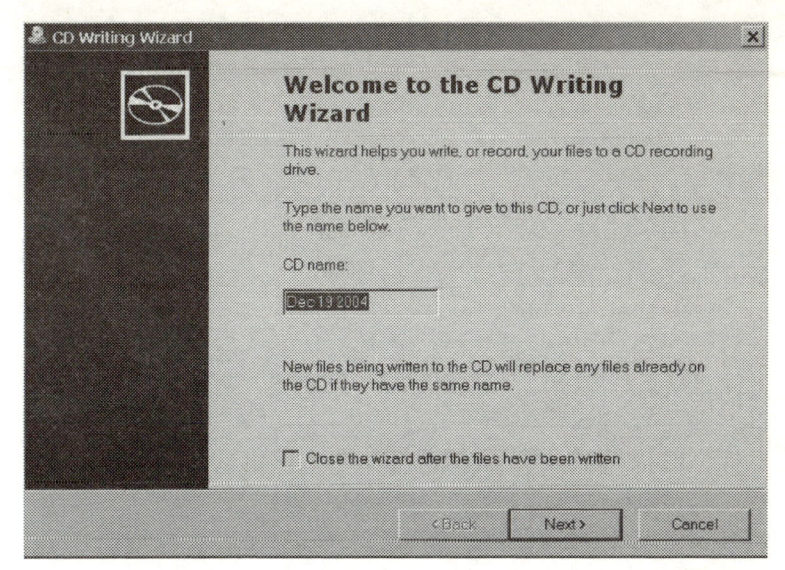

Fig.1.21 The Welcome screen for the CD Writing Wizard

writer plus a CD/RW disc effectively become a hard disc drive when using one of these programs.

The problem with this type of file copying is that writing data to a CD is a much more complicated affair than writing data to a hard disc drive. Making sure that the complex directory structure, etc., of the disc is maintained correctly can take longer than writing the data to the disc. Although modern CD writers are much faster than the early units, they are still very slow in comparison to modern hard disc drives. Using a CD/RW disc as a sort of pseudo hard disc drive is in many ways a convenient way of doing things, but it can be tediously slow at times. File browsers can become generally rather slow when a CD/RW disc is used in this way.

Although relatively crude, the method used by Windows XP has the advantage that things operate relatively quickly while you accumulate files that will eventually be written to the CD/RW disc. There will probably be a substantial delay when these files are eventually written to the disc, but one large write operation is much more efficient than numerous smaller ones. The best method to use depends on the reason for the files being copied and the way in which you prefer to work. An important

1 Basic data transfers

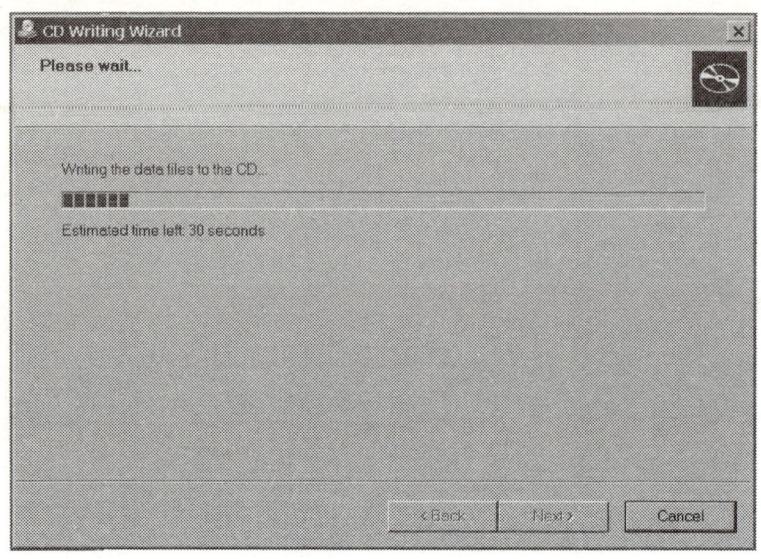

Fig.1.22 The usual bargraph shows how things are progressing

point to bear in mind is that files in limbo are not of any use for backup purposes. There are no backup copies until the files are actually copied to the disc in the CD writer. Until that has been done your files are vulnerable.

Writing the files to the disc it is very straightforward. One way is to right-click in an empty area of the window near but not on an icon for one of the files. This produces a small pop-up window (Figure 1.20) where the "Write these files to CD" option is selected. Another way is to select this option from the Edit menu. Either way, the CD Writing Wizard will be launched (Figure 1.21). Left-clicking the Next button results in the files being copied to the CD, and the customary bargraph shows how things are progressing (Figure 1.22).

The window of Figure 1.23 appears when the copying has been completed. The checkbox is ticked if you need to repeat the process and copy the files to another CD, but it is otherwise just a matter of operating the Finish button to close the window. Windows Explorer should then show the full icons for the copied files (Figure 1.24), rather than the "hollow" versions that were used previously. The text above the files should indicate that the files are on the CD, rather than waiting to be copied to it.

Basic data transfers 1

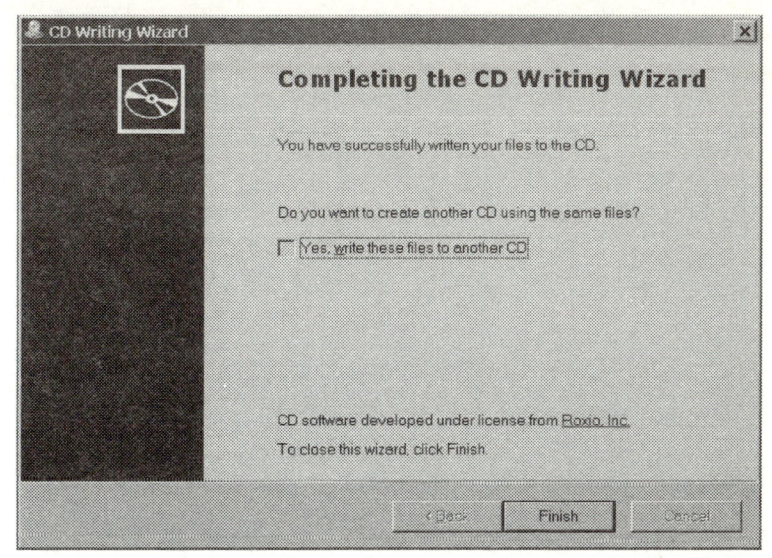

Fig.1.23 This window appears when the files have been copied

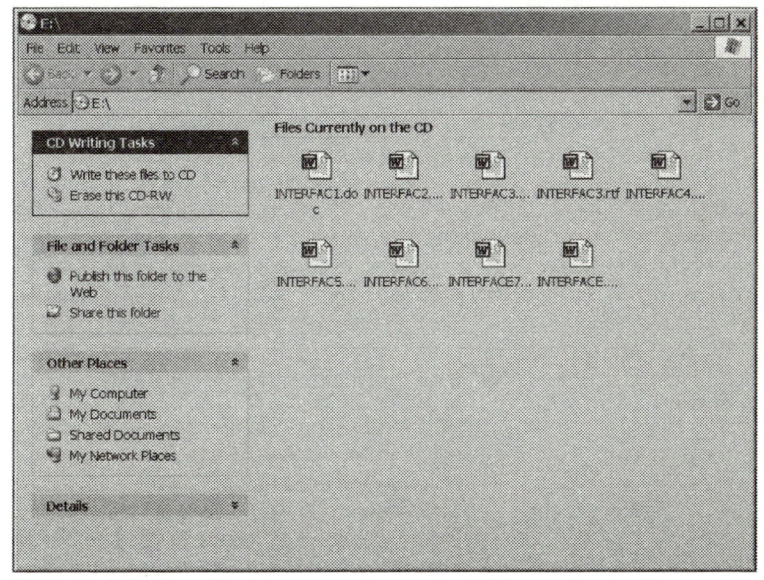

Fig.1.24 Windows Explorer now shows the full icons for the files

1   Basic data transfers

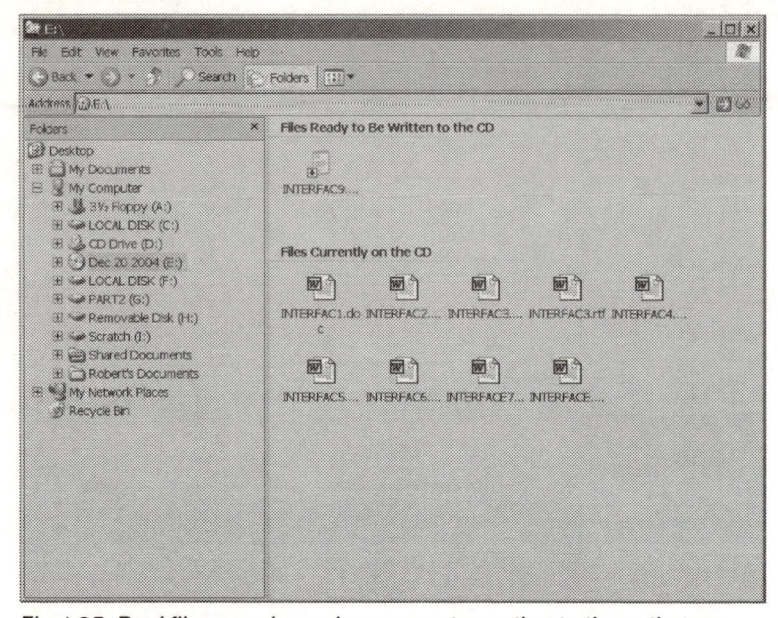

Fig.1.25 Real files are shown in a separate section to those that are pending

Temporary files will be left on the hard disc if you accumulate files to copy to a CD but fail to do so. These files can be removed by going into the appropriate drive using Windows Explorer and selecting "Delete temporary files" from the Edit menu. It is also possible to delete the "ghost" files that have not yet been written to a disc using the same methods that are utilised for the real thing. The deletion method has to be used if you need to remove some files while leaving others so that they can be copied to a CD. If you add files to a CD that already contains some files, the existing files and the ones that have not yet been written to the CD will be shown in separate sections (Figure 1.25). This should help to avoid any confusion over the true contents of the CD.

CD burning software

The built-in facilities of Windows XP are fine for simple file copying, but proper CD burning software is needed for more complex tasks. Using a program such as Nero it is possible to burn CDs from image files (ISO, BIN, CUE, etc.), produce audio CDs, video CDs, and so on. Much of this

Basic data transfers 1

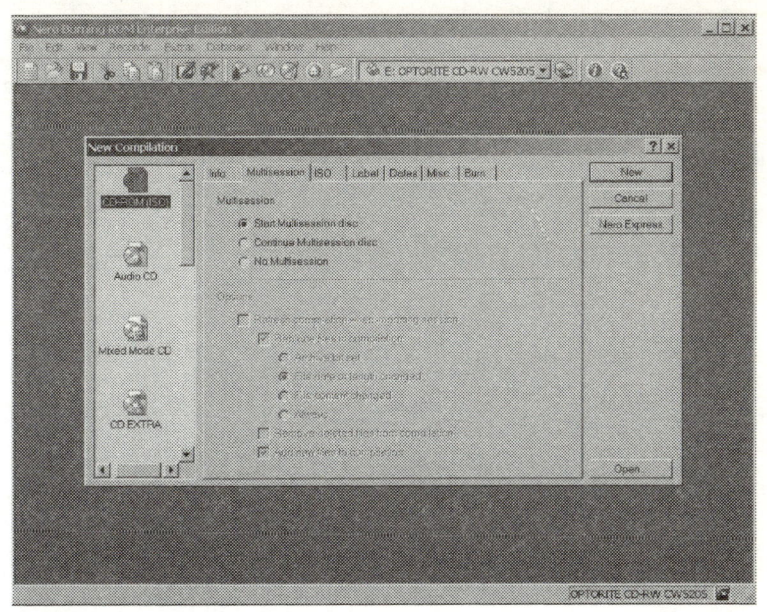

Fig.1.26 The opening screen of Nero 6.0

is irrelevant in the current context, where it is only basic file copying to permit file transfers that is of interest. A CD burning program should have facilities for selecting files and then copying them to disc.

In many cases the files that you need to copy will already be neatly grouped together in a single directory. In cases where the files are liberally scattered across the hard disc drive it would probably be a good idea to copy them into a temporary directory on the hard disc. Having made sure that all the files to be copied are present and correct, the temporary folder can be copied to a CD, after which it can be deleted. However, CD burning software does usually give the option of selecting files from numerous sources and burning them to a CD.

Figure 1.26 shows the opening screen for Nero Burning ROM 6.0. A column of icons down the left-hand side of the screen is used to select the type of disc to be produced, and the default (CD-ROM) option is the one that is needed for a data CD. The tabs, radio buttons, and checkboxes provide a bewildering array of options, but for most purposes the defaults can be accepted. It is the three radio buttons near the top of the Multisession section that are of most importance.

31

1 Basic data transfers

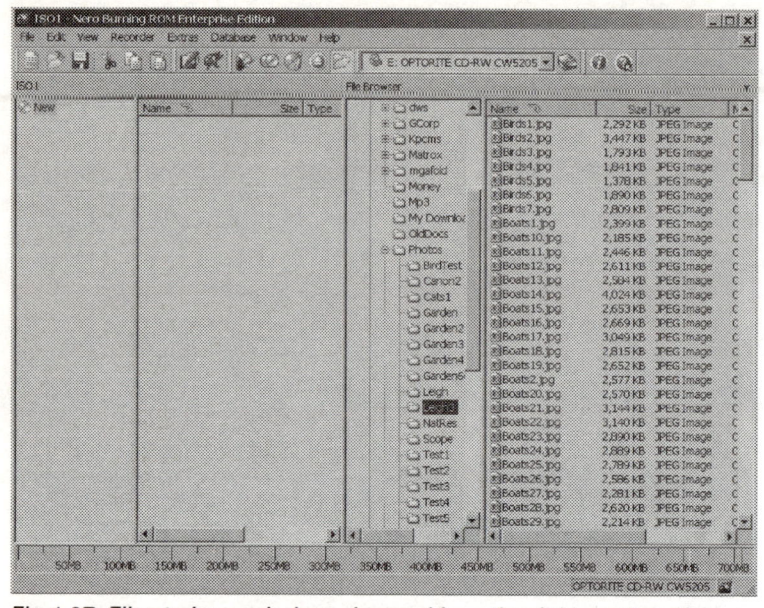

Fig.1.27 Files to be copied are dragged from the right section of the sreen to the left section

The "Start Multisession disc" button is selected by default, and this is used when starting a new data disc that you might wish to modify at some later time. Provided there is some unused capacity, more files can be added to a multisession disc. It is also possible to erase existing files. Note though, that erasing files does not free any storage space with a disc that is not rewritable. Erased files have their entries removed from the file allocation table, but they remain on the disc and they can not be overwritten by new files. Therefore, use rewritable discs if you will need to delete old files and replace them with new ones. Use CD-Rs if you will only need to add files to an archive, such as an on-disc photo album.

Existing multisession

The middle radio button is selected when you have an existing multisession disc that you wish modify. The bottom of the three buttons is selected when you need to create a disc that does not have multisession capability. In general, it is better to opt for a multisession disc, which

Basic data transfers

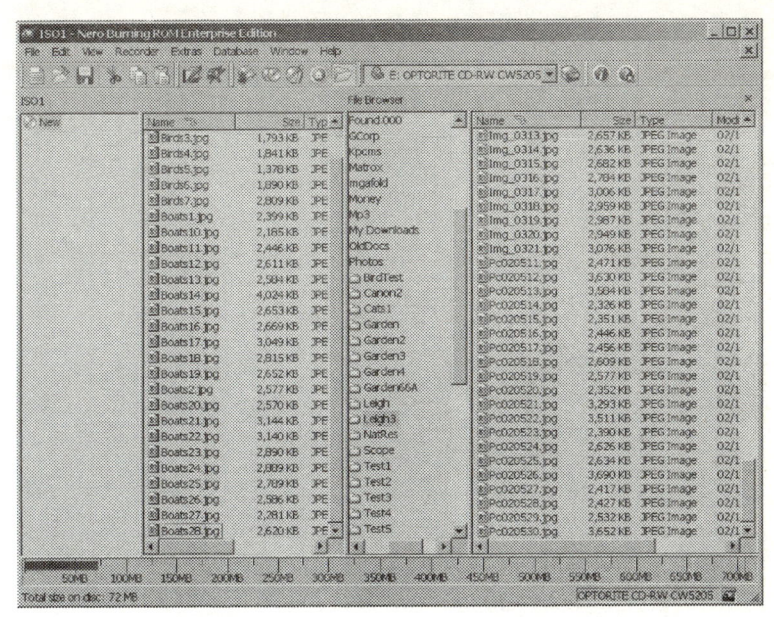

Fig.1.28 Some files have been selected and they are now ready to be copied to a CD

leaves you the option of adding more files later. Although you might have no immediate need for this facility, it is something that could prove useful in the future. If you do not opt to make a multisession disc, the completed disc will be a read-only type with no way of altering its contents. The only advantage of not opting for a multisession disc is that this provides a somewhat higher storage capacity.

For this example I opted to start a new multisession disc and then operated the New button. This moves things on to the screen of Figure 1.27, which is a form of file browser. The files or folders you wish to copy are selected in the right-hand section of the window, and then dragged to the main panel in the left-hand section. The usual file related functions such as Copy, Paste and Select All are available, should you need them. If you need to remove an item from your list of files in the left-hand section of the window, right-click on it and select the delete option. This will delete the file from the list, but will leave the original intact.

When the list of files is complete (Figure 1.28), the next step is to select Burn Compilation from the Recorder menu. This produces a new window

1 Basic data transfers

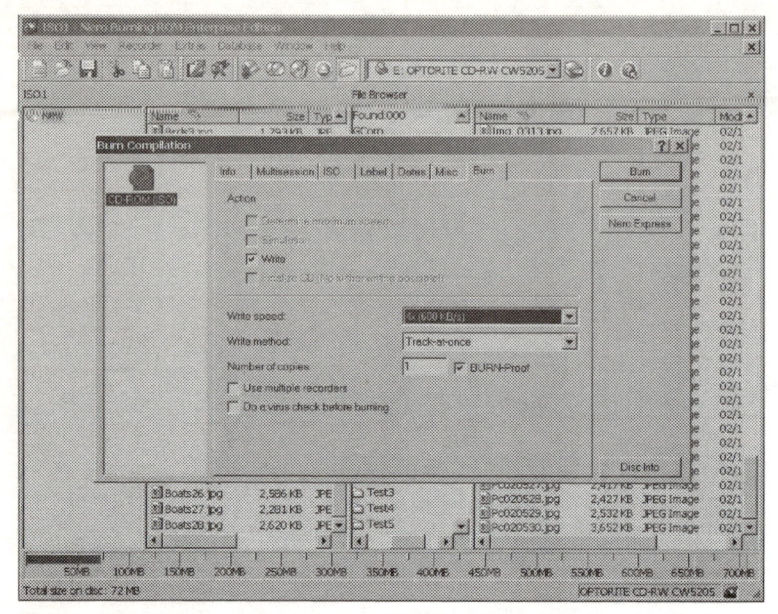

Figure 1.29 Various options are available prior to burning data to the CD

(Figure 1.29), and there are various options available here. In most cases the defaults will be satisfactory, but there could be one or two changes you would like to make. In particular, you might like to change the recording speed from the default setting. The default setting will probably be the highest one that your drive and media will support, but many users prefer to use a slightly slower writing speed.

The usual reason for doing this is that it is widely believed to give more reliable discs, and that the risk of something going wrong during the write operation is reduced if a slightly lower speed is used. Bear in mind that a problem during the production of a disc will result in it being unreadable. With a rewritable disc you can reformat it and try again, but the contents of the disc will be lost. With other types of disc there is no second chance. Whether using a slightly reduced writing speed really has any benefits is debatable, but dropping the speed from (say) 52x to 40x will not greatly increase the time taken to copy the files. I usually err on the side of caution and settle for something less than the highest possible speed when using fast discs in a high-speed drive.

Basic data transfers 1

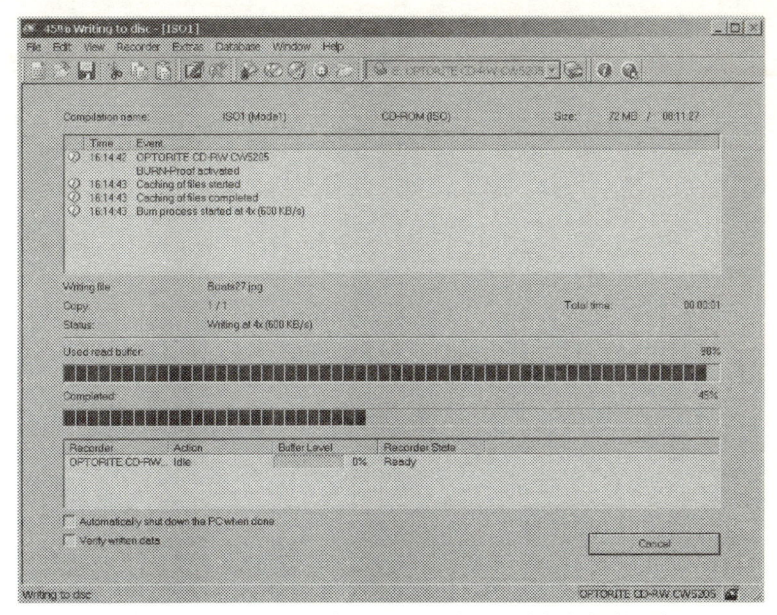

Fig.1.30 Status and progress information is provided during the burning process

When any required changes have been made to the settings, operating the Burn button initiates the writing process. A window like the one shown in Figure 1.30 appears, giving status information and showing how the copying is progressing. Once the files have been copied and the disc has been made ready for use, a message will indicate that the disc has been completed successfully (Figure 1.31). Operate the OK button to remove the message and then the Done button to return to the main program window.

Many CD and DVD burning programs offer more user-friendly ways of burning discs, and modern versions of the Nero program have the StartSmart program. This offers a more wizard like approach to producing discs, and the initial screen is shown in Figure 1.32. You start by selecting the appropriate task, such as making a data or audio CD. You are then taken into the appropriate Nero program where the task is carried out. In the example of Figure 1.33 I opted to make a data CD, with a view to adding files to a disc that already contained some data in one folder. The Add button is used to launch a file browser so that the new files can be selected and added to the file list. The Next button is then operated

1 Basic data transfers

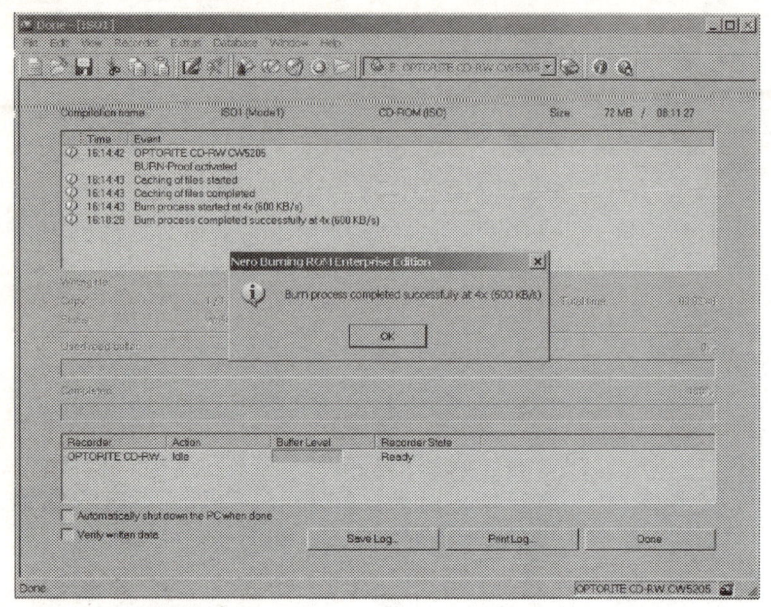

Fig.1.31 The pop-up message window indicates that the files were successfully copied to the disc

to move things on to the burning stage, and so on in standard wizard fashion. The wizard approach is probably the best one if you do not wish to get too deeply involved in burning CDs and DVDs.

UDF reader

There should be no problem when trying to read a CD-R disc using a PC that does not have a drive that can write to CDs. Even with a multisession disc, it should be possible to read it using an ordinary CD-ROM or DVD drive. In practice there can be problems with some drives finding it difficult to read certain discs. The modern discs that are almost silver in colour seem to be the least problematic, and can sometimes be read perfectly well using drives and audio players that are not guaranteed to be compatible with this type of disc. Discs that have a highly coloured coating, such as the bright blue variety, seem to be the most problematic.

Modern CD-ROM drives are generally very good at reading CD-R discs, but older units and DVD drives tend to be more troublesome. It might be

Basic data transfers 1

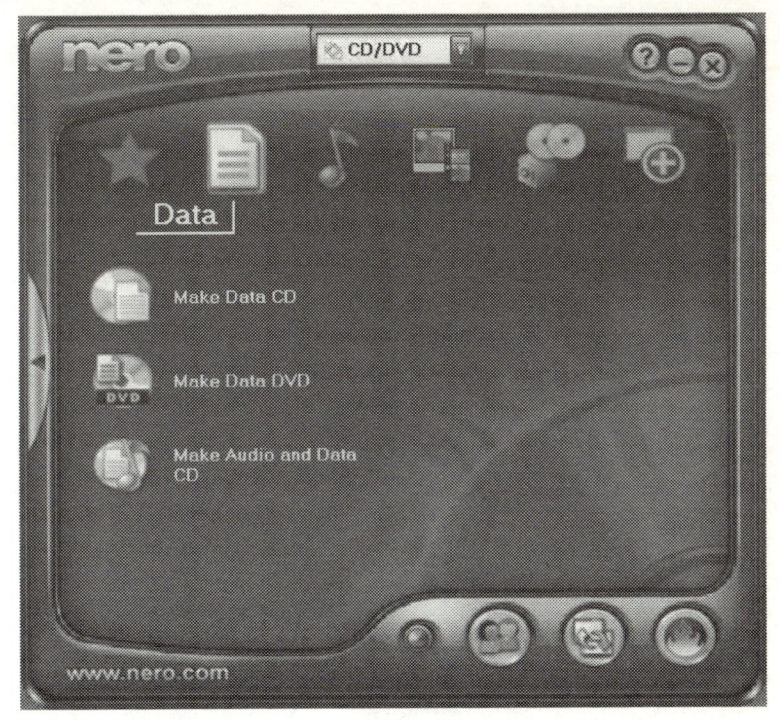

Fig.1.32 The opening screen of Nero's SmartStart front-end

necessary to experiment with discs of different makes in order to find a brand that gives perfect results every time with the particular equipment you are using. These days most PCs are equipped with a CD writer, and this should have no difficulty in reading any CD-R or CD-RW discs that are in serviceable condition. Where this type of drive is available, it therefore makes sense to use it when trying to read CD-R or CD-RW discs.

Reading any CD-RW disc on some PCs proves to be impossible, even though the computer is fitted with a drive that is guaranteed to be compatible with this type of disc. The same problem can occur with CD-R discs that have been used with certain forms of CD writing software. The problem often manifests itself as a disc that seems to work properly when it is first placed into a drive. However, the disc appears to contain no files or folders when its contents are examined using Windows Explorer

1 Basic data transfers

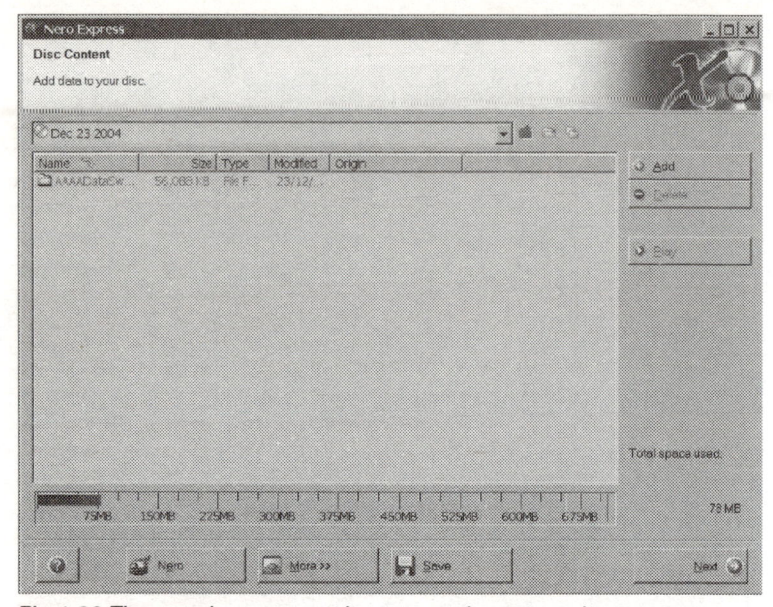

Fig.1.33 The opening screen takes you to the appropriate program

or a file browser. The disc is then found to be fine when it is returned to the PC that generated its contents.

In the case of a CD-R disc, it might be possible to render it readable on any PC with a multi-read CD drive. This is just a matter of closing the disc using the writing software. A better solution is to use an appropriate reader program on any PC that will need to read the discs. These programs are usually called "packet readers", "UDF readers", or "UDF packet readers". It is likely that your CD writing software was supplied with a program of this type, so it is worth looking through the documentation for installation details. If you run the installation disc it is possible that there will be an option for installing a UDF reader. In some cases it is necessary to go to the web site of the company that produced the CD writing program, where the reader is available as a free download.

UDF readers are also available from the usual sources of software downloads, such as www.downloads.com. However, make sure that you obtain a reader that is compatible with the software and operating system that you are using. Installing an inappropriate program can cause problems with reliability and can even cause boot problems.

Points to remember

Floppy discs are fine for transferring small amounts of data from one PC to another, but they are impractical when many megabytes or more of data are involved. Many PCs now lack a floppy disc drive, so it is not safe to assume that a recipient's PC will be able to handle a floppy disc.

A data compression program can reduce the amount of data to be transferred. This is potentially useful when using any method of transferring data. However, some types of data file have built-in compression and are unlikely to be significantly reduced in size by further compression.

External drives that are actually based on Flash memory are now quite cheap. They are available in the form of pen drives that have the memory and electronics in a single unit, or as a card reader that can be used with standard memory cards such as Compact Flash and Secure Digital cards. Both types provide a reasonably low-cost method of transferring several hundred megabytes of data.

Flash memory has a speed rating that is based on the one used for CD-ROM drives. A speed of X1 is about 150 kilobytes (0.15 megabytes) or so per second. It is normally only the faster cards that are marked with a speed rating. The speed of unmarked cards is usually between about X4 and X12.

With any external drive that uses a USB port it is as well to bear in mind that a USB 1.1 port only supports speeds of up to about 0.6 megabytes per second. This is adequate for many purposes, but will give long read and write times when gigabytes of data are involved. USB 2.0 and Firewire interfaces are much faster, and should not hinder the performance of any external storage device.

An external drive should be properly integrated with the operating system so that it has its own drive letter, just like an internal drive. With most types of drive, whether fitted externally or internally, it is possible to use the standard Windows Cut, Copy, Paste, and Delete functions.

1 Basic data transfers

Windows XP has built-in facilities for copying files to CD writers, and these are sufficient for many purposes. Other versions of Windows can only copy files to a CD writer with the aid of CD burning software, and additional software is also needed for DVD writers. It is likely that your PC or CD/DVD writer was supplied with a program of this type, such as a version of the popular Nero program.

It is not sufficient to have a compatible drive in order to read some CD-R and CD-RW discs. They can only be read using a PC that is equipped with a suitable UDF packet reader program. Do not install any program of this type unless you are sure that it is compatible with the version of Windows you are using.

2
Networks and direct connection

Missing link

Swapping data using high-capacity discs is a reasonably effective method, but it is also a bit fiddly, especially when a number of discs are involved. When dealing with large amounts of data it would clearly be much easier if the two PCs could be linked together so that files and folders could be freely exchanged. Taking things a stage further, it would often be a great asset if several computers could be linked so that data could be exchanged by any two computers in the system.

A basic swapping of data between two PCs or the linking of several PCs can be achieved using networking. This type of network is generally called a LAN (local area network). In other words, it is a network where all the PCs are in the same building, or at least close enough together for a connecting cable to be a practical proposition.

Networking PCs used to be a complex and expensive business, with few low-cost options. The few inexpensive methods of networking that were available often proved to be difficult to use, if they could be made to work at all! Matters are much easier these days, and networking two or more PCs is easy and quite inexpensive. Probably the best way of networking PCs is to use a standard Ethernet system, and this method is covered in detail later in this chapter. There are alternatives to using Ethernet ports, and these alternatives are covered in this chapter. Networking using Ethernet ports is covered in the next chapter.

2 Networks and direct connection

USB

A USB 1.1 port is not particularly fast with its maximum transfer rate of 11 megabits per second. It has to be borne in mind here that this speed is the number of bits that can be transferred in one second, and not the number of bytes. With eight bits per byte, the speed in megabytes per second is actually much less at just under 1.4 megabytes per second. A further complication is that a single USB device is permitted to utilise no more than half the bandwidth, which gives a maximum transfer rate of just under 0.7 megabytes per second. In practice it is likely that the transfer rate would actually be slightly less than this.

Although not fast, a transfer rate of this order is sufficient for many purposes. The speed problem when transferring large amounts of data via a USB 1.1 drive was covered in chapter one. With direct PC-to-PC transfers the situation is somewhat better, because only a single transfer is involved. When transferring data via an external drive it is necessary to transfer the data to the drive first, and then from the drive to the second PC. The direct method avoids the second transfer, but transferring a gigabyte of data would still take something like 25 to 30 minutes.

USB 2.0 offers much higher transfer rates, and it is potentially more than 40 times faster than a USB 1.1 interface. In theory, a gigabyte of data could be transferred in less than a minute. In practice it is unlikely that the PCs would be able to fully utilise the speed of the interface, but rapid data transfers should still be possible. Clearly USB 2.0 is preferable if you intend to swap large amounts of data via a USB link.

USB interfaces are not designed for networking, but on the face of it they are perfectly adequate for simple links from one PC to another. There is a major problem though, because USB interfaces are not designed for this type of link. The hardware is designed to accommodate one PC connecting to anything from one to several dozen peripheral devices. These devices can be practically anything, but would typically be "run of the mill" computing devices such as mice, printers, modems, and scanners. The PC controls the other devices in the system, which are usually relatively simple units. In the normal computer terminology, the PC is the master device and the peripherals are slave units.

Too many chiefs

Connecting two PCs via their USB interfaces causes a problem in that the system has two master devices and no slave units. A normal (A to B) USB cable has a large plug at the end which connects to the PC, and a

Networks and direct connection 2

Fig.2.1 A normal USB cable can not be used to connect two PCs

smaller plug at the other end for the connection to the peripheral device (Figure 2.1). This type of cable can not be used to connect two PCs. Even if two PCs could be linked via their USB ports, there would still be a problem because the hardware and operating system are not designed to cope with this setup.

There is a way around this problem in the form of special leads that contain some electronics. This is a form of "A to A" USB cable, and it has a large connector at each end. The electronics makes it appear as though each PC is connected to a slave device, and I suppose it is true to say that each PC really is connected to a slave unit. Each PC is actually connected to the electronics in the lead rather than direct to the other PC. The electronics provides a bridge between the two PCs, but it must be backed up by suitable software.

Leads of this type are sometimes supplied complete with the software needed to facilitate data transfers from one PC to another. Others are designed to work with third-party software such as one of the popular

2 Networks and direct connection

Laplink range of programs. Before buying the lead and the software separately you must make sure that it is possible to obtain both parts of the system, and that they are designed to work together. Buying a kit that contains the software and the special lead is the safest approach. Remember that a lead designed for use with USB 2.0 ports will only operate at full speed if both PCs have a spare USB 2.0 port. USB 2.0 equipment usually works with USB 1.1 ports, but only at the USB 1.1 speed.

Serial transfer

At one time it was quite common for ordinary RS232C serial ports to be used for simple PC links and even for simple networks. On the face of it a serial port is well suited to this application. It is capable of full-duplex operation, which simply means that it can send and receive data simultaneously. It is also designed as a general purpose communications link, so there is no major problem in using this type of interface to link two PCs. Simple and inexpensive connecting cables are perfectly adequate for serial links over short distances. Unfortunately, in practice there are major problems in using a standard serial interface to link two PCs.

One problem is simply that RS232C serial ports tend to be difficult to use, and serial links that should work well in theory do not necessarily work properly in the real world. This can necessitate a lot of trial and error in order to get a serial link to function correctly. Serial cables are quite inexpensive, but finding one that will work properly in this application can be difficult. Note that the usual "null-modem" serial cables will not work with a link from one PC to another. It is necessary to obtain a cable specifically intended for this application or to make your own. The do-it-yourself approach has a big advantage in that you can try altering some of the connections if it fails to work first time.

Another problem with an ordinary serial port is that it is not designed for high-speed operation. Serials ports can operate at a wide range of standard speeds, but the highest of these is 19200 baud, or 19200 bits per second in other words. PC serial ports can be persuaded faster than this, but in most cases the maximum usable baud rate is 115000 baud. Two or three additional bits are sent with each byte to aid synchronisation between the sending and receiving devices. This gives a maximum transfer rate that is likely to be about 10 kilobytes (0.01 megabytes) per second.

I used simple serial networks in the dim and distant past, but in those days a large amount of data was a few megabytes at most. Using a serial interface for a simple network is still a practical proposition where the transfer of small amounts of data is involved, but it is totally impractical where gigabytes of data are involved. Transferring large amounts of data in this way could take days or even weeks. Another point to bear in mind is that serial ports are gradually being phased out, so this method will not be an option in the not too distant future.

Parallel

The parallel ports originally fitted to PCs were only intended for sending data to a peripheral device such as a printer. Getting a parallel port to input data was actually possible, but only by using software that made use of a few clever tricks. Modern PCs have an upgraded version of the original port, and this can handle the inputting and outputting of parallel data. An advantage of the parallel approach is that data is sent and received as complete bytes rather than (literally) on a bit-by-bit basis. This gives the potential for faster transfers, and in its most advanced mode a PC parallel port can input or output data at about two megabytes per second. This is clearly much faster than the best rate available from a serial port, and it is actually faster than a USB 1.1 port. It is not possible to send and receive data simultaneously, but this is not usually a major drawback in practice.

The main problem with the parallel method is that the cables are quite expensive and can be difficult to obtain. Another point to bear in mind is that reliable operation is not possible using long cables. In fact it is usually necessary to use a cable of no more than about two or three metres in length. This is fine if the two PCs are in the same room, but links from one room to another are not usually possible using a parallel link.

Software

Using the MS-DOS operating system it is possible to copy files from one PC to another via a serial link without resorting to any special software. The standard operating system commands include the ability to send a file to a serial port and to copy from a serial port to a file. Windows seems to be rather less accommodating when it comes to simple file transfers, but it does have a more sophisticated alternative. It is possible

2   Networks and direct connection

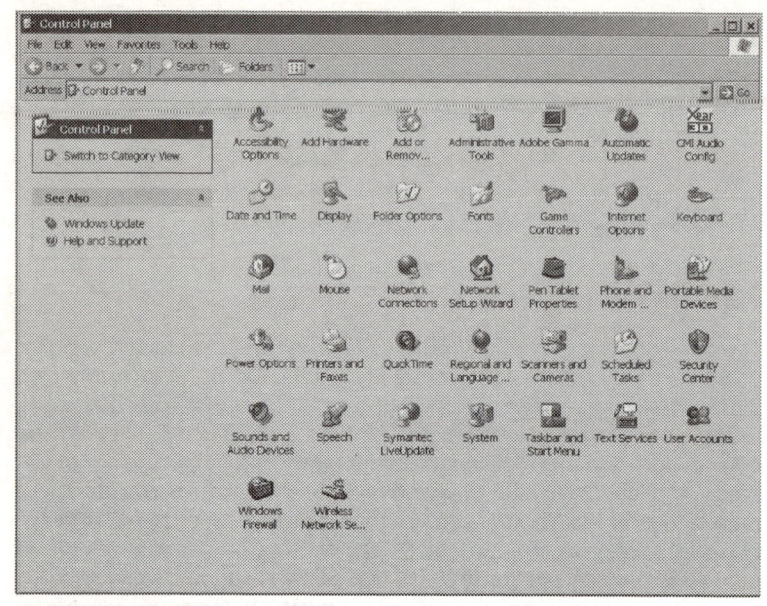

Fig.2.2 The Classic version of the Windows Control Panel

to use the networking facilities of Windows in conjunction with simple serial or parallel connections.

The relatively slow transfer speeds when using a serial interface mean that some of the networking facilities could be of limited use when using this type of connection. The higher speed of a parallel connection gives better results, but will still not be the equal of using a proper system of networking. Anyway, if you opt for this method it is quite easy to implement.

The first step is to go to the Windows Control Panel. The route to this depends on the version of Windows in use and the way it is set up, but with the "Classic" Windows setup it is accessed by going to the Start menu and selecting Settings, followed by Control Panel from the submenu. Another route is to double-click the My Computer icon, and then select the Control Panel link in the right-hand section of the new window that appears. The Windows Control Panel should look something like Figure 2.2, but the exact icons present will depend on the devices and software installed on your PC.

Networks and direct connection 2

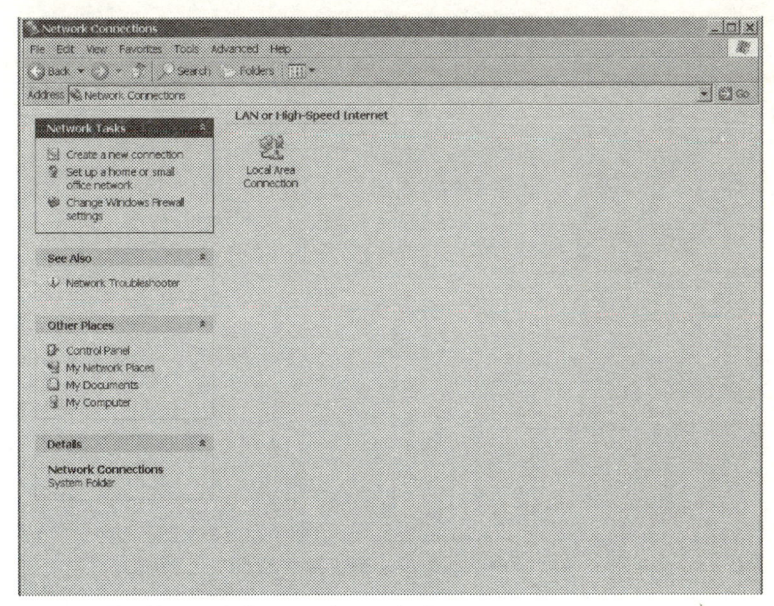

Fig.2.3 The Network Connections window

Start by double-clicking the Network or Network Connections icon. In the new window that appears (Figure 2.3) there should be a link called something like "Create a new connection" near the top left-hand corner of the window. Left-clicking this link should produce the New Connection Wizard (Figure 2.4). The initial screen is the usual type of Microsoft welcome screen that simply outlines the function of the wizard.

Things start in earnest at the next screen (Figure 2.5) where you select the connection type. This wizard is used when adding various types of network connection, so there are a number of options, each of which leads to further options. In this case the radio button nearest the bottom of the screen should be selected, as it is an advanced connection that is being set up. This leads two a couple of options at the next screen (Figure 2.6). In this case it is a direct connection to another computer via a serial or parallel port that is required, so the lower radio button is operated.

Moving on to the next screen (Figure 2.7) there are two more options. The two computers in the system must be set up for a direct network connection. They are set up slightly differently as one must be set as the

2 Networks and direct connection

Fig.2.4 The Welcome screen of the New Connection Wizard

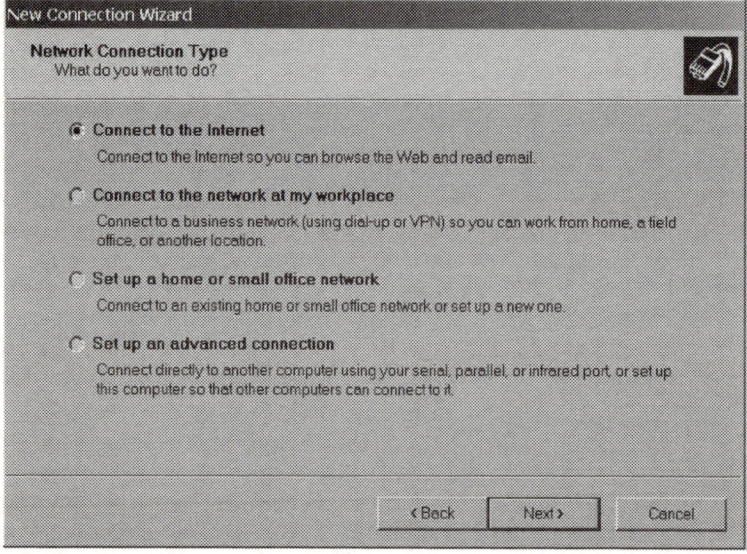

Fig.2.5 This screen is used to select the type of connection

Networks and direct connection

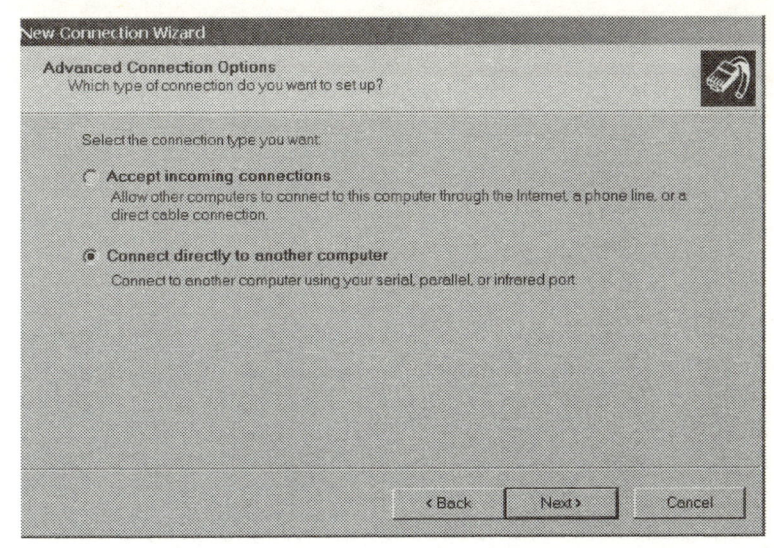

Fig.2.6 Use the lower radio button to select a direct connection

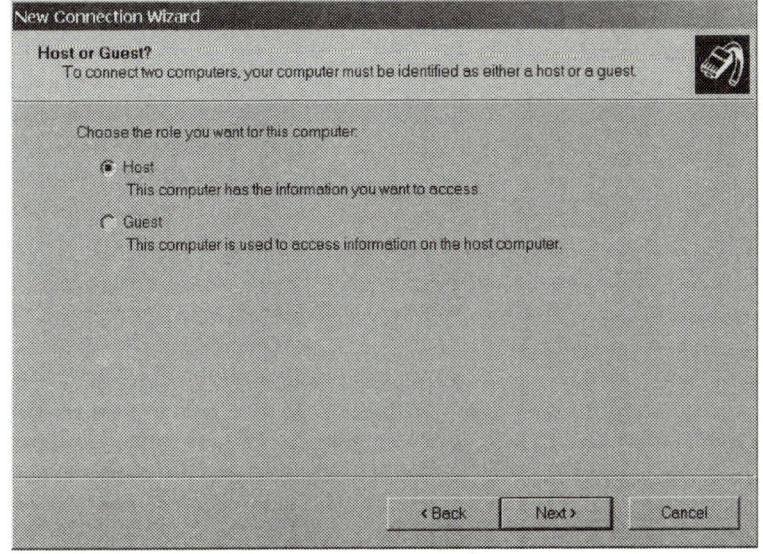

Fig.2.7 Host and Guest options are available from this screen

2   Networks and direct connection

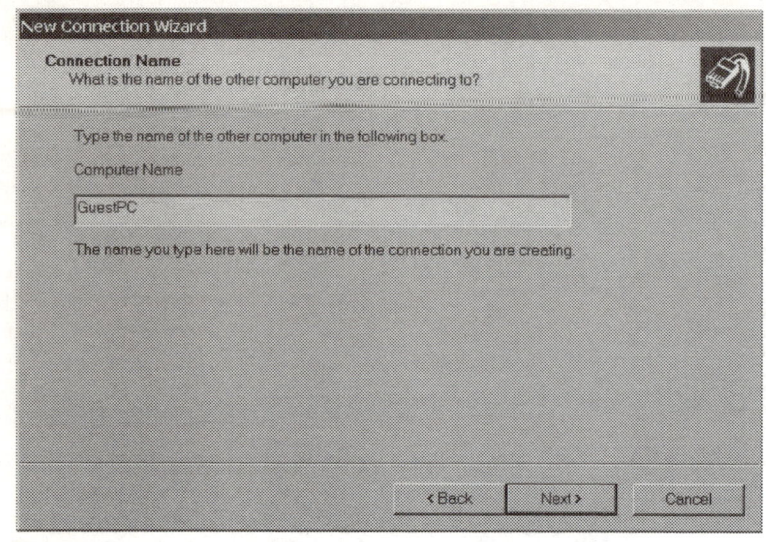

Fig.2.8 The computer must be given a unique network name

host and the other as the guest. The host computer is the one that contains the files that you wish to share, and the guest computer is the one to which the files will be copied. It is advisable to set up the host computer first and then the guest computer. The process is essentially the same for the two types of connection. In this example we will assume that the host PC has already been set up for a direct connection and that it is a guest connection that is being produced. It is therefore the lower of the two radio buttons that is selected.

Naming

With any network, including a very basic type such as this, each computer or other device in the system must be given a unique name. The name is added at the next screen (Figure 2.8). The name used is not of great importance with a simple two-PC setup, but it is always good to use network names that are brief and to the point. A menu is provided at the subsequent screen (Figure 2.9), and this is used to select the port that will be used for the connection to the other PC. There will typically be two serial ports (COM1 and COM2) and one parallel port (LPT1) on offer, but the exact options depends on the hardware fitted to your particular

Networks and direct connection 2

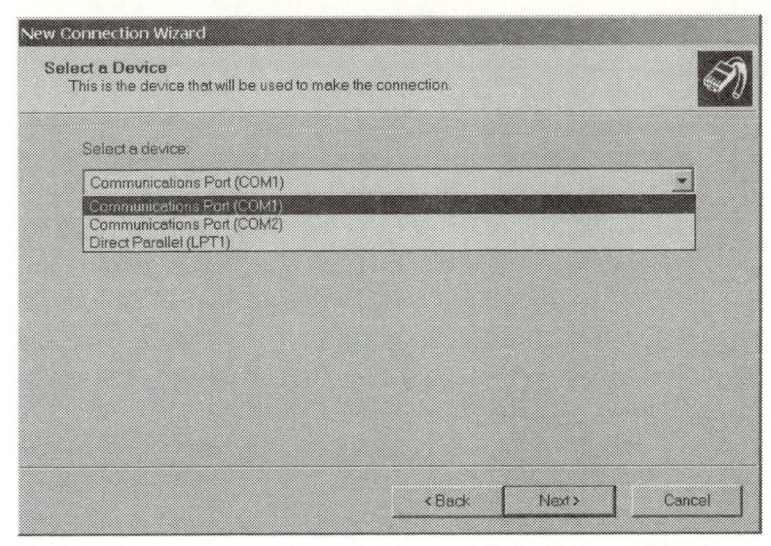

Fig.2.9 This menu is used to select the port that will be used for the connection

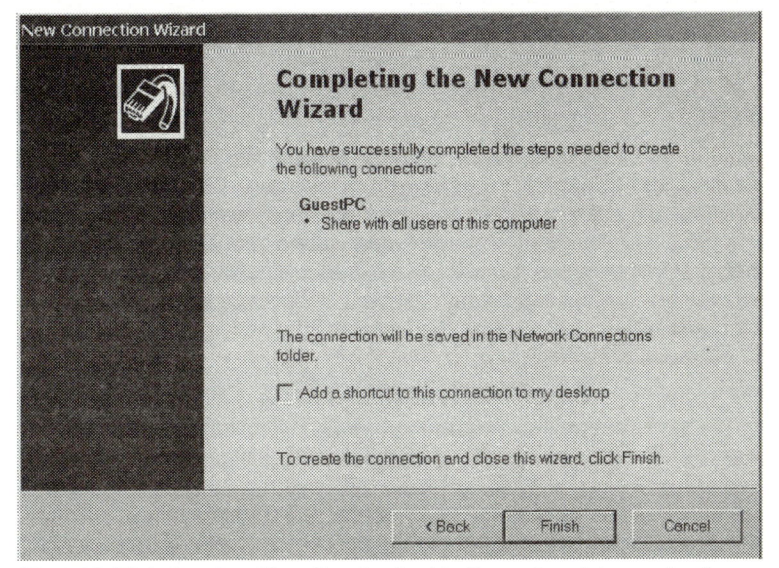

Fig.2.10 Tick the checkbox if a shortcut to the network is required

2 Networks and direct connection

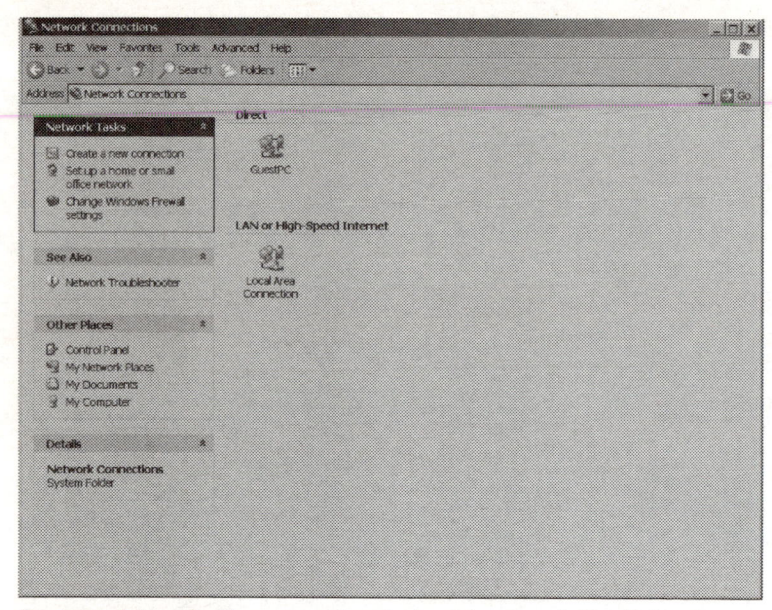

Fig.2.11 A icon for the new network should appear in the Network Connection window

PC. Simply select whichever port you are using for the network connection.

Moving on to the screen of Figure 2.10 gives the option of adding a desktop shortcut to the new network connection. Tick the checkbox if you wish to add this shortcut. Operating the Finish button completes the process. An icon for the new connection should be added to the Network Connections window. In the example of Figure 2.11 there was already one connection present, and this connection provides access to a broadband modem via an Ethernet port. The one in the Direct section is the newly added network connection.

If you did not opt for a desktop shortcut, it is still possible to access the new connection by double-clicking its icon in the Network Connections window. Accessing the connection produces the small window of Figure 2.12, and this will be launched automatically on finishing the setting up procedure. Although this is an extremely basic form of network connection it is still necessary to log onto the network. This requires a username and password to be entered into the appropriate textboxes.

Networks and direct connection   2

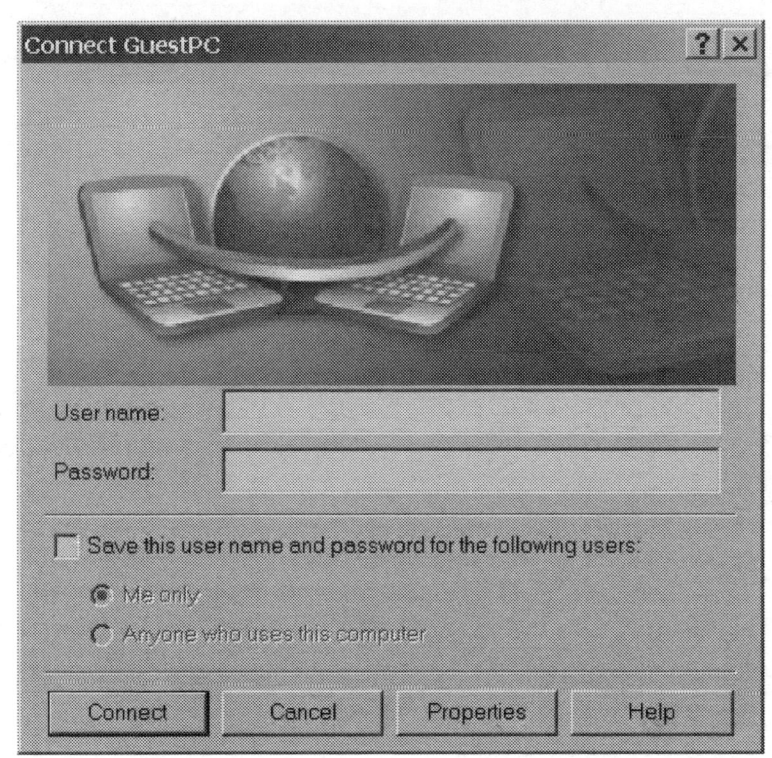

Fig.2.12 Accessing the network produces this window

Tick the checkbox if you would prefer not to enter these each time the network connection is used. The two radio buttons near the bottom of the window become active when this option selected. These permit the user name and password to be entered automatically only when the current user is operating the PC, or when any user is operating it. In this context a user is really a user account, and it will obviously not be applicable if the PC is set up with only one user account.

Properties

It is possible to alter the settings of the new connection by right-clicking its icon and selecting Properties from the pop-up menu. This produces the connection's properties window (Figure 2.13), which will show the

2 Networks and direct connection

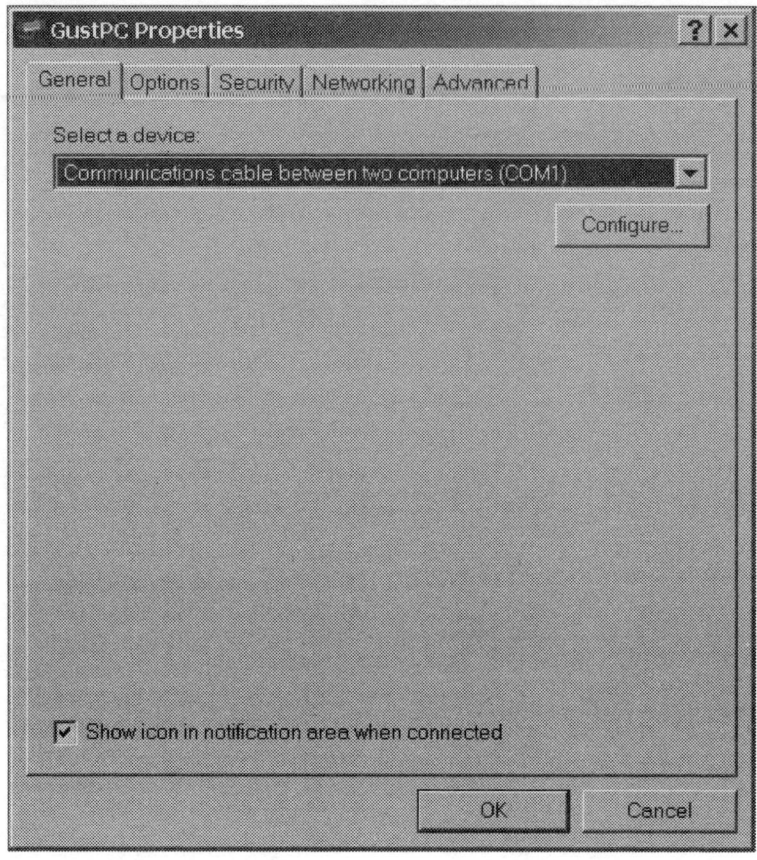

Fig.2.13 Changes can be made via the connection's Properties window

General page initially. The menu on this page enables a different port to be used for the connection. The Options section (Figure 2.14) provides control over the way logging on and dialling is handled. Obviously there is no dialling in the conventional sense in this case, and this term simply refers to the process by which the guest PC establishes contact with the host PC.

Operating the Advanced tab produces the window of Figure 2.15, where there is the option of sharing an Internet connection. This is good in theory, but it is probably not worthwhile unless a broadband connection

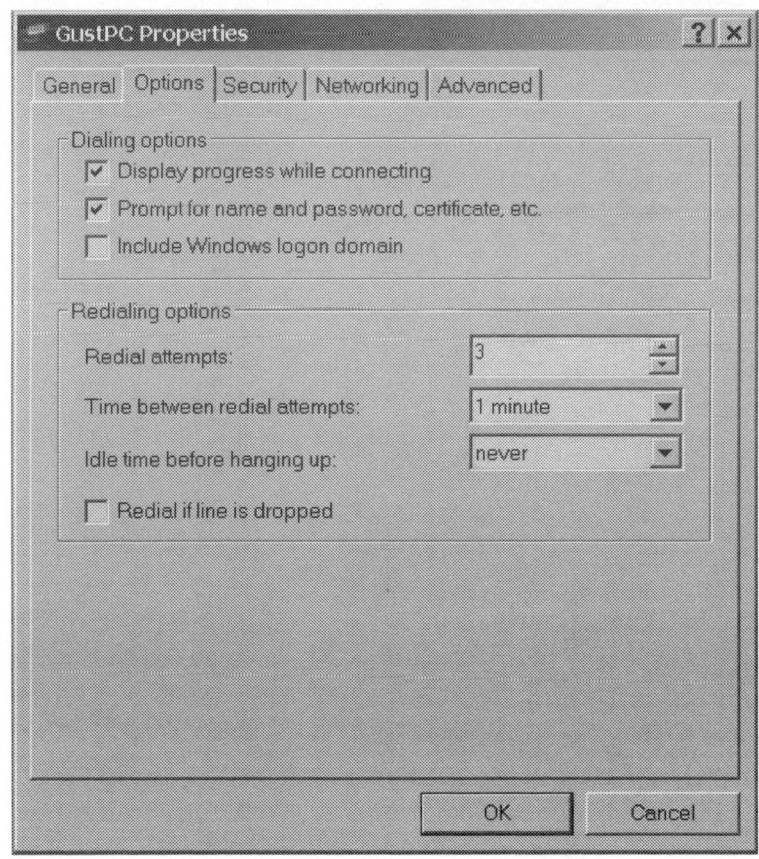

Fig.2.14 The Options section of the Properties window

is available. Even then it would be better to opt for a combined modem and router, and proper networking.

In general it is not a good idea to play around with the various settings available in the properties window, as this could result in a working connection being rendered inoperative. However, if you are using a serial connection it is certainly worth trying baud rates that are higher than the default. In order to do this, first go to the General page and then operate the Configure button. A menu offers various maximum bps (bits per second) speeds, and by default it will be set at 19200.

2 Networks and direct connection

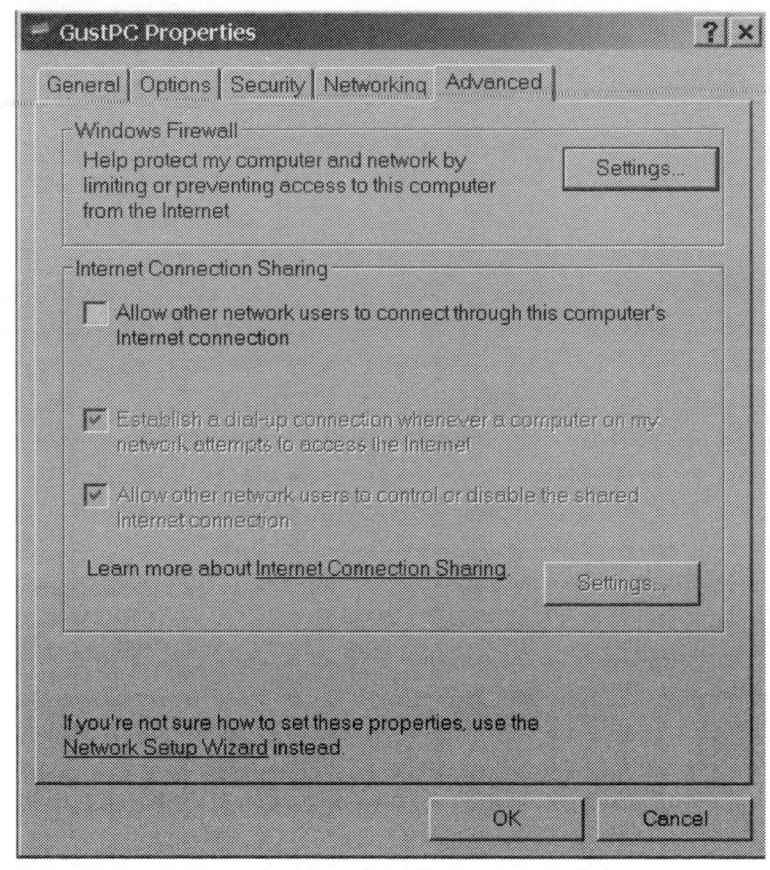

Fig.2.15 The Advanced section of the Properties window

As pointed out previously, this is the highest standard rate for serial ports, but higher rates can usually be achieved with PCs provided a long serial cable is not being used. With a cable of up to about three metres in length it is usually possible to operate the serial ports reliably at 115200 bit per second. It is apparently possible to use higher rates with some PCs, and these are available from the menu Figure 2.16). There is no harm in trying them, but I have never obtained usable results when using rates above 115200 bits per second. It is quite likely that the network will not work at all with one of the very high rates. Note that both ends of the system must be set to use the same rate.

Networks and direct connection 2

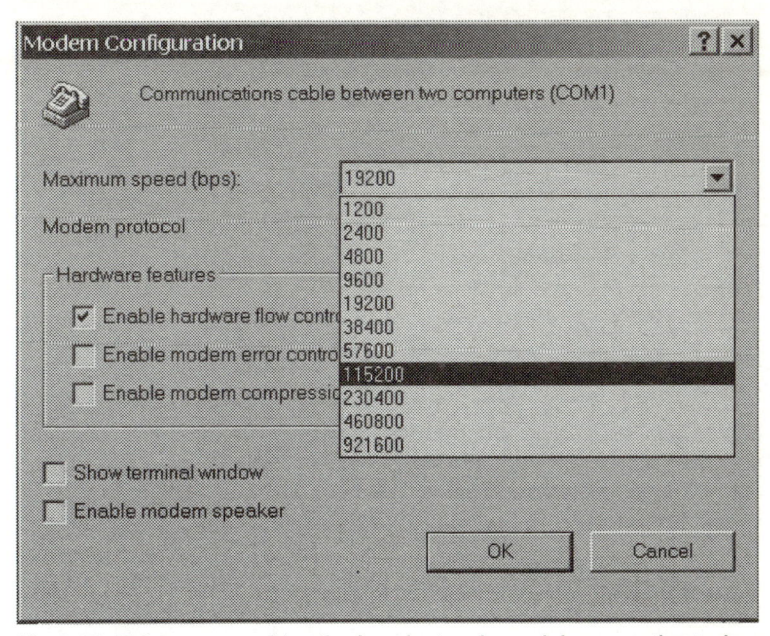

Fig.2.16 This menu enables the baud rate of a serial connection to be changed

Ports

With modern PCs the serial and parallel ports are almost invariably in the main cluster of ports at the rear of the unit. There is no proper standardisation of the layout because the actual ports present vary somewhat from one PC to another. Fortunately, the serial and parallel ports are easily spotted. Figure 2.17 shows the layout of a typical PC port cluster. The printer port is the large 25-way type, and the serial ports are the similar but smaller ports having 9-way connectors.

When using a serial port it does not matter which one is used for the network, and it is perfectly all right to use COM1 on one PC and COM2 on the other. Of course, the port setting in the network's properties window must match up with the port you use. Windows will not go in search of the right port if you accidentally specify the wrong one. It is probably best to use ready-made cables that are specifically designed for a direct serial or parallel port connection. Details of do-it-yourself

2   Networks and direct connection

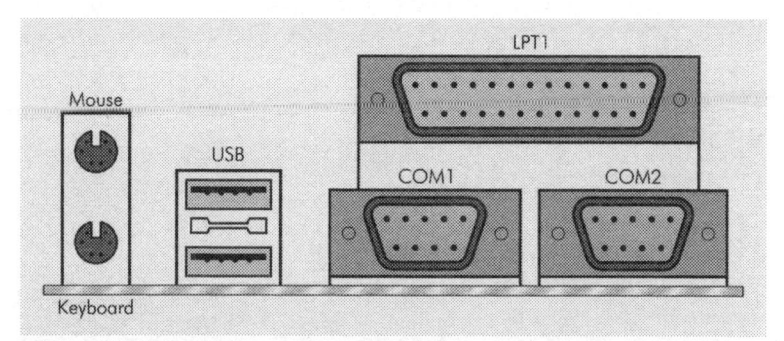

Fig.2.17 The layout of a typical port cluster on a modern PC

cables can probably be found on the Internet, but these days it is usually cheaper to buy ready-made cables. Using ready-made leads should also avoid the inevitable hassles that seem to occur when making your own.

The BIOS

Any PC should be set so that the serial ports are operational by default. The same is true of the parallel port, but the port will often operate in a basic mode by default. In order to operate at maximum speed in a networking application it is necessary for the parallel port to be set to one of the more advanced modes that provide high-speed bidirectional operation. Note that the network should work, but at a relatively low speed, if the ports are set to the standard mode.

If a parallel port network fails to establish a connection when it is first tried, it is likely that one or both of the ports are set to the wrong enhanced mode, or that there is a mismatch in the modes. The network will not work at all until this problem is corrected. With a modern PC the ports are controlled via a built-in program that is part of the BIOS (basic input/output system).

The BIOS performs some basic checks when a computer is first switched on, and it then boots the operating system if no problems are detected. It also provides routines and information that help the operating system to use the drives, memory, etc., in an error-free fashion. The BIOS Setup program enables the user to control some aspects of the PC's hardware, such as the memory timing, and the motherboard's power management facilities.

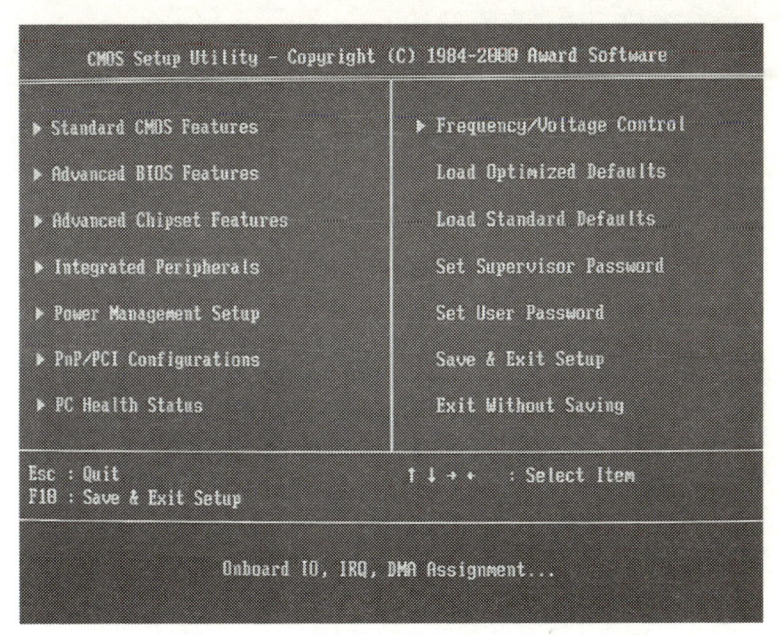

```
CMOS Setup Utility - Copyright (C) 1984-2000 Award Software
┌─────────────────────────────────┬─────────────────────────────────┐
│ ▶ Standard CMOS Features        │ ▶ Frequency/Voltage Control     │
│ ▶ Advanced BIOS Features        │   Load Optimized Defaults       │
│ ▶ Advanced Chipset Features     │   Load Standard Defaults        │
│ ▶ Integrated Peripherals        │   Set Supervisor Password       │
│ ▶ Power Management Setup        │   Set User Password             │
│ ▶ PnP/PCI Configurations        │   Save & Exit Setup             │
│ ▶ PC Health Status              │   Exit Without Saving           │
├─────────────────────────────────┴─────────────────────────────────┤
│ Esc : Quit                           ↑ ↓ → ←  : Select Item       │
│ F10 : Save & Exit Setup                                           │
├───────────────────────────────────────────────────────────────────┤
│              Onboard IO, IRQ, DMA Assignment...                   │
└───────────────────────────────────────────────────────────────────┘
```

Fig.2.18 The initial screen of an Award BIOS Setup program

I doubt if it is possible to damage any of the hardware by using inappropriate settings in the BIOS, but it is certainly possible to make the PC unusable until the erroneous settings are corrected. Do not be tempted to experiment with BIOS settings that you do not understand. If the worst should happen, with badly mangled BIOS settings it is usually possible to return to the default settings via an option on the main menu page. This might not get the PC operating at the peak of performance again, but it should get it working quite well once more. If you know you have made a mistake, you can simply exit the program without saving the changes. The BIOS Setup program can then be entered again, so that a fresh attempt can be made.

The BIOS Setup program is not part of the operating system, and in most cases it can not be accessed via the operating system. It is built into the PC and is contained in a memory chip on the motherboard. With most PCs the BIOS Setup program is entered by pressing the "Del" key at the appropriate point is the initial boot-up routine. However, there are plenty of alternative methods such as pressing the Esc or Ins key. Usually there is an onscreen message during the initial testing routine

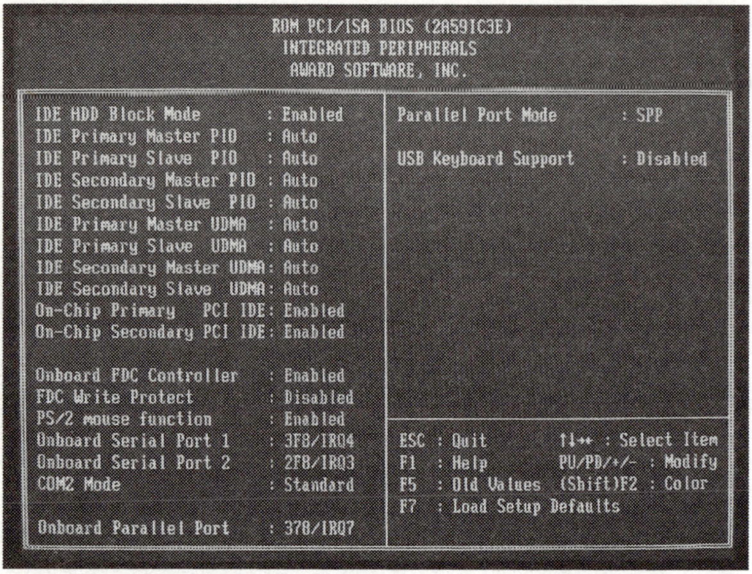

2 Networks and direct connection

Fig.2.19 The Integrated Peripherals section of an Award BIOS

that indicates which key or keys to operate. If in doubt you should consult the instruction manual for your computer or the manual for its motherboard.

BIOS changes

Modern Setup programs are quite large, and have the available options in half a dozen or so groups. Figure 2.18 shows the initial screen produced by an Award BIOS, and it is really an outsize menu. Use the cursor key to highlight the required option and then operate the Return key to enter that menu. The serial and parallel port settings are usually in a section called something like "Integrated Peripherals". Figure 2.19 shows this section of an Award BIOS. The address and IRQ (interrupt request) number for the port are set via the entry at the bottom of the left-hand section, but there should be no need to alter these. The parallel port's mode is set via the entry at the top of the right-hand section of the screen. In this case the cursor keys are used to select the required parameter, and the Pg Up and Pg Dn keys on the numeric keypad are then used to alter the setting. However, the exact method of control

Networks and direct connection 2

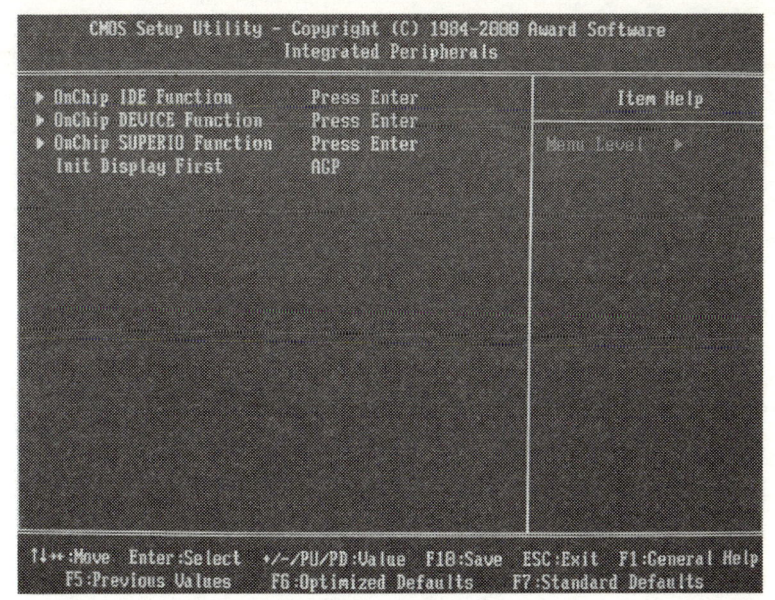

```
          CMOS Setup Utility - Copyright (C) 1984-2000 Award Software
                            Integrated Peripherals

 ▶ OnChip IDE Function           Press Enter              Item Help
 ▶ OnChip DEVICE Function        Press Enter
 ▶ OnChip SUPERIO Function       Press Enter           Menu Level  ▶
   Init Display First            AGP













 ↑↓→← :Move  Enter:Select  +/-/PU/PD:Value  F10:Save  ESC:Exit  F1:General Help
     F5:Previous Values    F6:Optimized Defaults    F7:Standard Defaults
```

Fig.2.20 This screen offers three submenus

varies from one BIOS manufacturer to another. There are usually onscreen prompts that indicate the functions of the important keys.

The size of a modern BIOS Setup program is such that it might be necessary to go into a submenu in order to find the section that deals with the parallel port. In the example of Figure 2.20 there are three submenus to choose from, and it is not immediately obvious which one gives access to the parallel port's parameters. The manual for the computer or its motherboard might provide some help, but if necessary you will have to do some exploring. With this version of the Award BIOS I found the parallel port's settings in the SUPERIO section (Figure 2.21).

Modes

The modes on offer are usually something like standard, SPP, EPP, and ECP. If you are using third-party software to facilitate the connection it will be necessary to consult the instruction manual in order to ascertain which mode or modes are supported. With a Windows Direct Connection network it is the ECP mode that is required for a high-speed connection.

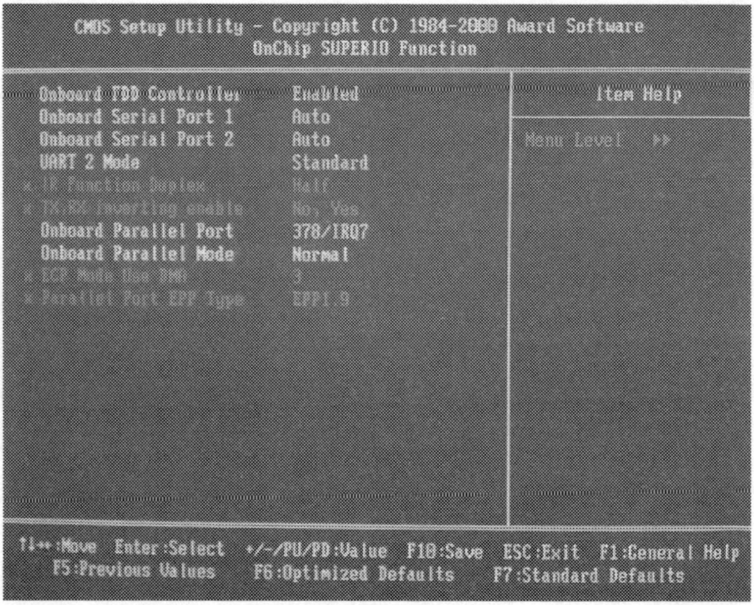

2 Networks and direct connection

```
          CMOS Setup Utility - Copyright (C) 1984-2000 Award Software
                           OnChip SUPERIO Function

   Onboard FDD Controller       Enabled                    Item Help
   Onboard Serial Port 1        Auto
   Onboard Serial Port 2        Auto               Menu Level    ▶▶
   UART 2 Mode                  Standard
 x IR Function Duplex           Half
 x TX,RX inverting enable       No, Yes
   Onboard Parallel Port        378/IRQ7
   Onboard Parallel Mode        Normal
 x ECP Mode Use DMA             3
 x Parallel Port EPP Type       EPP1.9




   ↑↓→← :Move   Enter:Select   +/-/PU/PD:Value  F10:Save  ESC:Exit  F1:General Help
        F5:Previous Values     F6:Optimized Defaults    F7:Standard Defaults
```

Fig.2.21 In this case the SUPERIO section has the required settings

Note that this mode might not be available using a PC that is getting "a bit long in the tooth", so it is as well to check that this mode is available before buying a parallel networking cable. Of course, in the absence of the ECP mode you can try a slower connection using the standard or SPP mode. Having set the correct mode for the parallel port, press the Escape key once or twice to return to the main menu. Then select the Save and Exit Setup option to save the changes, exit the program, and boot into Windows.

If the network still fails to establish a connection, the most likely cause is that the lead is not connected properly at one end of the system. Make sure that both connectors are fully pushed into place and are not fitted at an angle. Use the screws on the connectors to lock them securely in place. Note that serial leads that have two 25-way male connectors can be used to physically link two parallel ports, but they will not provide the correct interconnections. A parallel port network will only work using a cable designed specifically for this application.

Points to remember

It is possible to transfer files from one PC to another via a link provided by ordinary serial or parallel ports. Windows has a built-in facility that can use a connection of this type to provide a very basic form of networking. Bear in mind that PC serial and parallel ports are due to be phased out, so this method will become obsolete in the not too distant future.

Transfer speeds using parallel ports are reasonable, but are nowhere near as fast as those obtained using proper networking ports. In theory, an enhanced parallel port can transfer data at up to about two megabytes per second.

Ordinary serial ports are not intended for high speed data transfers. Even when using these ports beyond their normal maximum bit rates, data transfers are unlikely to exceed 10 to 20 kilobytes (0.01 to 0.02 megabytes) per second. This type of connection is therefore impractical when large amounts of data must be transferred.

Networking using parallel ports normally requires the ports to be set to one of their more advanced modes that provide high-speed two-way communication. This might require adjustment to the appropriate setting in the BIOS Setup program. The ECP mode is required for a Windows Direct Connection Network that uses parallel interfacing for a high-speed connection.

Do not be tempted to experiment with the settings in the BIOS Setup program. Using the wrong settings should not cause any damage to the hardware, but it could prevent the computer from operating until the errors are corrected.

If you should manage to seriously scramble the BIOS settings, the main menu normally has an option that sets them all back to the defaults. This should at least get the computer operating again, but it might not provide optimum performance.

2 Networks and direct connection

The network connection must be set up using the Network Connection Wizard, and the physical connection is of no practical value until this is done. Alternatively, a third party program such as an appropriate version of Laplink can be used to facilitate data transfers.

3
Setting up a LAN

Proper networking

In the past there was a big advantage in a simple form of networking such as the Direct Connection variety. Proper networking equipment cost a substantial amount of money, and it certainly cost more than most home and small business users were prepared to pay. The situation is rather different these days, and it is generally better to opt for a proper network.

The main drawback of these ultra-simple networking systems is that their expansion potential is strictly limited. In most cases it is nonexistent rather than limited, and they are only of use if you will never need anything beyond a simple link between two computers. Another drawback is that the cables tend to be relatively expensive, which negates the main point of using the computer's built-in ports. One of these basic links could actually cost more than using a "real" network. This will certainly be the case if your PCs have built-in network ports, and this is now quite a common feature

In the early days of PCs there were numerous interfaces designed specifically for networking, and some of these coexisted for many years. A standard port for networking gradually emerged in the form of the Ethernet type, which became more popular and the others gradually "fell by the wayside". No doubt there are still many PCs that are networked by way of an alternative interface, but Ethernet is the only type that is currently in widespread use with PCs. If you have a PC with a built-in network port it will certainly be an Ethernet type, and it is the only "real" networking method that will be considered in this book.

Ethernet ports are sometimes referred to as 10/100 networking ports. The two figures refer to the original speed of this interface and the speed of the improved version. They respectively operate at speeds of 10 and 100 megabits per second. Note that the speeds are in megabits per second and not megabytes. There are eight bits per byte, and with a practical networking system it is necessary to send more than just the

3 Setting up a LAN

Fig.3.1 The Ethernet socket is to the right of the two USB ports

raw data. Transfers at about 1 and 10 megabytes per second might be possible, but in practice it is likely that the transfer rates would actually be somewhat lower. Even being pessimistic about the performance of an Ethernet port, a 100 megabyte file could be transferred in less than 20 seconds, which is more than adequate for most purposes.

It is assumed here that the system can handle the higher operating speed, and any reasonably modern Ethernet port should be capable of doing so. When setting up a new network it is very unlikely that any 10-megabit equipment will be on offer from the retailers, and if any should be on offer it would definitely not be a good idea to buy it. Modern 10/100 Ethernet equipment costs so little these days that there is little point in bothering with old and inferior pieces of equipment. There is good compatibility between 10-megabit devices and the modern 10/100 variety, but as one would probably expect, a link only operates at the lower rate if one device is a 10-megabit type.

Note that 10 and 100-megabit cables are different. Although a 10-megabit cable will work with a 10/100 Ethernet system, it will only support operation at the slower rate. Again, the cost of a modern cable that operates at the higher speed is now so low that there is little point in using old 10-megabit cables. These days the 100-megabit cables are the only networking type that are likely to be available in the shops. If you are new to networking you can forget the 10-megabit option and regard an Ethernet port as a 100-megabit type.

Setting up a LAN 3

Fig.3.2 Removing a side panel gives access to the PC's interior

Adding ports

It might be necessary to install Ethernet ports in some of the PCs in the system, but check to see if any of the PCs are already equipped with this type of interface. Many PCs are supplied complete with an Ethernet port, and in the example of Figure 3.1 it is in the main cluster of ports, next to the USB types and below the PS/2 mouse and keyboard ports.

An Ethernet socket looks a bit like the type of telephone socket used in the USA and some other countries, and the sockets often used for broadband modems in the UK. Ethernet connectors are different though, and they are physically incompatible with any type of telephone socket. This is important, because some networking equipment has a socket to handle connections to a telephone line or a modem. Using incompatible connectors ensures that errors are avoided when installing the cables.

67

3 Setting up a LAN

Fig.3.3 Two common forms of blanking plate

Ethernet equipment uses RJ-45 connectors, and the cables are sometimes referred to as RJ-45 cables.

Adding an Ethernet port to a desktop PC is normally straightforward provided there is at least one PCI expansion slot free. The cost of generic Ethernet cards is extremely low, and those from the well-known manufacturers are not expensive. In order to add the card it is necessary to gain access to the interior of the PC, and this usually means removing the appropriate two or three screws at the rear of the unit. With some form of tower case this enables the left-hand side panel (as viewed from the front) to be pulled clear (Figure 3.2). Note that removing the other side panel will not give access to the expansion slots. With a desktop case it is the lid of the case that has to be removed.

There is usually a fair sprinkling of screws on the rear panel of the case, so look at the way the case is put together and be careful to remove the right ones. It is unlikely that any harm will be done if you should manage to remove one or two screws that (say) hold the power supply unit in place, but replace the screws immediately if a mistake is made. Fathoming some of the more stylish cases can be difficult, but if in doubt, the documentation supplied with the PC should explain how to gain access to the expansion slots.

Fig.3.4 This case has all seven of its brackets in place

Blanking plate

Before the network card can be fitted it is necessary to remove a blanking plate in the rear of the case for the particular slot you will be using. Cases used to be supplied with blanking plates that were screwed to a bracket at the rear of the case. This type is not used a great deal these days, but it is still to be found in some of the more up-market cases. Including the screw-fixing type, there are three main forms of blanking plate currently in use.

The original type is held in place by a single screw per blanking plate. A bracket of this type is shown on the right in Figure 3.3. If you undo the screw using a largish cross-point screwdriver the bracket should pull free without any difficulty. It is advisable to keep the bracket so the hole in the rear of the case can be blocked up again if you remove the expansion card at some later date. The bracket's fixing screw will be needed to hold the expansion card in place.

Probably the most popular kind of bracket these days is the type that is partially cut out from the rear of the case. In order to remove one of

3 Setting up a LAN

Fig.3.5 Here two of the brackets have been twisted slightly so that they can be broken free

these it is necessary to twist it to and fro until the thin pieces of metal connecting it to the main casing fatigue and break. Figure 3.4 shows the rear of a new case with all of the brackets in place. In Figure 3.5 two of the brackets have been twisted round slightly to show how they can be broken away from the main casing. There is little point in keeping this type of bracket since it can not be fitted back in place again.

The third method has brackets that clip into the screw holes in the main case. A bracket of this type is shown on the left in Figure 3.3. These can be twisted slightly and pulled free, and the process is reversible provided the bracket is not seriously distorted during removal. It is therefore worthwhile keeping these brackets as they can be fitted into the case again should the need arise.

With the metal bracket removed, the network card (Figure 3.6) can be removed from its anti-static packing and pushed into position on the motherboard. Some cards and slots fit together quite easily while other combinations are less accommodating. Never try the brute force method of fitting expansion cards into place. Using plenty of force is virtually

Setting up a LAN 3

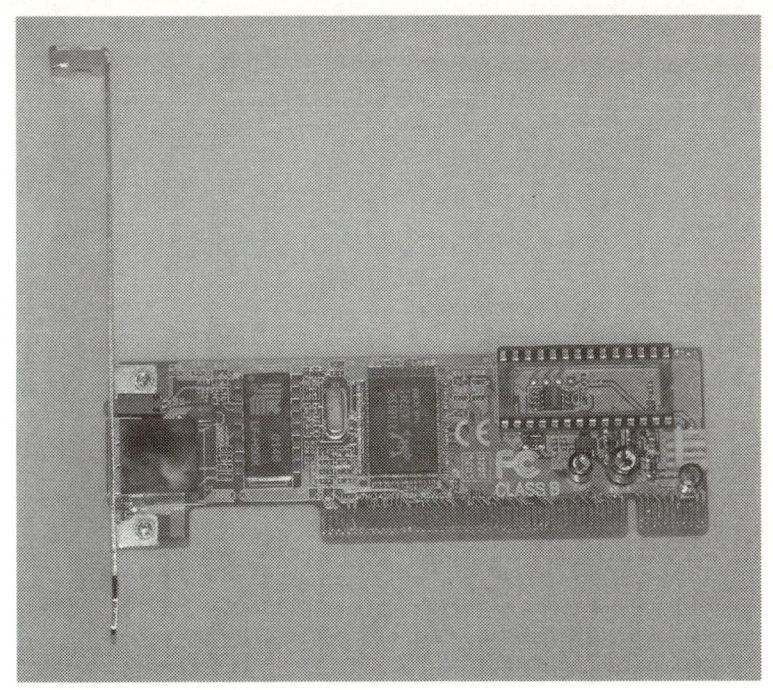

Fig.3.6 A low-cost PCI network card

always the wrong approach when dealing with PCs, but it is certainly asking for trouble when applied to expansion cards. Apart from the risk of damage to the card itself there is also a likelihood of writing off the motherboard.

Alignment

If a card seems to be reluctant to fit into place, check that the metal bracket is slotting correctly into place between the case and the motherboard. With some PCs the bottom end of the bracket has to be bent away from the circuit board slightly as it otherwise tends to hit the motherboard rather than fitting just behind it. Look carefully to see what is blocking the card. It can be quite dim inside a PC, so if necessary, get some additional light inside the PC using something like a spot-lamp or a powerful torch.

3 Setting up a LAN

Fig.3.7 The card's mounting bracket is bolted to the case

Probably the most common problem is the card being slightly too far forward or back. This is the same problem with the metal bracket, but manifesting itself in a different manner. The bracket is fitting into place correctly, but the rest of the card is then out of alignment. If the misalignment is only slight, you should be able to ease the card backwards or forwards slightly and then into place.

Where there is a large error it will be necessary to form the bracket slightly in order to get the card to fit properly. In one or two cases where all else has failed, slightly loosening the screws that fix the motherboard to the chassis has provided the solution. Presumably in these cases the motherboard has been bolted in place when it is fractionally out of position. Loosening the mounting bolts and then fitting the expansion card shifts it into the correct position. The mounting bolts are then retightened, and fitting further expansion cards should be perfectly straightforward.

The mounting bracket can be fixed to the bracket at the rear of the case (Figure 3.7) once the card is correctly in place. Where appropriate, use

Setting up a LAN 3

the screw removed along with the blanking plate. It is otherwise a matter of looking through the odds and ends supplied with the PC, which should include at least one fixing screw per free expansion slot.

Shocking truth

If you are new to handling PC components it is important to realise that most of them, including practically all expansion cards, are vulnerable to damage from static charges. I think it is worth making the point that it does not take a large static charge complete with sparks and "cracking" sounds to damage sensitive electronic components. Large static discharges of that type are sufficient to damage most modern semiconductor components, and not just the more sensitive ones.

Many of the components used in computing are so sensitive to static charges that they can be damage by relatively small voltages. In this context "small" still means a potential of perhaps a hundred volts or so, but by static standards this is not particularly large. Charges of this order will not generate noticeable sparks or make your hair stand on end, but they are nevertheless harmful to many electronic components. Hence you can "zap" these components simply by touching them, and in most cases would not be aware that anything had happened.

An obvious precaution when handling any vulnerable computer components is to keep well away from any known or likely sources of static electricity. These includes such things as computer monitors, television sets, any carpets or furnishings that are known to be prone to static generation, and even any pets that are known to get charged-up fur coats. Also avoid wearing any clothes that are known to give problems with static charges.

This seems to be less of a problem than it once was, because few clothes these days are made from a cloth that consists entirely of man-made fibres. There is normally a significant content of natural fibres, and this seems to be sufficient to prevent any significant build-up of static charges. However, if you should have any garments that might give problems, make sure that you do not wear them when handling any computer equipment or components.

Static sensitive components will be supplied in some form of anti-static packaging, and this is usually nothing more than a plastic bag made from a special plastic that is slightly conductive. There is quite a range of anti-static packaging currently in use, but an expansion card is unlikely to be supplied in anything more elaborate that a conductive plastic bag.

3   Setting up a LAN

This effectively short-circuits the edge connector of the card so that no significant voltage can build up between the terminals.

Although it is tempting to remove the components from the packing to have a good look at them, try to keep this type of thing to a minimum. Ideally it should be completely avoided. When it is necessary to remove the card from its packing, always make sure that both you and the plastic bag is earthed before the component is removed. Simply touching the earthed chassis of a computer while holding the component in its bag should be sufficient to ensure that everything is kept free of static charges.

The computer must be switched off and the power should also be switched off at the mains socket. The chassis of the computer will still be earthed provided the mains lead is connected to the computer and the mains socket. There is a risk of a charge gradually building up in your body, but touching the earthed chassis of the computer every minute or so will prevent this from occurring.

Wristbands

If you wish to make quite sure that your body remains static-free, you can earth yourself to the computer by way of a proper earthing wristband. This is basically just a wristband made from electrically conductive material that connects to the earth via a lead and a high value resistor. The lead is terminated in a clip that permits easy connection to the chassis of the computer. The resistor does not prevent any static build-up in your body from leaking away to earth, but it will protect you from a significant shock if a fault should result in the earthing point becoming "live". A variation on this system has a special mains plug that enables the wristband to be safely earthed to the mains supply. Earthing wristbands are available from some of the larger computer component suppliers, and from electronics component retailers.

A typical wristband, complete with lead and special earthing plug, is shown in Figure 3.8. Note that these are sometimes sold together as a kit, but they are also sold as separate items. Make sure you know what you are buying before you part with your money. The wristband on its own is about as much good as a monitor without the rest of the PC. It is possible to buy disposable wristband kits, but if you are likely to do a fair amount of PC upgrading from time to time it is probably worthwhile obtaining one of the cheaper non-disposable types. With intermittent use one of these should last many years. If you do not want to go to the

Setting up a LAN 3

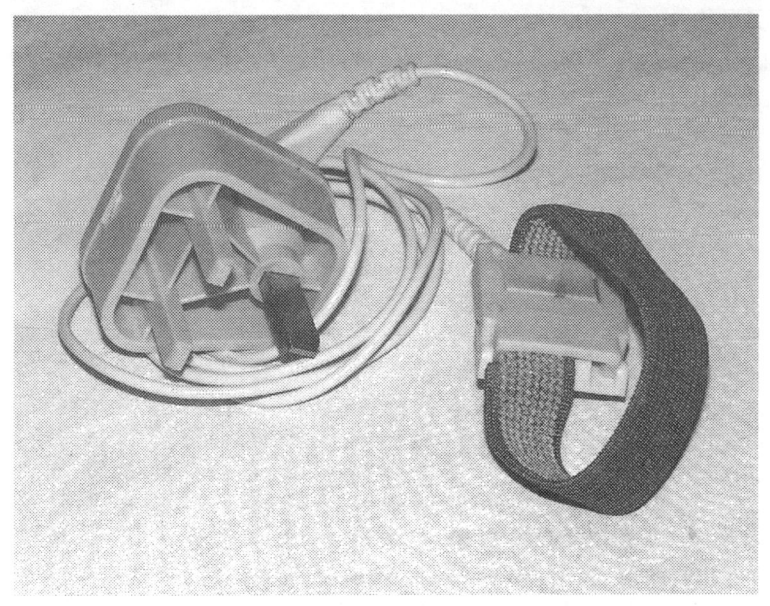

Fig.3.8 An earthing wristband, comple with special mains plug

expense of buying a wristband, the method of periodically touching the earthed chassis mentioned previously should be just as effective.

That is really all there is to it. Simply having a large chunk of earthed metal (in the form of the computer case) near the work area helps to discourage the build-up of any static charges in the first place. The few simple precautions outlined previously are then sufficient to ensure that there is no significant risk to the components. Do not be tempted to simply ignore the dangers of static electricity when handling computer components.

When building electronic gadgets I often ignore static precautions, but I am dealing with components that cost a matter of pence each. If one or two of the components should be zapped by a static charge, no great harm is done. The cost would be minimal and I have plenty of spares available. The same is not true when dealing with computer components. Each component costs at least a few pounds, and some cost in excess of a hundred pounds. Also, the computer could remain out of commission until a suitable replacement spare part was obtained.

3 Setting up a LAN

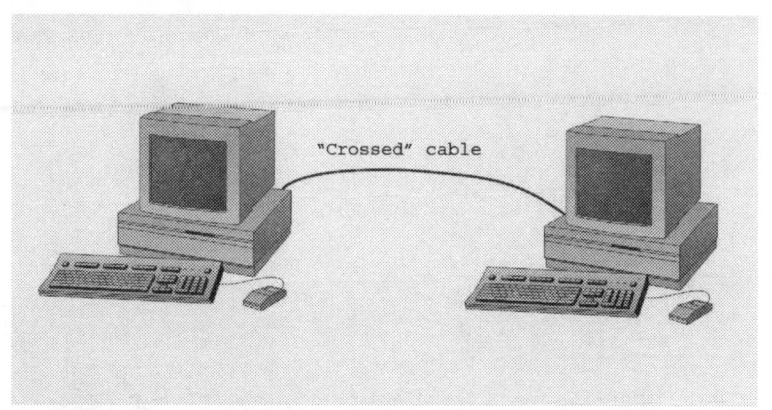

Fig.3.9 The most basic of networks does not require any extra hardware, but does require a special cable

Basic network

With all the PCs in the system equipped with Ethernet ports it is time to design and build the network. The most basic network barely justifies the "network" description, and it just consists of one PC connected direct to the other via their Ethernet ports (Figure 3.9). It is important to realise

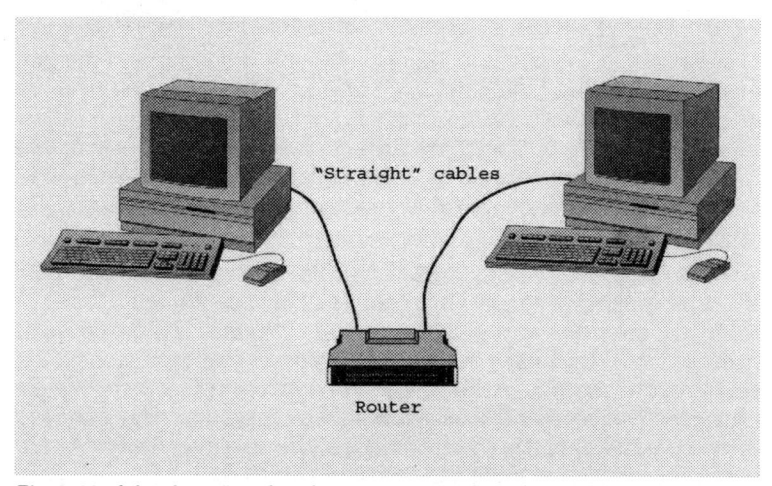

Fig.3.10 A basic network using a router and normal cables

Setting up a LAN 3

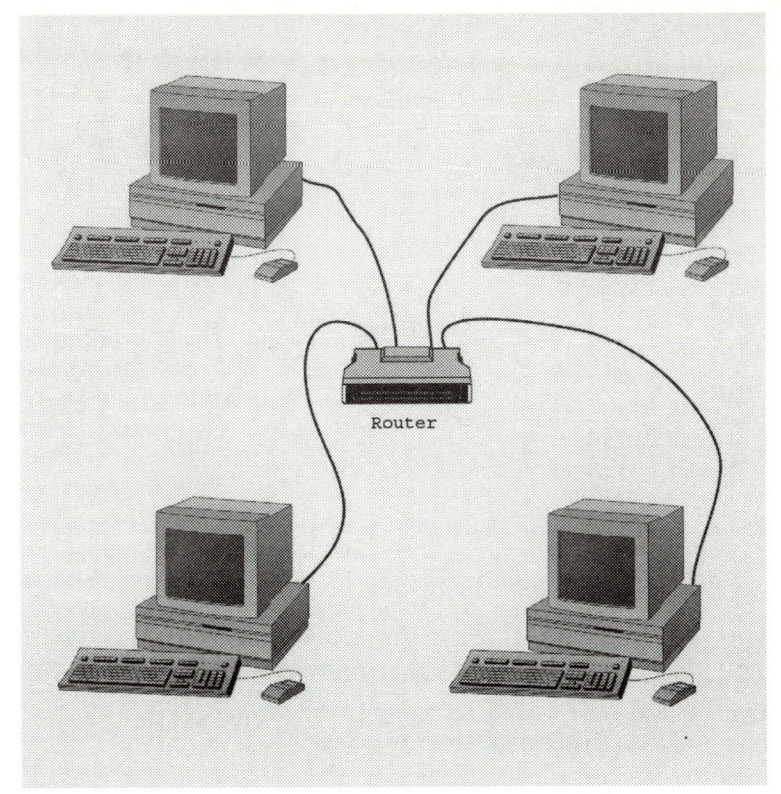

Fig.3.11 A network based on a router is easily expanded

that Ethernet ports are not primarily designed for this method of connection, and this setup will not work if a normal network cable is used. The cable required when linking two PCs is usually called something like a "crossed" or "crossed-over" cable. A normal network lead is usually described as a "straight" cable.

The setup shown in Figure 3.10 is essentially the same as the one of Figure 3.9, and it provides a link between the two PCs. The PCs are linked via a networking router, and the two cables are of the "straight" variety. In the arrangement of Figure 3.9 the crossed-over connections in the cable makes each PC "look" like a router to the other PC. This avoids the expense of the router and it is probably the better method if it will never be necessary to introduce other computers into the system.

3   Setting up a LAN

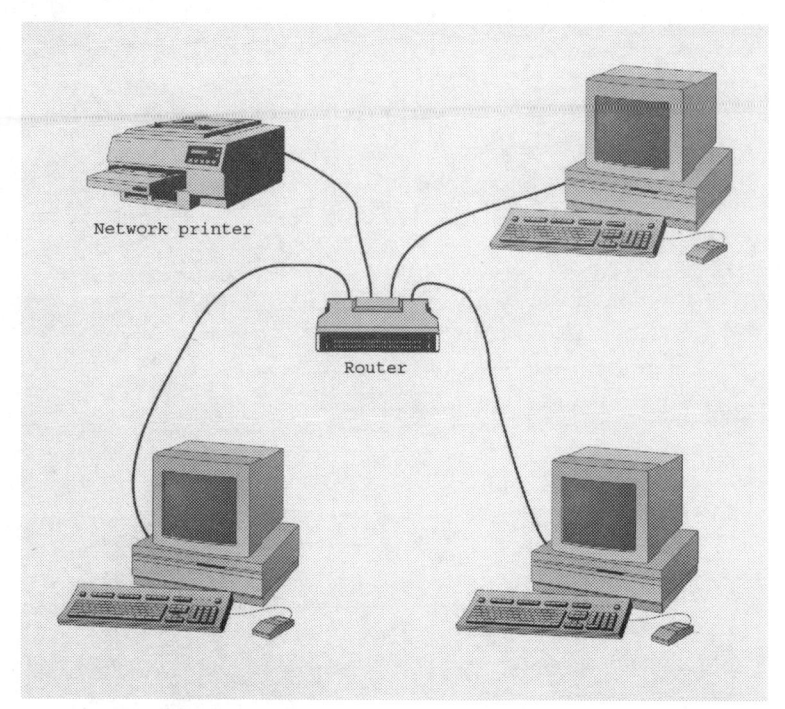

Fig.3.12 Sharing a network printer requires nothing more than a cable to connect the printer to the router

A big advantage of using a router is that it will typically have four or more Ethernet sockets, making it easy to add further PCs into the network. If you buy a laptop computer fitted with an Ethernet port, it can be connected to the router when you need to swap files with one of the other PCs in the system. Figure 3.11 shows a network having four PCs, and the setup of Figure 3.10 is easily expanded into this configuration. It could probably use the original router, since these mostly have four or more Ethernet sockets. Therefore, the only additional hardware required would be two cables, plus the two extra PCs of course. Networks can become quite involved, but for a home or small business network it should not be necessary to use anything more than a single router to bind the system together.

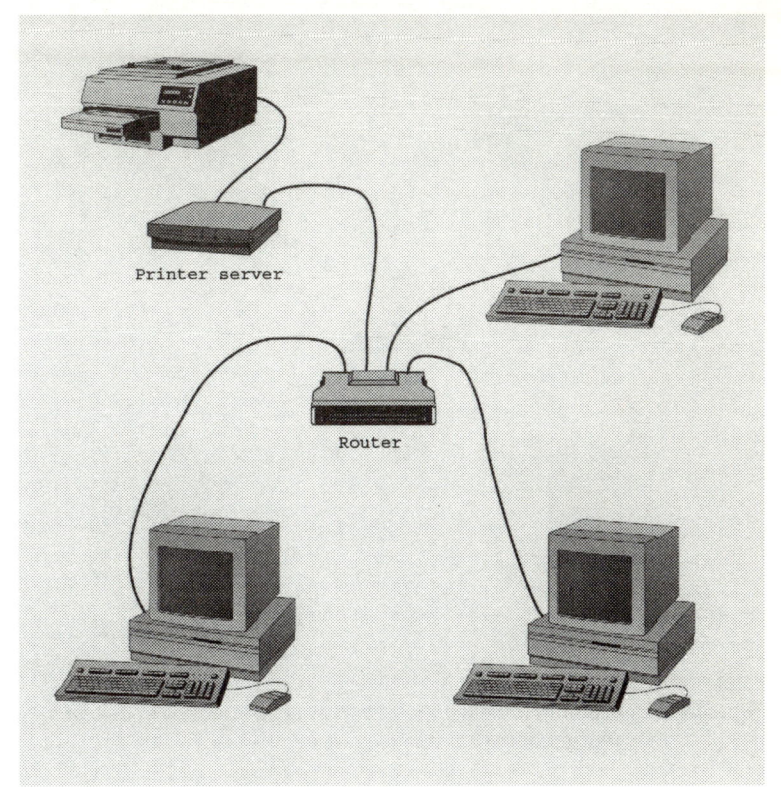

Fig.3.13 A printer server makes it easy to share an ordinary printer

Shared resources

As described so far, the system contains nothing other than the networking equipment and the PCs. This is fine for sharing files and folders, and a basic twin PC network is often used for games that can accommodate two players using separate PCs. However, most users wish to go beyond data sharing. Other resources can be shared, and in practice this usually means sharing a printer and/or an Internet connection.

Some printers are network enabled, which basically just means that they have an Ethernet port and can be connected into the system as in Figure 3.12. Heavy-duty printers for business use often have an Ethernet port

3 Setting up a LAN

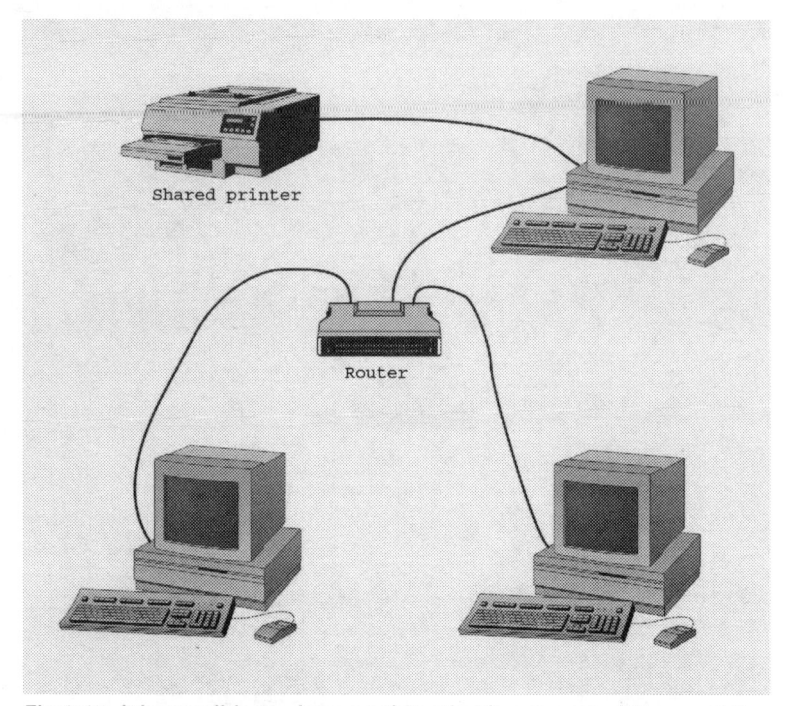

Fig.3.14 It is possible to share a printer that is connected to one of the PCs in the network

as standard, and it should certainly be available as an option. It is not included as standard with the printers used in most home and small business systems, and will probably not be available as an optional extra either.

With the aid of a suitable gadget it is possible to connect practically any printer into the network via the router, but it is not usually cost-effective to use this method. The gadget is called a printer server, and it simply goes between the router and the printer (Figure 3.13). Real-world printer servers often have the ability to drive more than one printer. This method has the major advantage of making the printer or printers available at all times to any network user. Furthermore, it does so without increasing the workload of any PCs that are not accessing a printer. The only real drawback is that the cost of a printer server is greater than that of many inkjet printers. These days it can even be higher than the cost of a budget laser printer.

The more common approach with small networks is to install the printer on one of the PCs in the usual way (Figure 3.14). The printer can then be designated as a shared resource and made available to any PC on the network. This system works well in most respects, but it does have one slight drawback. The printer will only be available to the network when the PC it is connected to is switched on. A printer that has its own network connection is available to the system at all times, as is one driven via a printer server.

With the setup of Figure 3.14 it can be necessary to switch on one PC so that another one can use the printer. Another slight drawback is that the PC which drives the printer has an increase in its workload when other PCs access the printer. Even so, this method is still the most practical for most home and small business networks.

Internet sharing

Sharing an Internet connection is probably the main reason for home and many small business users organising their individual PCs into a network. If you install a network for file sharing and you have a broadband Internet connection, it is definitely worth considering a shared Internet connection. It is only fair to point out that sharing an Internet connection does not work well with an ordinary dialup connection. An Internet connection that is already relatively slow can be virtually unusable if it is shared by several users.

The situation is very different with broadband, where connection speeds are much greater. A standard ADSL broadband connection has a download speed of 512k. The download speed in fringe areas is less than this, but for most broadband users the download rate is at least the stated 512k. This is at least ten times faster than the actual connection rate achieved with most 56k modems. Three users accessing the Internet simultaneously would each have an effective connection speed of just over 170k. In other words, they could still connect to the Internet at a rate more than three times better than a single user with a 56k modem.

It is only fair to point out that some broadband providers have terms of service that limit or ban the sharing of a broadband connection. It is unlikely that you will encounter any restriction of this type with a broadband package aimed at business users, but there are often "strings attached" to the low-cost deals for home users. The self-install broadband packages often have restrictions, and in some cases there is an outright ban on shared connections.

3 Setting up a LAN

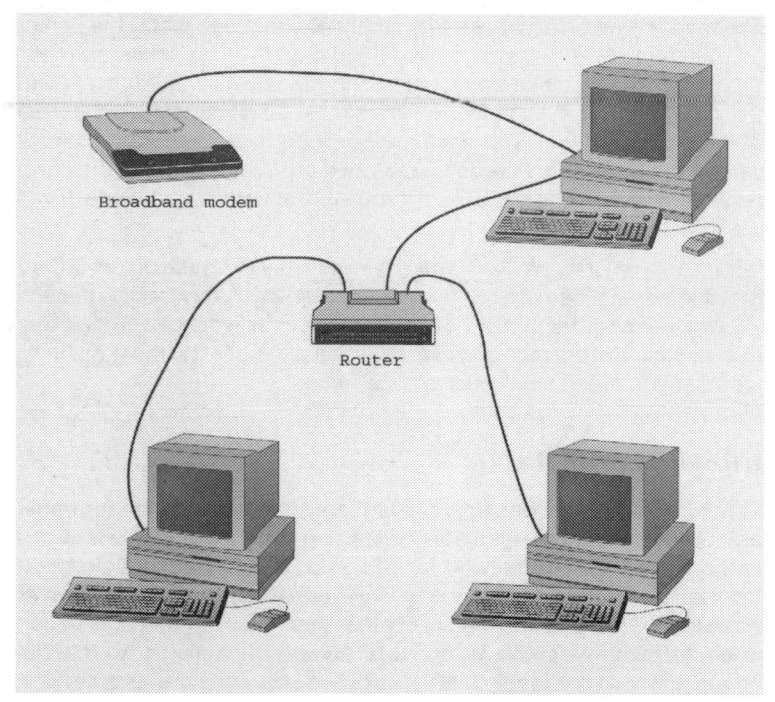

Fig.3.15 This simple setup permits the modem to be shared

Pressure from users and widespread flouting of the rules has led to some easing of the restrictions. Many providers now permit sharing between two or three users, but anything beyond this is likely to be outside the terms of service for low-cost broadband deals. Sharing a broadband connection between two or more households is unlikely to be permitted.

One way of sharing a broadband connection is to have the modem connected to one PC, with the Internet connection then being designated as a shared resource. This gives a setup of the type shown in Figure 3.15. Broadband modems are available in the form of PCI expansion cards, but the external USB type (Figure 3.16) is probably more popular. This method of sharing a broadband connection is cheap and easy if there is an existing network. You need little more than the modem and a microfilter for each telephone socket. The microfilters are needed to prevent the normal audio telephone signal from interfering with the high frequency broadband signal, and vice versa.

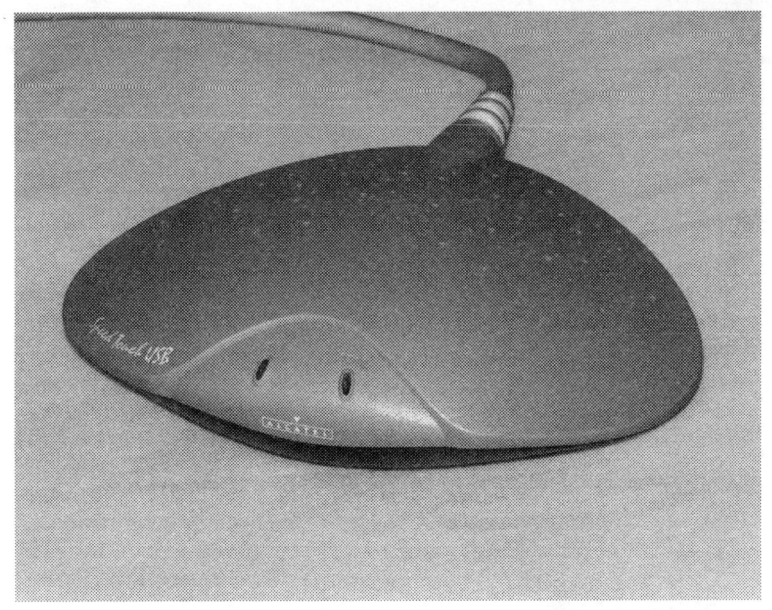

Fig.3.16 A typical USB broadband modem

Microfilter

A microfilter usually has a short lead that plugs into the telephone socket, and a couple of sockets on the main unit (Figure 3.17). One socket is for a telephone and the other is for the broadband modem. You can also obtain microfilters that look rather like a two-way telephone adapter (Figure 3.18), but one

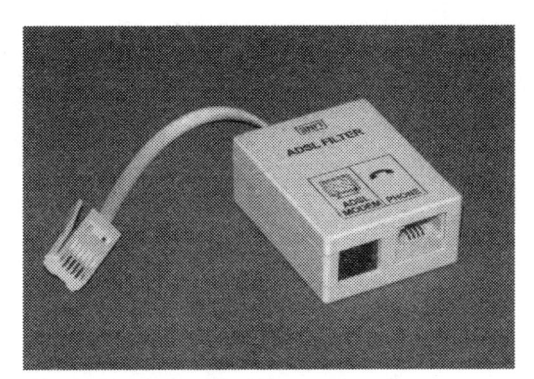

Fig.3.17 A microfilter has sockets for a modem and a telephone

3 Setting up a LAN

Fig.3.18 An alternative form of microfilter

of the sockets is for a broadband modem. Note that it is normally necessary to have a microfilter per telephone socket, and not just one filter at whichever socket happens to be used with the modem.

It is possible to use an ordinary modem with a telephone line that is broadband enabled, but the modem must be used via the ordinary telephone socket of a microfilter. It is possible that the filter will produce some loss of performance, although no problems were evident when I tried using a modem with two different microfilters. Although it is unlikely that you would need to use a dialup connection when a broadband type is available, an ordinary modem

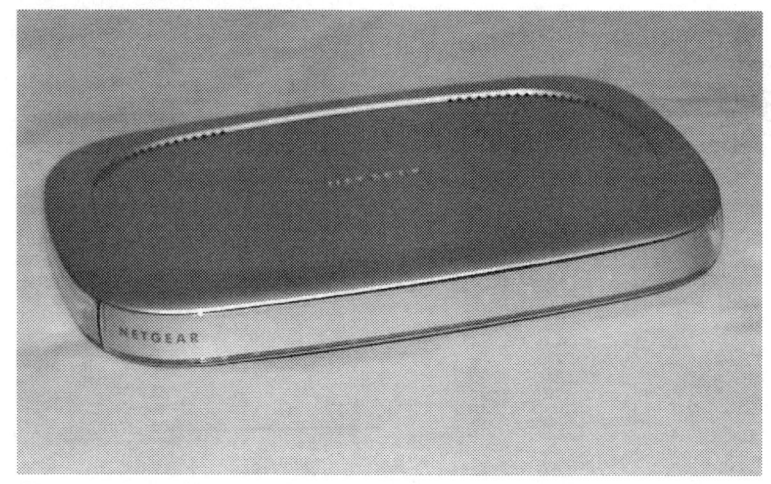

Fig.3.19 A combined broadband modem and router

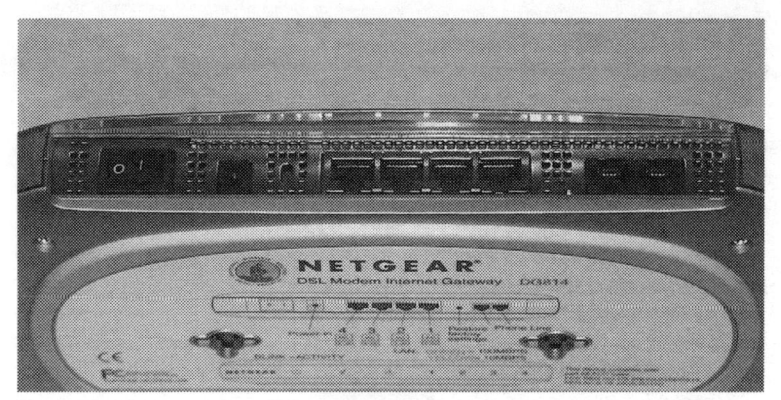

Fig.3.20 There are four Ethernet sockets at the rear of the modem

might still be needed for sending and receiving faxes. Also, it is a good idea to have a dialup connection available as a backup in case the broadband connection fails for some reason. Obviously the backup will be no use either if the lines goes "dead", but it does sometimes happen that the broadband connection is inaccessible while the line works fine in other respects.

A rather different scheme of things is normally used for a broadband connection that is installed by an engineer. The engineer usually installs a box that has an Ethernet socket on the front, and this is connected into the network by way of a suitable router. The ordinary telephone connections are left unchanged, and they do not require the use of microfilters. There is no exact equivalent of this for self-install systems, but it is possible to obtain a broadband modem that has an Ethernet socket for connection to the network. With this arrangement a microfilter is still required at each telephone socket.

Probably the most popular means of sharing a broadband connection between a few computers is to use a combined modem and router, such as the one shown in Figure 3.19, which has four Ethernet sockets on the rear panel (Figure 3.20). There is also a telephone socket which is connected to a telephone wall socket via a microfilter. A combined modem and router is used in a setup of the type shown in Figure 3.21. This is basically just a standard network, but with the important difference that any PC connected to the router is automatically provided with Internet access. It is possible to obtain much the same effect using a separate router and broadband modem (Figure 3.22), but combining the two units gives a neater solution.

3 Setting up a LAN

Fig.3.21 A combined modem and router is used much like a normal router

Compatibility

If you decide to use a setup like the one in Figure 3.22, bear in mind that you can not use any broadband modem with any router. The router must be one that is designed to be used in this way. Also, most routers have an Ethernet socket for the modem, and can only be used with modems that have an Ethernet socket. It could be difficult to track down a router that will work with a modem that only has a USB interface.

Using a gadget that combines a router and modem, possibly with a firewall or other functions, is certainly the best method. Setting up the network is generally much easier using an all-in-one solution, and it helps to reduce

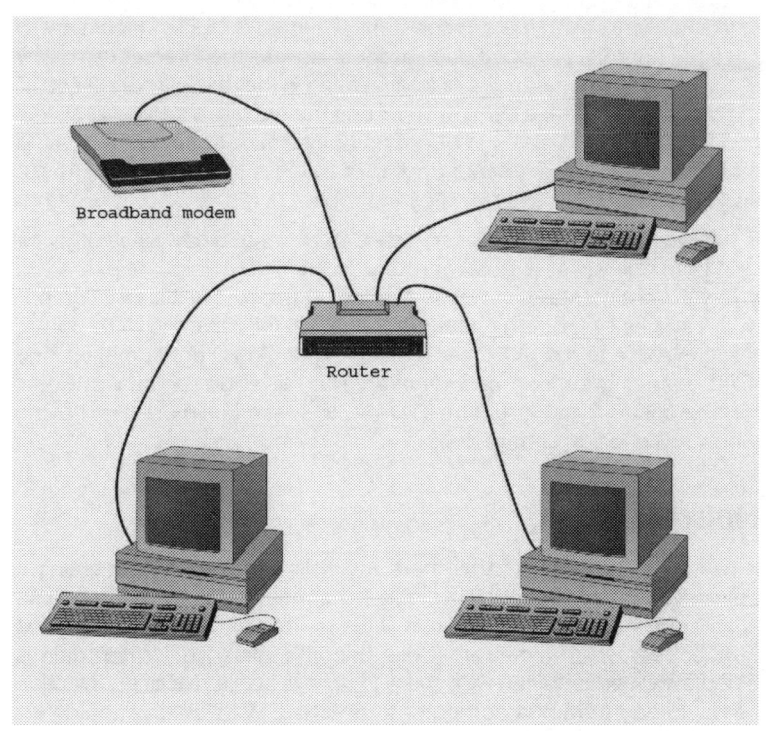

Fig.3.22 This setup requires a modem that has an Ethernet port

the amount of cabling. Most wireless networks have wired connections as well, but you must avoid having the wireless name become ironic! Try to keep everything neat and simple, with no more "boxes" and cables than is really necessary.

An advantage of the current low prices of computer hardware is that it is usually possible to design a system that accurately matches your requirements, rather than having to compromise due to cost considerations. Depending on the equipment you have to start with, a setup of the type shown in Figure 3.21 might cost a little more than one like Figure 3.15. The cost is likely to be small though, and the arrangement of Figure 3.21 is much better from the users' point of view.

With the setup of Figure 3.21 the modem/router is usually left running continuously, making an Internet connection always available to any PC in the network. With the arrangement of Figure 3.15 it is necessary to have the right PC switched on in order to access the Internet using any of the others. Another point to bear in mind is that the PC connected to the modem becomes a form of router, and this will place additional claims on its resources. Using a modem combined with or connected to the modem avoids any overhead on any of the PCs in the system. All the additional workload is handled by the router.

In the past it was common for an old PC to be given a new lease of life by using it to operate as a router or router/modem. This might appear to be a very environmentally friendly way of doing things, but it is less "green" than it seems. A modern router or modem/router consumes little power, and costs little to run. A PC has a much higher power consumption, and if left operating for long periods every day will soon run up significant running costs. In the long term it is likely to cost much more than buying a new router or modem/router.

Network risks

It has to be pointed out that there are risks involved in connecting a network to the Internet. With a single PC connected to the system there is only one PC at risk from hackers, viruses, Trojans, and the other types of attack for which the Internet has become infamous. When data is being swapped between PCs there is always some risk of an infection being spread from one computer to another. With data swapping via CDs, flash cards, etc., the risk is relatively low. There is a good chance of any infection being detected and dealt with before it has a chance to spread to another PC.

With a network there is the potential for a hacker to gain access to the entire system, or for some kind of infection to quickly spread itself across the system. By the time you discover that something is wrong it is possible that massive damage will have been done to numerous files on all the PCs in the network. When using a network it is important to be more careful about security, and even more care has to be exercised when using a network that connects to the Internet. With a shared broadband connection even more care has to be taken. It is essential to use a firewall to help keep hackers at bay, and an up-to-date antivirus program to combat viruses, Trojans, worms, and the other infections that seem to pervade the Internet.

Note that firewall and antivirus programs are not the same, and that they perform very different functions. Antivirus software scans the discs and

Setting up a LAN 3

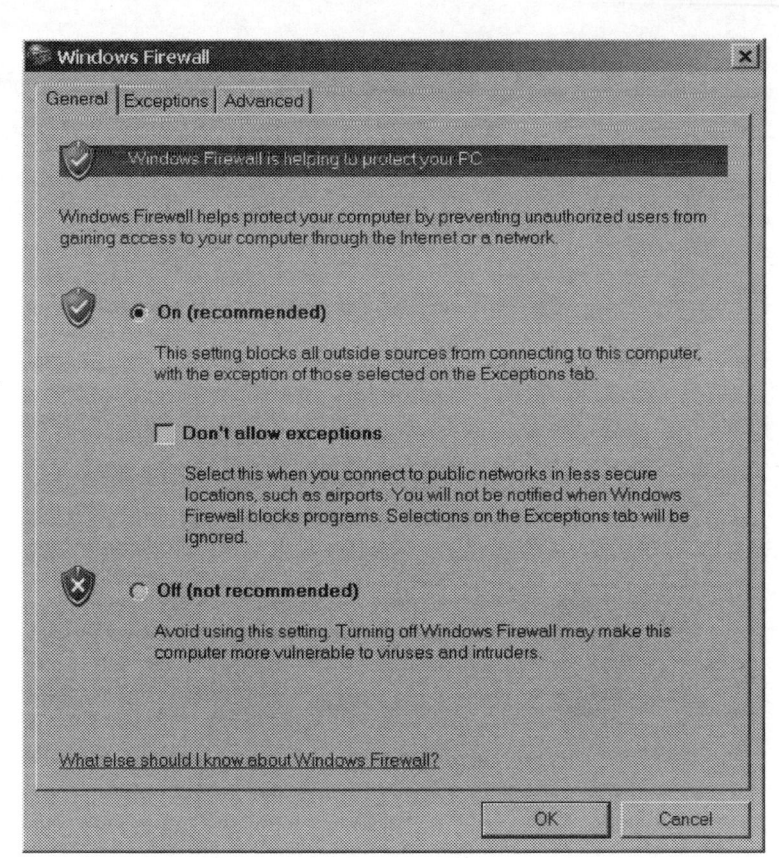

Fig.3.23 The firewall can be switched on and off as required

memory in search of viruses, Trojans, and various other types of infection. In most cases the software will also deal with any infection that is found. Programs of this type will also monitor Internet activity and try to block or otherwise deal with any malicious files that the user or the system attempts to download.

A firewall program monitors Internet and network activity in an attempt to block any unauthorised accesses. In other words, it tries to prevent hackers from gaining access to your PCs. Both types of program are needed in order to provide good security. Windows XP has a basic but effective firewall built into the system, and this is the minimum that should be used. In the interest of good Internet security it is essential to keep

3 Setting up a LAN

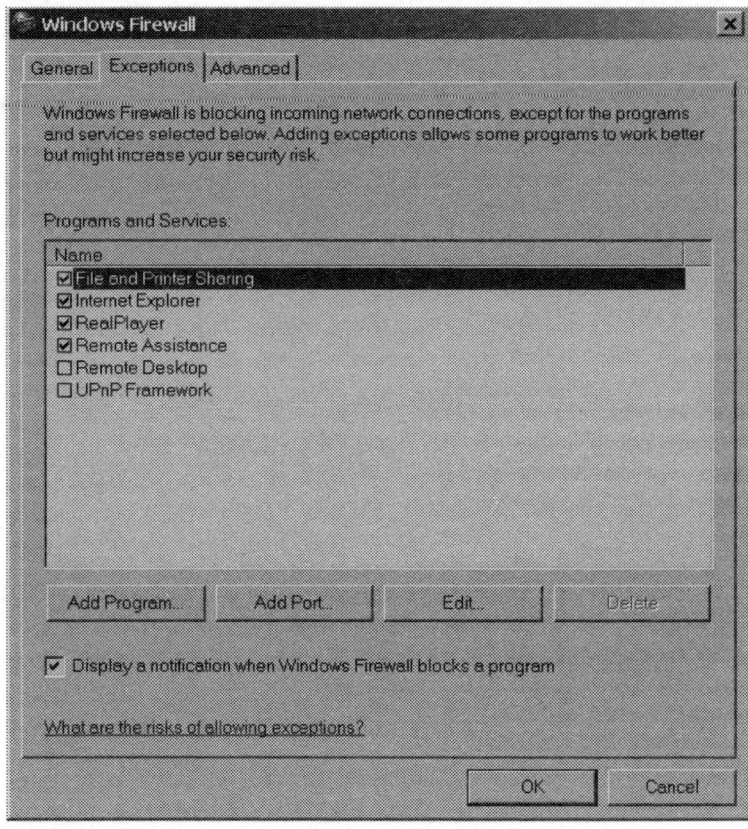

Fig.3.24 Programs listed in the Exceptions section

Windows up-to-date, and to install all the latest security updates. In particular, with Windows XP it is important to have Service Pack 2 (SP2) installed. This provides numerous improvements to the security of the Windows XP operating system.

When using Windows XP SP2, the built-in firewall program is enabled by default. It therefore protects the PC unless you switch off the firewall, which is definitely not a good idea unless another firewall program is in use. Using two firewall programs at once is probably not a good idea. Although it seemingly gives added protection, the two programs will to a large extent provide the same facilities. With this type of thing there is a real danger of the two programs preventing each other from operating

Setting up a LAN 3

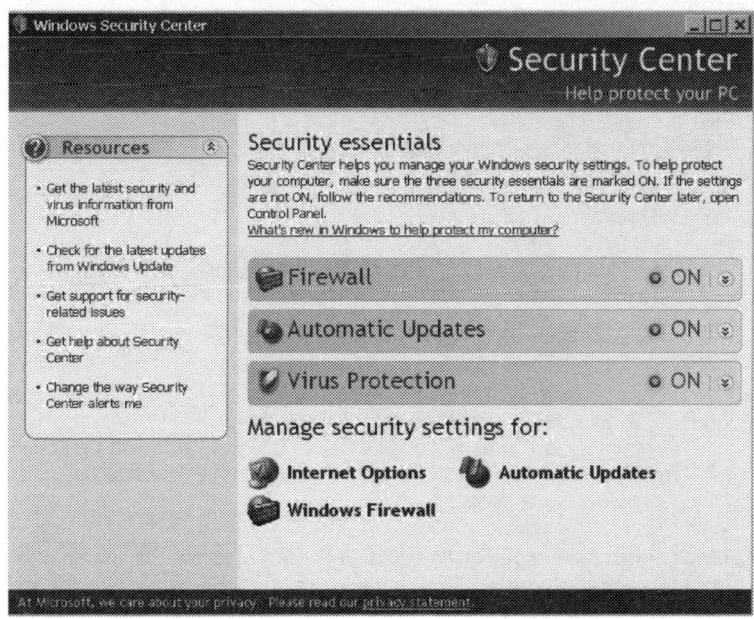

Fig.3.25 The Security Center is a new addition provided by Service Pack 2

properly. In addition to the risk of introducing security "holes", it could also make the system unstable.

Running two resident antivirus programs simultaneously is not a good idea either. Having two resident antivirus programs running simultaneously used to more or less guarantee serious problems, and in many cases it actually made the PC unbootable. These incompatibility problems are less severe these days, but it is still advisable to only use one resident antivirus program at a time. Having a resident antivirus program operational while using an online virus detection facility should not introduce any problems though.

If you should need to alter the Windows XP firewall settings, it is controlled by double-clicking the Windows Firewall icon in the Control Panel, which produces the window of Figure 3.23. The radio buttons enable the firewall to be switched on or off, as required. Operating the Exceptions tab produces a window like the one shown in Figure 3.24. The main part of the window lists the programs that the firewall grants Internet access. Remove the tick from the checkbox for any program that you would like

3 Setting up a LAN

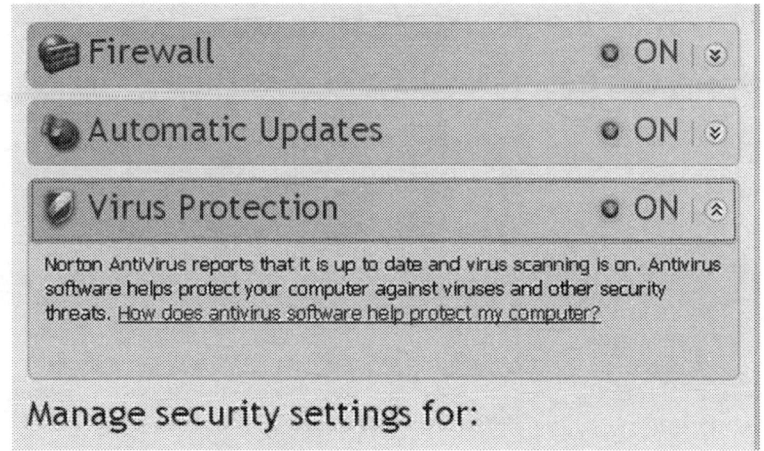

> **Firewall** ○ ON
>
> **Automatic Updates** ○ ON
>
> **Virus Protection** ○ ON
>
> Norton AntiVirus reports that it is up to date and virus scanning is on. Antivirus software helps protect your computer against viruses and other security threats. How does antivirus software help protect my computer?
>
> Manage security settings for:

Fig.3.26 Here the Virus Protection section has been expanded to provide more details

to block. With the firewall operational, it is normal to get the occasional warning message stating that a program has been blocked from accessing the Internet. Most of these attempted accesses are perfectly innocent, but it is advisable not to grant Internet access to any program unless you are sure that it is safe to do so.

Security Center

The Windows Security Center (Figure 3.25) is a new feature that is provided by Service Pack 2. It is accessed by double-clicking the Security Center icon in the Windows Control Panel. It uses a "traffic light" system that will show three green lights if the firewall is switched on, automatic updating of Windows is active, and the computer is using a recognised antivirus program. A red light indicates that the relevant feature is not "alive and kicking". A yellow light will be produced if the state of a facility is indeterminate, such as when an antivirus program has been detected but its update status can not be read.

More information from any of the three sections can be obtained by left-clicking on the relevant section. A drop-down panel then provides further details. In Figure 3.26 the Virus Protection section has been expanded, and this shows that Norton Antivirus is installed and has indicated that it is up-to-date. Left-click an entry again in order to remove the drop-down panel.

Setting up a LAN 3

Points to remember

Over the years many types of interface have been used for networking. These days the only interface commonly used for networking PCs is the Ethernet type, which is also known as a 10/100 network interface. The two figures in the 10/100 name refer to the speeds (in Mbits per second) of the original and current versions of this interface.

Many PCs now have a built-in Ethernet port as standard, but this facility is easily added to a desktop PC. It is just a matter of fitting a PCI Ethernet expansion card. It is also possible to obtain USB Ethernet adapters for use with desktop and portable PCs. Note that a USB 2.0 adapter is needed in order to utilise the full speed of the Ethernet interface.

If you add a PCI Ethernet or wi-fi card to a PC, take the necessary precautions to avoid damaging anything with static charges. A few simple handling precautions are all that is needed to avoid problems.

The most basic network consists of two PCs linked via their Ethernet ports. This requires a "crossed" cable and not the more usual "straight" type. In order to network more than two computers it is necessary to have a router, with the Ethernet port of each PC connected to the router by way of a "straight" cable.

It is not necessary to buy any software in order to implement a basic but useful network. The built-in networking facilities of Windows permit files, folders, or even complete discs to be shared. It is also possible for a printer connected to one PC to be used by other PCs in the network.

It is possible to share the Internet connection of one PC via the network. In practice this is not a very good way of doing things though. If the PC that has the Internet connection is switched off, all the other PCs in the network lose their Internet connection. The PC connected to the modem acts as a kind of router, and this can be a significant drain on its resources.

Using a broadband modem connected to a router (or a single unit that combines both functions) provides an always-on Internet connection for

3　Setting up a LAN

every PC in the network. It does so without increasing the workload of any PC in the system, and need not cost very much.

Antivirus programs are of limited use against hackers. In order to keep hackers at bay it is essential to use either a software or hardware firewall. Ideally, both should be used if you have some form of broadband connection, especially if it is of the "always on" variety.

4

Going wi-fi

Why wi-fi?

Although wireless networking technology has been in existence for some time, it has only gained widespread acceptance quite recently. This rise in popularity has no doubt been triggered by the substantial reductions in the prices of wireless networking equipment, or wi-fi equipment as it has become known. Some generic wi-fi adapters can now be purchased for just a few pounds. This makes wi-fi systems a practical proposition for home and small business users.

Although wireless networking is now reasonably inexpensive, it is still likely to cost somewhat more than an equivalent wired network. Is it worth the extra outlay? The obvious advantage is that it avoids the need to any install wiring. For many users this is really the only advantage of the wi-fi approach, but for most it is a major plus point. A short lead from a computer to a router or other piece of networking equipment is not difficult to implement, particularly if the two pieces of equipment are on the same desk. No do-it-yourself skills are likely to be required.

The situation is very different when the items to be linked are on opposite sides of the room. An "off the shelf" lead is all that is needed to connect the two pieces of equipment, but keeping the lead tucked away discretely out of sight is more difficult. This is not just a matter of making things look pretty, and there is the safety aspect to consider. A lead placed where people keep tripping over is obviously unsafe, although in practice it is probably the networking equipment that is most likely to suffer. It becomes increasing difficult to keep things neat and safe as more equipment is added to the network. A certain amount of do-it-yourself ability is needed in order to install the wiring properly, but it is not too difficult to make a good job of it.

Installing the wiring becomes much more difficult when leads have to be run from one room to another. This type of thing is still within the abilities of the average handyman with an electric drill, but it is not everyone's "cup of tea". Also, it is not a practical proposition unless you are prepared to have holes for the cables drilled in the walls, floors, and ceilings. Apart from aesthetic considerations, having a house entwined with various networking cables could adversely affect its resale value. In the case of a listed building, it is unlikely that permission to install the wiring would be obtained.

It is usually possible to use ready-made cables, but this could mean having to use some standard lengths that are substantially longer than you require. You then have to hide a few metres of cable safely out of the way where no one will trip over it. The bits and pieces needed to make your own custom cables are readily available, but this is a more difficult approach. Surprisingly perhaps, making your own cables can be relatively expensive when all the costs are taken into account.

Drawbacks

Having the longer links in a network provided by wi-fi equipment has a huge advantage for most network users. Even with short links, such as from a desktop PC to a laptop or notebook PC, not having to bother with connecting cables is a major advantage. However, there are a few disadvantages to take into account when considering the wi-fi option. The obvious one is the higher cost mentioned previously, although as technology becomes cheaper this becomes a less significant drawback. At the time of writing this book the additional cost is still significant, although for slower wi-fi equipment it is becoming much less of an issue.

With any relatively new and more expensive technology it is a matter of pricing the various options and making your own subjective assessment with the prices prevailing at the time. With a typical home or small business network there will often be just one or two links that could really benefit from a wireless connection, which should help to keep the additional cost well within reason.

The relatively slow speed of wireless systems is another potential drawback. Although a wired network has a notional speed of 10 or 100 megabits per second, in the real world any equipment you use will support the higher rate. A modern Ethernet system therefore works at 100 megabits per second and you can forget the lower rate. You will never use it. Wi-fi systems normally operate at 11 or 54 megabits per second.

In practice, even a transfer rate of 11 megabits per second could be perfectly adequate. For many users, the point of networking a system is to share a broadband Internet connection. A standard ADSL connection operates with a download rate of 512 kilobits (0.512 megabits) per second, with an upload rate of just half that figure. Even allowing for inefficiencies in the systems, both types of wi-fi link can easily handle the sharing of an ADSL broadband Internet connection. Some broadband connections operate at higher rates of one or two or four megabits per second, but this is still well within the capabilities of wi-fi equipment.

Wi-fi connections are also perfectly adequate for some types of file sharing. It is popular to use a home network to permit music files stored on one computer to be played on another PC in the system. Music files generally operate at about 64 to 256 kilobits per second, with a few operating at up to about 512k per second. This is again well within the capabilities of a wi-fi connection. Many of the videos played on PCs use a similar bit rate, but high quality video requires higher rates that could stretch a wi-fi system. This is not of significance to most home and small business users though.

The speed of a wi-fi system is likely to be sluggish when transferring large files or large numbers of files from one PC to another. In theory it is possible for a system operating at 11 megabits per second to transfer more than one megabyte of data a second, but in practice the transfer rate could be little more than half this rate. To transfer 500 megabytes of data would therefore take at least eight minutes, and could well take closer to 15 minutes. For this type of thing transfers at 54 megabits per second are preferable, enabling 500 megabytes of data to be transferred in around one and a half to three minutes. A wired network would complete the task in little more than half the time, but would still be something less than instant.

Although, on the face of it, a wi-fi link is more than adequate for most users, there is a "fly in the ointment" that should not be overlooked. The quoted speeds for wi-fi equipment are the highest that can be achieved, and they require quite strong signal levels. Do not be misled by the ranges quoted for wi-fi equipment, which are often something like 100 metres, and in some cases much higher figures are quoted. A usable signal may be obtained at a range as large as 100 metres, but only with clear air between the aerials. Where longer ranges are quoted, these are usually for operation at speeds well below the maximum transfer rate.

When using a wi-fi link from one room to another there will inevitably be walls, floors, ceilings, and all-manner of obstructions between the aerials. How much (or little) effect these have on the signal strength is not totally predictable, and the only way to find out is to use a "suck it and see" approach. Buildings that have large amounts of metal in their structure

4 Going wi-fi

can be problematic, but a reasonable operating range should otherwise be obtained. A range of 10 or 20 metres is usually possible, but at longer ranges the transfer rate is likely to be significantly less than notional 11 or 54 megabits per second.

When reduced speed is obtained, results should still be adequate for sharing a broadband Internet connection, audio files, etc., but a wired network would probably be a better choice for transferring large amounts of data. An unfortunate truism is that wi-fi equipment performs the worst in situations where it would be by far the most convenient solution. With a large distance plus walls and floors between the two units to be linked, using a connecting cable is very difficult. In this situation a wi-fi link is a much easier option that avoids the awkward wiring, but getting a strong signal is likely to prove difficult. In practice it is likely that many users will be prepared to put up with reduced speed in order to avoid the inconveniences of installing wiring.

Security

Computer security has become a major issue in recent years. There seems to be a significant number of criminals continually thinking up new scams or finding ways of reworking old ones. The early viruses were produced by individuals who were really just showing off, and trying to show how clever they were. It has now become rather more sinister, with people trying to find ways of extracting money from companies or private individuals using what we now know as cyber crime. All Internet users now have to take security very seriously, but it is particularly important to the growing band of users that have a broadband connection.

You do not have to be a computer genius to see that using wi-fi links has the potential to let hackers "eavesdrop" on your network or even gain access to it. At the most basic level, anyone operating a wi-fi equipped PC within the range of your system could have free Internet access by way of your network and Internet connection. This would probably not matter a great deal if you have an unlimited broadband connection. The unwanted guest would effectively reduce the bandwidth of the Internet connection, but probably not to a significant degree.

Someone using your Internet connection could prove costly if you have capped access, where extra has to be paid if more than a certain amount is downloaded each month. Either way, are you really unconcerned about others gaining access to your network for a bit of freeloading? Most of us value our privacy and would prefer to keep the network totally closed to outsiders, even if they have no really sinister intent.

Of course, some hackers trying to enter the network might have a sinister motive. With no security measures in use, someone could potentially hack into your network and gain personal information stored on the system, or even steal passwords or other sensitive information. Unless the network is used for purely unimportant applications such as games or entertainment, it is essential to take steps to keep it secure. Even if the system is only used for trivia, you would presumably still prefer not to have strangers using your Internet connection and accessing your PC.

In some cases wi-fi equipment can be installed with no setup information at all being provided by the user. However, equipment of this type is usually installed without any of the built-in security measures being implemented. There is a temptation to simply "let well alone", and not bother with implementing the security measures. With the network working well, why risk messing up the installation? Taking this attitude is definitely a mistake though, and it is a good idea to read the instruction manuals and get everything set up properly as soon as possible. Setting up a network to make it secure is quite simple and does not take long.

Interference

The range of frequencies available for use with wi-fi networks is quite narrow, but the allocation is broad enough to permit a number of channels to be accommodated. As will be explained later, there are actually two bands available for this type of equipment, and these are at frequencies near 2.4GHz and 5GHz. At present the vast majority of wi-fi devices operate in the 2.4GHz band, and it is primarily this type of wi-fi equipment that will be covered here.

Even though there are several channels, congestion is still a potential problem. This depends on where you live, and to some extent it is a matter of luck. I live in a part of the country that has quite a high population density, but my home wi-fi network has yet to detect any other wi-fi networks in the vicinity. Although the short range of this equipment is normally considered to be a drawback, in this context it is definitely an advantage. In fact a range of a few miles would render wi-fi networks unusable as in many areas interference from other networks would render most systems unusable.

The short operating range largely avoids this problem in suburban and rural areas, but if you operate a wi-fi network in a town it is quite likely that you will find that you are not alone. Switching away from the default channel should avoid any major problems with interference from other systems. As wi-fi becomes more popular it could be difficult to find a totally clear channel in heavily built-up areas, giving a more limited operating range. Also, bear in mind that having several systems nearby could reduce the range somewhat even if they are not operating on the same channel as your system.

Many wi-fi users are probably under the impression that a band has been set aside specifically for wireless networking. Unfortunately, this is not the case, and wi-fi shares the 2.4GHz band with several other types of equipment. These include such things as some cordless phone systems, baby monitors, Bluetooth devices, video senders, cordless headphones, and even microwave ovens. These devices all add to the congestion, and can potentially block some channels completely. They also add to the general noise on the band and tend to limit the maximum operating range. Again, in suburban and rural areas any problems should be minimal, but performance could be seriously compromised in some parts of towns.

Standards

Computer standards have tended to be something of a joke in the past. Standards have not only been a problem in the world of computing. The electronics industry in general has experienced problems with competing standards, which inevitably results in many people buying gadgets that soon become obsolete. In fact competing standards can ultimately kill the product, producing a situation where there are no winners and plenty of losers.

An additional problem with computer standards is that of manufacturers having tended to "do their own thing" rather than rigidly adhering to agreed standards. It is difficult to understand why a manufacturer would release a product that does not strictly adhere to the rules, but this was quite common in the past. Possibly it was the result of cost cutting, or perhaps it was just poor design work that was to blame. Anyway, even something as basic as trying to get a printer to work properly with a serial or parallel port used to be very difficult. Although "off the shelf" leads were usually available, these ready-made leads often proved to be inadequate.

Fortunately, the situation has improved somewhat over the years, and wi-fi is certainly free from many of the problems associated with wired interfaces. Inevitably though, there is more than one standard to contend with. The wireless networking equipment in common use conforms to the standards laid down by the Institute of Electrical and Electronics Engineers, or the IEEE as it is more commonly called. All the wi-fi equipment falls within the 802.11 standard, but there are three versions of it in common use (802.11a, 802.11b, and 802.11g). Table 1 summarises the important differences between the three 802.11 standards.

Table 1

Standard	802.11a	802.11b	802.11g
Maximum speed	54Mbits/s	11Mbits/s	54Mbits/s
Real-world speed	20Mbits/s	4.5Mbits/s	20Mbits/s
Range (outdoors)	30 metres	120 metres	50 metres
Range (indoors)	12 metres	60 metres	20 metres
Band	5GHz	2.4GHz	2.4GHz
Users	64	32	32
Total UK channels	8	13	13
Separate channels	8	3	3
Compatibility	-	802.11g	802.11b
Wi-fi certified	Yes	Yes	Yes

The ranges quoted here are theoretical, and would probably not be obtained in practice. These are the maximum ranges at the maximum operating speed, and longer ranges can be achieved at lower speeds. Bear in mind that ranges quoted for operation outdoors assume that there is clear air between the aerials. Walls, fences, and other solid objects between the aerials, particularly if they are made from metal, will substantially reduce the range.

I tried operating a 802.11b link between two systems about 100 metres apart, hoping that there would be a sufficiently strong signal to permit one system to use the broadband Internet connection of the other. In practice the two systems remained oblivious to each other, with neither system picking up a discernible signal from the other. There were a few trees and other obstructions between the two aerials, and that was sufficient to shield each aerial from the other unit's signal. The only way to find the maximum usable operating range is to try it and see, but slightly pessimistic forecasts are usually the most accurate.

4 Going wi-fi

As already explained, the maximum range indoors is heavily dependent on the type and number of obstructions between the two aerials. A couple of plasterboard walls are unlikely to have much effect on the range, but a few substantial brick walls could massively reduce it. A large metal radiator in the wrong place could totally block the signal. In difficult surroundings, 802.11b equipment probably offers the greatest chance of providing usable results.

802.11a equipment has the advantage of not operating in the overused 2.4GHz band, and it also permits twice as many users per access point. However, for a home or small business network it is unlike that more than 32 users will need to use an access point. There are some drawbacks to 802.11a equipment, and probably the most important one for most potential users is that the cost is much higher than for equivalent 802.11b and 802.11g equipment.

The economics of networking are at least as capricious as those for other aspects of computing, but at the time of writing this, opting for 802.11a equipment means paying more than twice as much for the privilege. Another important factor to bear in mind is that there is relatively little 802.11a equipment available, although choice and availability should improve in due course. Because 802.11a equipment operates on a different band, it is totally incompatible with the other two standards. 802.11b and 802.11g equipment can be freely mixed, but transfers will obviously be at the lower rate if one unit in a link is of the 802.11b variety.

Note that it is possible to obtain 802.11a equipment that is compatible with the other two standards. However, this compatibility is presumably obtained by combining 802.11a and 802.11g gadgets in a single box. As one would expect, the extra hardware required tends to make these units relatively expensive. They are extremely versatile though.

Channels

On the face of it, the 802.11a standard provides fewer channels than the other two standards. In reality it is actually better, since its eight channels do not overlap, and they are genuine channels. The 13 channels of the other two systems overlap to some extent, so significant interference between units operating on adjacent channels is quite possible. In fact the channel overlap problem is so great that it is only possible to have three totally separate channels. Together with its operation on the 5GHz band, this makes 802.11a equipment a safer choice in areas where there is severe congestion.

Wi-fi Alliance

In theory, equipment manufactured to conform to one of the three IEEE standards should work perfectly with any other equipment designed to meet the same standard (or a compatible one). In reality it is never as simple as this with such complex technology, and there have been incompatibility issues in the past. In some cases the level of performance obtained was below expectations, and in extreme cases no usable link was obtained.

The Wi-fi Alliance was formed in 1999, and its purpose was to certify that wi-fi equipment fully conformed to the appropriate standard and would operate properly with any equipment of the same or a compatible standard. A certified 802.11g access point should therefore operate perfectly with any certified 802.11b or 802.11g wireless adapter. Wi-fi certified equipment carries the Wi-fi logo, and it should also have a badge of approval (Figure 4.1). The badge shows which standard or standards the equipment is compatible with, and it also indicates whether it has protected access. In other words, it shows whether the equipment has built-in security measures to keep unauthorised users out of the system.

Is it essential to obtain equipment that has wi-fi certification? In theory it is safer to do so, but the fact that a unit lacks certification does not necessarily mean that it lacks full compatibility with the relevant standard. In fact, such equipment is likely to be perfectly usable. The wi-fi badge of approval is not as common as one might expect, and there is plenty of good quality equipment available that does not sport the wi-fi logo. On checking a mixture of "big name" and generic wi-fi units I found that very few had the badge of approval.

Fig.4.1 A typical certification badge

The cost of gaining approval has certainly deterred some manufacturers from seeking certification for their products. Added costs are obviously unwelcome when making any products, but they are particularly unhelpful when producing cheap generic devices. There is little chance of obtaining approved products if you take the cheap generic route, and customer support is often poor or nonexistent with these units. On the plus side, generic products are almost certain to be based on exactly the same chips as equivalents from the well-known companies.

For those with limited experience of dealing with computer hardware it is probably better to opt for equipment from one of the well-known manufacturers such as Netgear, Belkin, US Robotics, and 3Com. If the equipment is from a respected company and it also has certification, so much the better. If it does not have certification, at least there should be a proper customer support service to get things sorted out, and you are protected by your statutory rights.

Bluetooth

There is a common misconception that Bluetooth and wi-fi equipment are the same, or that they are to some extent compatible. The confusion is perhaps understandable, since Bluetooth equipment uses the same 2.4GHz band as most wireless networking equipment, and its function is much the same. It provides a wireless link between two pieces of electronic equipment. Despite the superficial similarities, the purpose of Bluetooth is very different to that of wi-fi equipment.

Wi-fi is an extension of the Ethernet networking system, and when using wi-fi equipment you have what is essentially an Ethernet based network. A typical wi-fi network will include some wired connections using standard Ethernet ports and cables. Bluetooth is not intended for networking, although it could probably be used to provide networking. Using Bluetooth equipment in this fashion would be doing things the hard way though, and wi-fi equipment performs this task much more efficiently.

The real purpose of Bluetooth is to link two devices, and it is a general-purpose system which is designed to accommodate practically any two pieces of equipment that could be usefully linked. Bluetooth is used for such things as connecting a computer to a printer, a laptop PC to a desktop computer, and a notebook PC to a mobile phone.

Wireless links have been used with PCs for many years in the form of IrDA infrared links. The main problem with the infra-red approach was that it was basically just a short range line of sight system, although for many purposes this was perfectly adequate. When uploading from a digital camera or a laptop computer to a PC for example, the two devices would probably be more or less side-by-side anyway. Another limitation of IrDA is that it is based on a standard serial port, and it has the relatively low bit rates associated with this type of port. The maximum transfer rate is usually about 115kbits (0.115Mbits) per second, and in some cases is much less than this.

Another problem is that IrDA interfaces are not normally included as standard, particularly with desktop PCs. Although most PCs have some built-in IrDA hardware and support, the extra parts needed to complete the interface often prove to be elusive. In many cases the easiest way, and possibly the only way of adding this facility to a PC is to ignore any built-in IrDA support, and instead opt to use a USB to IrDA adapter.

Bluetooth is designed to be a sort of universal version of an IrDA link, with a higher level of performance. It is designed to operate with low levels of power consumption, making it suitable for use with small portable devices such as phones and palmtop PCs. With a maximum transfer speed of only about 1Mbit per second, Bluetooth is not particularly fast by modern computing standards. It is only about one tenth as fast as an 802.11b link for instance. The transfer speed is adequate for many purposes though, and it is nearly ten times faster than an IrDA link. If you have gigabytes of data to transfer, forget IrDA or Bluetooth.

The range of a Bluetooth device is about 10 metres, and because it uses a radio link rather than infrared, the signal is able to pass through many types of object. It can be blocked by large pieces of metal though. It is possible to obtain signal repeaters that can boost the range to 100 metres, but Bluetooth is normally used in applications where a range of 10 metres is adequate.

Although Bluetooth devices have a very short operating range, they still need security measures in order to keep hackers at bay. Security measures are built into the system, and Bluetooth gadgets have unique identifying codes that can be used to prevent any unauthorised use. For instance, a Bluetooth mobile phone could be set up so that it would only connect to the Internet when used with your own Pocket PC.

Piconet

When Bluetooth devices lock-on to each others' signals they form what is termed a piconet, or a small network in other words. One gadget initiates contact, and this is the master device. This unit negotiates all data transfer paths between devices in the network, and there can be up to seven slave units in addition to the master. In practice it is unlikely that eight units would be networked using Bluetooth, and in most cases it is used with just two devices. However, it could be used in a situation such as a Bluetooth enabled printer being fed from several PCs.

Any Bluetooth device has the wherewithal to control a piconet, and the master – slave relationship has to be flexible so that the equipment can adjust to suit practically any situation. With a simple swap of data between two devices, the one that initiates the connection becomes the master device. Any other units that join the piconet will automatically operate as slaves.

This simple scheme of things does not suit all situations, and it would not work in the printer setup mentioned previously. The first computer to access the printer would become the master unit, but for this network to operate properly it is necessary for the printer to always be the master device. This enables the printer to properly control the flow of print jobs. The way around this is for a master device to be temporarily demoted to slave status when it links with a device that must have master status.

Channels

Bluetooth uses the same 2.4GHz band as 802.11b and 802.11g wi-fi units, but the channelling is arranged differently. The lower bit rate of Bluetooth permits a larger number of channels to be accommodated, and there are some 79 separate channels. There is no need to select a channel, since a system of channel hopping is used. Devices "hop" 1600 times a second in an attempt to avoid conflicts.

The system used with Bluetooth is called Adaptive Frequency Hopping (AFH), and it is designed to avoid interference from any devices that use the 2.4GHz band, and not just other Bluetooth equipment. As signals within the band come and go, Bluetooth devices will adapt to the changing situation in an attempt to make the best possible use of any free channels.

Bluetooth had quite a long gestation period, and when first launched its level of take-up was somewhat underwhelming. It is backed by the Bluetooth Special Interest Group (www.bluetooth.com), which has over 2000 members including huge companies such as Intel and IBM. It is gaining in popularity, but has yet to achieve its creators' aim of becoming a worldwide standard for short-range communications without cables. It seems likely that it will do so in due course, but only for applications where transfers at relatively low speeds will suffice.

Incidentally, Bluetooth is named after a Harold Bluetooth Gormson. He is not one of the brains behind the system, but was in fact the monarch of Denmark just over a thousand years ago. Apparently, he managed the difficult task of uniting two Baltic states, which seems to a rather tenuous link to modern wireless technology.

Getting connected

Any computer that will be connected to a network via a wireless link must be equipped with a wi-fi adapter of some kind. The available options depend on the type of PC, but for a desktop type the main options are a USB wireless adapter or a PCI type. Provided a spare USB port is available, the USB option is the easier to install. Some of these units are similar in appearance to the popular USB pen drives that contain flash memory, and a few of these devices do actually combine the two functions of wi-fi adapter and pen drive. There is normally no outward sign of an aerial with these units, as it is contained within the plastic case.

The adapter can be plugged straight into a USB port of the PC, or connected via a USB extension lead. Using any unit of this type directly plugged into a USB port is convenient, but it leaves the device vulnerable to damage. The risks are probably greater when the device is used with a heavy desktop PC. If someone should happen to knock against the adapter it is possible that the PC will remain in place and that the adapter will give way. This would probably render it unusable, and repairs are usually uneconomic with low-cost units such as these adapters.

I prefer to use a short extension cable with any small USB gadgets. In the current context this method has the added advantage of permitting the adapter to be moved slightly, which can be useful if a "blind" spot is giving problems with poor performance. Note that it is not a normal A to B USB cable that is required, but an A to A extension lead. This has the larger A type socket at one end and an A type plug at the other.

USB wi-fi adapters are also available in the form of a small box that sits on top of the PC and connects to the USB port via a short cable. Figure 4.2 shows a neat unit of this type made by Netgear. This type of adapter is connected to the USB port via a standard A to B cable, and the rear of the unit has the smaller B type USB connector. This is the type of cable this is used with scanners, printers, and most other USB gadgets, but a suitable lead is normally supplied with the adapter.

This style of wireless network adapter tends to be more expensive than the type that is designed to plug straight into a USB port, but one reason

4 Going wi-fi

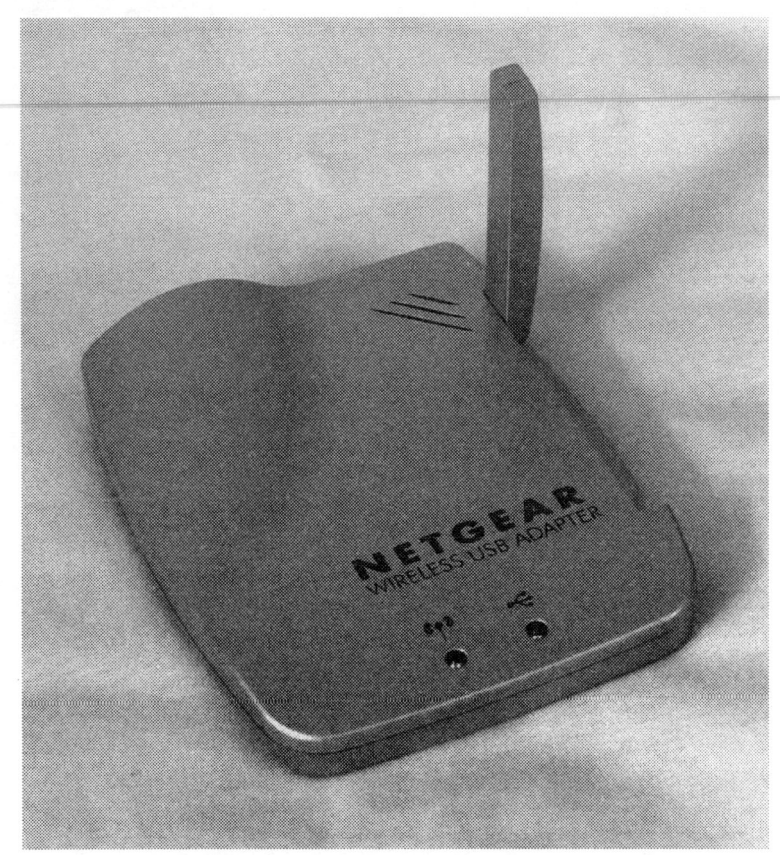

Fig.4.2 This Netgear adapter connects to the PC using an ordinary (A to B) USB cable

for this is that many of them are 802.11g devices. The cheap "pen drive" adapters are 802.11b devices. An advantage of the box and lead style adapters is that, as standard, the box part can be easily repositioned in order to find the position that gives optimum results. This is a definite advantage for an adapter that will be used with a desktop PC, but the pen drive type units are probably a better choice for use with portable PCs.

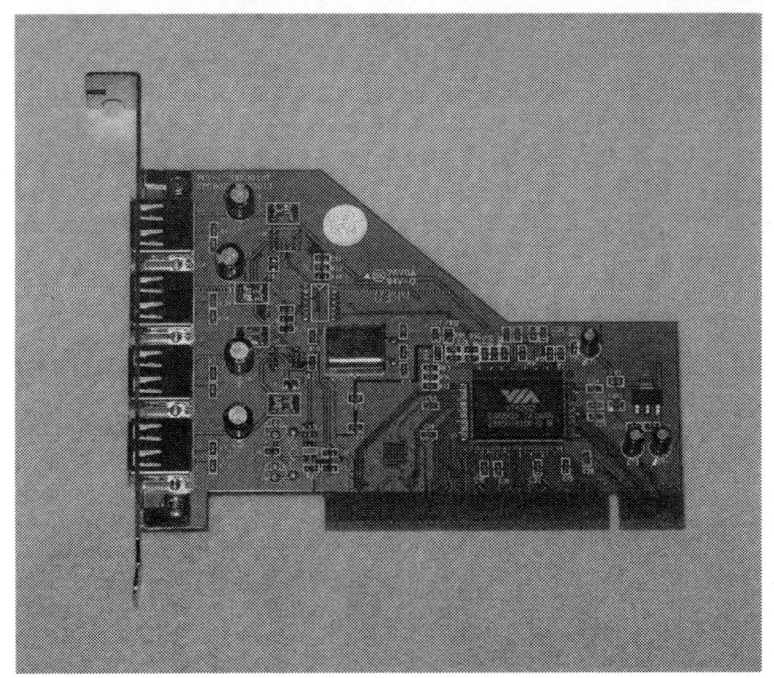

Fig.4.3 This PCI card provides four USB 2.0 ports

Speed

802.11b adapters usually have a USB 1.1 port, but they will work perfectly well with USB 2.0 ports. On the face of it, a USB 1.1 port is adequate for an 802.11b adapter, since it operates at more or less the same maximum speed as the adapter. In practice it is not quite as simple as that, because USB 1.1 only permits a single device to use half of the available bandwidth. This ensures that one device can not hog all the bandwidth to the detriment of the others. Unfortunately, it also means that USB 1.1 wi-fi adapters might not operate quite as fast as expected, although any shortfall is likely to be quite small.

There is little point in using USB 1.1 for an 802.11g adapter, because the speed of the USB port would be far too low to accommodate the transfer rates possible with the adapter. It is possible to use an 802.11g adapter with a USB 1.1 port if that is all that is available, but data transfers will be limited by the relative slowness of the USB port. USB 2.0 can handle bit

4 Going wi-fi

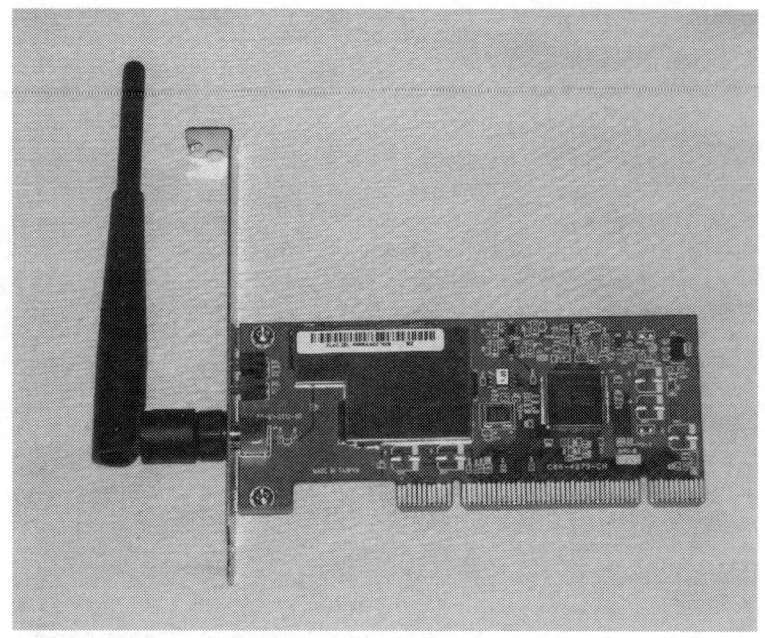

Fig.4.4 A PCI wi-fi adapter complete with aerial

rates well above the 54Mbits per second of the 802.11g standard. In fact USB 2.0 can handle rates of up to 480Mbits per second. An 802.11g USB adapter should therefore be capable of operating at full speed with a USB 2.0 port.

Note that it is possible to add USB 2.0 ports to a desktop PC that is only equipped with USB 1.1 ports. It is just a matter of adding a PCI expansion card that has what will typically be two or four USB 2.0 ports. The generic card shown in Figure 4.3 has four ports and cost only a few pounds. Of course, the PC must have at least one spare PCI expansion slot, but this will not be a problem with most PCs. Windows XP is designed to operate with USB 2.0 ports, but Windows ME is not. However, provided you are careful to obtain a card that is supplied with drivers for Windows ME, it should work perfectly well with this operating system.

Note that a USB wi-fi adapter that is powered from the USB port will probably not work if it is used via a passive hub. This is due to the fact that a passive hub has to share the power from the source USB port between however many USB outputs it provides. This will usually result in too little power being available for a wi-fi adapter. Connect the adapter direct to the PC or via a powered USB hub.

PCI adapter

In some ways a wi-fi PCI card (Figure 4.4) is a neater solution than using any form of USB wi-fi adapter. Apart from the aerial, everything is kept within the main housing of the PC. This avoids having to use a lead or having the adapter protruding well out from the rear of the PC. These days most PCs have a free PCI expansion slot, but USB ports soon seem to be used up.

There are drawbacks as well though, and one of them is that the aerial is not placed in a favourable position. It is in amongst the leads at the rear of the PC. Even if you can manage to keep most of the leads away from the aerial, it will still be very close to the metal case (Figure 4.5). This situation is considerably less than ideal, and is likely to compromise results. Matters are compounded by the fact that repositioning the aerial to avoid a "blind" spot means moving the entire base unit.

Fig.4.5 A PCI wi-fi card and a tower case in not a good combination

There is a possible solution, but this is dependent on the aerial having a standard fitting and being detachable from the card. Most PCI adaptors

4 Going wi-fi

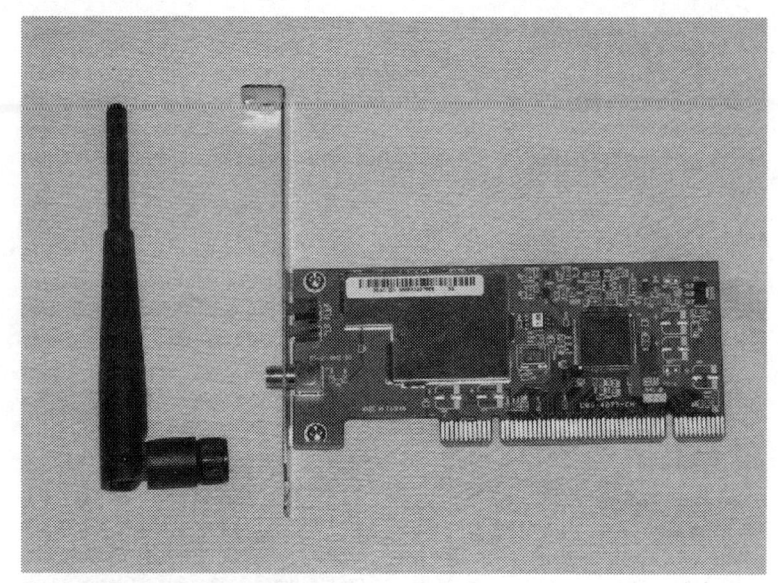

Fig.4.6 The aerial can be unscrewed from the card

do have a standard connector for the aerial, which is easily unscrewed from the card (Figure 4.6). Figure 4.7 shows a close-up of the connectors on the card and the aerial. Note that it is usually necessary to temporarily dismount the aerial so that the card can be installed in the PC.

One way of using the aerial away from the rear of the PC is to use an extension cable. An alternative is to obtain a new aerial complete with cable. The second method is likely to be much more expensive, but it might be possible to obtain an aerial that has a built-in stand so that it is easily mounted on top of a PC, on a desktop, etc. Unfortunately, aerials and extension cables are less widely available than the wi-fi adapters themselves, and they seem to be relatively expensive.

The obvious way of adding a wi-fi adapter is to have a device that connects to a standard Ethernet port. Strangely, I have not encountered a simple adapter that uses this method, although more complex wi-fi devices do use this method of interfacing. There is a drawback to using an Ethernet port for a wi-fi adapter, which is that it is not possible to draw power from this type of port. This would make it necessary to have a mains adapter to power the device, which would be less convenient than drawing power

Going wi-fi 4

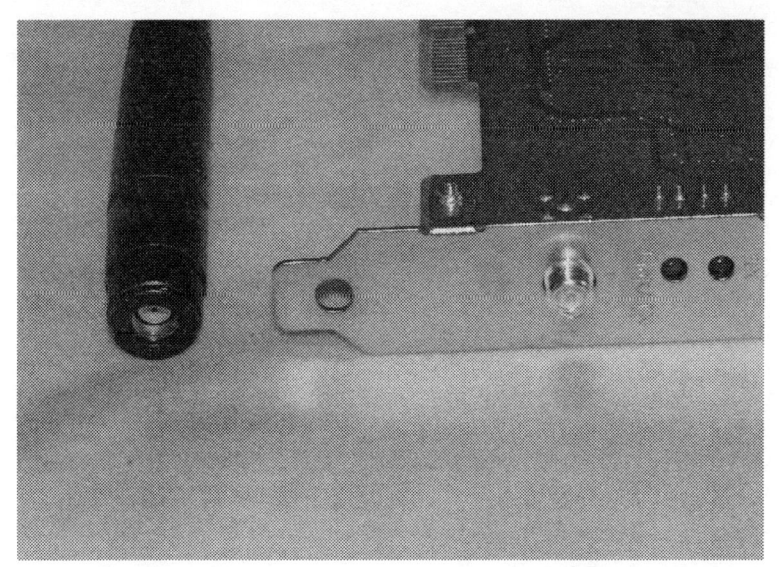

Fig.4.7 Close-up of the connections on the aerial and the PCI card

from the PC. Of course, no adapter is needed for PCI or USB wi-fi adapters.

Ad hoc

It is not essential to use an access point, and two wi-fi equipped PCs that can receive each others signals can establish a network in what is called "Ad Hoc mode". This is the wi-fi equivalent of two PCs being connected together using their Ethernet ports and a crossed-over cable. The wi-fi version is actually more versatile in that it enables easy communication between any two PCs that are within range, and no cable swapping is required. However, proper networking effectively provides a simultaneous connection between every unit in the system, and is even more versatile.

Although it is not without attractions, the Ad Hoc method of networking is inferior to using an access point, and is little used in practice. If you really need nothing more than a basic wireless connection between two PCs, then two adapters and the Ad Hoc mode will certainly do the job. You still have the option of adding an access point at a later date if you should need a more elaborate network.

4 Going wi-fi

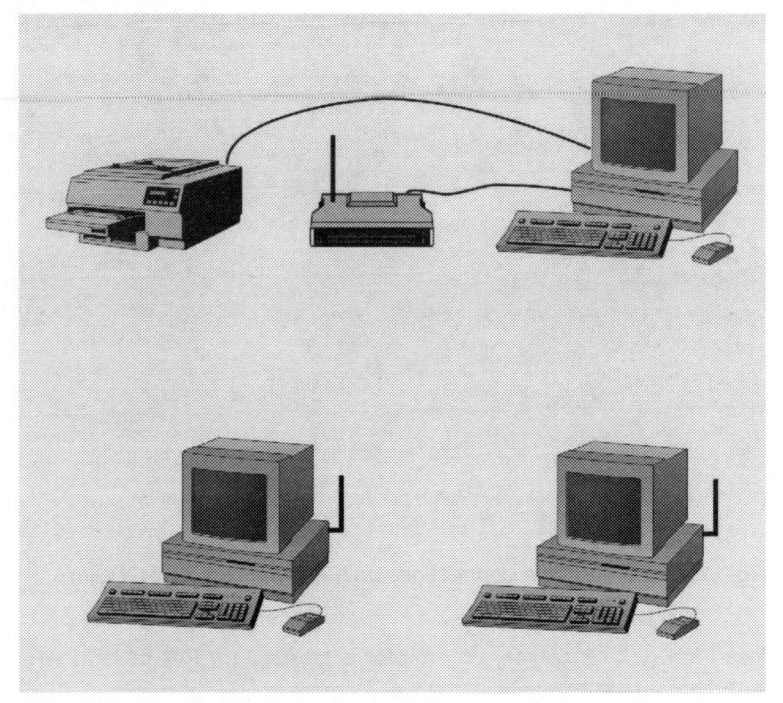

Fig.4.8 A typical wi-fi network has one PC wired to the access point and a printer, with the other PCs networked using wi-fi

Note that when installing and setting up a wi-fi adapter it might be necessary to specify the mode of operation that you wish to use. The adapter's control software then seeks signals from the appropriate type of wi-fi unit. With Ad Hoc mode selected, the software searches for signals from other wi-fi adapters, and will only communicate with that type of unit.

The other mode is called Infrastructure mode, and it is used to implement full networking. Infrastructure mode can only be facilitated with the aid of an access point. Some wi-fi adapters start in what is effectively Ad Hoc mode so that they can search for and list all the available wi-fi signals. By default they will probably connect to and use any access point that is found. As always, it is necessary to read the supplied documentation in order to determine the exact way in which the equipment operates.

As pointed out previously, the main advantage of using Infrastructure mode and an access point is that it enables communications between numerous devices to take place simultaneously. In effect, everything in the network is connected to everything else in the network all the time. In this respect it is the same as a wired network. With Ad Hoc working only two devices can be linked at any one time. Another advantage is that the access point can provide what is termed a "bridge". In other words, it can provide a bridge between wi-fi equipped devices and wired network devices. This is an important point, because few practical networks are purely of the wi-fi variety.

Of course, a wi-fi network can be purely that, with everything in the system communicating via radio links. No doubt there are many networks that perform very well using nothing but wi-fi links. In practice though, a totally wi-fi network is unlikely to be the best solution. With the access point on the same desk as one of the PCs, there is little point in using a wi-fi link between the two. A cable will do the job better and at a fraction of the price.

A typical wi-fi network would therefore use a setup of the type shown in Figure 4.8, with one PC wired to the access point and a printer, with the other PCs linked via wi-fi adapters. Apart from file sharing between the PCs in the system, it could also be set up to give all three PCs access to the printer. Obviously this arrangement can be modified to suit individual requirements. For example, there could be other PCs close to the access point, and a wired link might be more practical for these PCs. On the other hand, it could be inconvenient to have the access point very close to any of the PCs in the system, and a fully wi-fi network could then be used.

Extending range

As explained previously, the theoretical range of a wi-fi system and the real-world range are often very different, with the range obtained in practice tending to fall short of the theoretical maximum. In some cases it falls well short of the theoretical maximum. This does not necessarily matter, and in many situations there is no need for a large operating range. Unless a wi-fi system is being installed in a very large building, trying to stretch the system to its limits is unnecessary. However, there are gadgets available if you should need to extend the range of a link in the system.

Some of this equipment is fairly straightforward, such as aerials for outdoor use. Operating from one building to another often produces poor results even though the aerials seem to be within range. This problem is due to the use of indoor aerials that require the signal to go through at least two walls on its way from one end of the link to the other. The signal absorption can be quite high, giving a much lower than expected range.

By having both aerials outside it is often possible to have "clear air" between them, and something in the region of the full 100 metre operating range should be obtained. A significantly longer range is possible if reduced operating speed can be tolerated, but it is probably best not to take some of the claims for these aerials too seriously. For one thing, the greater the operating range, the lower the chance of having a path between the aerials that is totally clear of obstructions.

Directional

The simple aerials normally used with wi-fi networks are omnidirectional, which means that they transmit with equal strength in all directions. When receiving signals, they are equally sensitive in all directions. The omnidirectional term is not strictly accurate, because immediately above and below the aerial (which should be vertical) there are two "blind" spots. With most types of radio communication this is unimportant, but it should be borne in mind when installing a wi-fi network on two or more floors of a building.

In addition to the "blind" spots, signal strengths tend to be reduced when an aerial is higher or lower than the aerial at the access point. The range obtained on floors above and below the access point could therefore be less than the range obtained on the same floor. In fact this is almost certain to occur, because there is the added signal absorption of the floors and ceilings when a link is established between different levels of a building. These factors almost certainly account for the disappointing results that are sometimes obtained when using wi-fi equipment in a multi-storey building.

A directional aerial gives better results in one or possibly two directions. With several pieces of equipment using a wi-fi link to the network, omnidirectional operation is essential for the access point. It has to communicate with various pieces of equipment scattered around the building. It is highly unlikely that they will be conveniently placed so that they are all in more or less the same direction relative to the access point.

The situation is different when there are only two devices to be linked. A directional aerial is then acceptable at both ends of the link. When there are more than two wi-fi units in a network, a directional aerial can normally be used for anything other than the access point. Unless Ad Hoc operation is used, all the other devices in the system communicate via the access point, and do not directly communicate with anything else in the network. They can therefore communicate with the network by way a directional aerial aimed at the access point.

We are all familiar with directional aerials. Ordinary television aerials and satellite dishes are common examples of directional aerials, and for good results they have to be aimed quite accurately at the transmitter or satellite. The point of a directional aerial is that it provides gain. In other words, using a directional aerial produces a stronger signal when transmitting. A stronger transmission in one direction is obtained by having a weaker signal radiated in other directions. Increased sensitivity is obtained when a directional aerial is used for reception, but only in one direction. The sensitivity of the aerial is lower in all other directions. The more highly directional an aerial is made, the greater the gain that can be obtained.

Using a directional aerial can significantly increase the operating range of a wi-fi system, but it also makes it more difficult to get everything set up correctly and working well. Also, directional aerials are relatively difficult to obtain and expensive. It might be necessary to search online for a specialist supplier of wi-fi equipment in order to find something that suits your requirements.

Try to organise the network in a way that minimises the risk of range problems occurring. The access point should be somewhere near the middle of the building so that it is reasonably close to all the wi-fi enabled devices. Having the access point at one end of the building maximises the chances of problems, especially where there will be one of more wi-fi devices at the other end of the building.

Accelerators

The maximum speed possible using 802.11 wi-fi equipment is the 54 Mbits per second provided by 802.11g equipment, but you might find equipment advertised as offering something more like 100 or 108Mbits per second. The increase in speed is obtained by using some form of accelerator technology, which seems to mean changes to the way in which the packets of data are encoded and decoded. The radio side of

4 Going wi-fi

things is just uses standard 802.11 technology. Faster versions of 802.11b and 802.11g devices are produced. Note that in order to take advantage of the speed increase it is necessary for all the wi-fi devices in the network to use the same accelerator technology.

Points to remember

The main advantage of wireless networking is the obvious one of avoiding the need to thread cables around the house or office. This is a huge advantage for a home system where unsightly cables are deemed to be unacceptable, or where adding cables is simply not allowed for some reason.

The ranges quoted for wi-fi systems have to be taken with the proverbial "pinch of salt". The quoted ranges might be achieved in practice, but typical operating ranges seem to be somewhat less than the specifications would suggest. Operation is still possible with low signal strengths, but not at anything like the full quoted transfer rate.

Inefficiencies in the system mean that data can not be transferred at the quoted rates. In practice it is likely that the actual rate will be a little under half the quoted figure. Note also that the rates are in bits per second, not bytes per second. Divide speed figures by eight in order to obtain a transfer rate in bytes per second.

There is only one standard for wi-fi equipment, which is the IEEE 802.11 standard. However, matters are complicated by having three different versions of it (802.11a, 802.11b, and 802.11g). While the 802.11a equipment has potential advantages, it relatively expensive, difficult to obtain, and is incompatible with the other two.

It is 802.11b and 802.11g equipment that are used in most home and small office wi-fi systems. The faster 802.11g equipment is compatible with the 802.11b variety, but when a link uses the two types of equipment it obviously operates at the slower rate.

The short operating range helps to avoid problems with interference due to there being too many wi-fi users in the vicinity, but it is still a potential problem in heavily built-up areas. The problem is worse with 802.11b and 802.11g equipment which has fewer non-overlapping channels, and shares the 2.4GHz band with other types of equipment.

4 Going wi-fi

Many wi-fi equipment manufacturers now have their devices approved by the Wi-fi Alliance, but some do not bother. It is obviously reassuring to have approved equipment in your wireless network, but gadgets from any of the large manufacturers should have full compatibility with the relevant standards. As always, cheap generic equipment is a bit more risky and often lacks worthwhile customer support.

Bluetooth is not used for true networking, and is not really an alternative to 802.11 wi-fi equipment. It can be used for something like wireless printer sharing, but in most cases it is only used to provide a link between two devices such as a notebook PC and a mobile phone. It has a relatively low maximum data transfer rate of 1 Mbits per second, but this is adequate for many tasks.

A basic wireless adapter for a desktop PC can be in the form of a PCI expansion card or an external USB device. USB 2.0 is required in order to make full use of the speed available from an 802.11g adapter. Most USB wi-fi adapters will not work in conjunction with a passive USB hub.

A notebook or laptop PC can be interfaced to a basic wi-fi adapter using a USB port, but a PC card is the more popular choice. Some other portable computing devices can be wi-fi enabled, and a common ploy is to use a special version of a Compact Flash card. Many of these wi-fi gadgets only suit a limited range of devices, so always check compatibility with your particular PDA (or whatever) before buying anything.

Most practical wi-fi networks are based on a device called an access point. This acts as a sort of control centre, with all other devices in the network communicating via the access point rather than directly. The access point often provides other facilities, such as bridging to wired network devices, a firewall, and possibly even an ADSL broadband modem.

It is possible to network devices without using an access point, and this method relies on using the Ad Hoc mode of operation. This gives only a very simple form of networking, with two devices at a time communicating directly. Although potentially useful, this mode is little used in practice.

5

Installation and security

Installation

The amount of installation and setting up required in order to get a data link working will vary enormously depending on the exact equipment and method you are using. At its most simple, a link requires very little setting up. Suppose you have two PCs that are already equipped with Ethernet ports. Presumably the ports will already be installed physically, and in Windows. In order to produce a working link it is merely necessary to join the two Ethernet ports using a "crossed" lead, and then set up the network in Windows. Note that no additional software is needed in order to use any reasonably modern version of Windows with an Ethernet based network. The built-in networking facilities of Windows are perfectly adequate for most needs.

Things are nearly as simple with a Bluetooth link. It is usually just a matter of installing the software provided with the Bluetooth adapter, shutting down and switching off the PC, physically installing the adapter, and then booting up the PC again. The Plug and Play facilities of Windows then complete the installation. Bluetooth adapters for PCs are normally in the form of a USB "dongle", so the physical side of installation involves nothing more than plugging it in. Bluetooth is used with a wide variety of gadgets these days, but the software provided with the various bits of hardware you are using should handle basic file swapping. However, it will probably be necessary to delve deep into the instruction manuals in order to determine the precise manner in which the file swapping is accomplished. The manuals should also detail any special facilities or limitations of the data link.

Having completed the physical installation of a wi-fi network it is usually necessary to do a certain amount of setting up in a control program before the network itself can be set up properly. The wi-fi links have to

5   Installation and security

be installed and working before the network can be made fully operational, as do any wired network links. The first part of this chapter therefore deals with getting the wi-fi links set up and operational. Setting up the network in Windows is covered in the second half of this chapter.

Reading matters

Before installing any computer hardware, including Ethernet and wi-fi devices, it is essential to read the instruction manual. Realising that few people can be bothered to read the manual, many manufacturers now include a "Quick Start" leaflet, or something similar. At the very least you should look through the leaflet to determine the recommended method of installation. Failure to do so can result in a lot of wasted time due to a failed initial installation, and everything then having to be uninstalled and reinstalled correctly. With the more awkward devices it can be difficult and time consuming to get everything working once an installation has failed. Windows just keeps going back to the incorrect version despite your best efforts.

Most manufacturers now seem to recommend that the software is installed first, with the hardware being added once the drivers are safely installed. In theory it should be perfectly all right for the hardware to be fitted first. The Plug and Play facility of Windows should then find the hardware and install the driver software. In practice this method can be problematic, with Windows trying to install the wrong drivers, failing to recognise the right drivers, or continually detecting the hardware and trying to install the already installed drivers. Following the manufacturer's installation instructions "to the letter" should minimise the risk of running into problems with the drivers.

It would seem reasonable to assume that the drivers supplied with the new hardware will be fully tested and working. Matters are often very different in practice, with minor problems often occurring when the supplied drivers are used with some PCs. Also, it has been known for manufacturers to rush out new hardware with the drivers not being tested as comprehensively as they should be. This can cause major problems for anyone that tries to install them. I have obtained one or two pieces of cheap generic hardware where the supplied discs were clearly for another and totally different piece of hardware!

It is a good idea to search the manufacturer's web site for any updated drivers before trying to install any new hardware. If you do find more recent drivers, read any installation instructions that come with them.

The installation method often differs from that for the drivers supplied with the hardware. Even where the supplied drivers work all right, there might be improved drivers that provide more features, faster operation, or whatever. It is always a good idea to use the latest driver software that can be found.

In the case of generic hardware there might not be a manufacturer's web site where you can seek new drivers and other support. The drivers supplied with this type of software are often those provided by the producer of the chips on which the hardware is based. A computer chip manufacturer's web site will usually have the latest drivers for their products. Failing that, the retailer's customer support service is the only hope. Generic hardware is cheap, but you are unlikely to obtain the same sort of support that is available when "big name" products are purchased.

Firmware

With the more complex networking equipment you will sometimes find that there is more than just improved driver software available. Complex networking devices such as combined routers and modems are based on a microcontroller, which is essentially a fairly basic but capable computer on a single chip. This computer runs a program that is built into the hardware. Because the program is a mixture of hardware and software it is usually termed "firmware".

In addition to improved driver software it is now quite common for manufacturers to make better firmware available. The firmware is usually stored in some form of flash memory. Unlike normal computer memory, this type retains its contents when the equipment is switched off, but it can still be reprogrammed. Sometimes the firmware upgrades provide improved performance or extra features, but they are mostly used to fix minor bugs.

It is certainly a good idea to look for firmware upgrades and install any that you find. A firmware upgrade is not something to be undertaken lightly though, and mistakes can render the equipment unusable. Read the manufacturers installation instructions very carefully at least once, and follow them precisely. Installing new firmware is usually a very simple process and it should all go smoothly provided silly mistakes are avoided. Probably the most popular silly mistake is to download the wrong upgrade. Computing equipment tends to be sold under a range of similar

5 Installation and security

names and numbers, so be careful to ensure that the download is for the exact piece of equipment you are using.

A manufacturer sometimes recommends installing a firmware upgrade before using a piece of equipment in earnest. This is unusual though, and usually means that a serious bug has been found in the original firmware. Unless an equipment manufacturer recommends otherwise, it is probably best to get the equipment installed and working before undertaking any firmware upgrades. A detailed description of downloading and installing new firmware is covered at the end of this chapter.

Setting up

Both wired and wi-fi networking equipment can require a lot of complex setting up before it is ready for use. Fortunately, the equipment manufacturers have realised that most users would prefer not to spend months becoming an expert on networks just so that they can install and set up a simple home or small business network. Consequently, practically all modern networking equipment is supplied with drivers and other software that makes setting up and using the network as simple as possible. The installation software will usually scan the PC, Internet connection, etc., and then go through a largely automatic setting up procedure. There could still be some work to do in order to get things working really well and securely.

It is advisable to install the access point before adding anything else to the network. In general, wi-fi adapters are very easy to install, and the process is largely automatic. However, without an access point to communicate with it is difficult for a wi-fi adapter to set itself up correctly and do anything worthwhile. It is assumed here, that there will be at least one PC that has a wired connection to the access point. In a fully wi-fi network it is clearly necessary to have at least one PC with an installed wi-fi adapter before it is possible to contact and set up the access point. It is still probably best to have the access point switched on before installing the wi-fi adapters, but it is advisable to check the access point's instruction manual for guidance on this matter.

Setting up the access point is different depending on whether it is an add-on to an existing wired network, a type having a built-in router, or one having both a router and broadband modem. The process also varies somewhat from one manufacturer to another, and can even be different for various models from the same manufacturer. One example is provided here, and it demonstrates some basic principles, but it is essential to read the instruction manuals before installing any wi-fi equipment. The manuals should give concise guidance and fully explain any unusual aspects of installation. The examples given here can do no more than give some idea of the stages involved in setting up a wi-fi network.

Standalone

It is important to realise that the access point is unlikely to appear in the list of installed units in Device Manager. As part of the setting up process you might have to install a control program for the access point on one of the PCs, but this will be an ordinary piece of software and not a set of device drivers. After installing new hardware it is normal to look for its entry in Device Manager to check that there are no problems. Looking in the Network Adapters section of Device Manager will show an entry for the Ethernet or wi-fi adapter fitted to that PC (Figure 5.1), but there will be no entry for the access point.

The reason for this is simply that the access point is not a device installed on one of the PCs. It has its own built-in microcontroller, and it has to be regarded as akin to a PC in the system. The same is true of a printer server and any other standalone units in the system. Obviously it is necessary to have some means of making adjustments to the access point's settings, and this is normally achieved using either a control program in one of the networked PCs or using web-based configuration software. Either way the process is usually handled by a wizard, and will probably be largely automatic. It is probably best to avoid units that do not offer a user-friendly method of installation and setting up.

The so-called web-based method of configuration is increasingly common, and as such it does not use a configuration program in one of the networked PCs. Instead, you run browser program such as Internet Explorer, and then use a special web address. It then appears as though you are configuring the device via a series of web pages, but these pages are embedded within the device's firmware, as is any supporting software for them. The configuration is therefore achieved using an ordinary browser running on one of the networked PCs, together with firmware within the access point.

5 Installation and security

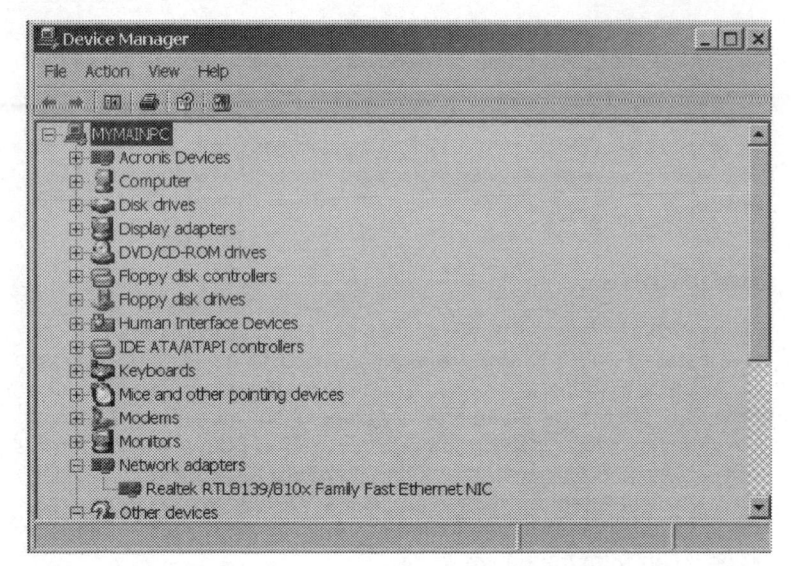

Fig.5.1 The Ethernet adapter is listed in Device Manager, but a device such as a router or access point will not be found here

Settings

A web-based setup program is used for the Netgear DG834G, which is an all-in-one 802.11g access point, ADSL modem, router, and firewall. The setup pages can be accessed by typing the appropriate address into a browser, or by clicking the link on the page that is launched when the installation disc is run. Either way, it is necessary to use the supplied username and password when prompted (Figure 5.2). The initial setting up procedure is largely automatic, but with a device that contains a modem it is necessary to supply basic connection information, such as the username and password for your broadband account. This information should have been provided by your Internet service provider (ISP) when you signed on to the account.

The connection information is stored in the modem and there is no need for you to provide it in order to gain access to the Internet. Normally the unit is left running continuously, so once it has connected to the Internet it stays connected. Any PC in the network then has instant access to the Internet at any time. Of course, things can go wrong, and over a period of time it is likely that for one reason or another, the Internet connection will be lost. Switching the unit off, waiting a few seconds, and then

Installation and security 5

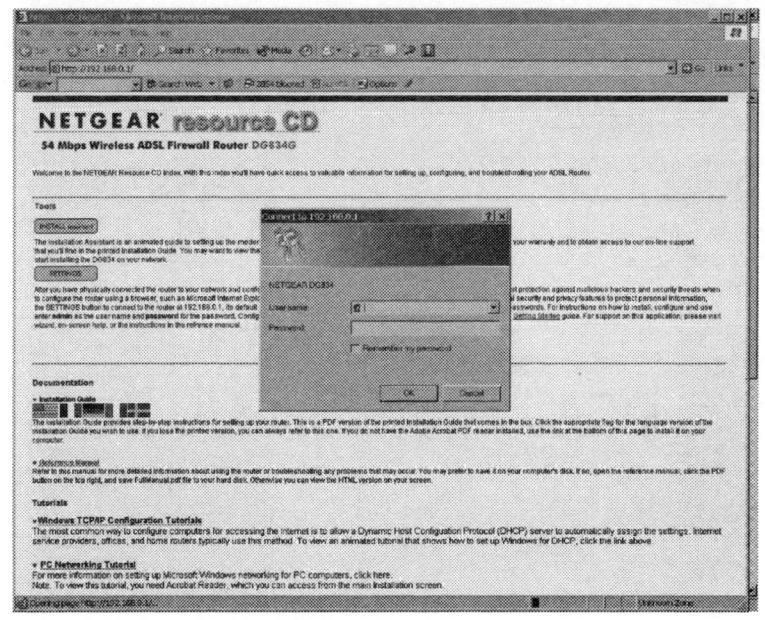

Fig.5.2 The supplied username and password are required in order to start the web-based configuration process

switching it on again will force it to reconnect, using the stored username, password, and other connection data.

A page like the one in Figure 5.3 is displayed once the initial setting up has been completed. This page shows the current settings in the main section, and there are some menus in the right-hand section. A scrollable Help page is available on the opposite side of the screen. Operating the Connection Status button near the bottom of the screen produces the small window shown in Figure 5.4. This confirms that a connection to the Internet has been made, and provides two buttons that enable the modem to be disconnected and reconnected. The Show Statistics button produce a small window like the one of Figure 5.5, which shows things like the number of data packets handled by various parts of the system.

It is the menus down the left of the screen that are of importance in the current context, as these give access to screens that control numerous settings. Most of these should not be altered, and it is definitely not a good idea to start experimenting with settings that you do not understand. There are some settings that can be usefully altered though, and one of

5 Installation and security

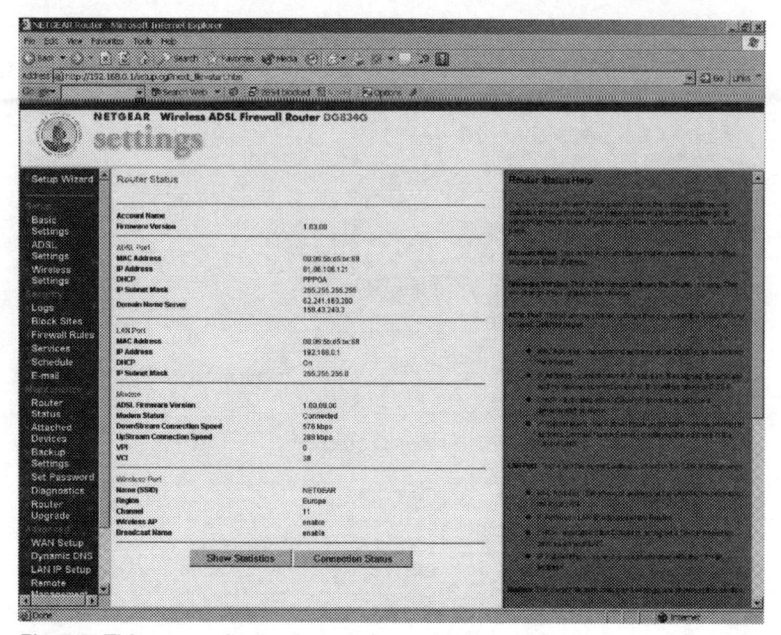

Fig.5.3 This page shows the current settings

these is the password used to access the setup pages. The default password is the same for every unit, so you must change it in order to genuinely password protect the system. Operating the Password menu option brings up the page of Figure 5.6. This operates in the standard fashion, with the old and new passwords being entered, followed by the new password again in case a mistake was made the first time.

Security

Note that this password is the one used to gain access to the setup program so that changes can be made to the configuration of the modem, router, etc. This password does not provide protection against hackers gaining access to the network via a wi-fi link. Any reasonably modern access point should offer at least two types of protection against hackers, and in this case the security settings are accessed via Wireless Options in the Setup menu. This brings up the page shown in Figure 5.7.

Installation and security 5

Most of the settings here are the basic ones for a wi-fi link, such as the region, channel number, and name of the access point. It is not essential to change the name, but there is obviously scope for confusion if you live in an area that has several wi-fi networks in operation. With everyone using the default name it is likely that the same name will be used for two access points in the same area.

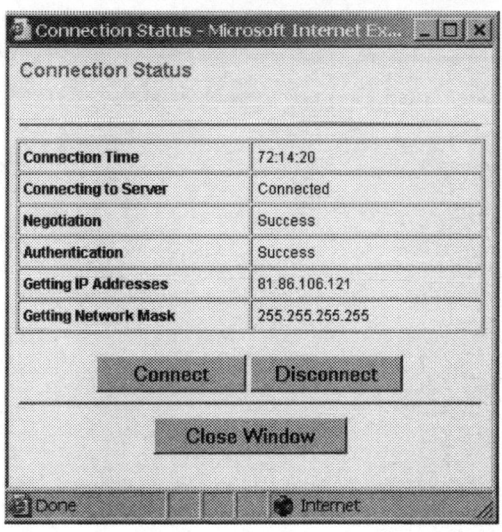

Fig.5.4 The Connection Status window

The DG834G is an 802.11g device, and as such it is compatible with 802.11b units. One of the menus enables it to be restricted to 802.11b or 802.11g operation. It can be advantageous to change the channel used by the system, and the reasons for this are discussed in the next chapter. The rest of the system adjusts to the channel used by the access point, so changing the channel used by the access point effectively changes the channel used by the entire network.

Three security options are available in the lower part of the screen, and the default option is for security measures to be disabled. It is best to use this setting initially, since it gives unrestricted access to the system, making it easy to get it working with the other wi-fi

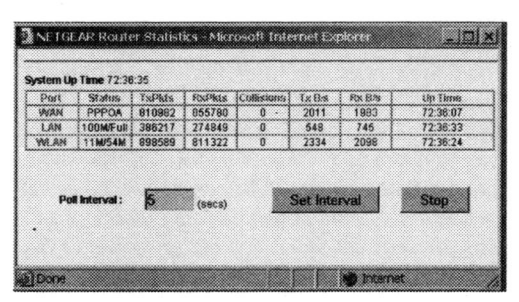

Fig.5.5 The Router Statistics window

5 Installation and security

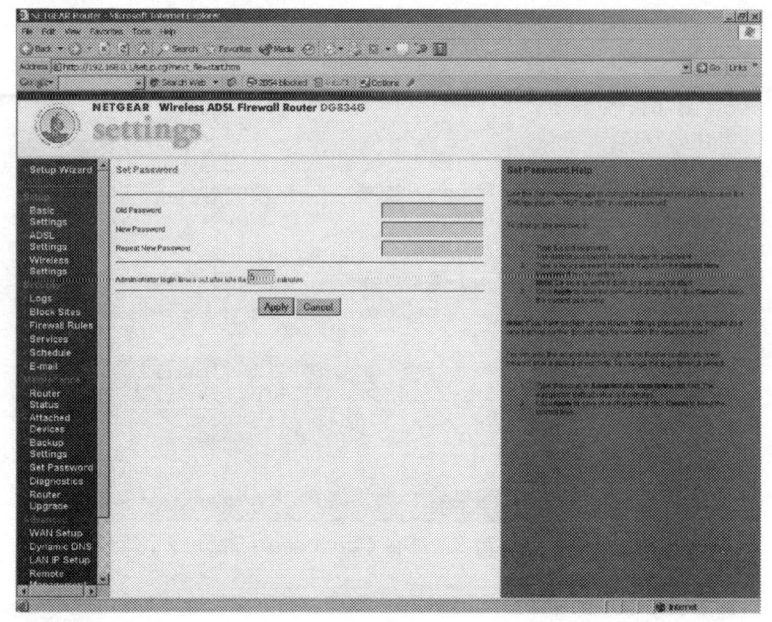

Fig.5.6 The unit is not secure until the password has been changed

units in the network. It is important to implement one of the security measures at an early stage though, especially if the PCs in the network are used for anything where security is important. This includes online ordering of goods and services, online auctions, Internet banking or other online financial dealing, and private correspondence.

WEP

The original and most basic form of wi-fi security is called Wired Equivalent Privacy, or WEP. This has been used with wi-fi equipment from the outset, and it is based on an encryption and decryption technique. The idea was to make wi-fi links as secure as the wired variety, and it is from this that the name of the system is derived. For WEP to work it is necessary for each wi-fi unit to have it enabled and to use the same key. The key is a large number used in the encryption and decryption process, and it is the WEP equivalent of a password.

An advantage of WEP is that any wi-fi gadget should be capable of using this security system, regardless of its precise function and which company

Installation and security 5

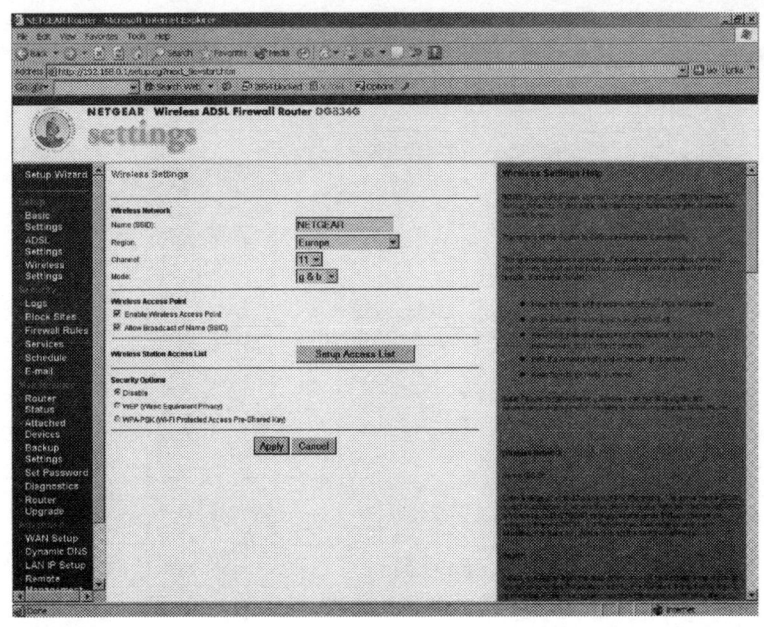

Fig.5.7 Most access points offer two types of security

produced it. Note that WEP is only used for wi-fi links and not for the wired variety, which are intrinsically more secure. Even where a network has a mixture of wired and wireless links, WEP security will only be used for the wireless links. Also note that the encryption and decryption process will reduce the speed of data transfers.

The level of security obtained depends on the number of bits used by the encryption process. Older equipment sometimes supports nothing beyond 64-bit operation, but modern wi-fi devices support at least 128-bit encryption. Obviously you should use the highest level of encryption that your equipment supports, but note that all the devices must use the same level. If some devices support 256-bit operation while others offer no more than 128-bit encryption, the whole system has to use 128-bit encryption.

In the DG834G setup program, the bottom section of the page changes when the WEP option is selected, with some new menus and textboxes appearing (Figure 5.8). One of the menus offers 64-bit or 128-bit encoding, and provided the other wi-fi units support it, 128-bit encoding

5 Installation and security

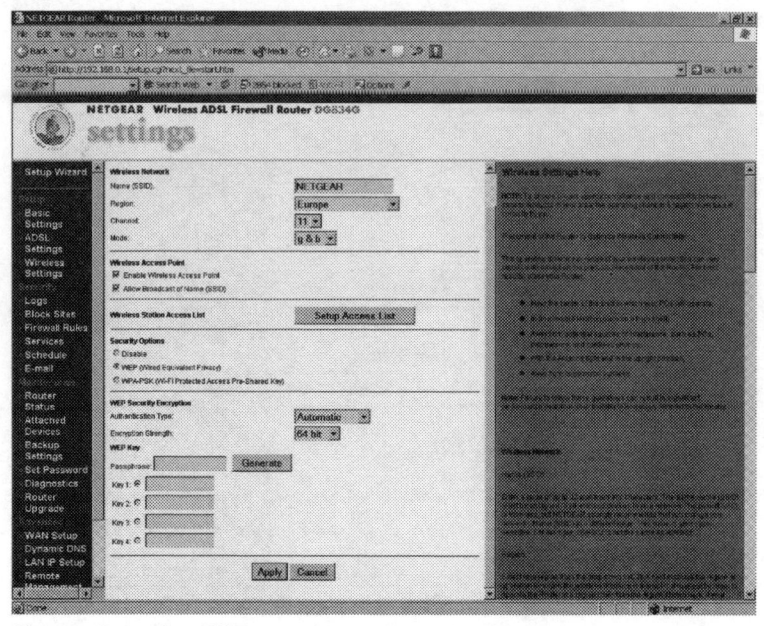

Fig.5.8 Selecting WEP security produces further options

should be used. The encoding type can be either Open System or Shared Key, and all units in the system must use the same setting. In this case there is an automatic option as the default. This can be changed to one of the other settings if automatic operation fails to work properly.

A WEP key can be generated by typing a short phrase into the appropriate textbox and operating the Generate key. Four keys are produced for 64-bit operation, but only one is generated for 128-bit encryption. The key will usually be in hexadecimal, which means that it will be comprised of numbers from 0 to 9 plus the first six letters of the alphabet (A to F). If it is generated in the form of a hexadecimal number by the access point's software, make sure that the software for your wi-fi adapters is set up to accept the key in the same form.

WPA

While WEP is adequate to keep casual hackers out of a home or small business network, it is vulnerable to determined hackers armed with the

Installation and security 5

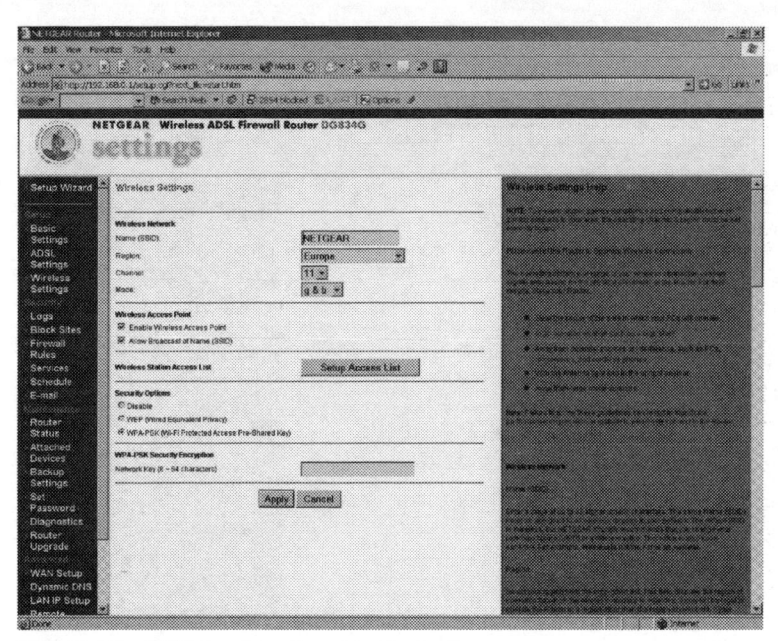

Fig.5.9 The WPA key is entered in the textbox

appropriate tools. This deterred larger business users from installing wi-fi links in their networks. With systems carrying sensitive information that could be worth millions to competitors, it was clearly not a good idea to use links that were anything less than totally secure. The equipment manufacturers' answer to this problem was a new and improved form of security called WPA-PSK (Wi-Fi Protected Access Pre-Shared Key). These days it is often just called WPA.

In this example there is a WPA-PSK security option, and selecting it produces a textbox (Figure 5.9) where the net key is added. This must be at least 8 characters, and can be up to 32 ASCII characters (numbers, letters, etc.) or up to 64 hexadecimal digits (0 to 9 and A to F). One reason for the better security provided by WPA is that the user enters the same key when setting up the network, but the key used for encryption and decryption is periodically changed by the system. The idea is that it is more difficult to find patterns that give away the key if it is changed from time to time. Also, by the time a hacker has found a key it is likely that the system will no longer be using it.

133

5 Installation and security

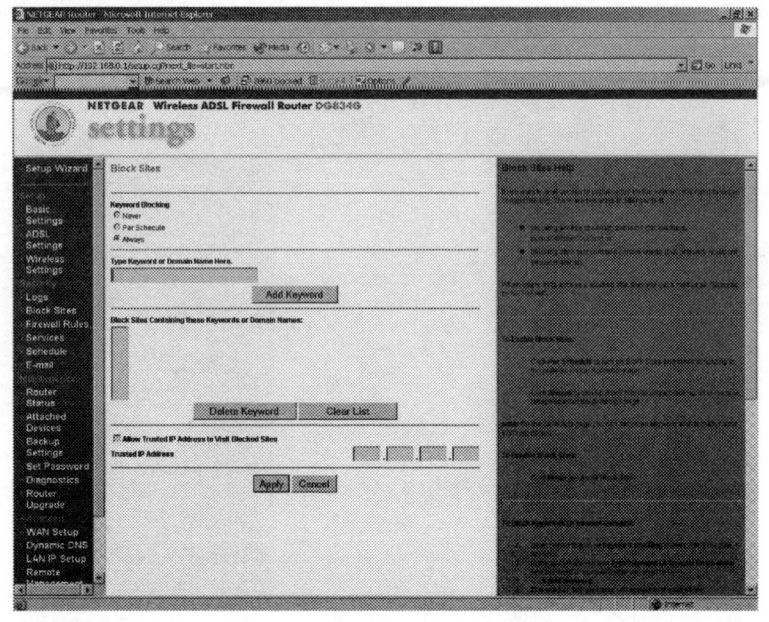

Fig.5.10 Addresses can be blocked using this page

It is clearly a good idea to use WPA where it is felt that the basic security provided by WEP is inadequate, but there can be practical difficulties in using WPA. The obvious one is that it is not part of the original wi-fi scheme of things, and it is not available with all wi-fi units. Note though, that it might be possible to add this facility via a firmware download.

802.11i

WPA was produced by the Wi-Fi Alliance rather than by the IEEE, and as such it does not form part of any 802.11 standard. The IEEE has been working on the problem of security, and during the course of writing this book its solution was finalised. It is known as 802.11i, but this is not a wi-fi standard of the same type as the other 802.11 standards. It is concerned with security and not with frequencies, transfer speeds, and the like.

Commenting on 802.11i is difficult because there are no products that use it available in the shops at the time of writing this piece. No doubt 802.11i devices will be available by the time you read this, and it will

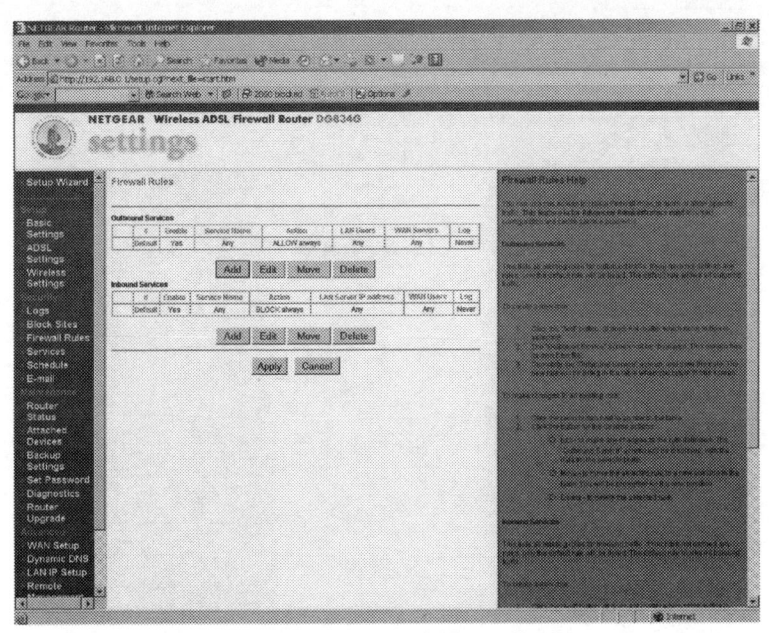

Fig.5.11 This page is used to edit or add firewall rules

probably be available as a firmware upgrade for some existing products. It should be an improvement compared to both WEP and WPA, and is the obvious security system to use provided your equipment supports it. Where optimum security is of paramount importance it clearly makes sense to obtain equipment that does support the 802.11i standard.

Other settings

There will probably be other types of setting available via the configuration program, and there could be large numbers of them if the access point includes features such as a built-in modem and firewall. Most of these can simply be left at the default settings, and you should definitely not "play" with them. It is worth investigating any firewall settings, and it might be necessary to adjust these in order to get everything working in a fashion that suits the way you use the Internet. Even if the default settings prove satisfactory, there could be some useful additional features available from the firewall.

5　Installation and security

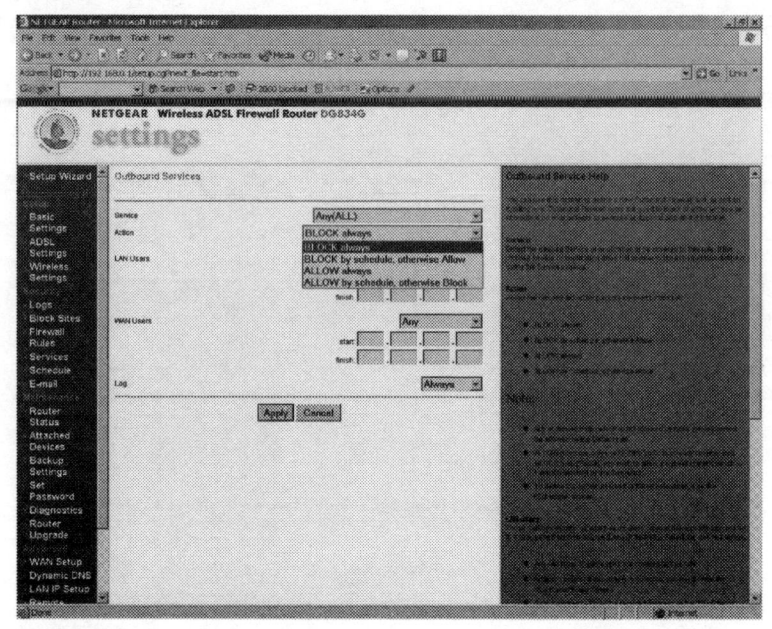

Fig.5.12　This page is used when defining your own firewall rules

The DG834G has the ability to provide some basic content filtering. It can be set to block sites that contain a certain text string in the domain name, or it can block specified addresses (Figure 5.10). A specified PC in the network can be given access to the blocked sites. Further control over the firewall is provided by the Firewall Rules page (Figure 5.11). The existing rules can be edited and it is also possible to add your own (Figure 5.12). It sometimes necessary to add rules or alter the existing rules in order to make firewalls work successfully with services such as video conferencing, and some peer-to-peer file sharing systems.

Adapter installation

Installing a wi-fi adapter is usually more straightforward than installing an access point, because the adapter is much more limited in scope. An access point is "its own boss", and often acts as much more than just an access point. A wi-fi adapter is just an ordinary peripheral, and it is essentially just a wireless version of an Ethernet port. Unlike an access

Installation and security 5

point, a wi-fi adapter is installed in the normal fashion, it will use device drivers, and it will have an entry in Device Manager.

Before installing any PC add-on it is advisable to check the manufacturer's web site for updated drivers. Most device drivers seem to go through various changes during the lifetime of the supported products. Follow the installation instructions "to the letter", especially when dealing with USB devices, which can be a little pernickety.

Note that it is not necessary to remove an Ethernet card or switch off a built-in Ethernet port in order to install a wi-fi adapter. The two can successfully coexist in the same computer, but obviously you should only use one or the other to connect to the network. There is a slight advantage in removing or switching off the Ethernet port. Leaving an Ethernet adapter installed and operational results in the computer's resources being consumed by a port that is not used. On the other hand, having a working Ethernet port in each PC and a long network cable is useful insurance. If a wi-fi link becomes troublesome, a wired connection can be used until the problem has been sorted out.

Control program

Double-clicking on the adapter's entry in Device Manager will bring up a properties window, and this might have sections that give control over such things as the default channel, the country setting, and the network type. Clearly this is very useful, but it is not used for everyday control of the adapter. There will be a control program that scans the band for access points and will automatically connect to the network if it finds the correct access point. This might be the only means of controlling the adapter. The control programs are all different, but some basic features are common to all of them.

Figure 5.13 shows the control program for the Netgear WG121 802.11g wi-fi adapter. This program has four sections, and the four tabs near the top of the window are used to switch between them. The Networks section is shown in Figure 5.13, and this scans for networks and lists those that are found. In this case just one network has been located. The information on this page shows that it is operating on channel 11, it is being received at full strength, and that the connection is operating at the full 54Mbits per second. It also shows that this network is not using any form of security (encryption). Two of the buttons at the bottom of the screen enable the band to be scanned again, and the PC to be connected to the selected network.

5 Installation and security

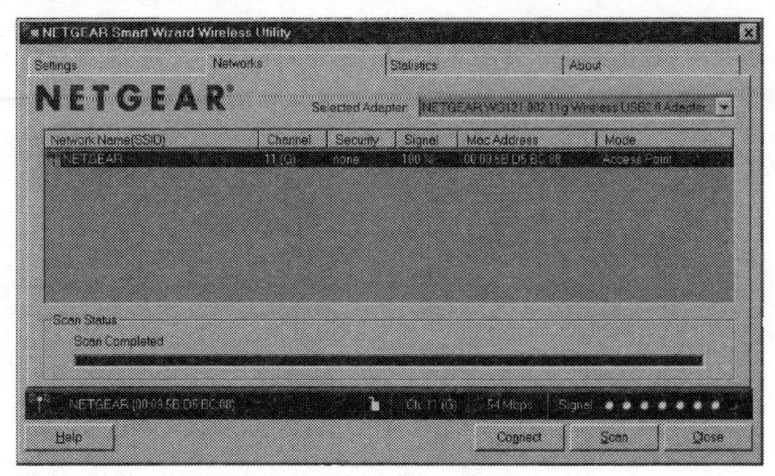

Fig.5.13 The program scans for access points

The statistics page (Figure 5.14) provides information such as the number of packets that have been received. There is also a display that provides a graph showing the amount of activity, and a bargraph that shows the percentage of the adapter's capacity that is being used. The About section (Figure 5.15) just gives some basic information about the adapter, such as its firmware version and driver details. This information will be needed if you look for updated drivers or firmware on the manufacturer's web site. Note that details of the current drivers can be obtained from the relevant section in Device Manager, but the firmware version is unlikely to be included here.

The Settings section (Figure 5.16) is an important one that controls a number of vital parameters. You can select Infrastructure mode for operation with an access point, or Ad Hoc mode for direct connection to another PC. The ability to define profiles is a standard feature, and one that is supported by this software. The idea is to have a profile defined for each network that you use. You can then switch from one network to another by selecting the appropriate profile.

Obviously a desktop PC will normally be used with a single network. It could still be useful to define a profile for that network. If there should be other networks within range, the program will automatically connect to the one for which there is a profile, and it will ignore the others. If encryption is introduced at an access point it will be necessary to set the

Installation and security 5

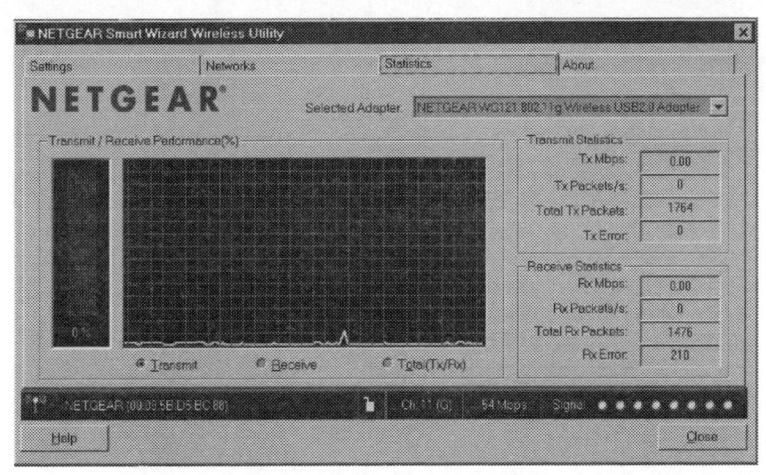

Fig.5.14 The Statistics section includes a graph showing the amount of data that has passed through the link

same encryption in the profile for that access point. In this example it was WEP encryption that was activated at the access point. WEP encryption with the same network key must therefore be activated on this adapter, and the others in the system.

WEP is actually the only security option offered by this adapter, and the others in the system. This renders the WPA option at the access point of

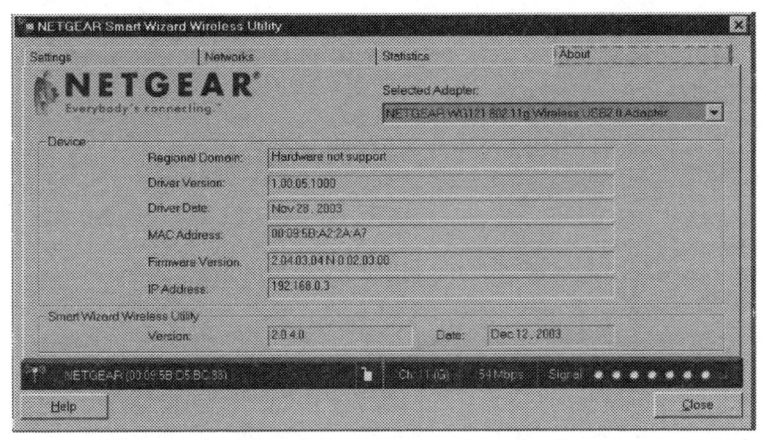

Fig.5.15 This section gives information such as the firmware version

5 Installation and security

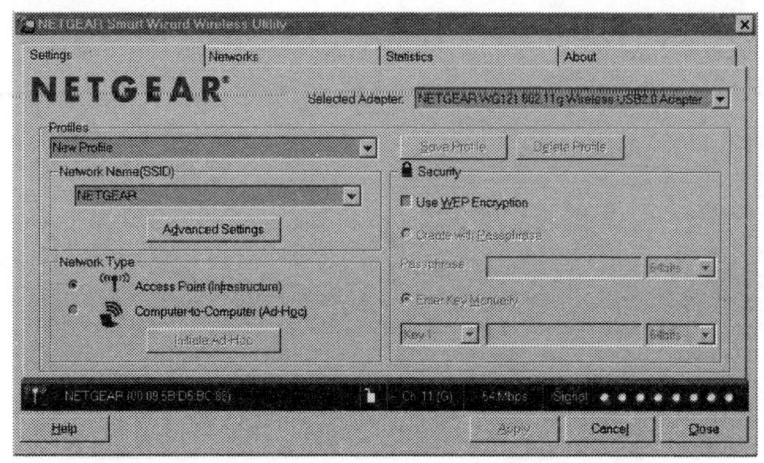

Fig.5.16 As one would probably expect, the Settings section is used to control the operating mode and other important settings

no practical value. In order to activate WEP encryption at this adapter it is necessary to first tick the Use WEP Encryption checkbox. Then 64-bit or 128-bit operation is selected using the small pop-down menu. Like the access point, this adapter is made by Netgear, and it offers the same

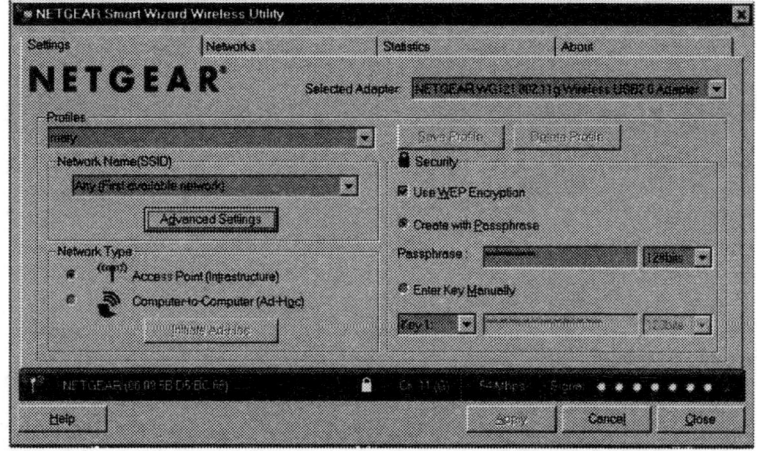

Fig.5.17 This control program includes a "passphrase" facility

Installation and security 5

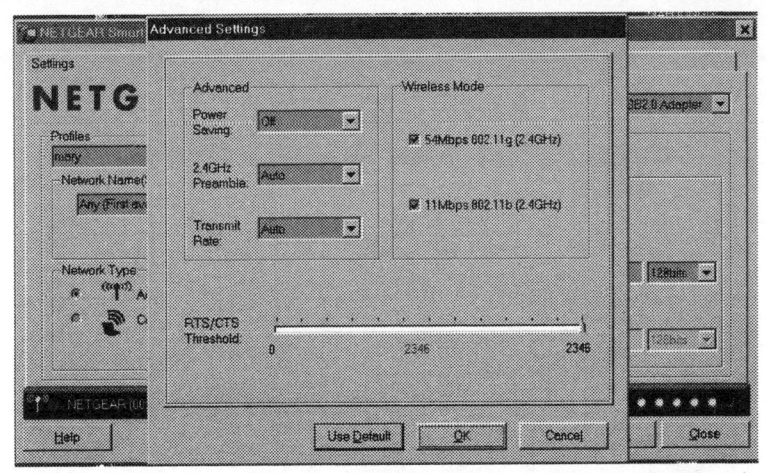

Fig.5.18 802.11b and 802.11g modes are both enabled by default

"passphrase" method of entering the net key. It is just a matter of operating the upper radio button and entering the same text string that was used at the access point. The software then converts this into the appropriate key and enters it in the text box (Figure 5.17). Manual entry of the key is also possible. Operate the lower radio button and type the network key into the textbox.

Operating the Advanced button brings up another window that offers further settings. There is probably little here that can be usefully altered though. The two checkboxes enable 802.11b and 802.11g operation to be enabled or disabled.

Another PC in the example network has a generic PCI adapter, and this also has software that can scan for access points (Figure 5.19). In order to make a connection to a network it is just a matter of selecting its entry in the main part of the window and then operating the Connect button. It will be necessary to enter the network key if the access point uses WEP security (Figure 5.20). In this case there is no "passphrase" option, and it is a matter of selecting 64-bit or 128-bit operation and then typing the key into the textbox.

The software has support for profiles, and a new profile can be added by selecting a network and then operating the Add Profile button. If WEP security is used, it is necessary to add the network key into the window

141

5 Installation and security

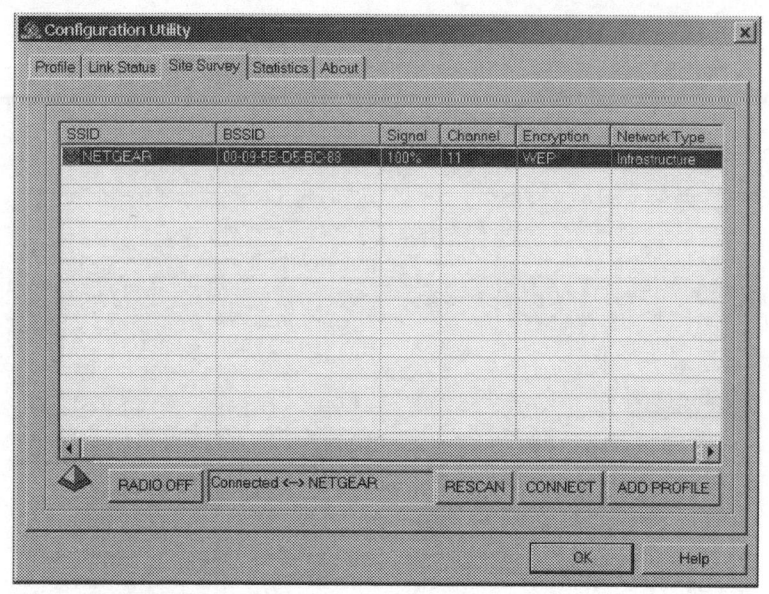

Fig.5.19 This control program also scans for access points

that pops up. However, the key is stored as part of the profile, and the network can be accessed thereafter without having to enter the key again. The newly added profile should be listed on the appropriate page of the program (Figure 5.21).

Sharing

With the access point set up correctly, the wired and wi-fi links in place, and everything working nicely, the network is in a sense fully operational. As things stand it has only one minor drawback, which is that it is not possible to share any resources such as files and printers. The resource sharing facilities built into any modern version of Windows are sufficient for most users, so there should be no need to buy any networking software. However, it is essential to get Windows set up correctly in order to get the network to do anything useful.

When Windows is configured and set up correctly, the shared resources can be used on any PC in the system in the same way as if they were actually part of that PC and its peripherals. Shared files and folders on

Installation and security 5

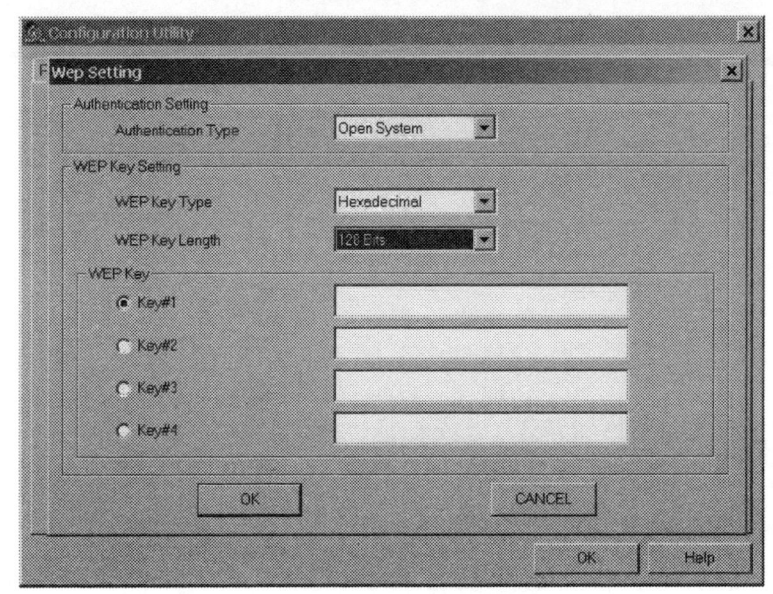

Fig.5.20 This window is used to enter the WEP key

other computers, for example, can be accessed using Windows Explorer, or via the standard file browsers built into applications software. They appear in the My Network Places folder, but not all the files and folders on other PCs in the network will appear here. Resources are only shared if they are specifically designated as shared resources.

Although most programs will use shared files and folders just as if they were on a local drive, there are actually a few applications programs that will not use them, or will do so in a restricted fashion. Sometimes restrictions on the use of shared files are due to security issues. In other cases it is simply that the speed of the network is inadequate. For example, burning a CD-ROM using data obtained via a wi-fi link might provide an inadequate flow of data, even at fairly low burn speeds. In order to burn a CD-ROM using data obtained over the network it would probably be necessary to copy the data to a local drive first. It would then be transferred to a CD-ROM from the local drive, after which the file on the local drive could be deleted.

5 Installation and security

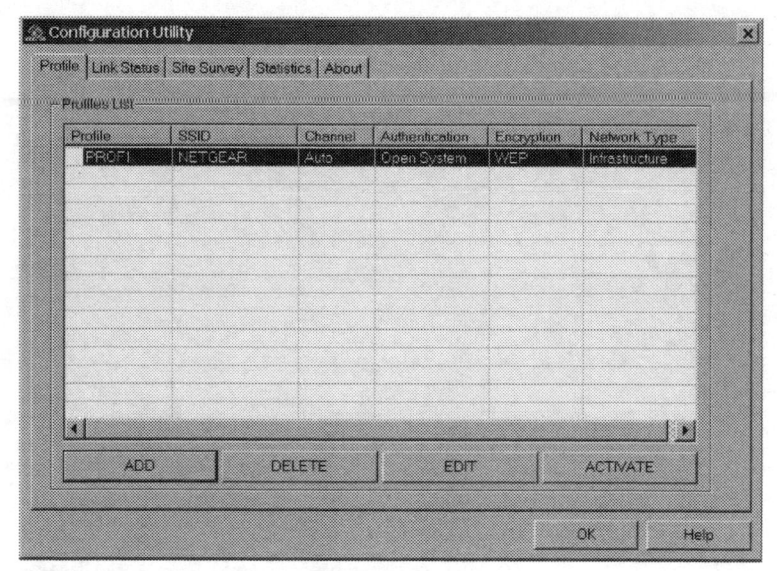

Fig.5.21 A facility to use profiles is included

Disc sharing

Although it would in many ways be easier if all the hard discs in the system were shared in their entirety, this is definitely not considered to be a good idea. It is actually much easier to use the network if files that will be shared are kept in a few special folders. This makes it easy and quick to find the files that you require. With access to all the folders on every hard disc in the network it could take a long time to locate the particular files you require. The sheer number of files and folders would make finding the right files a bit like "looking for a needle in a haystack". Another important point is that users of the system will probably not wish to make all their files available to the network. Most of us would prefer to keep most files private and only share certain material.

It is particularly important not to share all the files and folders if the network has an Internet connection, which in practice means practically every network. The problem with sharing everything in the system, or even large parts of the system, is that it makes life very easy for anyone who manages to hack into the network. With large scale or even total access to the system, they will probably be able to steal any files that take their fancy, and damage any files at will. For security reasons it is best to

Installation and security 5

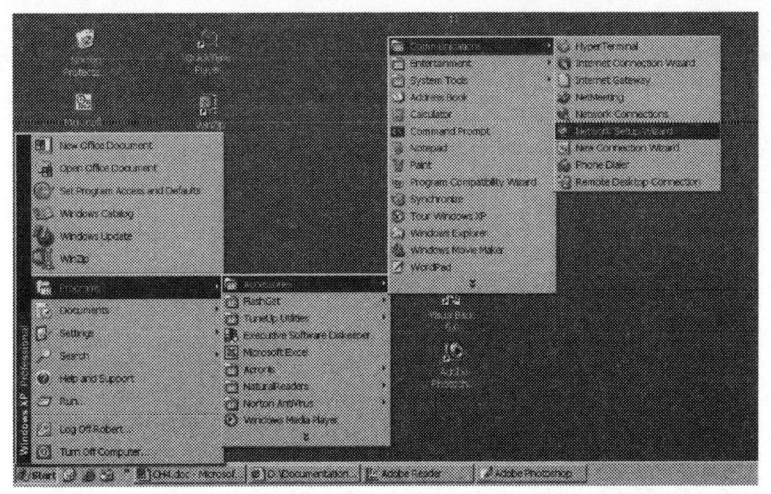

Fig.5.22 The Network Setup Wizard is deep in the menu structure

share the minimum amount of files and folders that permits the network to be used efficiently.

Naming

Each computer in the network has to be given a computer name, and each group of computers has a workgroup name. The computers will appear in file browsers under their computer names, and will look much the same as folders. On opening the "folder" for a computer on the network you will only see files and folders that have been designated as shared resources. All other files and folders on the computer are invisible to the network, and they can not be accessed by other computers in the network. Workgroup names are only of significance when networks are networked, but each workgroup must always be named.

When selecting names it is essential to choose a different name for each PC. Apart from the fact that having two computers operating under the same name would be confusing for users of the system, it more or less guarantees that the network will not operate reliably. Having two PCs operating under the same name would be equally confusing for Windows! The names can have up to 15 characters, which should be letters and numbers. Spaces are not permitted, but the underline character can be

5 Installation and security

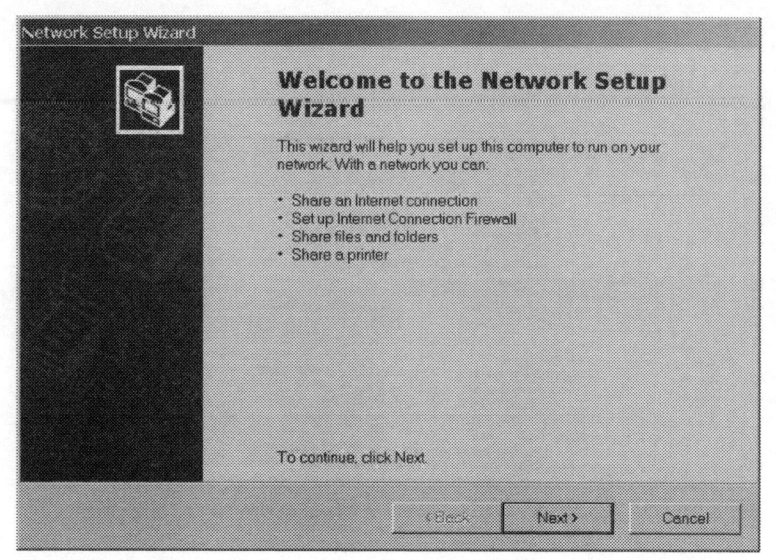

Fig.5.23 The Network Setup Wizard starts with the usual Welcome page

used. Therefore, naming a PC "My Old PC" would not be allowed, but it could be called "My_Old_PC". Although up to 15 characters can be used, it is more practical to settle for a maximum of eight or so. Use names that will enable every user of the network to easily associate each name with the PC it represents.

Network Setup Wizard

The easy way to set up networking on PCs running Windows XP and ME is to run the Network Setup Wizard. This is buried quite deep in the menu structure, but it can be accessed by going to the Start menu and then selecting Programs, Accessories, Communications, and Network Setup Wizard (Figure 5.22). The Windows XP and ME versions are slightly different in points of detail, but they are very similar. The Windows XP version is used as the basis off this example.

The initial page (Figure 5.23) simply gives a brief explanation of what the Network Setup Wizard will do. The next page (Figure 5.24) provides an opportunity to obtain background information from the Help system. It also explains that everything in the network must be fully installed,

Installation and security 5

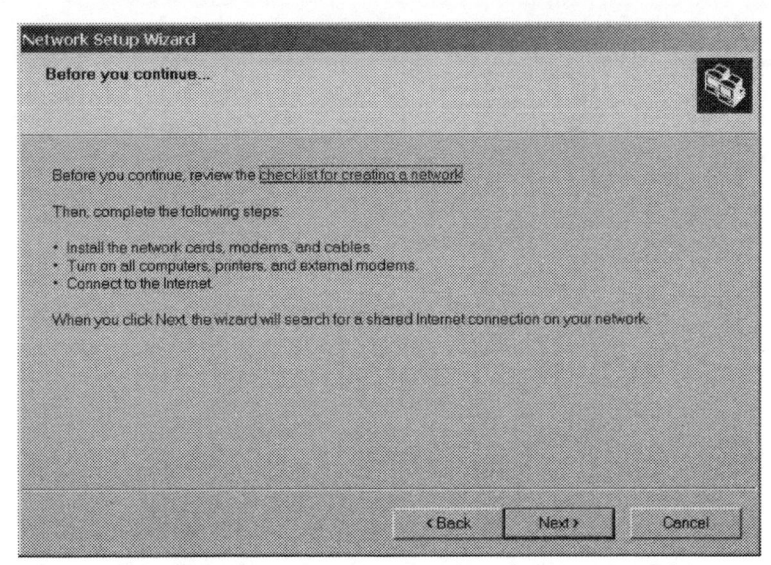

Fig.5.24 This page gives easy access to the relevant parts of the Help system

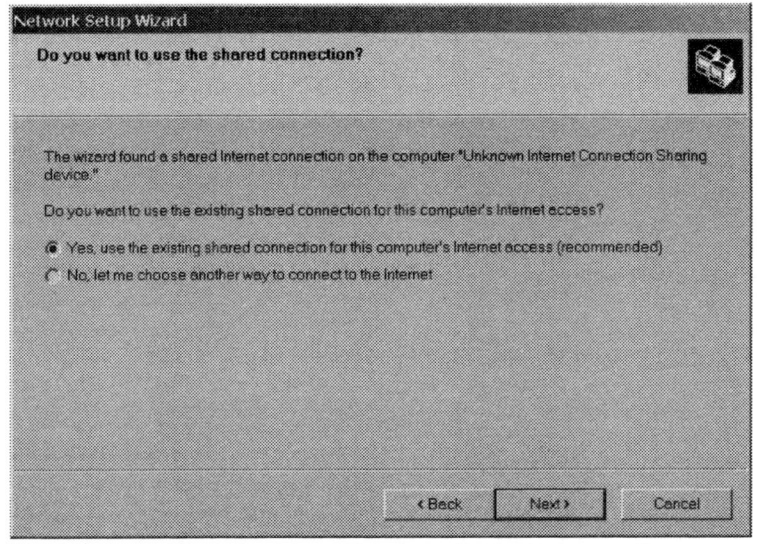

Fig.5.25 The wizard has detected a shared Internet connection

5 Installation and security

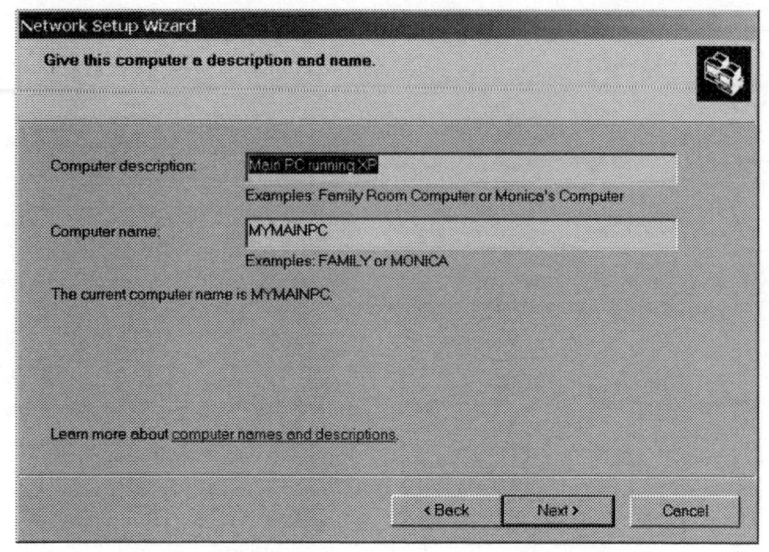

Fig.5.26 Use this page to name the computer and provide a brief description

connected together, switched on, and ready to use. The wizard will not help with such things as setting up an Internet connection or installing device drivers for Ethernet or wi-fi cards. It just sets up the network once installation has been completed.

On the next page (Figure 5.25) the setup process starts, and the wizard has detected a shared Internet connection. This is actually provided by a combined access point, router, and ADSL modem. A different Internet connection can be selected or the existing one can be used. In this case there is no alternative available, and the existing Internet connection has to be used. On the following page (Figure 5.26) the computer is given the name that will be used for it on the network, and a brief description can also be added here.

The network (workgroup) name is provided at the next page (Figure 5.27), or you can simply settle for the default name (MSHOME). This completes the setting up process, and a page that shows the selected settings is displayed (Figure 5.28) when the Next button is operated. Windows then does some reconfiguring of itself before displaying the page shown in Figure 5.29. This gives various options for setting up

Installation and security 5

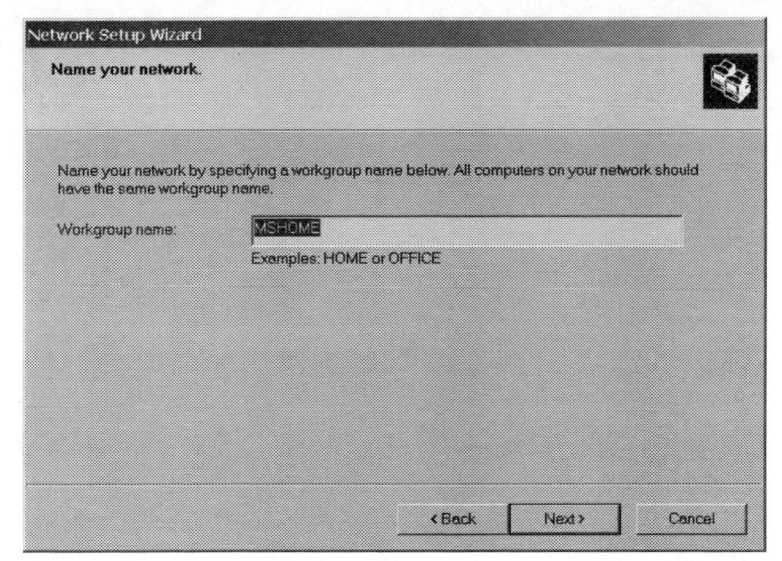

Fig.5.27 Here the name for the workgroup is entered in the textbox

networking on the other PCs in the system. You can simply exit the wizard if the other PCs in the network are running Windows ME and/or XP, and then run the Network Setup Wizard in the usual way on those PCs. Finally, the page shown in Figure 5.30 confirms that the process has been completed.

Sharing folders

A network is only worthwhile if some resources are shared, but it is not essential to have shared resources on every computer in the network. In order to share the resources of a computer it is necessary to have the appropriate type of sharing enabled. With Windows ME it is possible to disable sharing, and in the interests of good security it is advisable not to enable sharing unless it will be used on the PC in question. Note that it is not necessary to have sharing enabled in order to use a PC to access resources on other PCs. Any PC in the system can be used to access shared resources on other PCs. You only have to enable sharing on a PC that will make resources available to the network.

5 Installation and security

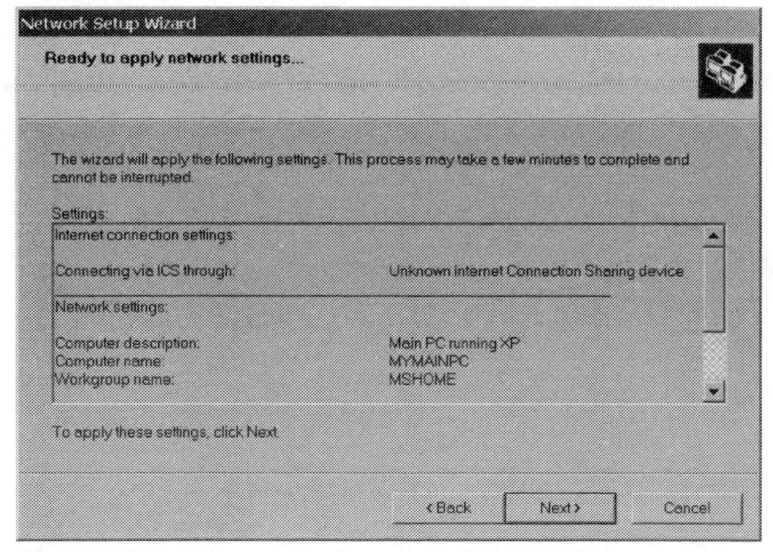

Fig.5.28 This window enables the selected settings to be reviewed

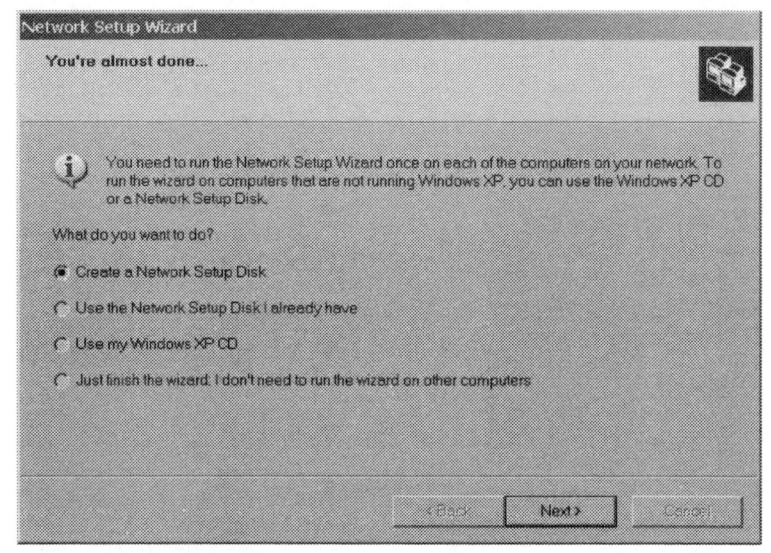

Fig.5.29 There are various options for setting up the network on the other PCs in the system

Installation and security 5

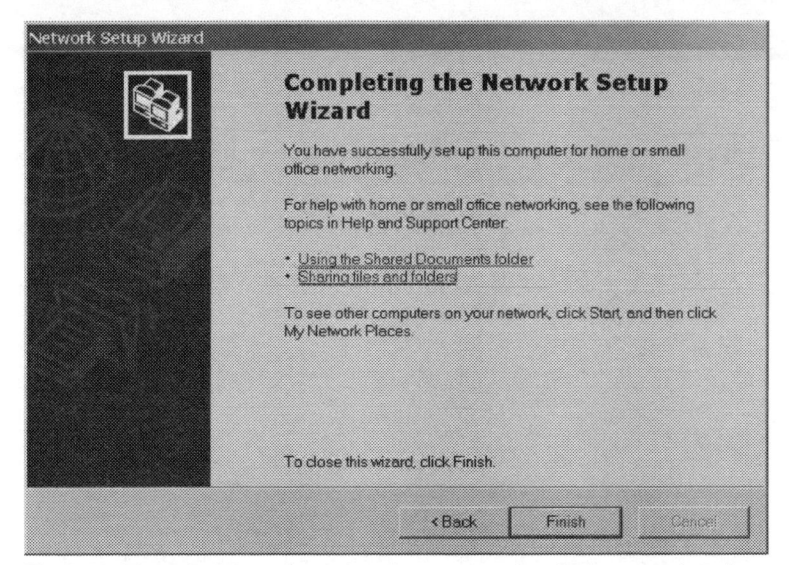

Fig.5.30 The wizard confirms that the process has been completed

To enable or disable sharing in Windows ME it is first necessary to go to the Windows Control Panel and double-click the Network icon. Left-click the Configuration tab and then operate the File and Print Sharing button. This launches a small window (Figure 5.31) where two checkboxes provide individual control over file and printer sharing. Operate the OK button when the required changes have been made, and then the OK button on the Network window.

Windows XP Home has a new system of file sharing called "simple file sharing", and this is the default setting for Windows XP Professional. Simple file sharing can be turned off in Windows XP Professional by double-clicking the My Computer icon on the desktop, and the selecting Folder Options from the Tools menu. Left-click the View tab and then scroll down the list in the main part of the window until you find the entry that reads "Use simple file sharing (Recommended)" (Figure 5.32). Remove the tick from its checkbox and then operate the Apply and OK buttons. For most purposes the default setting will suffice, and it is assumed here that the simple file sharing method is used.

5 Installation and security

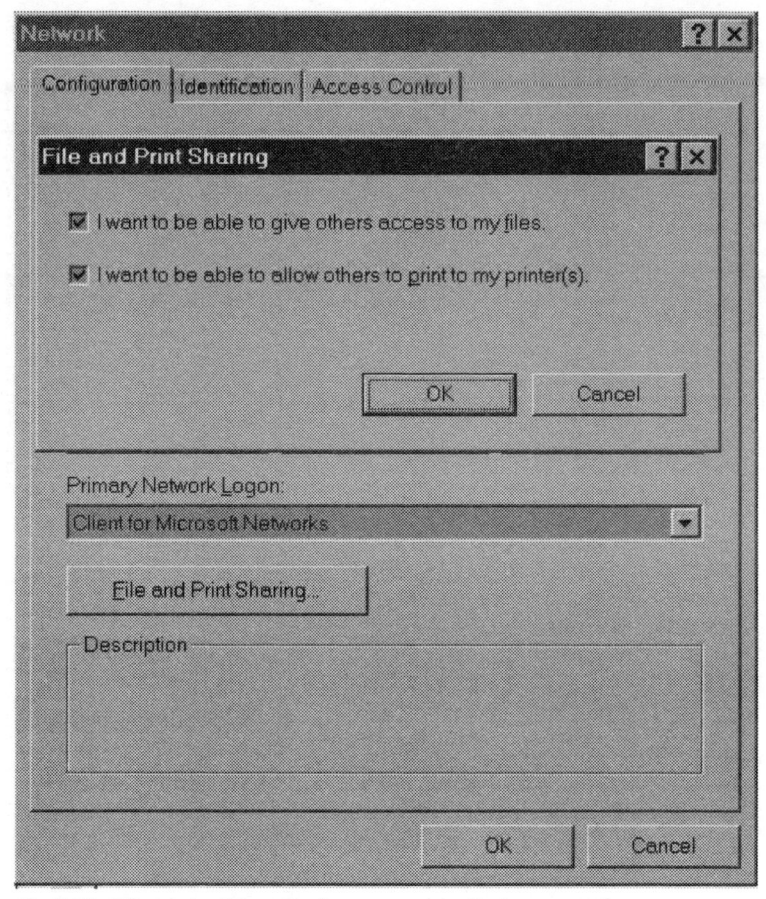

Fig.5.31 File and printer sharing are controlled separately

In order to share a folder, first locate it using Windows Explorer, and then right-click on its entry. From the pop-up menu select Properties, and then operate the Sharing tab in the properties window (Figure 3.33). Place a tick in the "Share this folder on the network" checkbox in order to make the folder available to the network. By default, the contents of the folder can be read via the network, but they can not be altered. Full access to the folder can be provided by ticking the "Allow network users to change my files" checkbox. The folder can be shared under its normal

Installation and security 5

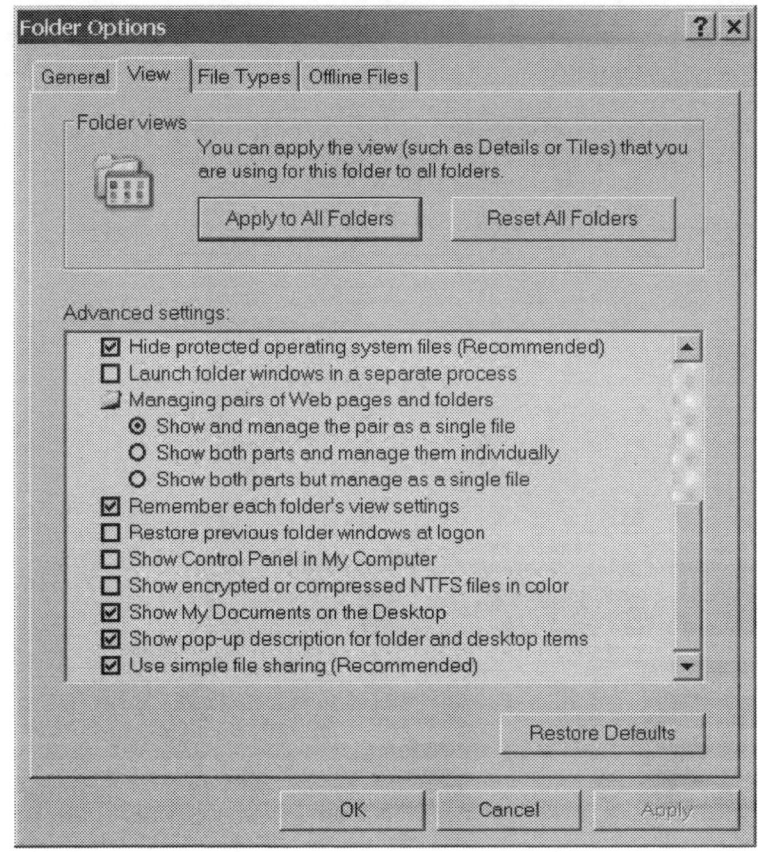

Fig.5.32 The "Use simple file sharing" option is suitable for most users

name, or a different name can be typed into the Shared name textbox. Operate the Apply and OK buttons to exit the window and make the changes take effect.

Essentially the same method is used to share a complete disc. However, on entering the Sharing section of the disc's Properties window you obtain a warning message (Figure 5.34). If you wish to continue anyway, left-click the link text and the properties window will then change to the normal sharing type. It can then be shared in the same way as a folder (Figure 5.35), but in most circumstances this method of sharing is definitely not a good idea.

5 Installation and security

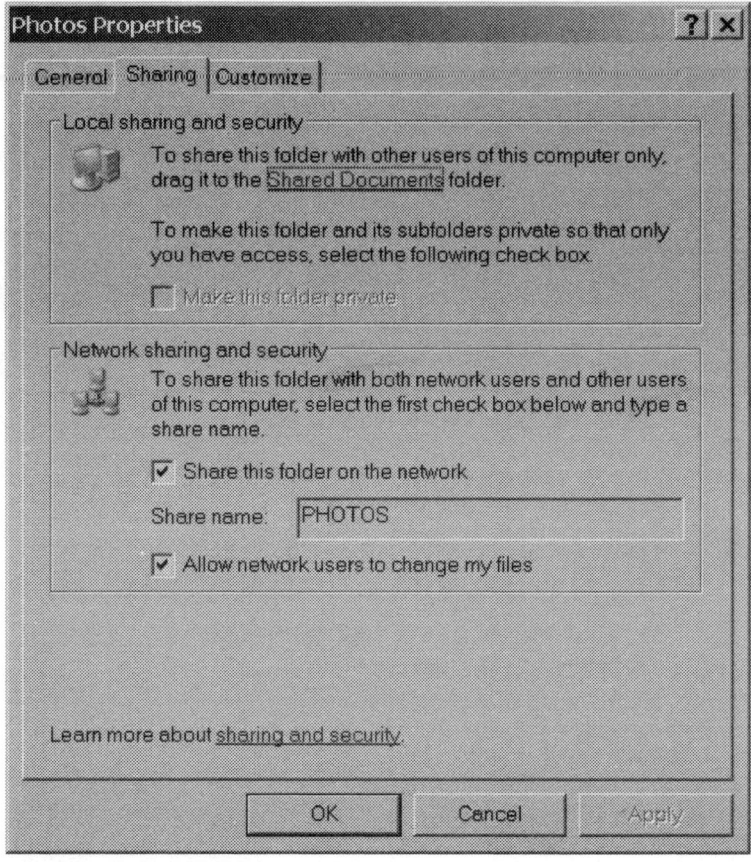

Fig.5.33 Use this window to enable sharing of a folder

Network Places

Having shared a disc or folder, the shared resource can then be added to the Network Places of any PC that will need to access it. Start by double-clicking the My Network Places icon on the desktop. The PC used for this example already has a couple of network places added (Figure 5.36), but when starting "from scratch" the right-hand section of the My Network Places window will be blank. Left-click "Add a network place" in the upper left-hand section of the window, which will launch a

Installation and security 5

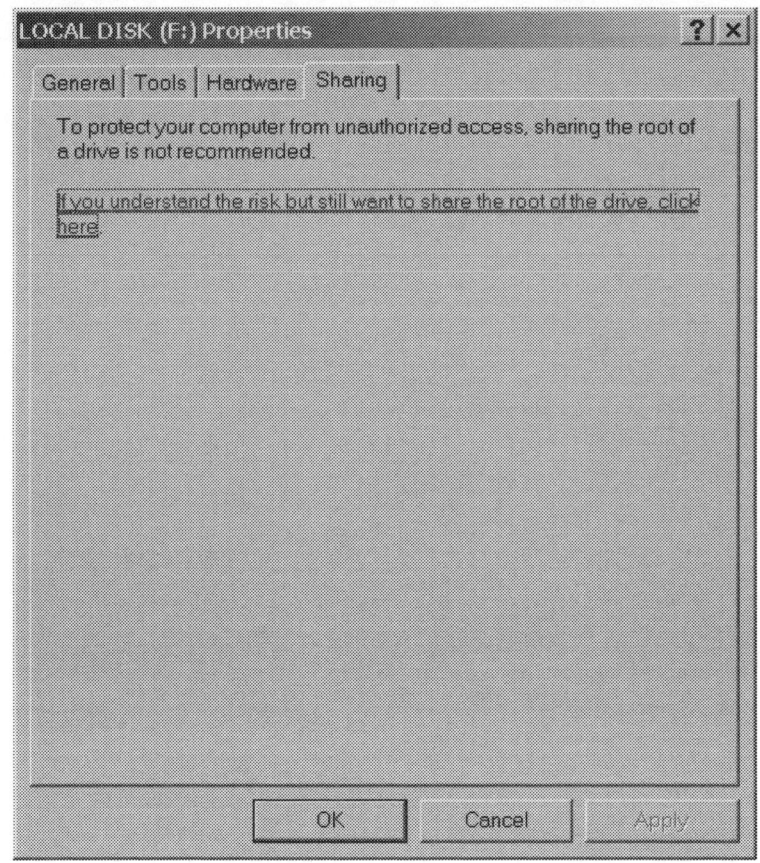

Fig.5.34 This warning message appears if you try to share a disc

new window (Figure 5.37). This is just a Welcome screen, so operate the Next button to move on to the window of Figure 5.38.

Windows will search for new network places, but it will not find very much. Consequently, you have to choose the option that lets you specify a network location. This moves things on to the window of Figure 5.39, where it is advisable to operate the Browse button and then use the file browser to search for the new network place. The browser provides access to all available parts of the network, and the required PHOTOS folder on Mymainpc was easily located (Figure 5.40). Having selected

5 Installation and security

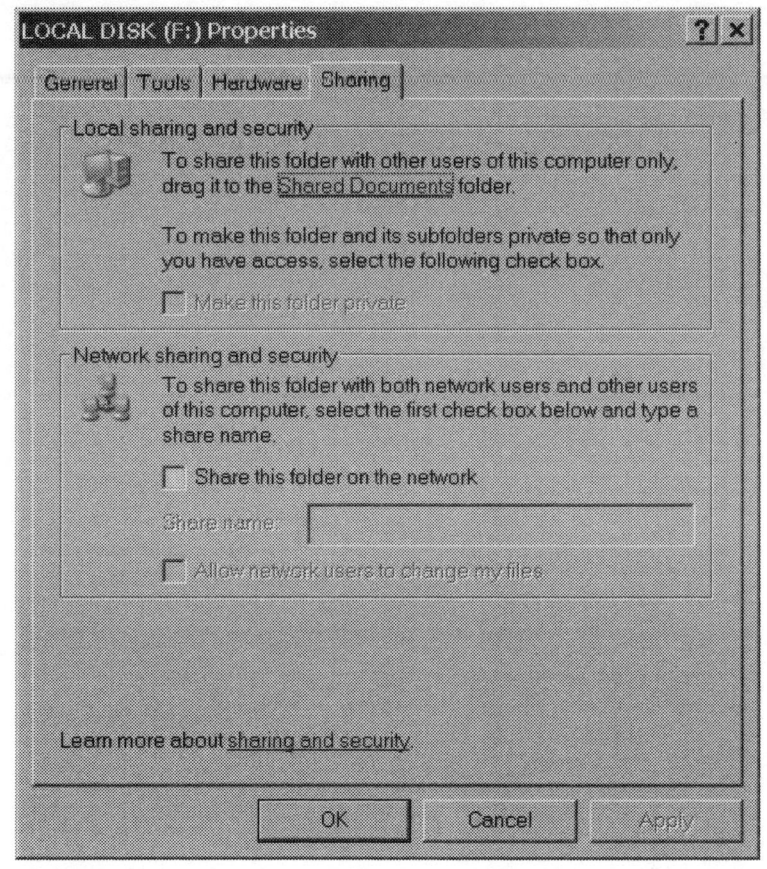

Fig.5.35 A disc can be shared, if you are prepared to accept the risks

the correct folder, operate the OK button and the network address will be added to the textbox in the main window (Figure 5.41).

A name for the new network place can be added in the textbox at the next window (Figure 5.42), or you can settle for the suggested default name. The next window (Figure 5.43) simply informs you that the task has been completed. Tick the checkbox if you wish to open the newly added folder in Windows Explorer when the Finish button is operated.

Installation and security 5

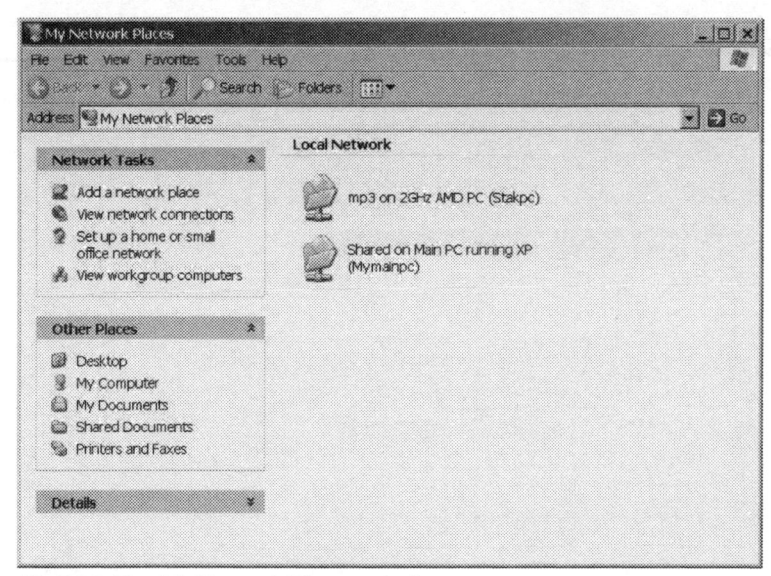

Fig.5.36 The My Network Places window

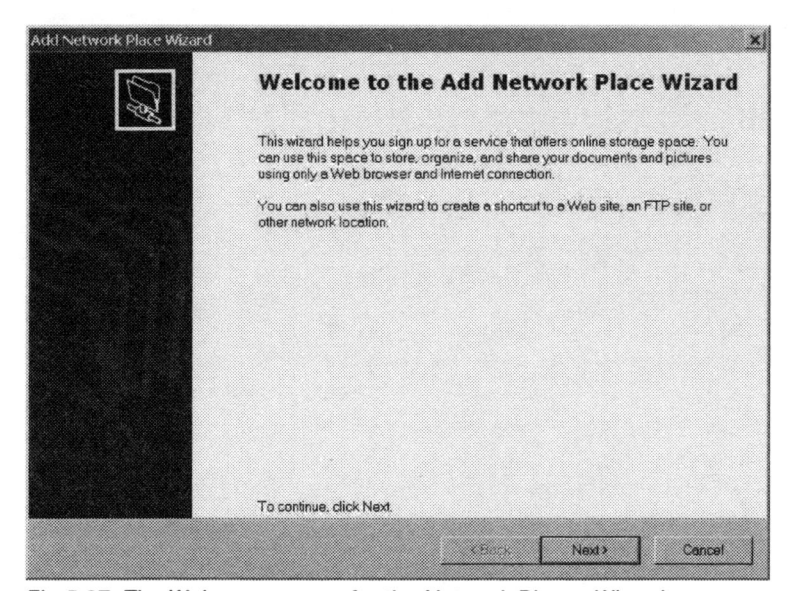

Fig.5.37 The Welcome screen for the Network Places Wizard

5 Installation and security

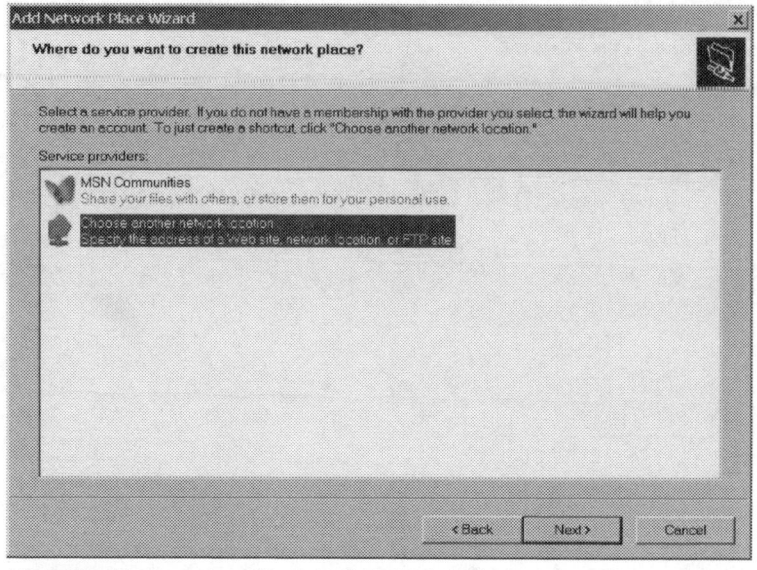

Fig.5.38 Windows is unlikely to find the location you require

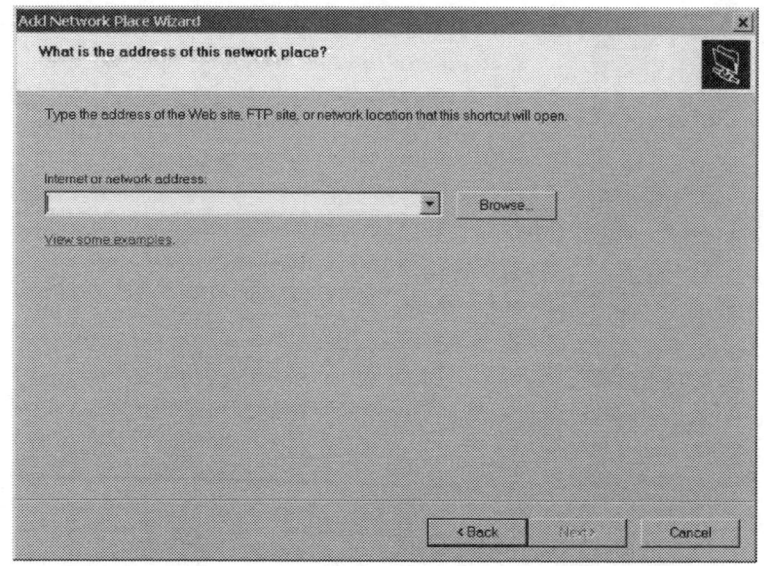

Fig.5.39 Use the Browse button to search for the required folder

Installation and security 5

The new network place can be easily accessed using Windows Explorer or the standard Windows file browser built into most applications programs. As one would expect, it will be found in the My Network Places folder, together with any other network places that are installed. In Figure 5.44 the PHOTOS folder has been located in the file browser of Photoshop

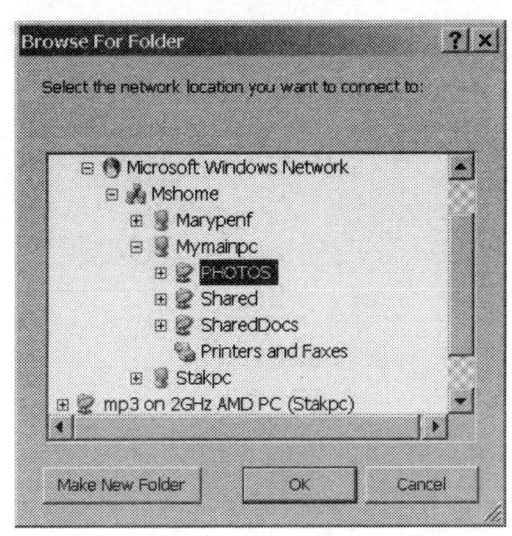

Fig.5.40 The required folder has been found

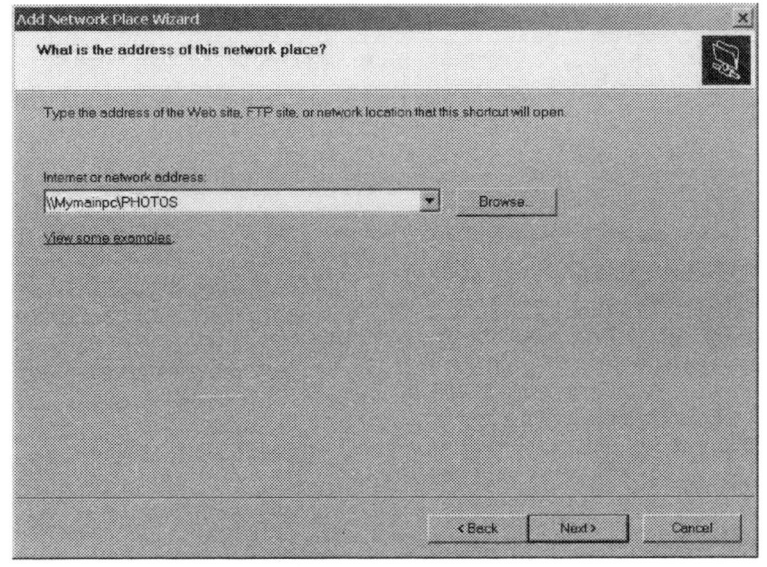

Fig.5.41 The correct folder has been selected

5 Installation and security

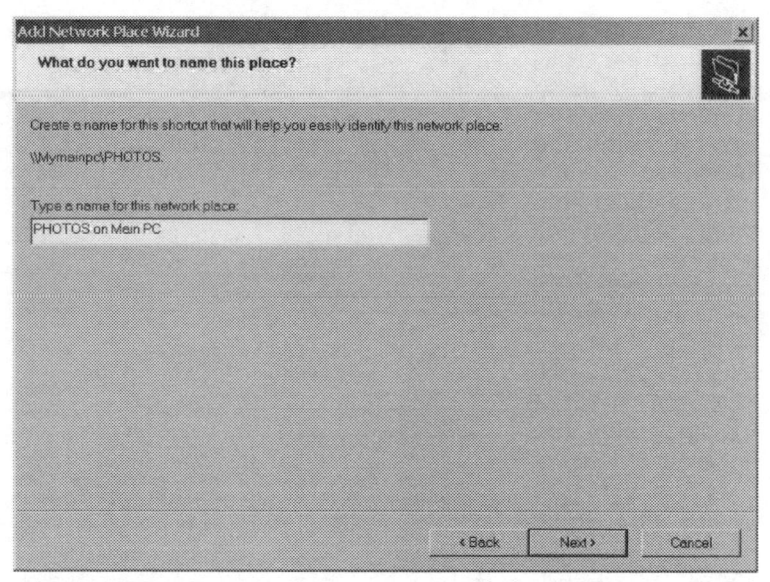

Fig.5.42 A name for the network place can be provided here

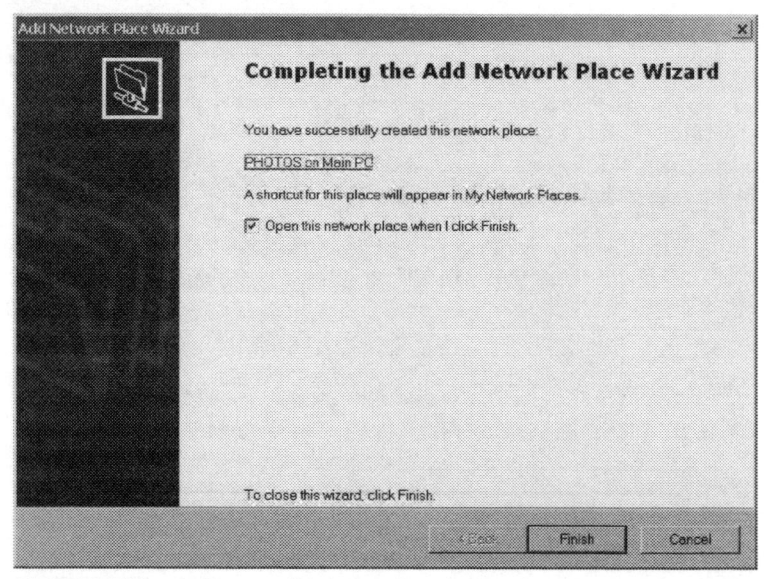

Fig.5.43 This window confirms that the process has been completed

Installation and security 5

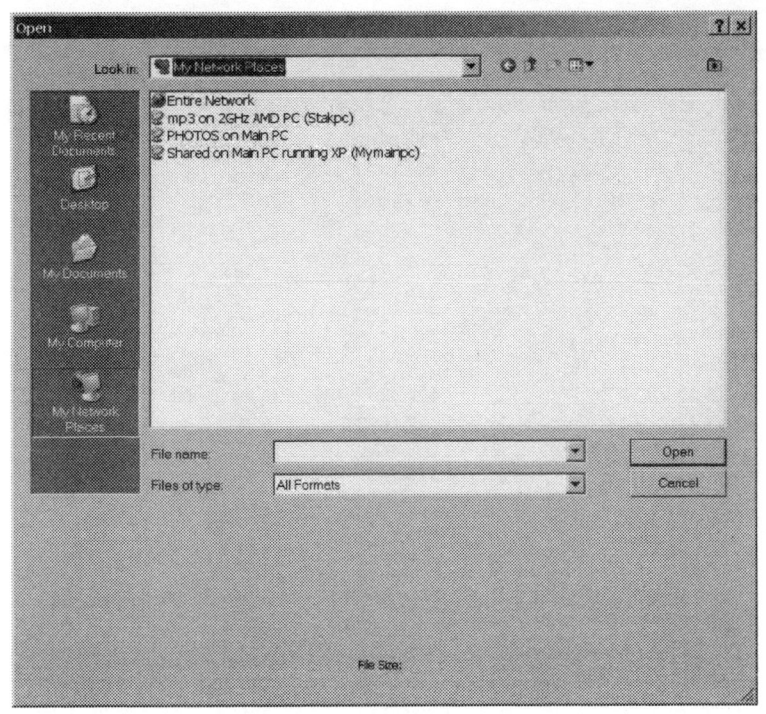

Fig.5.44 The shared folder is available in file browsers

CS. It can be opened in the usual way, and then a file can be loaded (Figure 5.45).

Note that it will only be possible to read files, unless you opted to permit changes to files when setting the sharing options for the folder. If changes are permitted, it is then possible to change files in an applications program and save the changes in the usual way. Where permission to alter files has not been given, it is still possible to load and edit them. The edited files must be saved to another folder though, so that the original files are left untouched.

Printer sharing

It is possible to get by without printer sharing, but implementing this feature is often the easiest way of handling things. Suppose you have a

5 Installation and security

Fig.5.45 A file from the shared folder has been loaded into Photoshop

notebook PC that can connect to your home network via a wi-fi link. In order to print out a file from a printer on the network you could upload the file to one of the networked PCs, open the file on that PC, and then print it out. This is actually a reasonably easy way of handling things provided there is a PC on the network that has the appropriate application program installed. However, it would probably be quicker and easier if the file could be printed from the notebook. Printer sharing facilitates direct printing from the notebook PC, or any other PC in the network.

The first task is to determine whether the printer you wish to share has sharing enabled. Go to the PC to which the printer is directly connected, launch the Windows Control Panel, and then double-click the Printers and Faxes icon. This will produce a window something like Figure 5.46, but its exact appearance will depend on the particular printers and faxes that are installed on the computer. Any printers that have sharing enabled will have a picture of a hand included in their icons.

In this example an HP Photosmart 7200 series printer will be shared, and as things stand, it is not set for shared operation. To enable sharing, right-click the printer's icon and select Sharing from the pop-up menu.

Installation and security 5

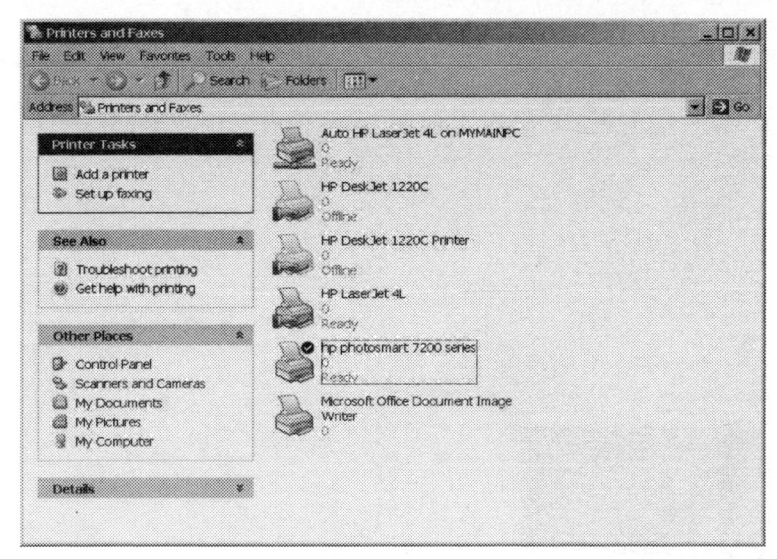

Fig.5.46 The Printers and Faxes window

In the new window that appears (Figure 5.47), operate the "Share this printer" radio button, and add a name for the printer in the textbox.

Operating system

At this stage you can operate the Apply and OK buttons if all the PCs in the network use the same operating system. Matters are complicated slightly if you will need to use the printer with a PC that has a different operating system to the one that is normally used with the printer. A different operating system will almost certainly require a different set of device drivers. Where appropriate, these drivers must be installed before proceeding.

Operating the Additional Drivers button produces a small window, similar to the one shown in Figure 5.48. This lists all the available device drivers for the printer, and there is a tick in the checkbox for those that are already installed. Tick the boxes for any more that need to be installed, and then operate the OK button. The window of Figure 5.49 then appears, and you have to direct the installation program to the source for the drivers. This will usually be the CD-ROM provided with the printer, or files downloaded from the Internet. Anyway, the usual installation process is

5 Installation and security

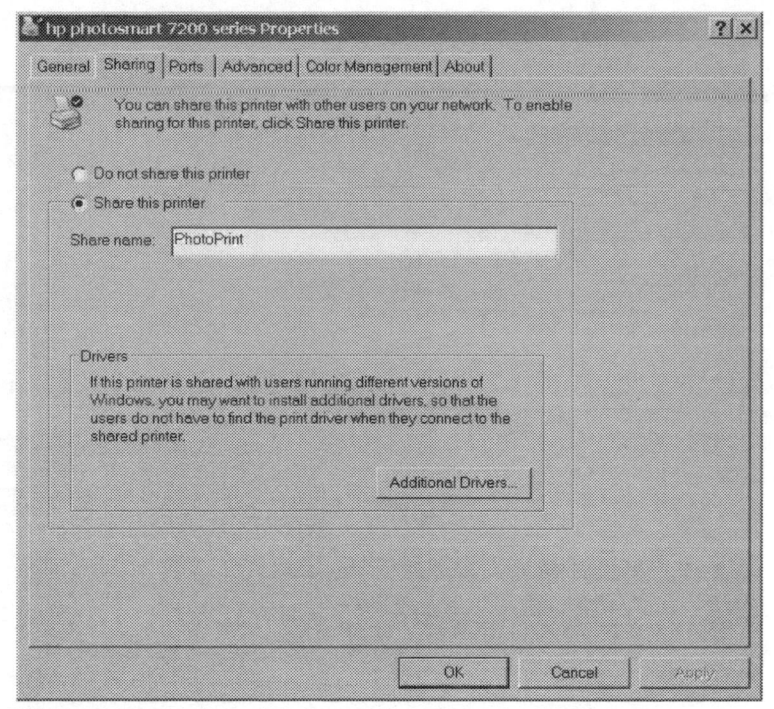

Fig.5.47 Sharing is enabled using the appropriate radio button and a name for the printer is then added in the textbox

then followed, and you should eventually arrive back at the Printers and Faxes window, which will show that the printer is set up for sharing (Figure 5.50).

Printer installation

Before a shared printer can be used on another PC, it must be installed on that PC. The installation process for a networked printer is different to that for a local printer (one driven direct from the PC). Start the process by going to the Printers and Faxes window in the PC that is accessing the printer via the network. This has icons for the currently installed printers and faxes, with no icon at this stage for the Photosmart printer (Figure 5.51).

Installation and security 5

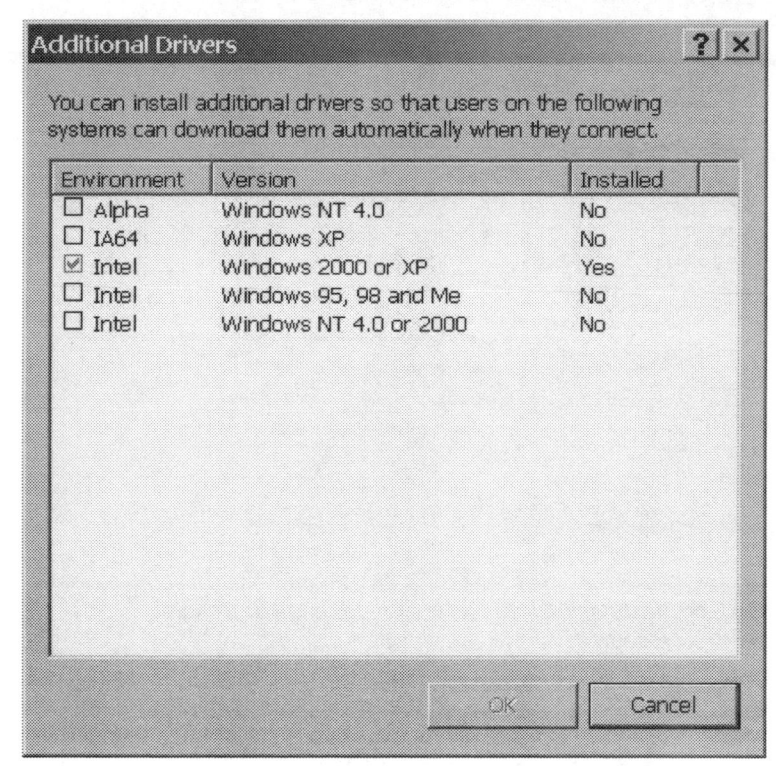

Fig.5.48 A list of the supported operating systems is displayed

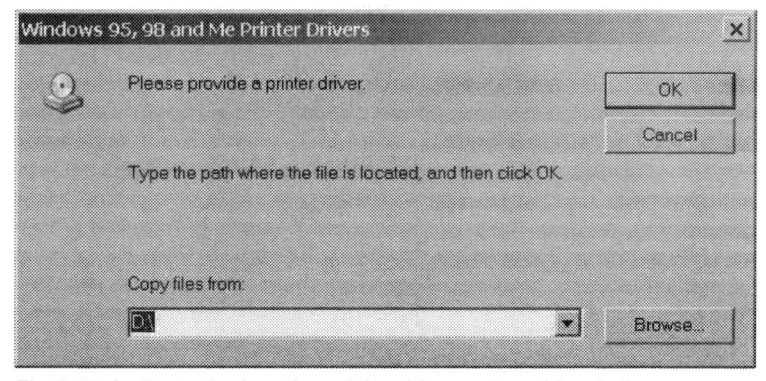

Fig.5.49 Indicate the location of the drivers when this window appears

5 Installation and security

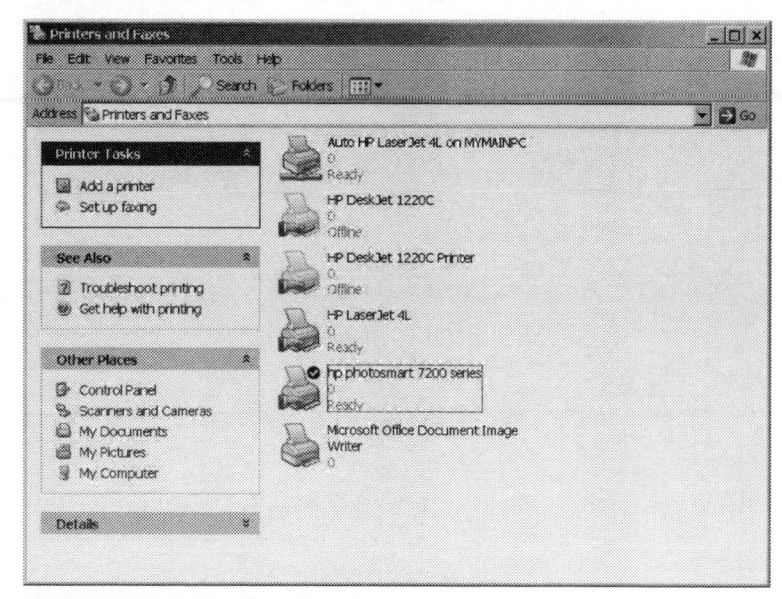

Fig.5.50 Its icon confirms that the printer is set as a shared resource

Start the installation process by operating the Add Printer link near the top left-hand corner of the window. This launches the Add Printer Wizard, and the first page is, as usual, the Welcome screen (Figure 5.52). At the next page (Figure 5.53) there is the option of installing a local or network printer, and in this case it is clearly the radio button for a network printer that is used.

It is then necessary to indicate the printer you wish to install, and it is advisable to use the browse option here (Figure 5.54). Having located the correct printer using the browser (Figure 5.55), operate the Next button. A standard virus warning screen will then appear (Figure 5.56), but there will presumably be no risk in downloading a driver from one of your own PCs. Finally, left-click the Yes button to go ahead and install the device drivers for the printer. There is no need to have the drivers disc for the printer, because the drivers will be obtained from the network PC that already has them installed. Note that an error message will be produced if this PC does not have the device drivers for the correct operating system.

Installation and security 5

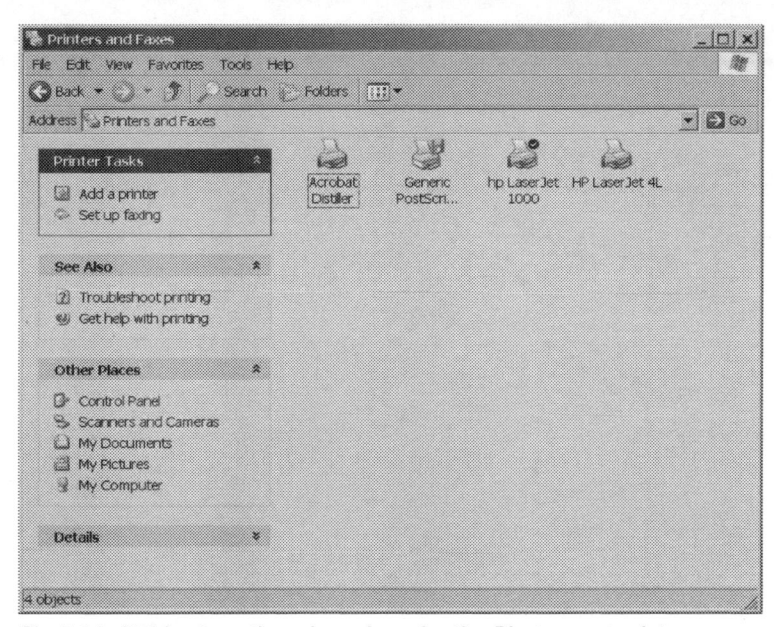

Fig.5.51 At this stage there is no icon for the Photosmart printer

Fig.5.52 The Welcome screen of the Add Printer Wizard

5 Installation and security

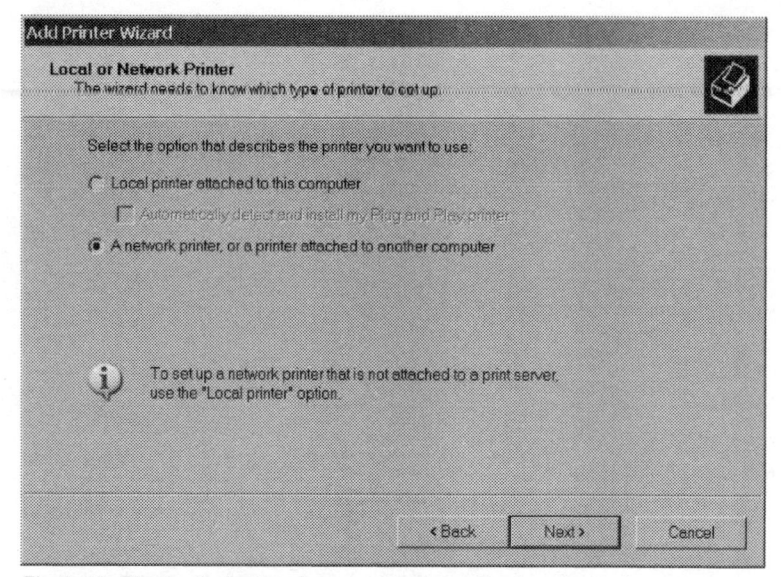

Fig.5.53 The radio button for a network printer is selected

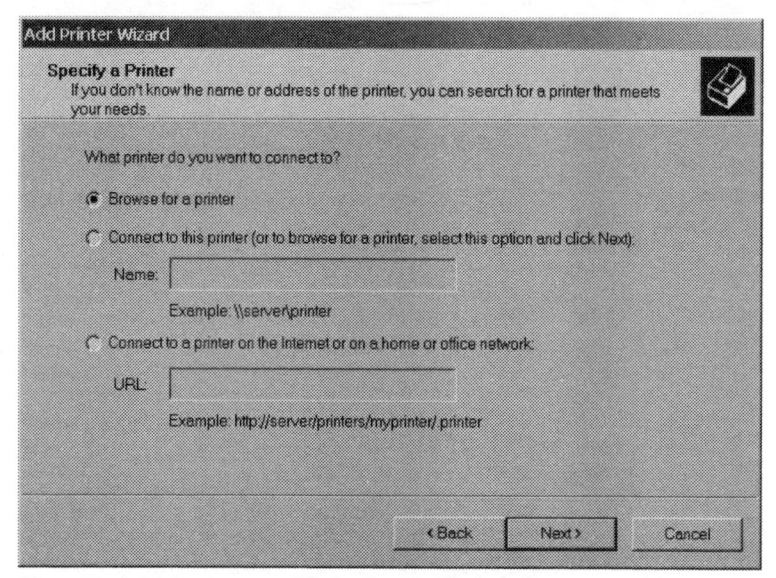

Fig.5.54 Specify a printer or use the browse option

Installation and security 5

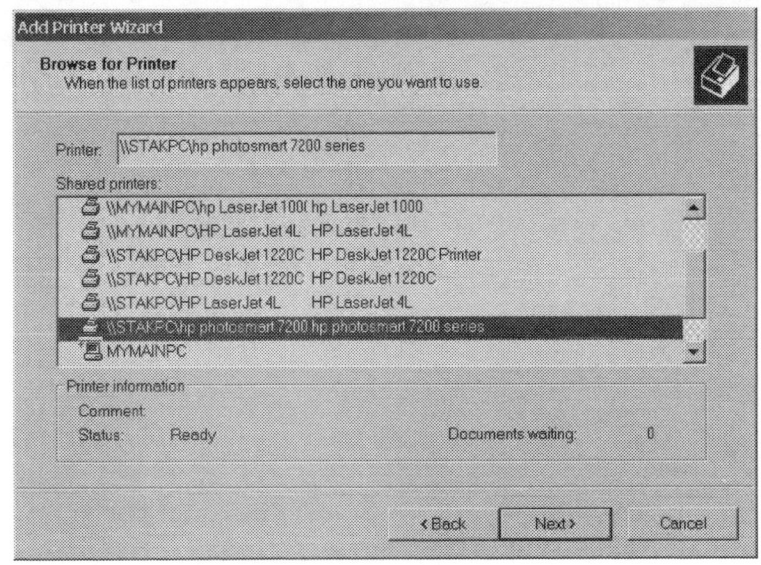

Fig.5.55 The correct printer has been found by using the browser

Default printer

To complete the installation you must decide whether the newly installed printer should be set as the default type (Figure 5.57). In other words, should it be set as the printer that will be used unless Windows is instructed otherwise? Finally, the page of Figure 5.58 informs you that the installation has been completed successfully. It is advisable to go back to the Printers and Faxes window to ensure that an icon for the

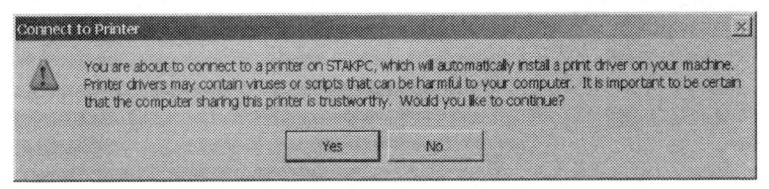

Fig.5.56 It should be safe to ignore the standard virus warning

5 Installation and security

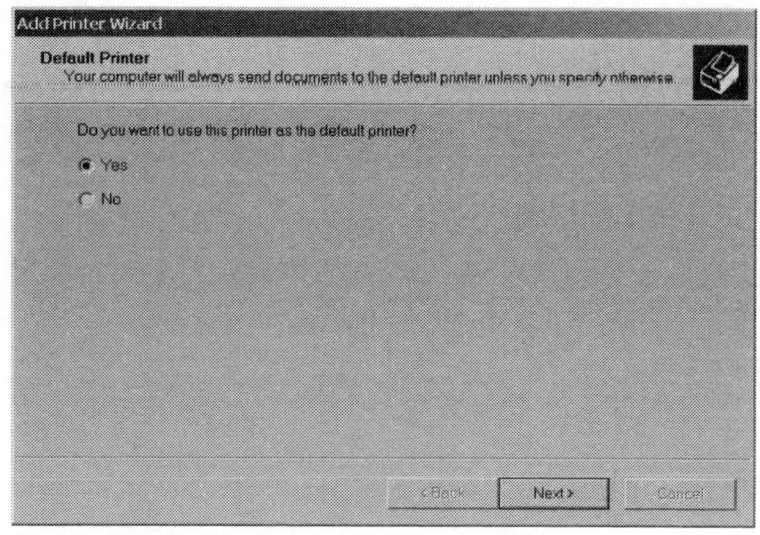

Fig.5.57 The printer can be the default unit if desired

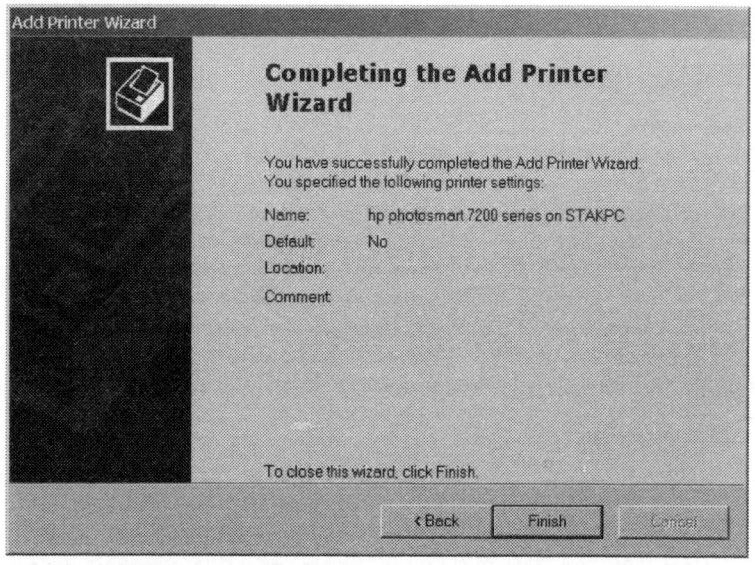

Fig.5.58 This screen confirms that the networked printer has been successfully installed

Installation and security 5

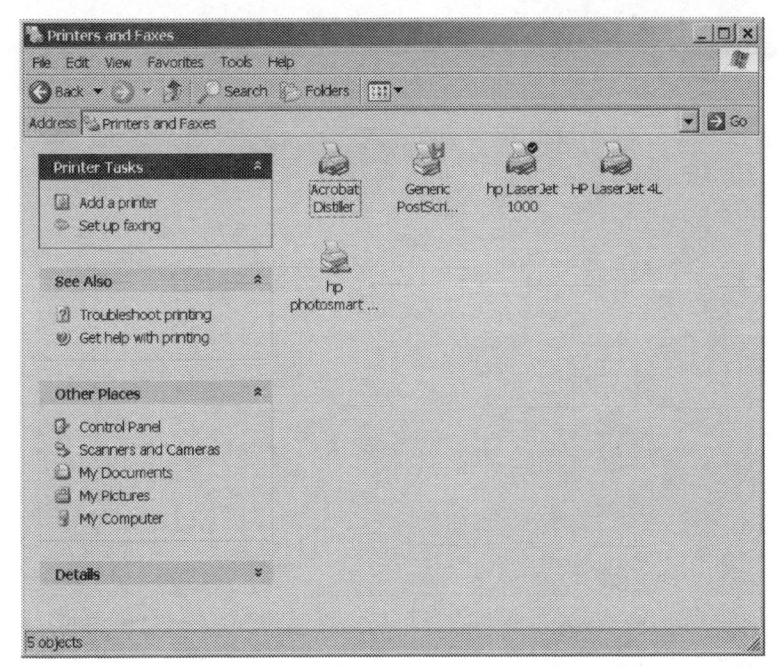

Fig.5.59 There is now an icon for the newly installed printer

newly installed printer is present and correct. In this case everything has gone to plan and the icon is present (Figure 5.59).

The printer can then be used in much the same way as if it was a local printer. Of course, it can only be used when the PC it is connected to is actually switched on. Less obviously, it is likely that "Out of paper", "Low ink", and similar status or error messages will appear on the screen of the PC that drives the printer. This is not very convenient if you are using a printer that is on a different room on another floor of the building, but you just have to learn to live with this limitation.

The newly networked printer should be listed when you try to print from an applications program (Figure 5.60). Having selected the printer it should then be possible to launch its properties window (Figure 5.61) so that the paper type, print quality, etc., can be selected. The amount of data sent to a printer can be massive, so results are likely to be obtained more quickly using an 802.11g or wired network connection. Printing can be noticeably slower when using a poor quality 802.11b link.

5 Installation and security

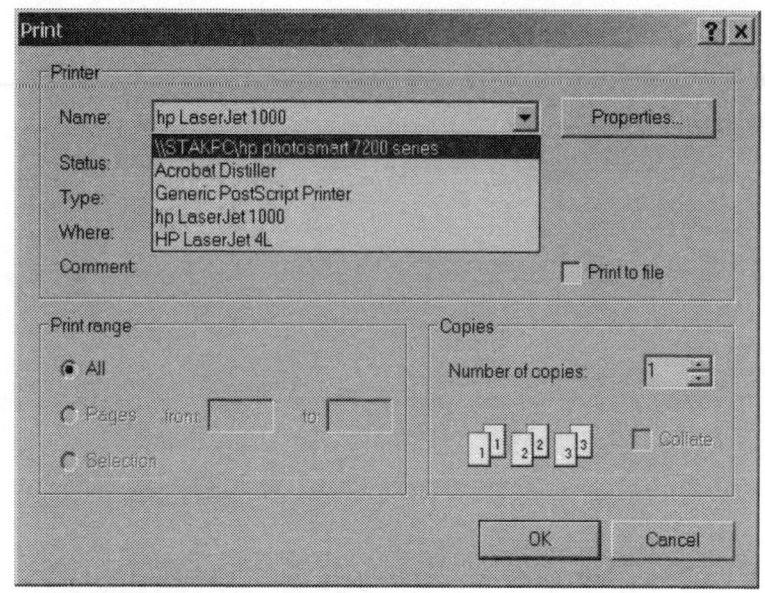

Fig.5.60 The newly installed printer should be available when using any Windows application that has a Print facility

Firmware upgrades

With the system "up and running" it is advisable to check the relevant manufacturer's web sites from time to time in case there are any driver or firmware updates. These are often needed in order to sort out minor problems that become apparent when the products are used in earnest by thousands of users. In some cases there are definite faults in the original software or firmware. Often the problems are more obscure, and typically they only occur when certain combinations of hardware or hardware and software are used.

Where a network is running well it is not necessarily a good idea to install firmware updates, but it is probably as well to install any improved drivers that are available. There is little risk involved in using updated drivers, and the Roll Back Driver feature of Windows XP makes it easy to return to the previous drivers if the new ones should prove to be problematic. The Roll Back Driver facility is accessed by going to the relevant entry in Device Manager, right-clicking it, selecting Properties from the pop-up window, and then operating the Driver tab in the Properties window. Then

Installation and security 5

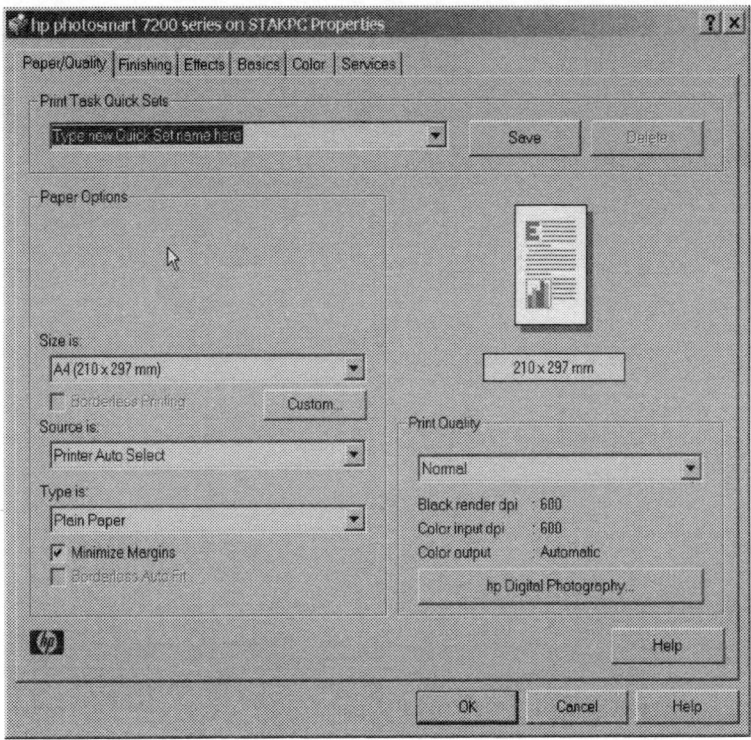

Fig.5.61 The Properties window can be accessed in the usual way

operate the Roll Back Driver button near the bottom of the window (Figure 5.62). In theory, the Update Driver button in the same window is used when installing a newer driver. In practice it is more usual for the updated driver to be installed via its own installation program. Always follow the installation instructions provided by the manufacturer.

It is advisable not to upgrade the firmware unless some real benefit will be gained in doing so. There is a slight risk involved when upgrading firmware. If the process should go wrong it is possible that the upgraded unit would be left unusable. It might then be necessary to return it to the maker to be repaired. The risk is actually very small. If you should happen to download the wrong data file, it is likely that the upgrade routine would spot the error and refuse to go ahead with the upgrade.

5 Installation and security

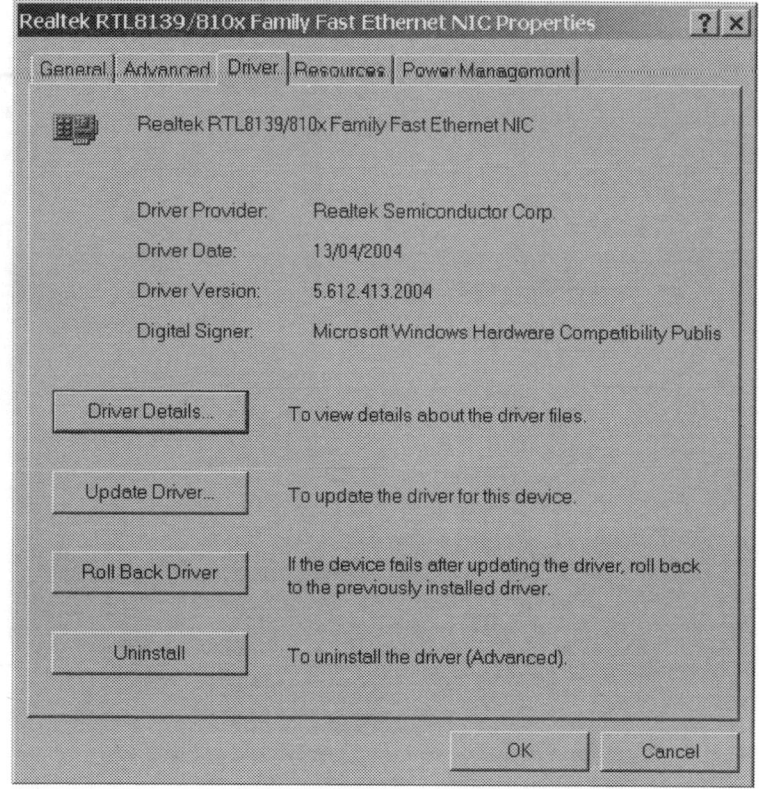

Fig.5.62 A Roll Back Driver option is available in Windows XP

The main danger is that something will interrupt the process, resulting in the unit having a combination of old and new firmware. This is almost certain to leave it in an unusable state. You would have to be very unlucky indeed for a power cut to occur during the few seconds it takes to complete an upgrade. There is probably a greater risk of interrupting the upgrade by accidentally knocking a connector out of place or switching something off. During the upgrade, keep still and touch none of the equipment or wiring.

Note that with some units it is not possible to go back to an earlier version of the firmware. I am not sure why this should be the case, but where there is no way back to the original version it would definitely not be a good idea to upgrade the firmware if the current version is working well.

Installation and security 5

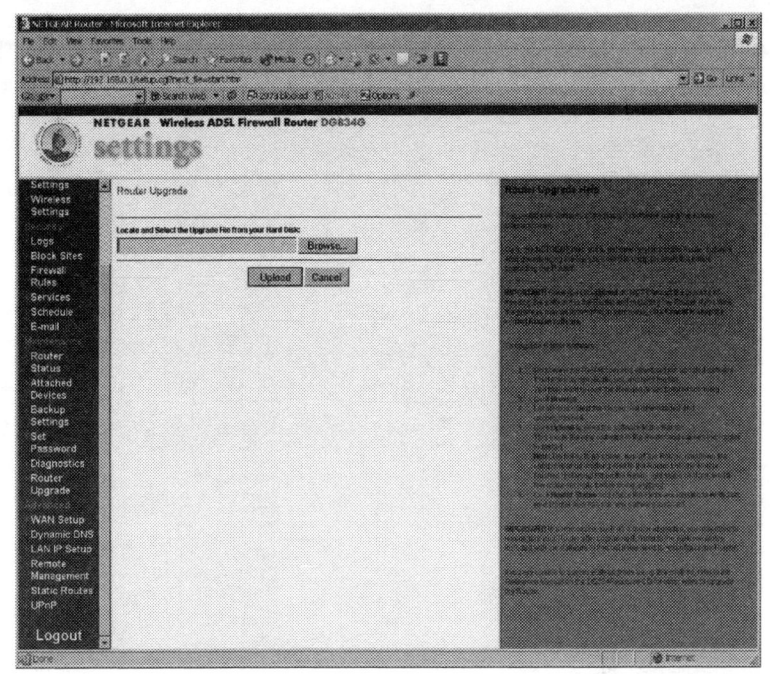

Fig.5.63 The DG834's control software includes an Upgrade section

Upgrading would involve a slight risk of introducing bugs into a unit that previously worked flawlessly, with no way of going back to a fully working version of the firmware. It might be worth the slight risk if the new firmware has added features such as improved security options, but it is otherwise not worth the risk. It is definitely a case of "if it ain't broke, don't fix it".

If you find a firmware upgrade and decide to go ahead with it, there are two normal methods of upgrading firmware. The simpler of the two is where the downloaded file is an executable program that contains embedded data. A file of this type will have an exe extension, and will be categorised as an "Application" in Windows Explorer. With this type of upgrade you just run the program and it updates the firmware. You can use the Run option in the Start menu, but double-clicking its entry in Windows Explorer is easier.

The unit that is being upgraded will usually have to be connected to the PC in a direct manner. For example, a USB wi-fi adapter would probably have to be upgraded via its USB interface and not by way of a wi-fi link

175

5 Installation and security

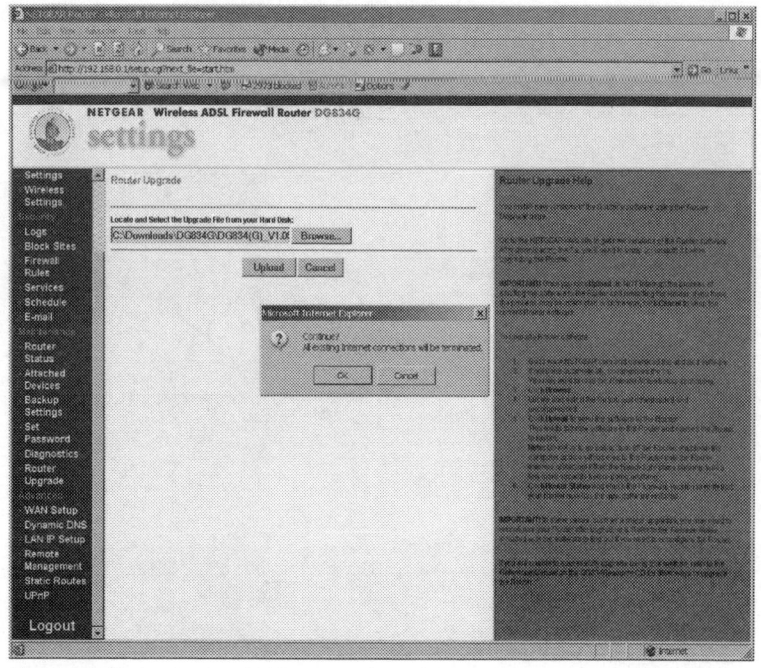

Fig.5.64 Operate the OK button when this warning message appears

from another PC in the system. With something like an access point it might be necessary to use a wired (Ethernet) connection rather than a wi-fi link. Always read the "fine print" before carrying out a firmware upgrade, and make sure that everything is being done in accordance with the manufacturer's recommendations.

With the second method of upgrading, the file you download is the data for the flash memory in the device that is being upgraded. A program is needed in order to program the data into whatever you are upgrading. A suitable program might have been supplied with the equipment, or it might be available as a download. It is also possible that the configuration software supplied with the unit has a facility for performing firmware upgrades. It is again a matter of finding the upgrade instructions and following them "to the letter".

In the case of the DG834G access point, the upgrade file I downloaded from the web site was a Zip file that had to be decompressed to extract

Installation and security 5

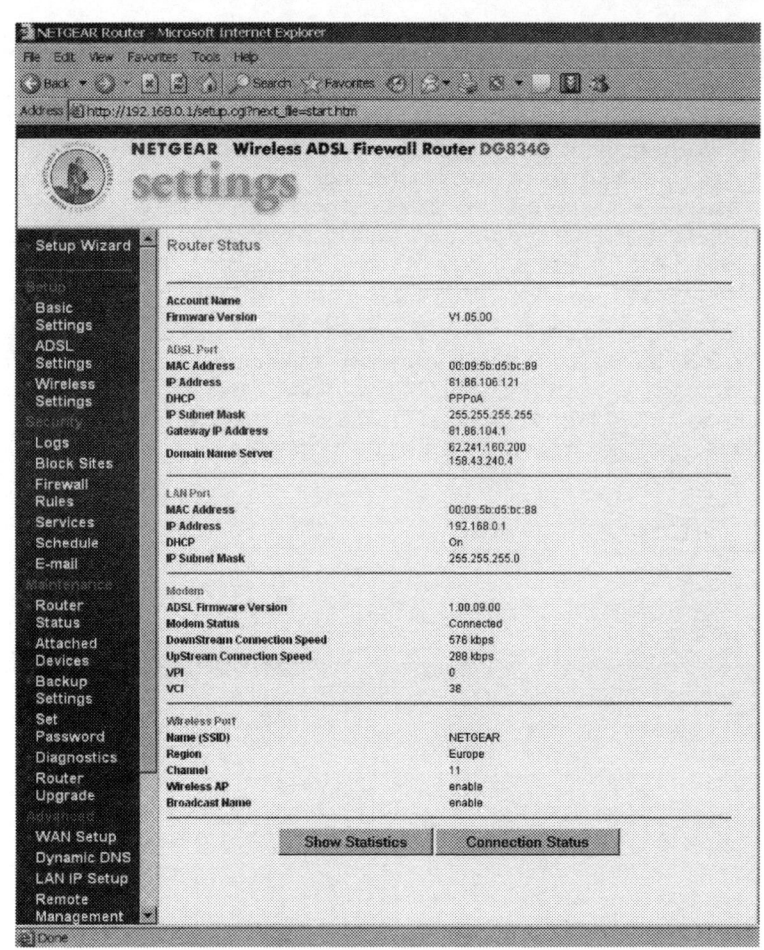

Fig.5.65 This page of the control software confirms that the upgrade has been completed successfully

its contents. A program such as WinZip is needed to do this, and programs such as this are widely available on the Internet. The extracted files were instructions in the form of an Adobe PDF file, and the image file containing the new data. The DG834G's web-based configuration program is used to perform the upgrade, and it has a Router Upgrade section specifically for this purpose (Figure 5.63).

5 Installation and security

The upgrade is performed by operating the Browse button, and then using the file browser to locate and select the appropriate file. It is unlikely that the program will go ahead with the upgrade if the wrong file is selected, but it would be as well to avoid errors just in case. With the right file selected, it just a matter of operating the Upload button, followed by the OK button when a warning message appears (Figure 5.64). This message just points out that all Internet connections will be terminated so that the upgrade can proceed. Writing to flash memory can be quite slow, so it might take a minute or two for the upload to be completed. The upgraded device is then ready to be put back into service again.

After completing any firmware upgrade it is a good idea to check that the firmware has indeed been upgraded. In this case the initial screen of the control software (Figure 5.65) gives some basic information about the device and its settings. The firmware version is given near the top of the screen, and this confirms that the upgrade has been carried out successfully.

Installation and security 5

Points to remember

Read the manufacturer's installation guide before installing any new hardware. It can be time consuming to sort things out if you get the installation of the device drivers wrong. Before installing any supporting software it is advisable to check the manufacturer's web site for updated drivers, support software, and firmware.

The easy way of setting up a PC to operate with networking is to run the Windows Network Setup Wizard on each PC in the system. However, once this has set up the PCs to use networking, there is still some work to do in order to implement file and printer sharing across the network.

Each PC in the network is given a name so that it is easily located when using other PCs in the system. Make sure that each PC is given a different name. The network as a whole is also given a name.

Files and folders are easily shared using the built-in facilities of Windows XP or ME. By default, folders are not shared. Consequently, you must enable sharing for any folder that you wish to make available to the network. Then add the folder to the My Network Places of any PC that will use the folder.

It is possible to share an entire hard disc, but for security reasons it is not a good idea to do so if the network is connected to the Internet. In normal use it is not necessary to share a complete hard disc anyway. Something like one shared folder for music files and another one for documents and other files is sufficient for most purposes.

Any printer that is installed on a PC in the network can usually be shared and used by any other PC in the network. However, the printer can only be shared using a PC that is running an operating system for which a suitable printer driver is available. This should not be a problem if all the PCs are running a modern version of Windows, but Linux and other operating systems might not be supported.

5 Installation and security

There is a very slight risk of rendering a unit unusable when upgrading its firmware. Unless a firmware upgrade will provide useful new features, it is probably not worthwhile upgrading a unit that functions perfectly. Always follow the manufacturer's upgrade instructions "to the letter".

6

Transferring settings

The easy way

I suppose that in an ideal world it would be easy to set up a new PC so that it had all the programs and settings of your old PC. You would simply link the two PCs via some form of network connection, and then tell Windows to make one PC operate just like the other. Windows would then copy programs from one PC to the other, and make the necessary changes to the Registry. The support files needed by any customisation of the programs would be copied to the appropriate folders on the new PC's hard drive. Perhaps all your data files would also be copied to the new PC. Unfortunately, Windows has no built-in facility of this type. However, as explained later in this chapter, it can provide some help in setting up one PC to mimic another.

There are actually third-party programs available that can copy programs, data, and settings from one PC to another. There are numerous programs that will just transfer settings from one PC to another. Unfortunately, many of these programs are difficult or impossible to obtain in the UK, and the ones that try to fully clone your old PC seem to be especially difficult to obtain. One would probably expect this type of software to be in big demand, since it is potentially useful for anyone upgrading from one PC to another. This does not seem to be the case though, and it can be difficult to track down any program migration software.

One possible reason for the scarcity of this software is that much of it has a reputation for being something less than user-friendly. A more likely reason is that many users take the opportunity to start afresh with a clean and uncluttered PC when they upgrade to a new one. However, as PCs become more heavily customised, the "clean sweep" approach becomes more difficult and time consuming. With a heavily customised PC it is possible that you would never get the new one set up in exactly the same way as your old PC. Finding out how to implement every little

6 Transfering settings

tweak could take too long, and you might never remember how some of the changes were originally implemented.

Anyway, if you have a heavily customised PC it might be worthwhile tracking down some program migration software if the alternative methods do not meet your requirements. The expense is probably not justified if your old PC has not been subjected to a fair amount of customisation. Installing everything from scratch is almost certainly the best approach where your old PC has little or no customisation. The time taken to install all the software should not be too great, and the "clean" installation should ensure that the new PC operates at the peak of efficiency.

Transfer Wizard

Even when installing everything from scratch, most Windows users would probably like a quick and easy means of transferring some basic settings from the old PC to the new one. Using special software to transfer some settings should not have any significant affect on the performance of the new PC, even if the old computer is not running at maximum efficiency. The types of setting that are normally transferred are very basic things such as screen colours, and the homepage used by Internet Explorer. Most settings transfer programs do not handle things that could have a major effect on the new PC's performance. Transferring settings of this type would be risky and could easily bring the new PC to a standstill.

Users of Windows XP do not need to buy any software in order to transfer files and some basic settings from one PC to another. It has an integral facility of this type in the form of the Files and Settings Transfer Wizard. Unfortunately, this facility was introduced with Windows XP, and is not available when using earlier versions of the Windows operating system. Various means of file transfer are supported, including a direct cable connection, copying to a home network drive, and removable media such as floppy discs or Flash cards and a card reader.

The method recommended by Microsoft is to use a home network, as this is likely to be the quickest and easiest. The wizard automatically detects a suitable direct cable connection and configures itself accordingly, so this method should also work quite well. Although floppy discs might seem to be impractical in an application of this type, the amount of data transferred to the new PC will often be quite modest. The number of discs required to complete the transfer is typically about half a dozen to a dozen. Even so, using floppy discs is relatively slow and inconvenient, so it is probably best not to use this method if an alternative is available.

One reason that floppy discs are just about a practical proposition is that the wizard does not actually transfer very much to the new PC. It can still save a large amount of time, since transferring files and settings via the wizard should be quite fast. Having to manually set up dialup connections, various Windows settings, etc., would almost certainly take much longer. The amount of time saved depends on how many settings have been altered on your old PC. Clearly there will be relatively little to gain by using this wizard if few settings have changed from their defaults. A great deal of time can be saved if you like changing anything that can be customised.

What types of setting will the wizard transfer to your new PC? Anything concerned with the appearance of Windows will almost certainly find its way onto the new PC. In addition to the obvious things such as the colour scheme and wallpaper, changes in the Windows sounds will also be copied to the new PC, as will mouse and keyboard settings. Most Internet settings will be transferred, including the ones that govern the way your PC connects to the Internet. Settings associated with Internet Explorer will also be changed, such as your homepage, security settings, and favourites. Cookies will also be transferred. Most PCs accumulate huge numbers of cookies over a period of time, so it might be advisable to clear unwanted cookies from the old PC prior to using the wizard.

Outlook Express

Email settings will be transferred to the new PC, but only if you use Outlook or Outlook Express. On the face of it, users of popular Email services such as Yahoo! and Hotmail will have to make other arrangements. However, the settings for these web-based Email services are stored on the server, and not on the users' PCs. You should therefore find that an Email service of this type is exactly the same, regardless of which PC is used to access it. Some facilities might be dependent on cookies stored on the user's PC, but these cookies should be transferred by the wizard.

The biggest weakness of this wizard is that it does not transfer the settings for most application programs. Windows itself will operate much as it did on your old PC, but the same might not be true for the word processor, image editor, accounting program, etc. As one would expect, the popular Microsoft programs such as Word, Access, and Excel are catered for. Some of the very popular programs from other software companies will

6 Transfering settings

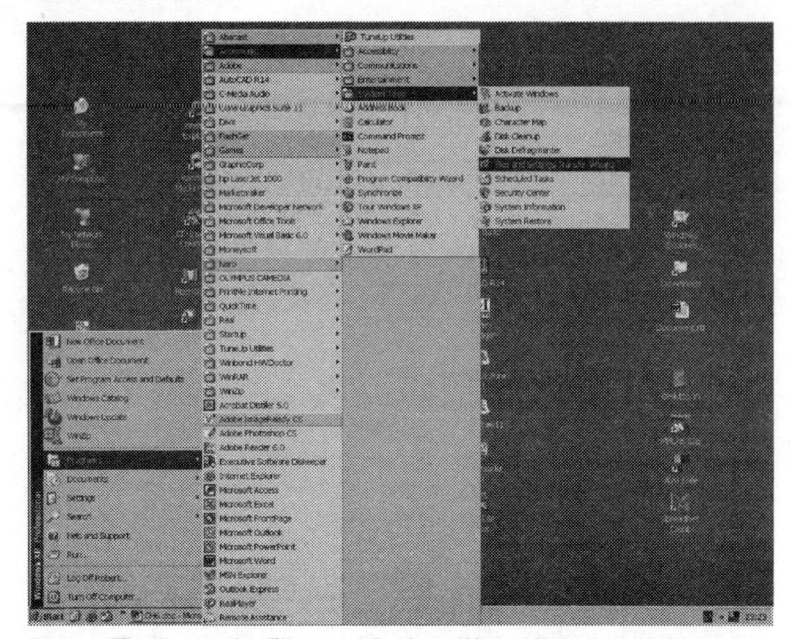

Fig.6.1 The link to the Files and Settings Wizard lies deep in the menu structure

also have their settings transferred. The Real Player program, for example, will have its settings moved to the new PC. However, few other non-Microsoft applications are supported. Note that it is only the settings for these programs that are transferred, and not the programs themselves. The programs must be installed on the new PC in the usual way before the settings are transferred.

Getting started

The Files and Settings Transfer Wizard is buried deep in the menu structure (Figure 6.1). Go to the Start menu and then choose Programs (or All Programs), Accessories, System Tools, and finally Files and Settings Transfer Wizard. This will launch the initial window of Figure 6.2. This is just the usual Welcome screen, but operating the Next button moves things on to the window of Figure 6.3, where the process starts in earnest. How you proceed from here depends on what you are trying to achieve, and the exact method to be used.

Transferring settings 6

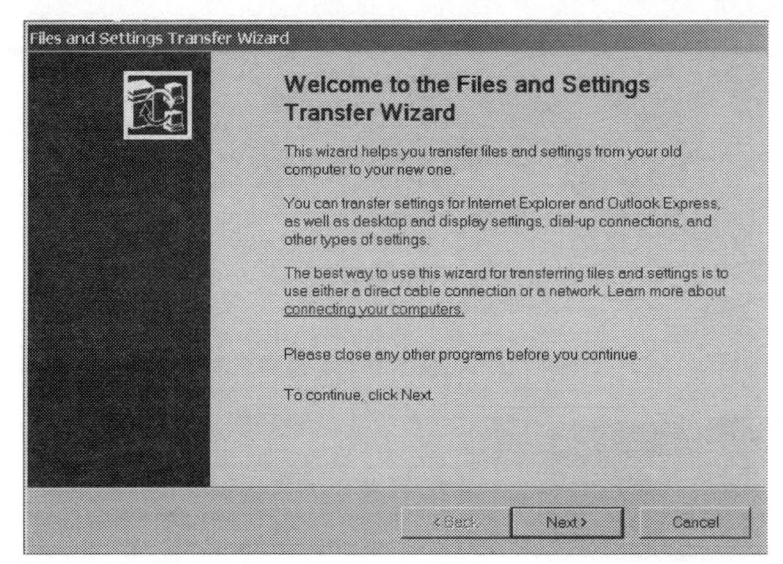

Fig.6.2 The Wizard starts with the usual Welcome screen

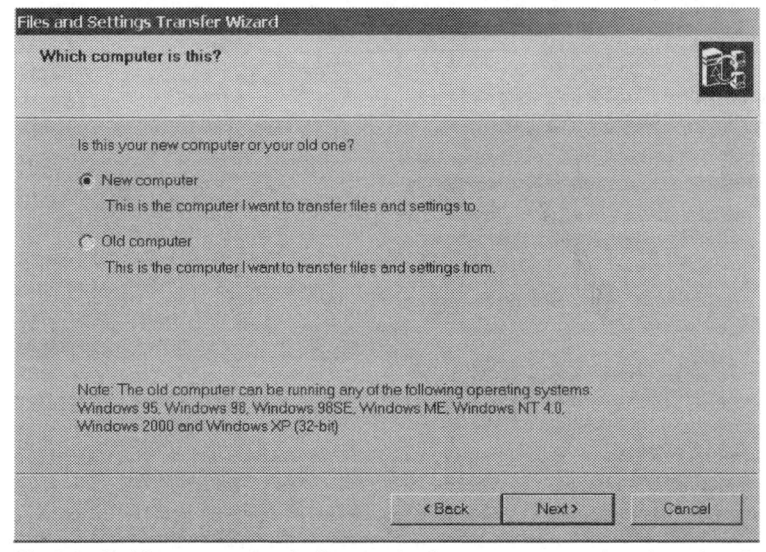

Fig.6.3 At this screen you indicate whether you are running the wizard on the old computer or the new one

6 Transfering settings

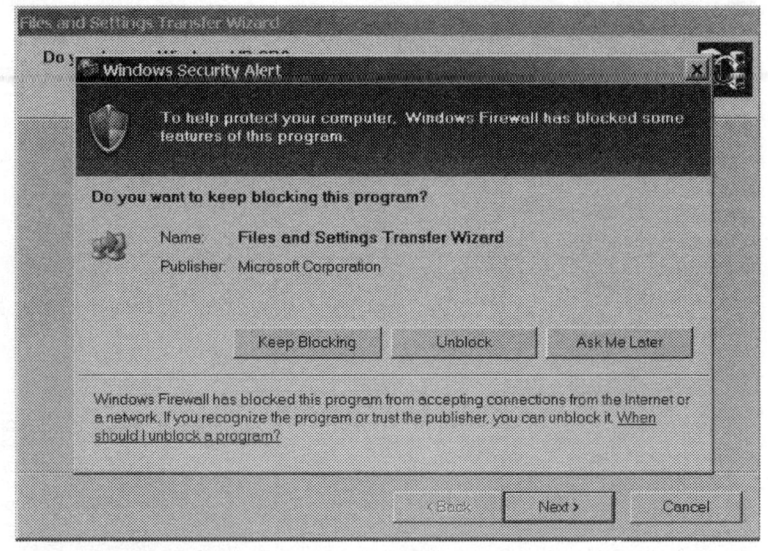

Fig.6.4 This warning message will probably appear if you are running Windows XP SP2

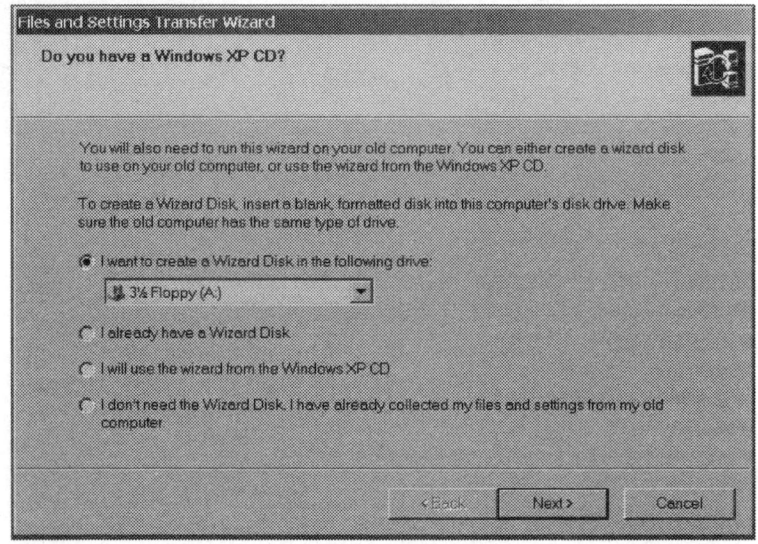

Fig.6.5 A program disc enables the wizard to be run on another PC

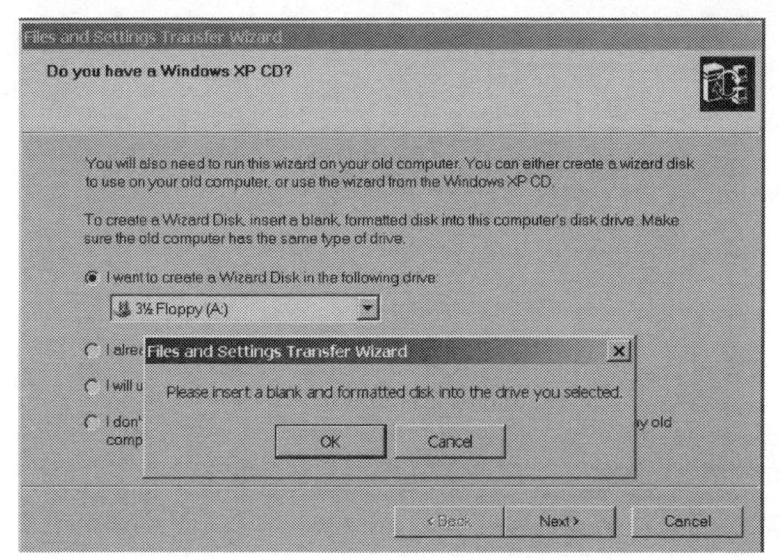

Fig.6.6 Insert a disc into the floppy drive when prompted

For the sake of this example we will assume that you are running the wizard on a new PC that has Windows XP as its operating system. You therefore need to transfer the files from your old PC to this new one. On the face of it, the transfer is not possible if your old PC is running under an earlier version of Windows, such as Windows ME, since earlier versions of Windows do not have the Files and Settings Transfer Wizard. This would render the settings transfer facility completely useless to many users. Fortunately, there is a way around the problem. Windows XP can make a program disc that will run under earlier versions of Windows, enabling the transfer to be made.

At the window of Figure 6.3, make sure that the New Computer radio button is selected, and then operate the Next button. When running Windows XP with Service Pack 2, it is likely that the warning window of Figure 6.4 will appear on the screen, even though the wizard is a Microsoft program. Operate the Unblock button so that the wizard can continue to run properly. This should move things on to the window of Figure 6.5. It is not essential to make a program disc if you have the proper Windows XP installation disc, as this disc contains the wizard program. However, many PCs have Windows preinstalled and are not supplied with a Windows installation disc. Even if you do have a Windows installation

6 Transfering settings

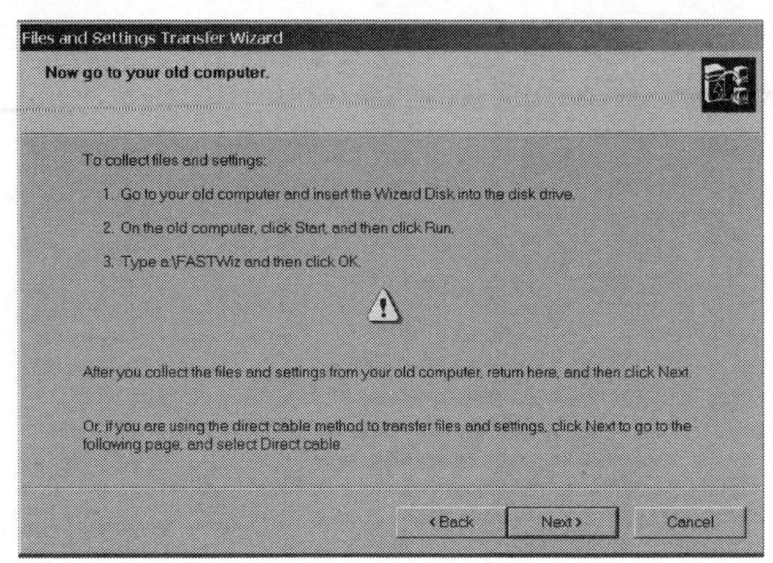

Fig.6.7 This screen appears once the program disc or discs have been completed

disc, it might still be easier to make the program disc. Doing so will avoid the need to go through drawers and cupboards searching for the Windows disc!

To make a wizard program disc, first make sure that the top radio button is selected. Use the menu immediately below this to select the appropriate drive, which in most cases will be drive A (the floppy disc drive). Operate the Next button to move on to the next stage, and insert a floppy disc into drive A when prompted (Figure 6.6). Note that the program is too large to fit onto a single 1.44-megabyte floppy disc, so it is better to use a higher capacity disc such as a Flash type wherever possible. I used a Compact Flash card

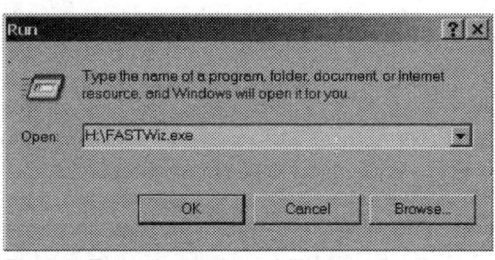

Fig.6.8 Enter the path and filename for the wizard program

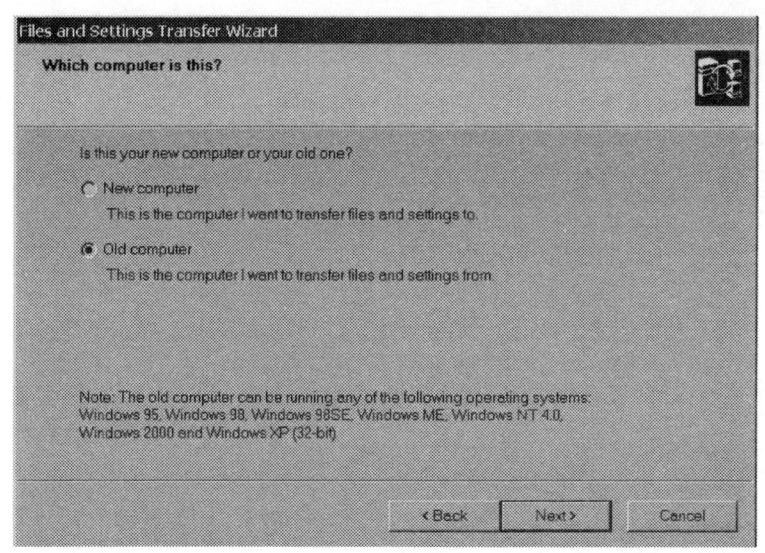

Fig.6.9 This time it is the "Old computer" radio button that is selected

and a card reader for this example. The window of Figure 6.7 will appear when the program has been copied to the disc or discs.

The next step is to run the wizard program on the old PC, and collect the files that will be transferred to the new PC. In order to run the program, select Run from the Start menu, and then type the path to the program and its name. Alternatively, operate the Browse button and then use the file browser to locate the program. Once the textbox has the correct path and filename (Figure 6.8), operate the Run button. You will then get a feeling of déjà vu, with the Welcome page for the Files and Settings Transfer Wizard appearing again. As before, operate the Next button to move on to the first "real" window of the wizard, but this time select the Old Computer radio button (Figure 6.9).

There will probably be a brief wait, during which the window shown in Figure 6.10 will be displayed. Eventually the window shown in Figure 6.11 should appear on the screen, and it is then a matter of selecting the method that will be used to collect the files. In this example it is removable media that is being used, and it is therefore the third radio button from the top that is selected. The appropriate drive is chosen from the drop-down menu, and then the Next button is operated.

6 Transfering settings

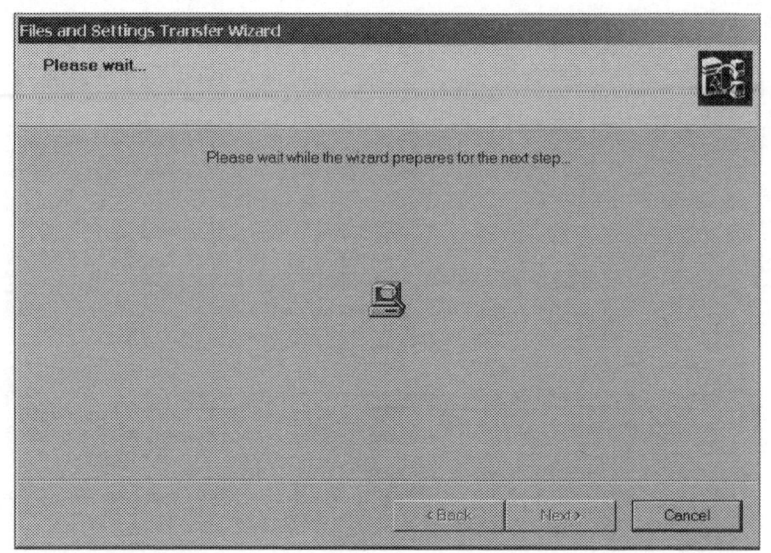

Fig.6.10 There will be a short wait, during which this window will be displayed

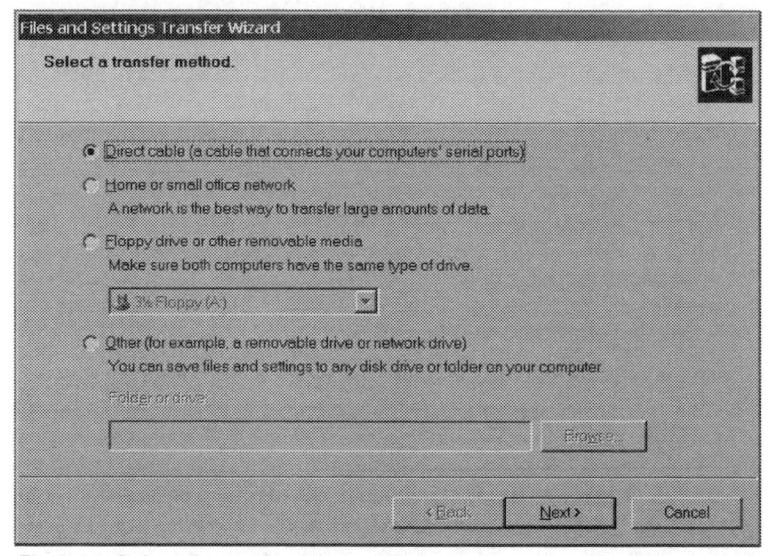

Fig.6.11 Select the method that will be used to collect the files

Transferring settings 6

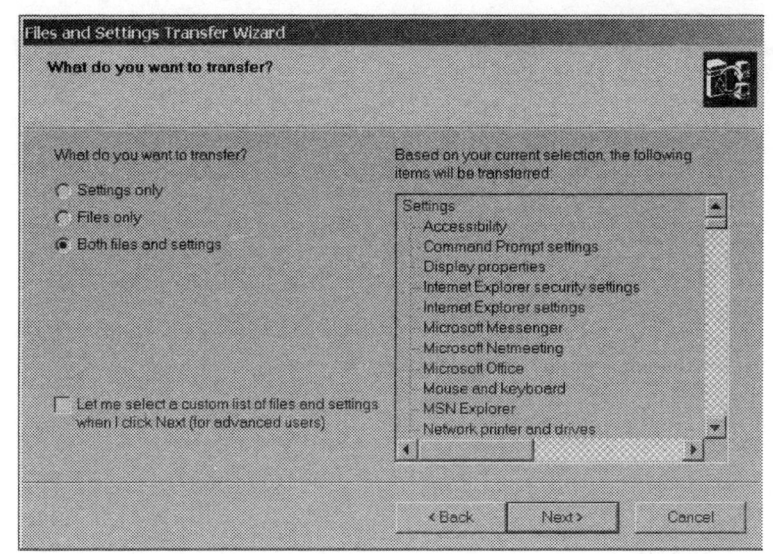

Fig.6.12 Here you have the option of selecting the files and settings that will be transferred

Decisions

You then have to select which files and settings will be copied to the disc or discs (Figure 6.12). The default is for settings and files to be transferred to the new PC, but the radio buttons enable only one or other of these to be selected. Ticking the checkbox enables the user to select which files and settings will be transferred to the new system. The scrollable list in the right-hand section shows the files and settings that will be selected by default. There will usually be little or nothing to be gained by using anything other than the default selection.

One possible exception is where a large number of files are selected by default. This is unlikely to be a problem when using a network or direct connection to transfer the files, but it could be awkward when using some types of removable disc. Transferring large amounts of data via this route might be very time consuming, and could require a large number of discs. If you opt to select the files and settings manually, the window of Figure 6.13 is obtained at the next stage. This enables files or settings to be deleted from the list, new files to be added via a file browser, and so on.

6 Transfering settings

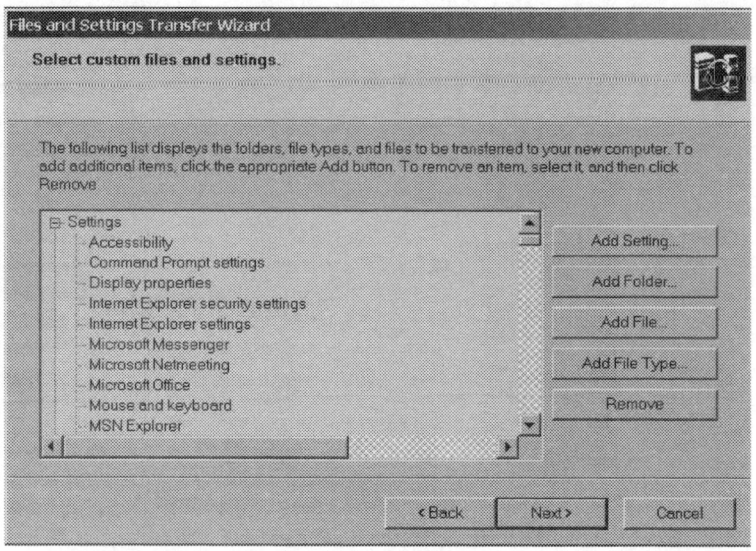

Fig.6.13 This window is used to select the required files and settings

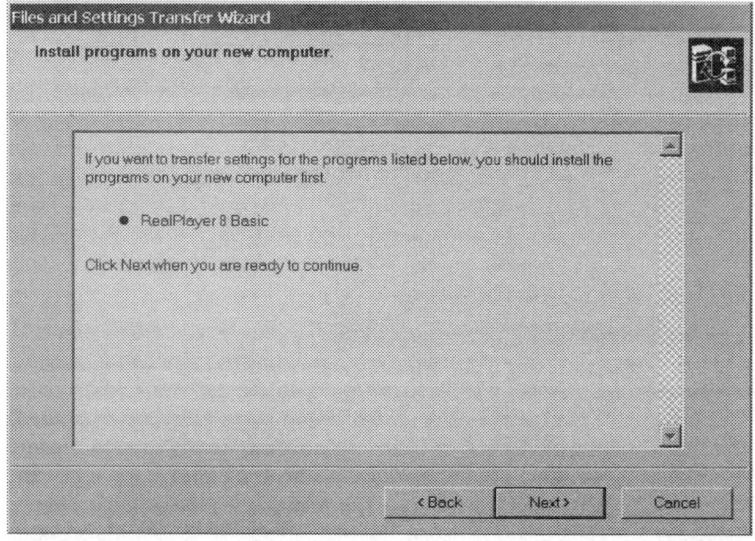

Fig.6.14 This screen warns that the relevant software must be installed on the new PC before the settings can be transferred

Transferring settings 6

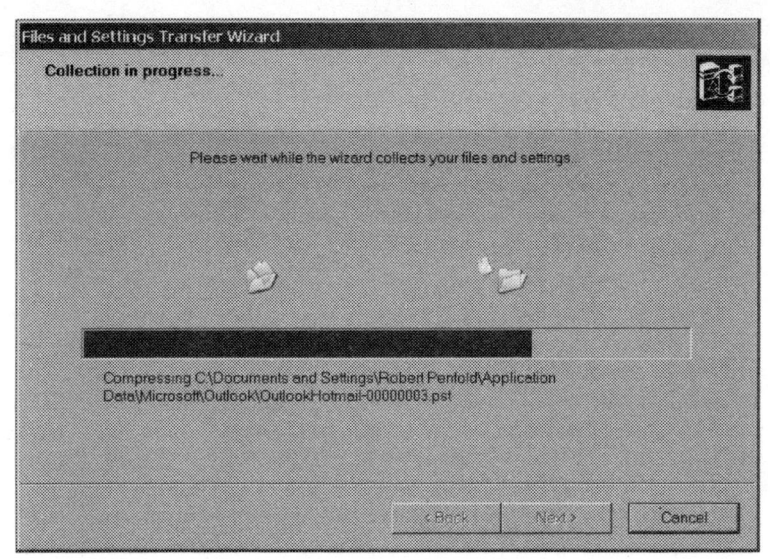

Fig.6.15 This screen shows how the copying process is progressing

In this case it is only the settings that have to be transferred. Any files that are needed on the new PC will be manually selected and copied to a CD, and then copied from there to the hard disc of the new PC. Accordingly, the Settings Only radio button was selected and the Next button was operated. A warning was provided at the next window (Figure 6.14), but this will only be produced if settings for non-Microsoft software will be transferred. As one would probably expect, the relevant software must be installed on the new PC prior to transferring the settings from the old PC.

After moving on from any warning screen, the familiar bargraph will appear (Figure 6.15) while the files are collected and copied to disc. There may be pop-up windows that provide information about the amount of data that has been gathered, the number of discs required, and this sort of thing. Simply follow any onscreen instructions that are provided. The window of Figure 6.16 is displayed once the files have been copied successfully. Operate the Finish button to close the window, and then return to the new PC.

6　Transfering settings

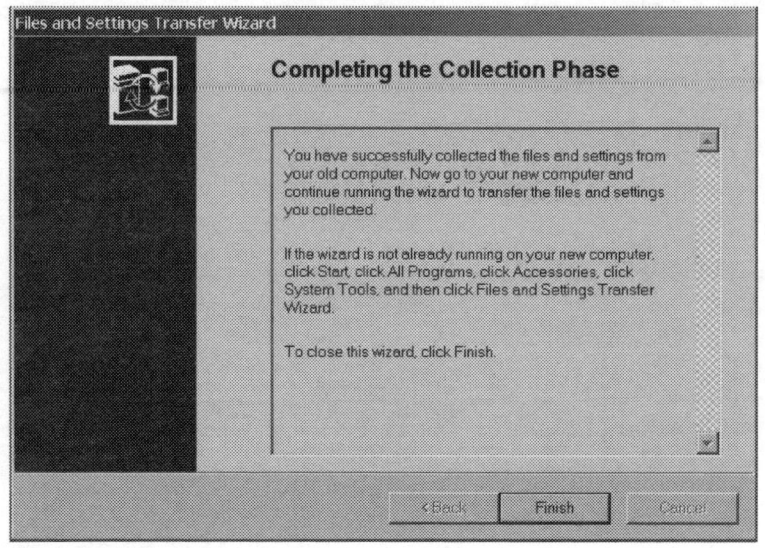

Fig.6.16 This screen indicates that everything has been copied successfully

Making the transfer

Now it is time to return to the new computer. Note that it is not essential to leave the wizard running while you gather the files and settings data from the old PC. You can close the wizard and then run it again when you are ready to transfer the data to the new PC. When you get to the screen of Figure 6.17, make sure that the bottom radio button is selected and then operate the Next button. This takes you to the screen of Figure 6.18. The same screen should be obtained if the wizard is left running and the Next button is operated.

The radio buttons are used to select the appropriate method of transferring the files to the new computer, and in this case the removable media option is required. The middle radio button is therefore selected, and then the appropriate drive is selected from the menu. A message like the one in Figure 6.19 will appear, and this prompts you to insert the first disc into the drive. Note that this message will appear even if the files are stored on a single "disc" such as a Flash card. Where appropriate, in due course you will be prompted to insert discs two, three, four, etc. Once again, a status window will show how far the process has progressed (Figure 6.20).

Transferring settings 6

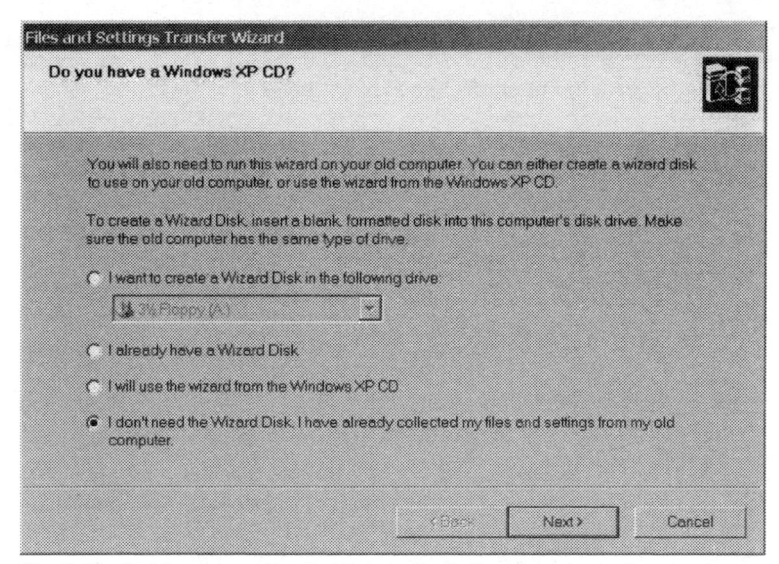

Fig.6.17 At this screen the bottom radio button is selected

Fig.6.18 Select the appropriate method of file transfer

6 Transfering settings

Eventually the process will be completed, but this can take a few minutes even if relatively small amounts of data are involved. This is presumably due to the large number of changes that have to be made to various Windows configuration files. In this case the window of Figure 6.21 informed me that the transfer had been completed, but it also indicated that there was a problem with one of the settings. Any settings that have not been transferred correctly must be sorted out manually. In this case there was a problem with a network printer, and it was due to the printer being connected direct to the new PC and not via the network. There was actually nothing to sort out and everything worked fine.

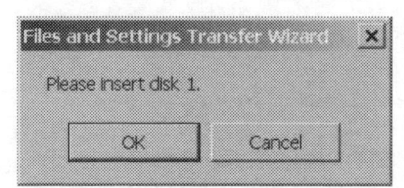

Fig.6.19 Insert a disc when prompted by this pop-up

The wizard will produce a final message such as the one in Figure 6.22, indicating that the changes will not take effect until you log off or reboot the computer. It is advisable to log off and on again or reboot the

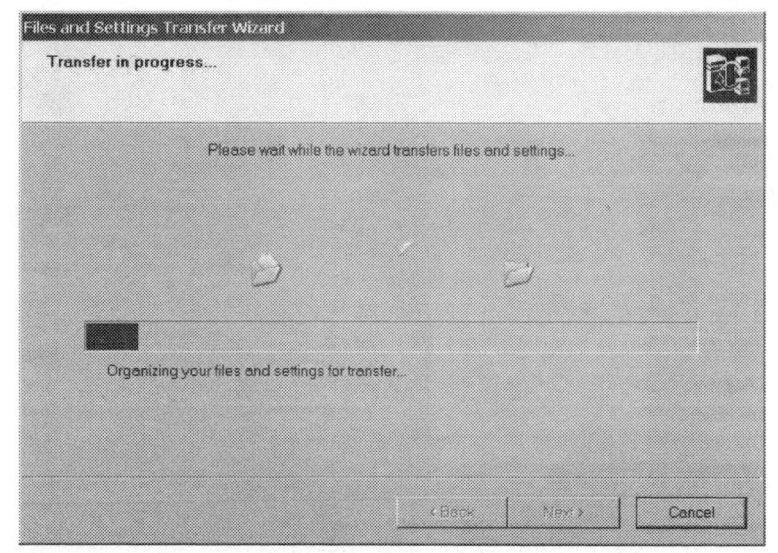

Fig.6.20 A status window shows how far the transfer process has progressed

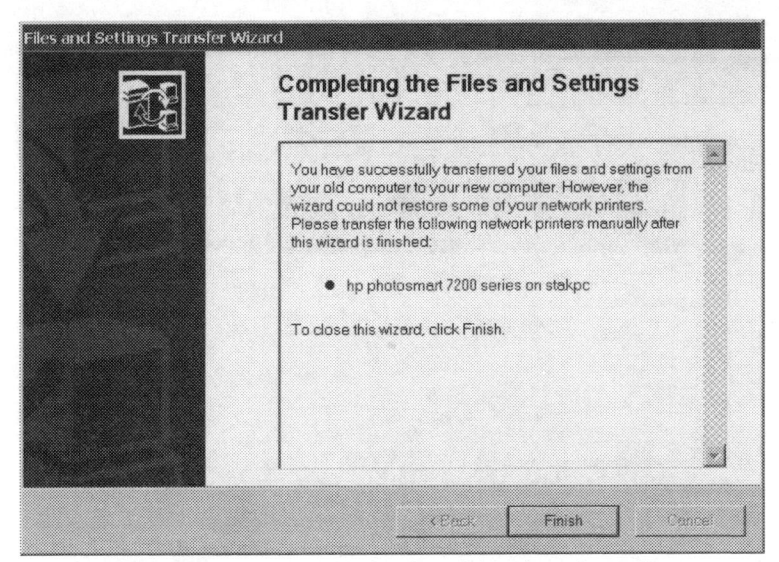

Fig.6.21 The transfer has been completed, but there is a minor problem

computer so that the system can be checked. As a quick check, try going on to the Internet to see if the homepage of the new computer matches that of the old PC. In this example the two pages matched correctly (Figure 6.23 and 6.24), and the list of favourites had also been transferred correctly.

Some things, such as the customisation of the toolbars in Microsoft Office applications, will not be transferred. Consequently, there will still be some manual changes to make, but using the Settings and Files Transfer Wizard should substantially reduce the amount of manual changes required. It can potentially save a great deal of time and effort. There is little to be

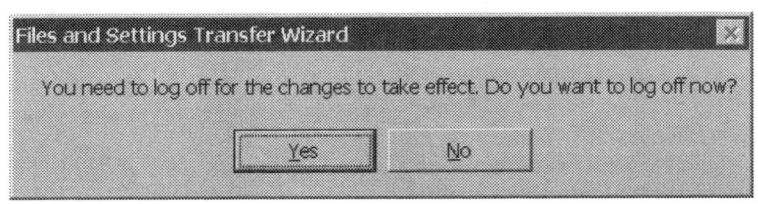

Fig.6.22 The changes will not take effect until you log off or reboot the PC

6 Transfering settings

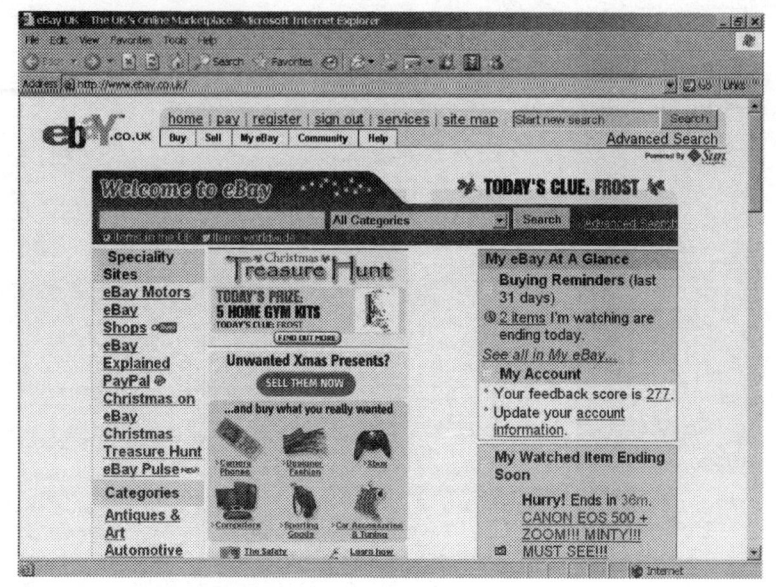

Fig.6.23 The homepage of the old PC

lost by trying this little known feature of Windows XP. In the unlikely event that it all goes horribly wrong, it should be possible to return the PC to its former state using the System Restore function.

Address backup

Some programs have built-in facilities that enable some types of setting to be transferred from one PC to another. With Windows XP you are probably better off using the Settings and Files Transfer Wizard, where this will have the desired effect. With other versions of Windows, and where the Settings and Files Transfer Wizard does not have the desired effect, there is probably no alternative to any built-in transfer facilities of your applications programs. The obvious drawback of this method is that the transfers have to be done one-by-one, which could be quite time consuming. Also, you are likely to be using some of the more obscure facilities of your application programs. Finding out whether the required facility exists, and how to use it if it does, could require a lot of time consuming research.

Transferring settings 6

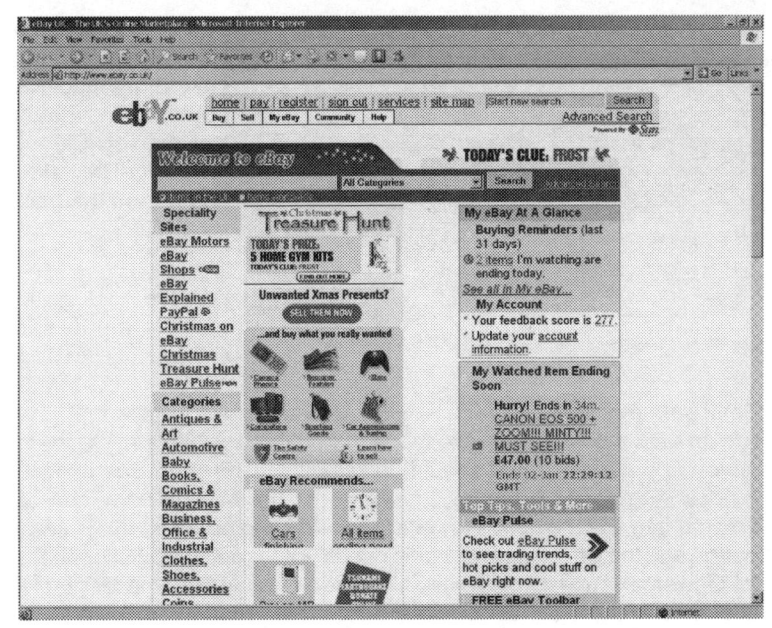

Fig.6.24 The new PC now has the same homepage

Email address books are a common problem when moving on to a new computer. Many users have the problem of getting their existing Outlook Express address book transferred to the new PC. With only a few addresses it would not take too long to enter the data manually, but even with a few entries things are quicker and more reliable if the address book is exported from one PC to the other. It is actually possible to import and export an address book, and it is not a bad idea to make a backup copy of the data. If your PC crashes and the data on the hard

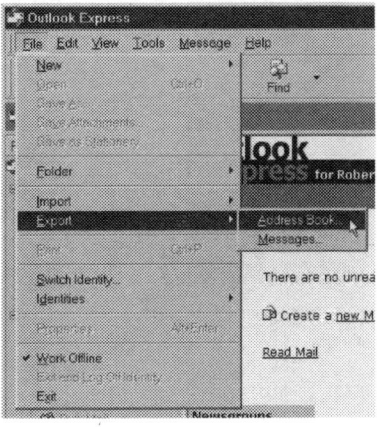

Fig.6.25 Select Address Book from the submenu

199

6 Transfering settings

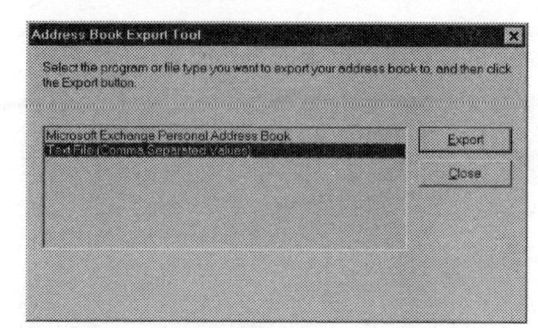

Fig.6.26 Select the Plain Text File option

disc is lost, you can restore your backup copy of the address book which should be stored on a floppy disc, CD-RW, etc., and not on the hard disc.

To export the address book go to the File menu and select Export followed by Address Book from the submenu (Figure 6.25). A window like the one in Figure 6.26 should then appear. Two types of file are available, and the lower option (the plain text file) should be selected. This produces another window (Figure 6.27) where a filename for the backup copy can be entered into the textbox. However, I would suggest using the Browse button and the file browser that this brings up (Figure 6.28). Choose the folder where you wish to save the file, type a suitable filename for the file, and choose the "csv" option for the file type. Then operate the Save

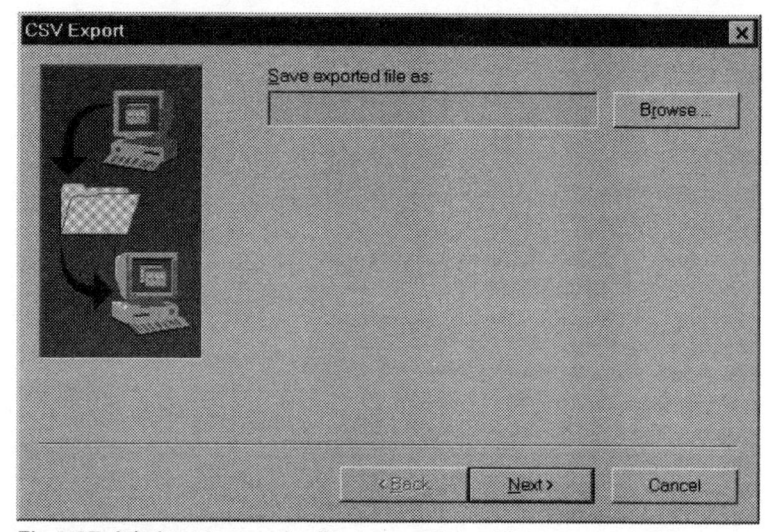

Fig.6.27 It is best to use the Browse option when you reach this window

Transferring settings 6

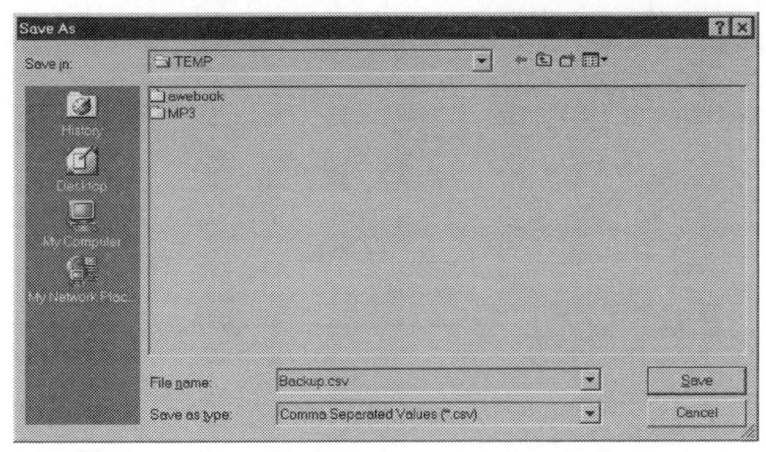

Fig.6.28 Choose csv as the file type

button to return to the previous window. Operate the Next button, which brings up a window like the one of Figure 6.29, where you can select the fields that will be exported. If in doubt select everything! Operate the Finish button and the backup copy will be saved to disc.

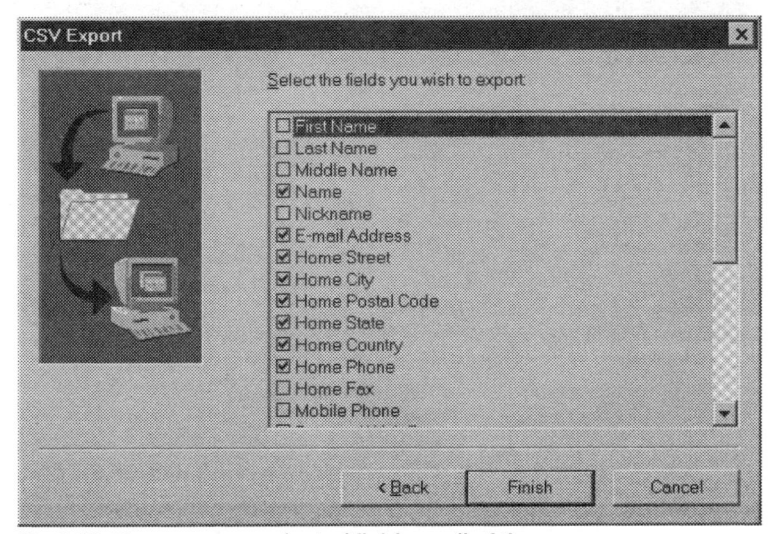

Fig.6.29 You can save selected fields or all of them

6 Transfering settings

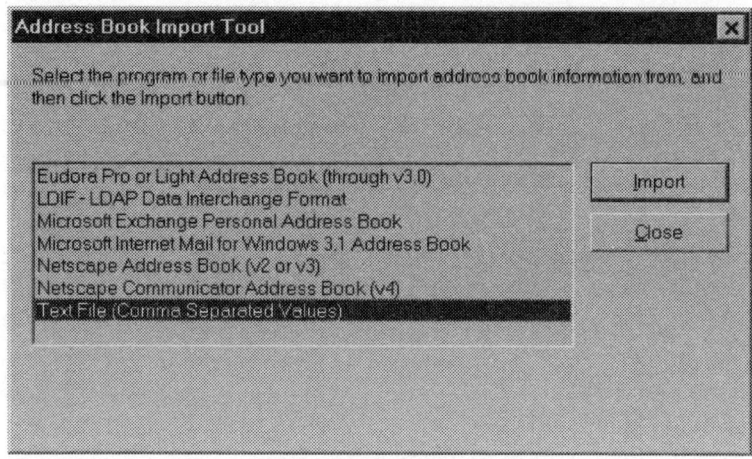

Fig.6.30 Select the correct file type, which is a text file in this case

The importing process is the same whether you are restoring a backup copy after a system crash or putting an existing address book on a new computer. Go to the File menu and select Import, followed by the Other

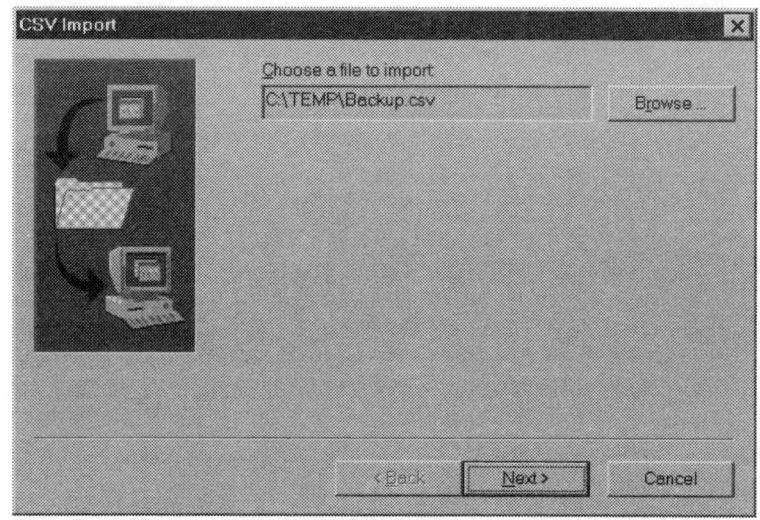

Fig.6.31 Type the full filename or use the browse feature to locate the correct file

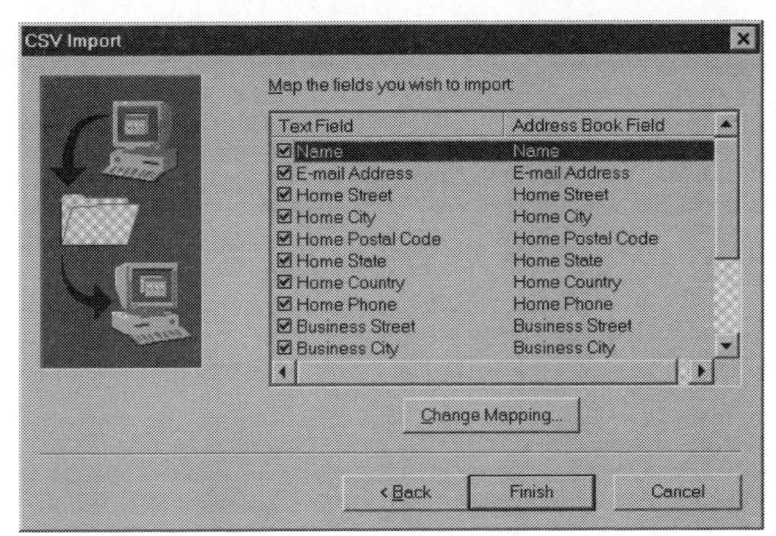

Fig.6.32 Select the fields that you wish to import. The default is for all available fields to be imported

Address Book option. In the new window that appears (Figure 6.30) select Text File from the list of importable file types. Then operate the Import button, which brings up a window like the one shown in Figure 6.31. Either type in the full name of the backup file including the path and extension, or use the browser to locate and select it. Operate the Next button to bring up a window like the one of Figure 6.32, where you can select the fields that will be imported. Left-click the Finish button to complete the process and import the address book.

Finally

Any facilities that can be used to transfer settings, etc., from one PC to another will obviously vary from program to program. With a voice recognition program for example, it might be possible to save the speech profiles to disc and then transfer them to the new PC. This avoids having each user go through the training process before the program can be used properly. With some programs it might be necessary to use a little ingenuity, as in the previous Outlook Express example. Facilities for backing up settings or customised features can often be used as a means of transferring them from one PC to another.

6 Transfering settings

A ploy that often used to work in the past was to install the application program on the new PC, and then overwrite the program's folder with its equivalent on the old PC. It was important to install the program on the new PC so that the appropriate changes were made to the Windows Registry. Without having the program properly installed in Windows there was little chance of it running properly. Overwriting the new installation with the old one transferred any customisation of the program to the new PC.

Unfortunately, this method is unlikely to work with a modern version of Windows. It used to be normal for programs to use configuration files to control their settings and customised features. However, this way of handling things has now been largely phased out, and most or all of the settings are now stored in the Windows Registry. For this reason, overwriting the program's folder with a copy of the old one is unlikely to have the desired effect. There will probably be no configuration files in the folder for the old installation, so no configuration information will be copied to the new computer. The most likely result is that the program will not have any settings transferred, but it will become unstable and produce error messages!

Points to remember

It is possible to buy programs that will transfer settings from one PC to another, but some of these programs do not seem to offer anything more than the facilities that are built into Windows XP. The more advanced migration programs will copy programs, settings, and even data from the old PC to the new one. Unfortunately, these programs seem to be very difficult to obtain in the UK.

The Files and Settings Transfer Wizard is a little known facility of Windows XP that can be used to transfer Windows settings and files from one PC to another. The settings of some application programs can also be transferred, but few non-Microsoft programs are catered for.

The transfer can use a network, a direct connection link, or removable media such as floppy discs or a Flash card in a reader. In most cases the amount of data transferred to the new PC is quite small, so using something as basic as a few floppy discs is a practical proposition.

On the face of it, the Files and Settings Transfer Wizard is only usable if the old PC is running under Windows XP. This is not the case though, because the Wizard can produce a program disc that will run under earlier versions of Windows. Running the wizard on the old PC and gathering the files to be transferred is therefore a straightforward task.

In general, any settings that affect the appearance of Windows will be transferred by the Files and Settings Transfer Wizard. This includes things such as the screen colours, and even the sounds that Windows uses. Things such as dial-up connections will also be transferred, as will the Favourites list and homepage of Internet Explorer. Some changes will have to be made manually though, including customised toolbars in Office applications.

Where appropriate, application programs often have facilities for transferring settings from one PC to another. It can be necessary to use a little ingenuity though. For example, a facility that is primarily intended

6 Transfering settings

as a means of backing up and restoring settings is likely to be usable as a means of transferring them from one PC to another.

When using a modern version of Windows it is unlikely that simply copying a program's folder from one PC to another will transfer any settings. These days the settings and customisation information are normally stored in the Windows Registry, not in configuration files. This copying method could easily result in the program becoming unstable and generating error messages.

7
Hard disc cloning

Back to basics

Transferring settings from one PC to another is useful, but it will not produce a true copy of the original system. Starting with a new PC it might be necessary to install Windows from scratch before any Windows settings can be transferred, or Windows might be preinstalled. Either way, application programs then have to installed, together with your data files and any small utilities that you use. Where possible, settings for the application programs can then be transferred as well. Finally, any final customisation must be completed, making manual changes and adjustments where no automated option is available.

Even with a fairly basic setup, installing everything from scratch or starting with a "bare" Windows installation is likely to involve a fair amount of time and effort. At one time it was quite common for "power" users to reinstall everything from scratch from time to time. The idea of this was to give a "clean" installation that was efficient and operated as quickly as possible. Going back to an uncluttered installation still has its advantages, but for most users it is simply not a practical proposition. It would take too long, and it could be difficult to precisely duplicate the original setup even given a suitable long period of time to complete the task.

Setting up a new PC to operate as a clone of an existing PC is likely to be just as time consuming, and would probably be more than a little difficult as well. You have a slight head start if Windows is preinstalled on the new PC, but installing the application programs and customising everything is where most of the work lies. An obvious shortcut is to simply copy the contents of the old PC's hard disc to the hard disc of the new PC. In effect, you take a backup of the old hard disc and restore it to the disc in the new PC. The new PC then operates in exactly the same manner as the old one, complete with all your data, customisation, and settings. The only difference is that the new PC should operate much more quickly than its ageing predecessor.

7 Hard disc cloning

In practice there are a couple of major problems with this approach. Simply copying all the files on the hard disc to CDRs or another form of mass storage will not enable the system to be restored to its original condition. The files can be copied back to the hard disc, but they will not be in the same places on the restored disc. This is likely to be academic anyway, since it is virtually certain that the new and old discs will have different characteristics. As a result of this the PC will not be able to boot from the disc. In order to precisely restore a disc to its previous state it is necessary to produce what is termed an image of the disc. It requires special software to produce the image file and restore the disc from this file. Power Quest's Drive Image and Norton's Ghost are two popular programs of this type. There is a rather less sophisticated backup and restore feature included as part of the Windows operating system.

Hardware differences

The second problem is that the hardware of the old and new computers will be different. Windows seems to need driver software for practically every piece of hardware, including things like soundcards, video boards, modems, and various pieces of hardware on the motherboard that handle the IDE drives and this type of thing. This will inevitably get Windows a bit confused the first time you boot the new PC using the cloned installation. It will find various drivers that do not match the hardware fitted to the PC.

In the days of Windows 95 it was unlikely that the PC would ever work properly with a massive mismatch of this type. You tended to go around in "ever decreasing circles", with new drivers being installed again and again, but the computer never managing to boot into Windows properly. More recent versions of Windows are better at sorting out changes in the hardware, and some of the new hardware might be installed automatically. In most cases though, it will be necessary to supply the appropriate installation discs when prompted, so that the driver software can be installed. This can take quite a little time and effort, but before too long the PC should be working properly.

It has to be pointed out that there is no guarantee that this method will work, but in the vast majority of cases it is not too difficult to get the cloned installation working well on the new PC. Many Windows users have successfully upgraded their PCs on a grand scale without reinstalling Windows, and transferring a cloned system on a new PC is not too far removed from this. In both vases it is necessary for Windows to adjust to numerous items of new hardware.

The driver software for all the hardware should be supplied with the new PC, but it is worth searching the Internet to see if any more recent versions are available. The process of installing the new hardware into Windows can result in some settings being returned to their default values. The resolution and colour-depth of the graphics card, for instance, could be set to something fairly basic. However, this type of thing is easily changed using the normal Windows facilities, and you may wish to make changes anyway in order to take advantage of the new hardware's capabilities.

It is important to note that many PCs are supplied with a version of Windows that is only usable with the PC it is bundled with. This can cause problems when large changes to the hardware are made. For example, users sometimes upgrade an old PC by fitting a new motherboard, processor, and memory. This is sufficient to convince Windows that it is running on a new PC, and it refuses to work. Transferring a system of this type to a new PC produces much the same result, and it is not worth trying if you are using a "tied" version of Windows.

Note that it is not a problem related to Windows product activation. Large changes to the hardware can necessitate a telephone call to Microsoft in order to reactivate Windows, but you should be able to get an activation code provided you are not trying to run more copies of Windows than you legitimately own. A "tied" version of Windows looks for the appropriate code in the BIOS chip on the motherboard, and it will not boot unless the correct code is found. In general, this means it is impossible to run that version of Windows on anything other than a PC of the correct make and model.

The version of Windows running on the new PC is not of importance in the current context, because it will be overwritten by the old system and will not be used. It is important to note that you must not run more copies of Windows than you have actually bought. Running the old version of Windows twice is all right provided you are not using the Windows operating system supplied with the new PC. If no Windows operating system was supplied with the new PC, the system on the old PC should be deleted once the cloning to the new PC has been completed.

Copying methods

There are two general approaches to transferring the image of the hard disc in your old PC onto the hard disc in the new PC. The obvious

7 Hard disc cloning

approach is to do a direct copy from one disc to the other. This method has the advantage of speed, but it can be difficult to implement in practice. It is definitely less than ideal for those with limited experience of dealing with computer hardware.

The second approach is to do a normal backup of the existing system onto CDRs or some other form of removable mass storage media. This backup can then be restored to the new PC. This avoids the need to delve into the hardware of your PCs, but it could take a large amount of time if there are many gigabytes of data to backup and restore. It could also require a large number of discs, although the cost of CDRs and some other types of mass storage media are now quite low. The actual cost involved could be quite modest. Although it could be time consuming, using this method could still be much easier and quicker than installing and setting up everything from scratch.

On the face of it, an advantage of the backup and restore method is that it gives you a backup of the system that can be used to restore the customised system and some data if disaster strikes. Unfortunately, having restored the system it would then be necessary to redo any changes to the driver software and settings that were enforced by the different hardware in the new PC. Having properly set up the new PC by whatever means, it is a good idea to do a complete backup of the system so that it can be quickly and easily returned to a fully working installation.

Bear in mind though, that a backup on (say) CDR discs will only provide a so-called "snapshot" of your PC at the time the backup copy was made. Going back to the system stored on the CDRs with not restore any data made since the backup was taken. It is therefore important to take copies of data produced since the main backup was taken, so that the data can be copied onto the hard disc once the basic setup has been restored. The program used to make the image of the hard disc might have facilities to backup data made thereafter. If not, it is up to you to ensure that copies of any important data are made onto CDRs or some other form of external storage.

In this chapter the direct copying method and the backup/restore approach will both be described. Copying directly from one hard disc to another can only be recommended for those having some experience at dealing with PC hardware. Copying from one hard disc to another should not be too difficult if you have done a few PC upgrades or repairs yourself. Those with no previous experience of upgrading or repairing PCs would be well advised to use the indirect method of disc cloning.

Fig.7.1 The initial screen of the Backup and Restore Wizard

Windows Backup

Using backup programs it is possible to save selected files, directories, directory structures, or the entire contents of the hard disc drive. It should also be possible to make an image of the hard drive so that an exact and bootable copy of it can be restored at a later date. I think I am correct in stating that every version of Windows is supplied complete with a backup program that has the imaginative name of Backup. Although basic compared to some programs of this type it does the job well enough for many users. Its lack of popularity possibly stems from the fact that the equivalent facility in Windows 3.1 was something less than user friendly, causing many users to look elsewhere for a backup utility.

Perhaps the problem is simply that the Backup program is a part of Windows that has often been easy to overlook. Anyway, the Windows XP version is more user-friendly and powerful than previous versions, and it is definitely there if you seek it out. With the Professional version of Windows XP it is installed by default, but with the Home Edition it will probably have to be installed from the Valueadd\Msft\Ntbackup folder on the installation CD-ROM. The Backup program might be absent if

7 Hard disc cloning

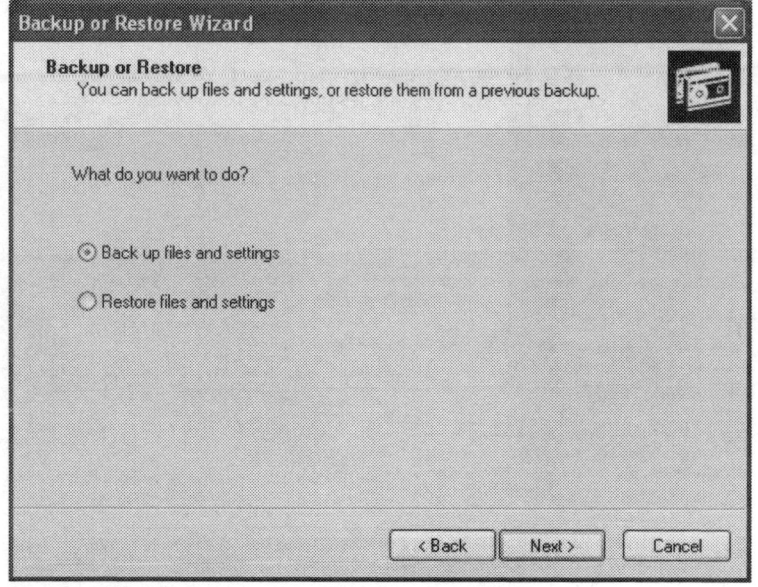

Fig.7.2 This window provides Backup and Restore options

you have a preinstalled version of Windows XP, but in such cases the computer is sometimes bundled with an alternative backup utility.

Backup Wizard

Once installed, the Backup program is run by selecting All Programs from the Start menu, followed by Accessories, System Tools, and then Backup. By default the Backup Wizard (Figure 7.1) runs when this program is launched, and initially it is probably best to use the wizard. Operate the Next button to move on to the first stage of using the Backup Wizard (Figure 7.2). Here you have the choice of backing up or restoring data, but it is obviously necessary to produce a backup disc before anything can be restored. Therefore, initially the Backup radio button has to be selected.

The next window (Figure 7.3) is used to select the data to be backed up. The top option produces a backup of the My Documents folder plus some system settings and cookies. The second option is similar, but it provides a backup of the documents and settings for all users. Using

Hard disc cloning 7

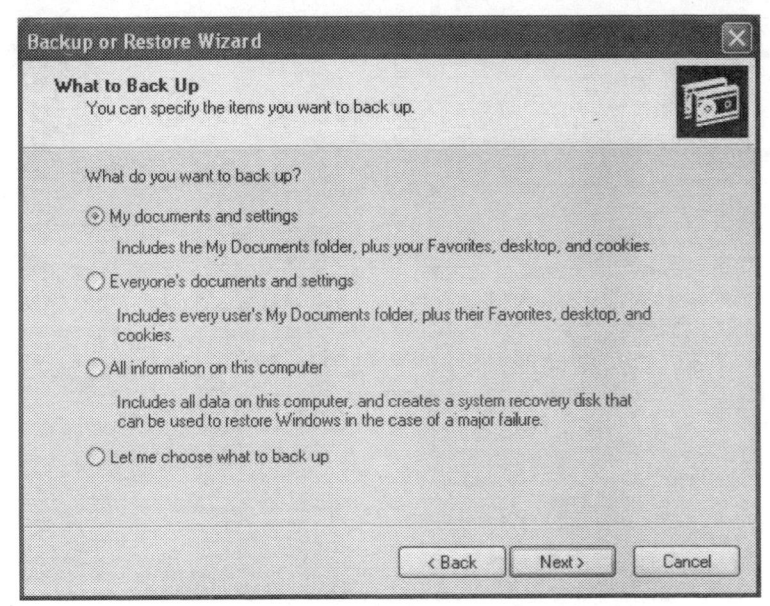

Fig.7.3 Use this window to choose what you wish to backup

the fourth option produces a file browser (Figure 7.4) so that the user can select the files and folders that will be backed up. The third option is the one that is of most use if the system becomes seriously damaged or the hard disc becomes unusable. It permits the whole system to be backed up, and it also produces a recovery disc that enables it to be easily restored again. In fact the restoration process is almost totally automated. It is the third option that will be considered here.

The next window (Figure 7.5) enables the backup drive to be selected, and a variety of drive types is supported. These include Zip discs, local hard drives, and some tape backup systems. Unfortunately, CD writers are not supported. Sometimes there are ways of working around this limitation, but it is probably best to opt for a third party backup program if you wish to use CD-R or CD-RW discs to hold the backup files. Use the menu or the Browse option to select the correct drive. If you select a device that is not supported by the Backup program, an error message will be produced when Windows tries to create the file. This will simply state the backup file could not be produced.

7 Hard disc cloning

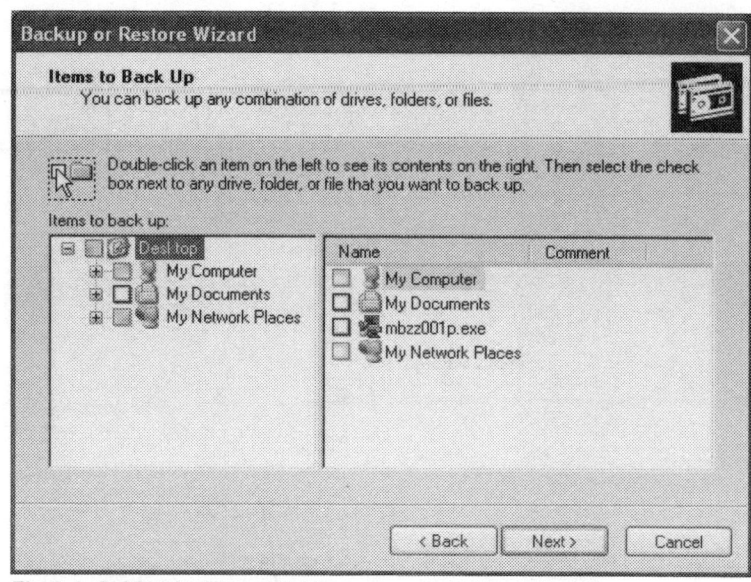

Fig.7.4 Select the files or folders you would like to backup

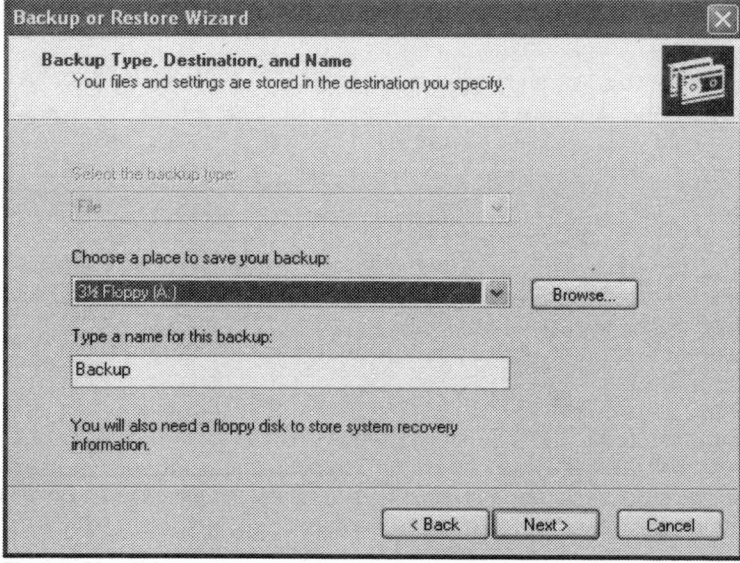

Fig.7.5 Use this window to select the backup drive

Hard disc cloning 7

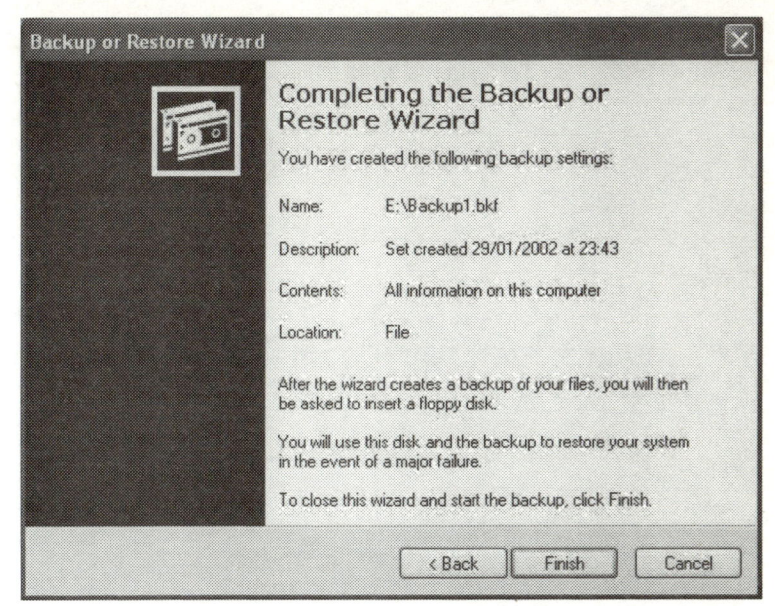

Fig.7.6 The selected options are shown before the backup is started

In the current context the best option is to use some form of external storage device as the backup device. This makes it easy to transfer the backup to the new PC. If an internal hard disc drive is used as the backup drive, there is the complication of installing it in the old PC and then transferring it to the old PC. The old system would then have to be restored on the new PC from this backup copy. This has to be regarded as doing things the hard way, and directly cloning the old drive from the new one would be quicker and easier.

By default, the backup file is called "Backup" but the name in the textbox can be changed to any valid filename. Operating the Next button moves things on to a window like the one in Figure 7.6. This shows the options that have been selected, and provides an opportunity to change your mind or correct mistakes. Use the Back button if it is necessary to return to earlier windows to make changes, or operate the Finish button to go ahead and make the backup file.

A window like the one shown in Figure 7.7 will appear, and this shows the progress made by the Backup program. It provides an estimate for the time remaining until the task is completed, and this will vary massively

7 Hard disc cloning

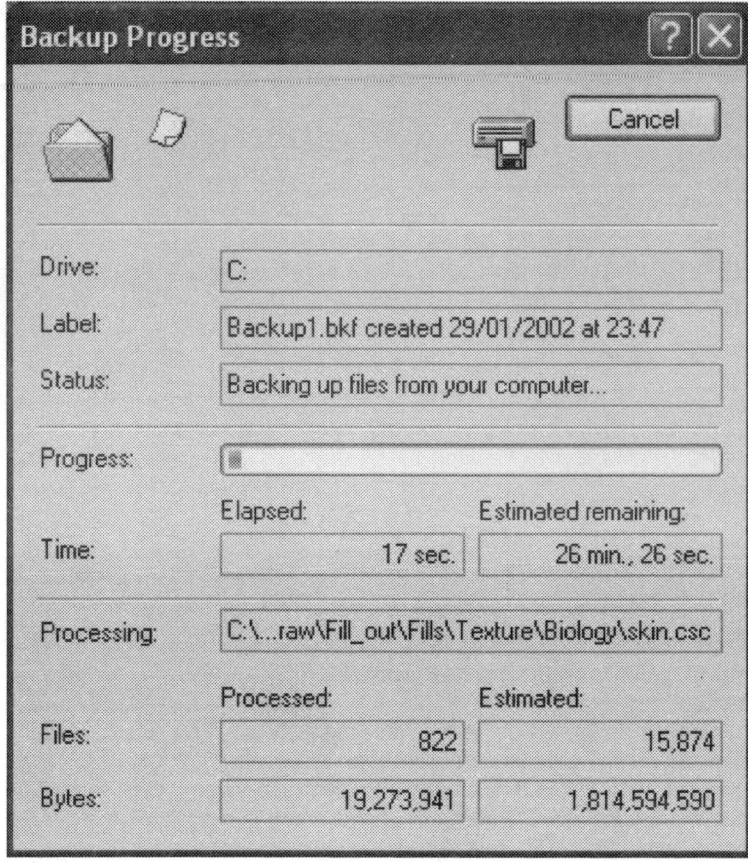

Fig.7.7 This window shows how the backup is progressing

depending on the amount of data to be saved and the speed of the backup device. With many gigabytes of data to backup it is definitely a good idea to use a fast backup device. With a slow backup device the process can take many hours, and in the current context it would probably not be the best way of handling things. Where appropriate, you will be prompted when a disc change is necessary. With multiple disc backups, always label all the discs clearly. You will then be able supply the right disc each time when restoring the backup copy. Do not worry if the size of the backup file is substantially less than the total amount of data on

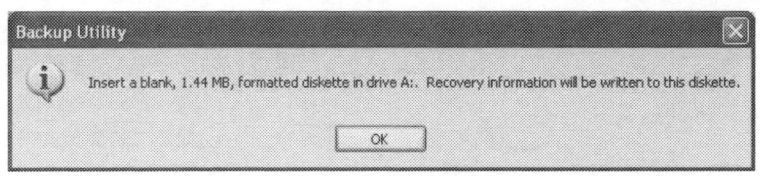

> **Backup Utility**
>
> (i) Insert a blank, 1.44 MB, formatted diskette in drive A:. Recovery information will be written to this diskette.
>
> [OK]

Fig.7.8 The floppy disc is inserted into drive A: when this message appears

the hard disc. The backup file is probably compressed, or perhaps no backup copies are made of standard files that are available from the Windows XP installation disc. Anyway, it is quite normal for the backup file to be significantly smaller than the source.

The message shown in Figure 7.8 will appear towards the end of the backup process. The floppy disc is needed to make an automatic recovery disc. This disc is needed in order to restore the system from the backup disc, and the backup is relatively little value without the recovery disc. Insert a 1.44-megabyte floppy disc into drive A: and

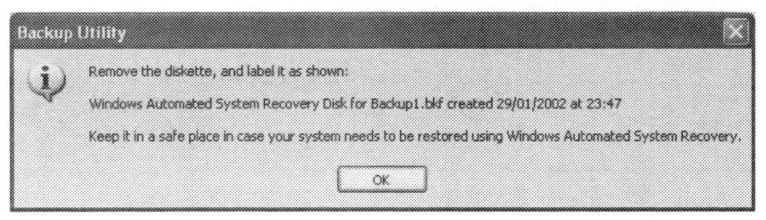

> **Backup Utility**
>
> (i) Remove the diskette, and label it as shown:
>
> Windows Automated System Recovery Disk for Backup1.bkf created 29/01/2002 at 23:47
>
> Keep it in a safe place in case your system needs to be restored using Windows Automated System Recovery.
>
> [OK]

Fig.7.9 This message indicates that the backup has been completed

operate the OK button. The message of Figure 7.9 appears once the recovery disc has been completed. Label the disc as indicated in the message and store it safely. The automatic recovery process is not possible without this disc. Finally, you are returned to the Backup Progress window (Figure 7.10), which should indicate that the backup has been completed successfully.

Restoring

There is little point in having a means of restoring the backup that requires the computer to boot normally into Windows XP, since this will often be impossible when the restoration feature is needed. The Windows XP

7 Hard disc cloning

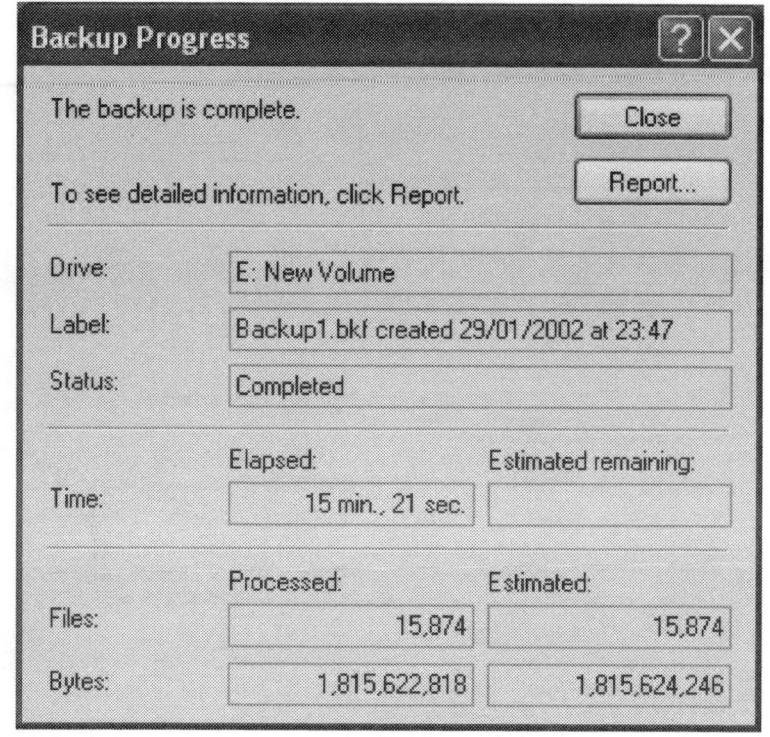

Fig.7.10 The Backup Progress window provides some statistics

method of restoring a full system backup is more straightforward than the Windows 9x equivalent. In fact the Windows XP method makes the process about as simple as it is ever likely to be. It is termed the Automated System Recovery, and it certainly lives up to the automated part of its name.

The first task is to boot from the Windows XP installation CD-ROM, and the BIOS must be set to boot from the CD-ROM drive before it tries to boot from the hard disc drive. If the boot sequence is the other way around, the computer will probably start to boot from the hard drive and the CD-ROM drive will be ignored. With the installation disc in a CD-ROM drive and the correct BIOS settings, a message saying "Press any key to boot from CD-ROM" will appear for a few seconds at the beginning of the boot process. Press any key while this message is displayed or the computer will revert to booting from the hard disc drive.

Hard disc cloning 7

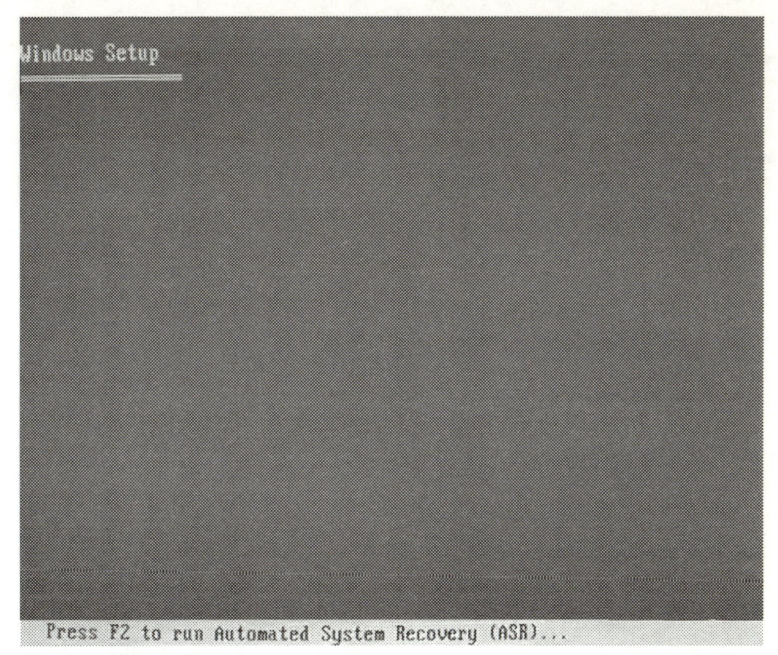

Fig.7.11 Press F2 as soon as this message appears at the bottom of the screen

Messages appear along the bottom of the screen when the computer starts booting from the CD-ROM. Look for the one that says "Press F2 to run Automated System Recovery (ASR)", as in Figure 7.11. This message only appears briefly, so press F2 as soon as you see it. After some disc activity the message of Figure 7.12 will appear, and the floppy disc produced when backup was made must be placed in drive A:. Then press any key to continue. The restoration process requires little intervention from the user, but it is as well to keep an eye on things in case something goes wrong.

First the partition used by the system is formatted, which effectively wipes all data from the partition. If there is any data on the disc that has not been backed up, it is lost forever at this stage. With a brand new PC this will presumably not be a problem, but remember to backup any data if you should happen use the new PC prior to installing the clone of the old system. The formatting will take several minutes, and an onscreen "fuel gauge" shows how far the formatting has progressed (Figure 7.13).

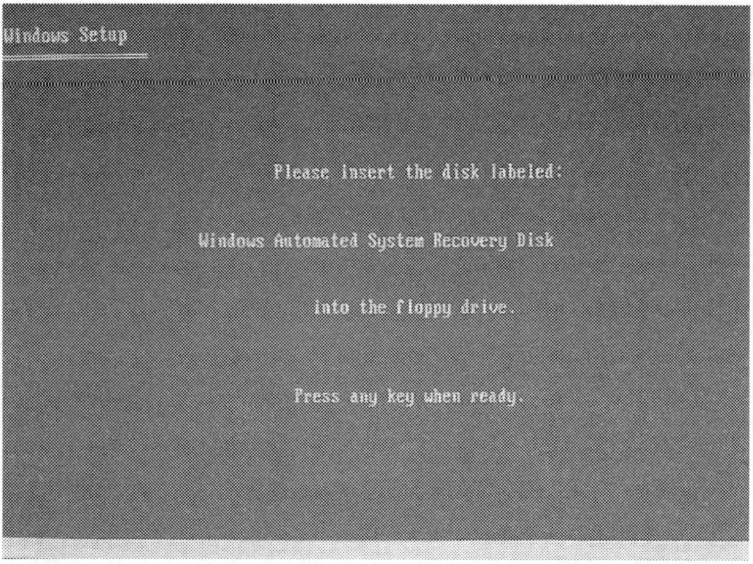

7 Hard disc cloning

Fig.7.12 Insert the backup disc in drive A: when this screen appears

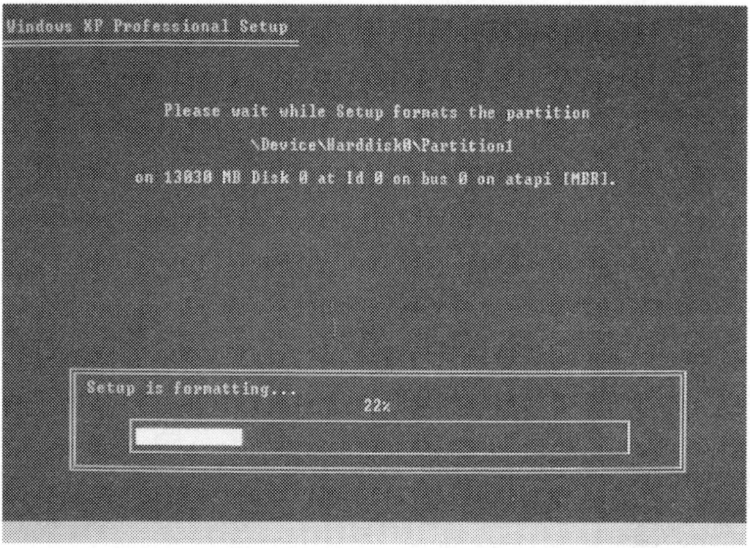

Fig.7.13 Formatting erases all the data stored in the partition

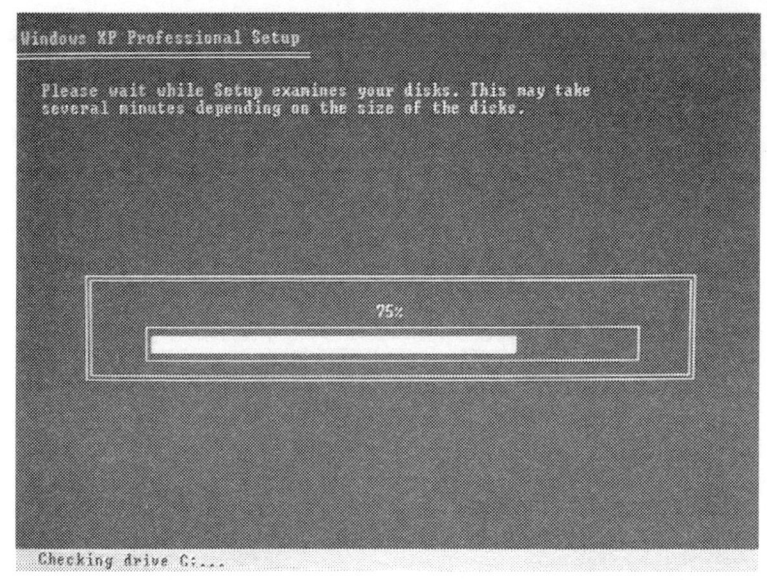

Fig.7.14 The Setup program briefly examines the disc drives

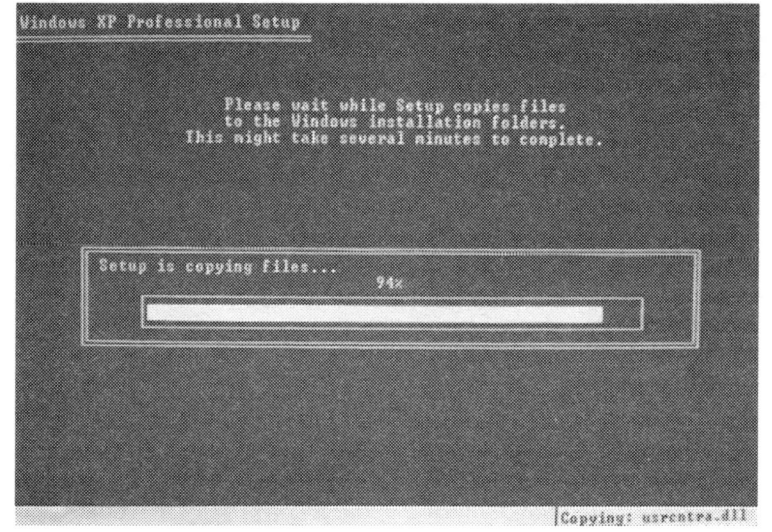

Fig.7.15 It takes a few minutes for the installation files to be copied

7 Hard disc cloning

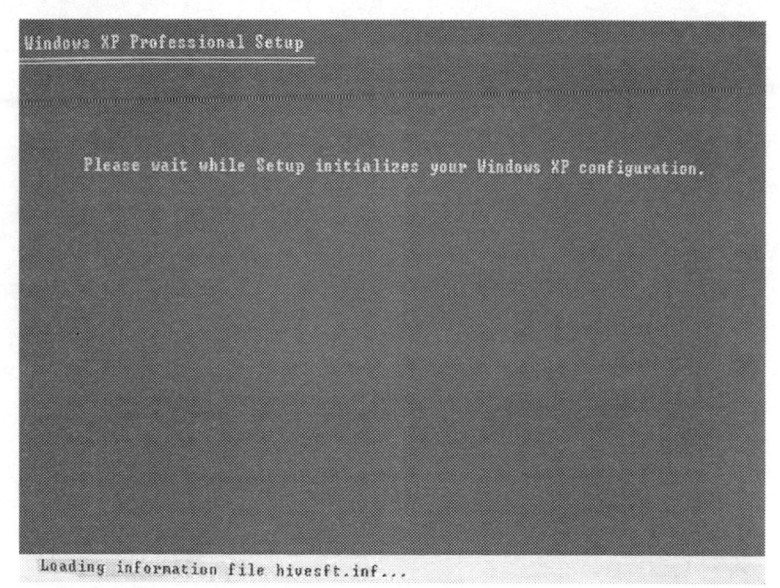

Fig.7.16 More files are loaded

A similar gauge is used at the next screen (Figure 7.14), where the program examines the disc drives. This is usually much quicker than formatting the restoration partition, and this screen may only appear for a second or two. A further gauge appears on the next screen (Figure 7.15), and here the program copies some files to the hard disc. Next the program loads some more files (Figure 7.16). The computer is then rebooted, and it will reboot after several seconds even if you do not press Return to restart the computer (Figure 7.17). Note that the Automated System Recovery disc in drive A: must be removed at this stage. The computer might try to boot from this disc if it is left in the drive, and this would probably prevent the computer from rebooting properly. If the reboot should stall because the disc is left in drive A:, removing it and pressing any key should get things underway again.

Windows is installed on the appropriate partition when the computer has rebooted, and a screen like the one in Figure 7.18 shows how the installation is progressing. Once Windows has been installed, the Automated System Recovery Wizard runs (Figure 7.19). This does not require any input from the user though, and you can just sit back and watch while your files are restored to the hard disc (Figure 7.20). Once

Hard disc cloning 7

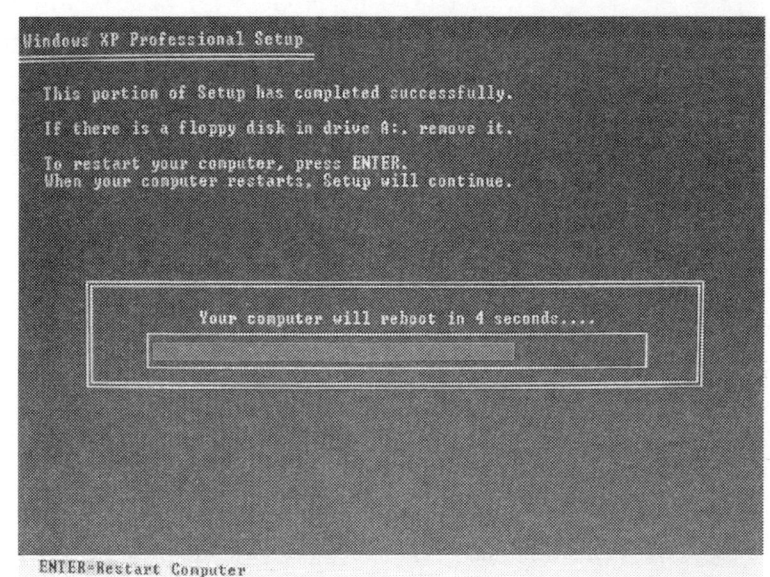

Fig.7.17 The computer will reboot automatically if the Return key is not operated

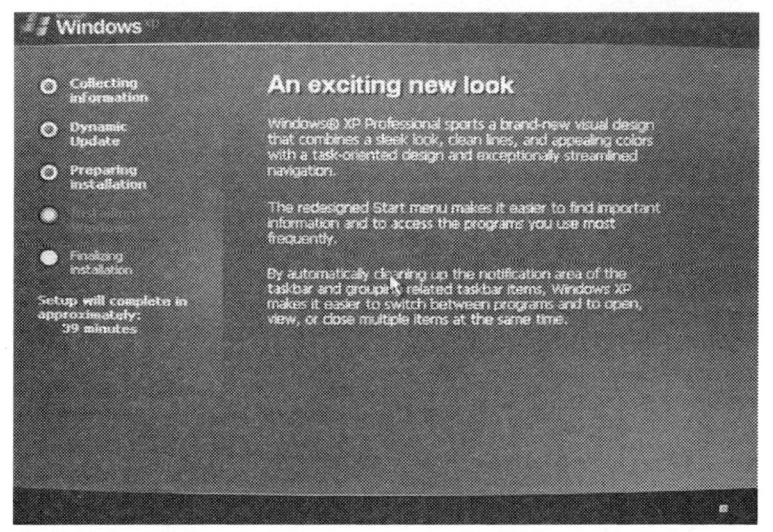

Fig.7.18 Installation starts in earnest once the PC has rebooted

7 Hard disc cloning

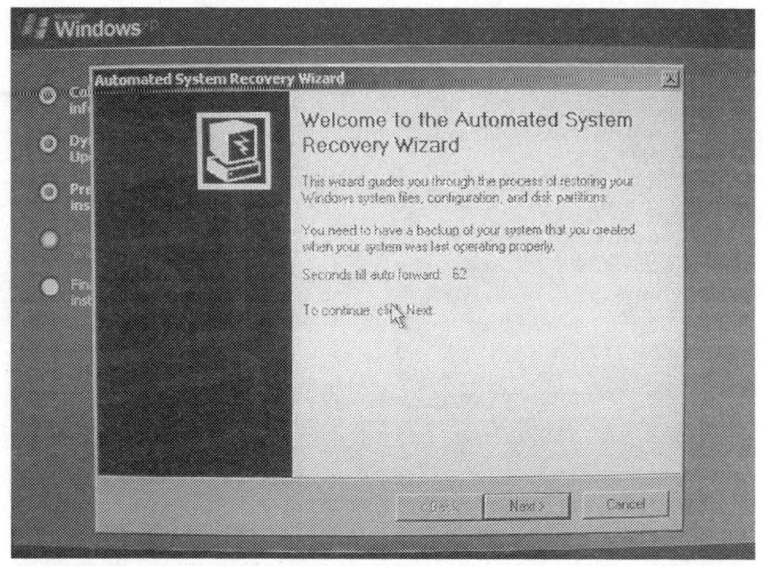

Fig.7.19 The Automatic System Recovery Wizard runs automatically once Windows XP has been installed

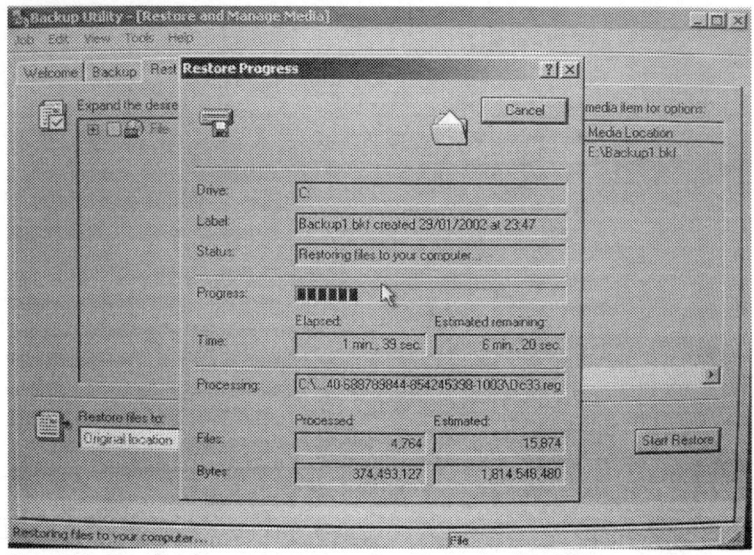

Fig.7.20 The Restore program copies file to the hard disc

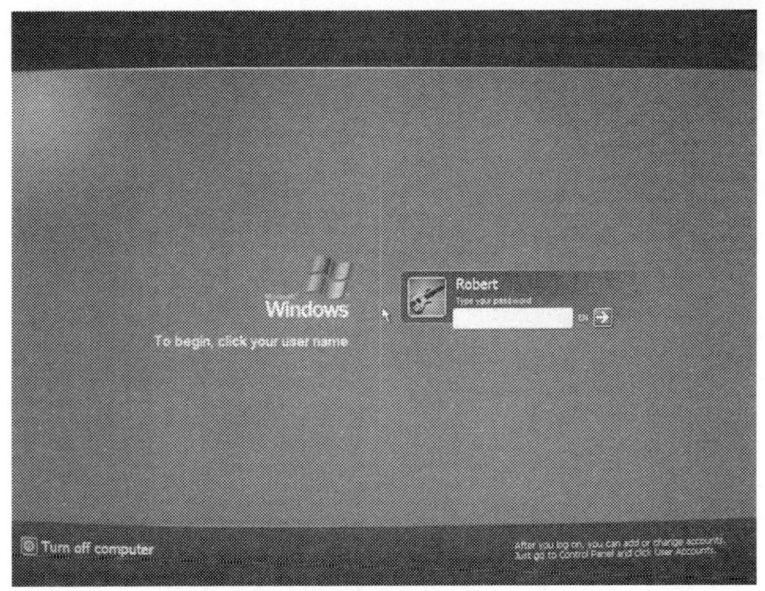

Fig.7.21 Login normally once the files have been restored

this has been completed, the usual login screen (Figure 7.21) appears. You login using your normal password, and the computer then goes into Windows XP (Figure 7.22). This should look the same and have the same settings that were in force when the backup was made. Any programs, data, etc., on the partition that was backed up should be included in the restored installation.

In practice there might be one or two minor differences to the system. In particular, any passwords or other data hidden on the disc in "invisible" files will not have been placed on the backup disc. Files of this type are very secure, but they are "invisible" to the Backup program. It is therefore unable to save them in the backup file. This should no be of any major consequence, because the relevant applications can be run, and the passwords (or whatever) can be stored on the hard disc again.

Of course, any data files produced after the backup was made will not be automatically restored to the hard disc. They must be restored manually. Clearly it is a good idea to make the transfer as soon as the backup has been made so that any manual restoration of data can be avoided. As explained later in this chapter, differences between the

7 Hard disc cloning

Fig.7.22 Windows XP should now look and work as before

hardware of the old and new computers will make it necessary to install drivers for the new hardware. Some of this might be done automatically by Windows, but in most cases some manual intervention will be needed.

Advanced mode

Use of the Backup Wizard is not mandatory, and the Backup program can be controlled directly by the user. Start running the program in the usual way, but left-click on the "Advanced mode" link. This produces a window like the one in Figure 7.23, and two of the buttons give access to more advanced versions of the Backup and Restore wizards. The third button provides another route to the Automated System Recovery Wizard. The tabs near the top of the window provide manual operation of the Backup and Restore programs, and to scheduled backups.

Figure 7.24 shows the window for the Backup program. The files and folders to be backed up are selected in the upper section of the window, while the backup drive and filename are entered in the textbox near the bottom left-hand corner of the window. The usual Browse facility is

Hard disc cloning 7

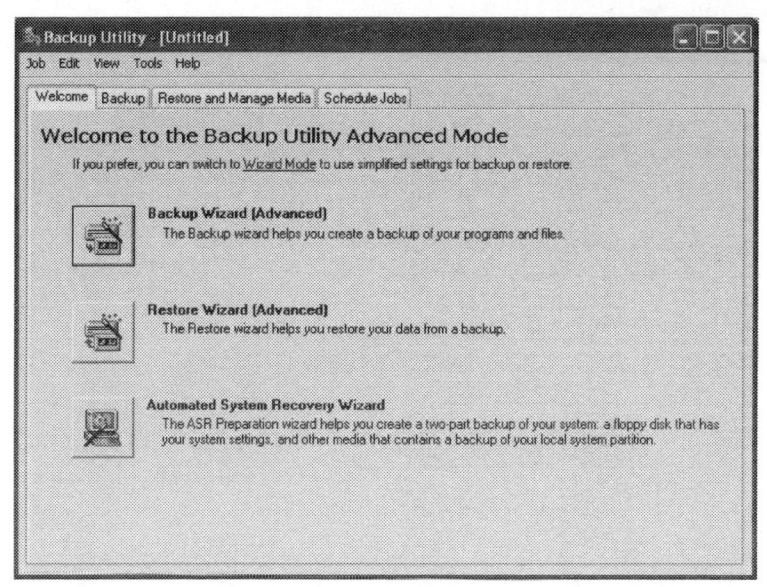

Fig.7.23 Three options are offered when Advanced Mode is selected

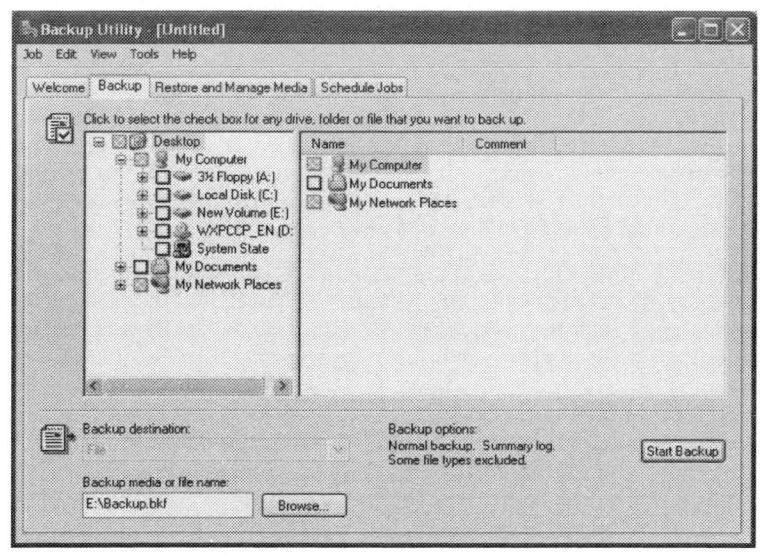

Fig.7.24 The source program enables the source files to be selected

7 Hard disc cloning

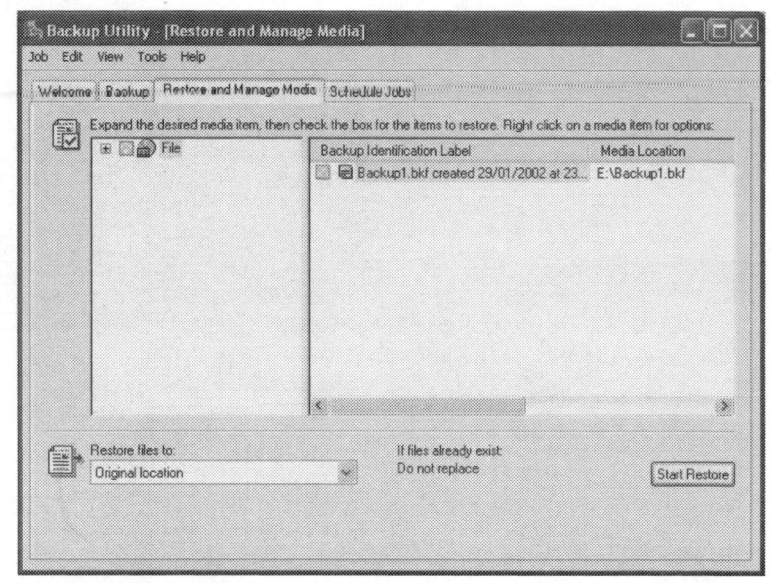

Fig.7.25 The Restore program enables the backup file and destination to be selected

available here. Once everything has been set up correctly, the Start Backup button is operated. The Restore program's window is shown in Figure 7.25. The upper section of the window is used to locate and select the backup file, and the lower section is used to select the destination of the restored backup. This will usually be the original location, but it can be restored to an alternative location. Once everything has been set correctly, the Start Restore button is operated.

The Backup and Restore programs are not difficult to use, and are certainly more user friendly than the equivalent functions in some previous versions of Windows. However, for a complete backup and restore operation it is probably best to use the wizards. These should ensure that you do not overlook anything, and that backup files can always be successfully restored. The Automated System Restore facility makes the whole process very easy. In the past it has been slow, difficult, and expensive to implement this type of backup system. With this facility and a suitable drive fitted to the PC, the entire system can be backed up quite rapidly and then restored to the new PC.

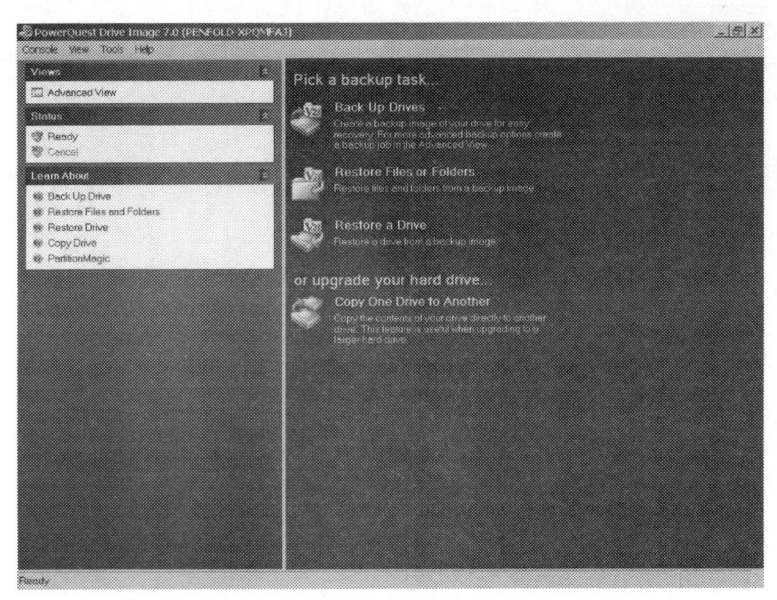

Fig.7.26 *The initial screen of Drive Image*

Alternatives

For most users it is preferable for the backup to be made onto CD-R or CD-RW discs, since a suitable drive is included as standard on most modern PCs. Unfortunately, this needs a third party backup program. CD-RW discs have the advantage that they can be reused, but they are more expensive than CD-R discs. Another point to bear in mind is that an ordinary CD-R can be read using any form of CD-ROM drive without the need for any special drivers. The same is not true for CD-RW discs, or for DVD media. Most other forms of high capacity disc also need special driver software in order to get the disc drive functioning properly.

On the face of it, this is not a problem when you have a fully working computer that is will boot into Windows properly. It is only problematic if you have a computer that will not boot into Windows and you are trying to revert to a backup copy of the installation. In practice it is possible that the backup program will not run under Windows when making a backup and restoring it. Instead, programs of this type often reboot into MS-DOS or the program's own simple operating system when making or restoring a backup. You need to do some careful checking before

7 Hard disc cloning

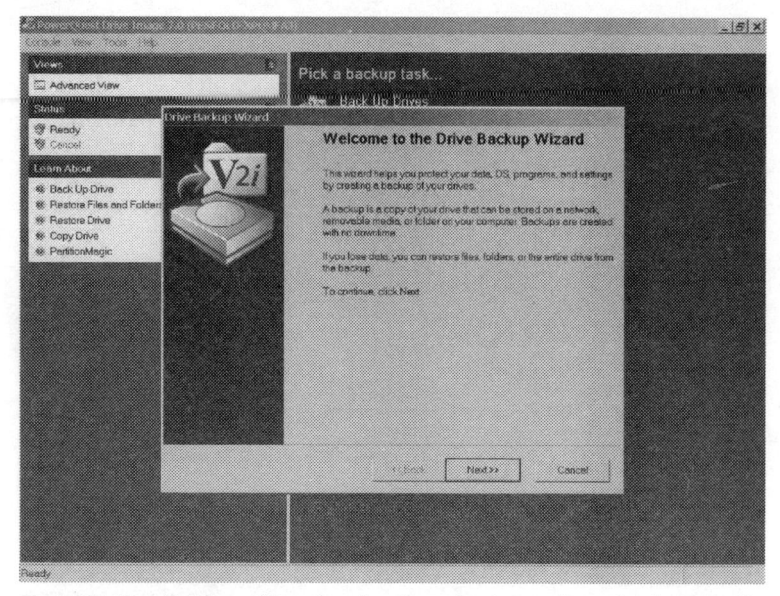

Fig.7.27 The Backup Wizard makes it easier to produce the backup file

using any form of backup that relies on anything other than a standard form of disc for storage. There is no point in carefully producing sets of backup discs if the image they contain can never be transferred to another PC or restored to the old PC if its installation comes to grief. If in doubt, stick to standard disc types, which really means a hard drive or CD-Rs.

Power Quest's Drive Image 7 is used in this example of producing a backup to CD-Rs and restoring it. There are other backup programs that no doubt work very well, and I am using Drive Image 7 here simply because it is the one installed on my PC. When this program is run under Windows XP it is possible to produce a backup from within Windows. As pointed out previously, not all backup programs operate in this way. With some backup programs and when using older versions of Windows, it is often necessary to exit Windows and reboot into a MS/DOS or a similar operating system. This ensures that Windows does not restrict access to any files on the disc, but is obviously not very convenient. However, with most modern backup programs the reboot into a basic operating system is taken care of by the program, and the process may well be completely automatic.

Hard disc cloning 7

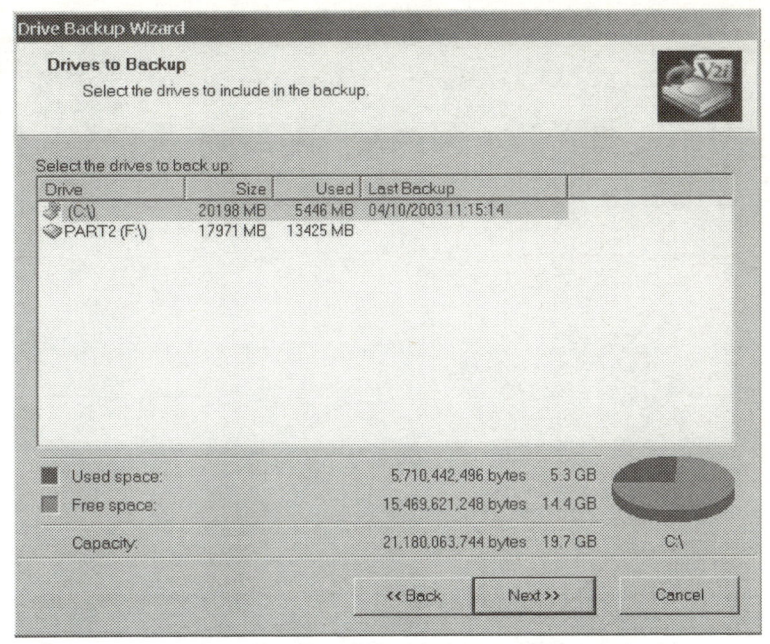

Fig.7.28 The first step is to select the drive to be backed up

Launching Drive Image 7 produces the initial screen of Figure 7.26, and the Backup Drives option is selected in order to start the backup process. Making the backup is made easier by the use of a wizard (Figure 7.27). Operating the Next button moves things on to the window of Figure 7.28 where the drive to be backed up is selected. Actually, in a multi-drive system it is possible to select more than one drive if desired. In this example only the boot drive (drive C) will be backed up, because the other hard drive is itself a backup drive.

The destination for the backup is selected at the next window (Figure 7.29). The Local File option is used when the backup will be onto another hard disc drive. Obviously the Network option is used where the PC is on a local area network (LAN) and the backup will be placed elsewhere on the network. In this case the backup will be made to a CD-RW drive, so it is the third option that is selected. The required drive can be selected using the usual file browser if the Browse button is operated.

7 Hard disc cloning

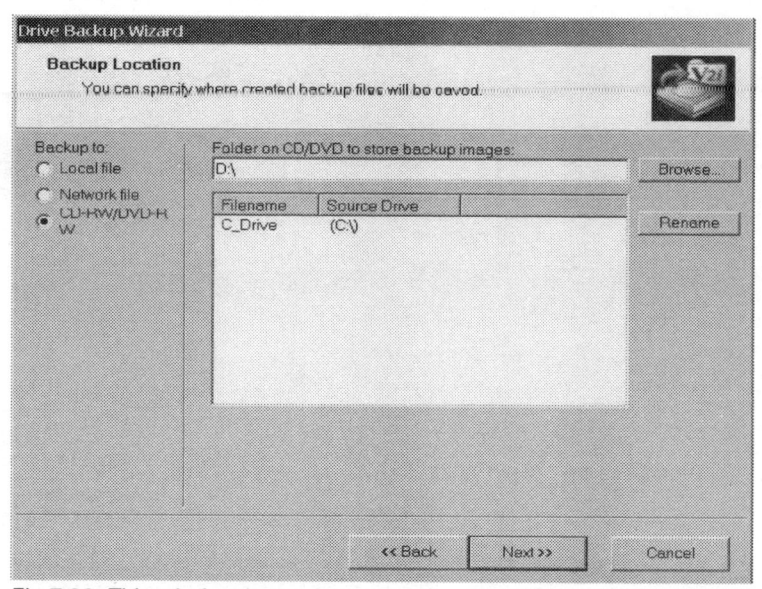

Fig.7.29 This window is used to select the destination for the file

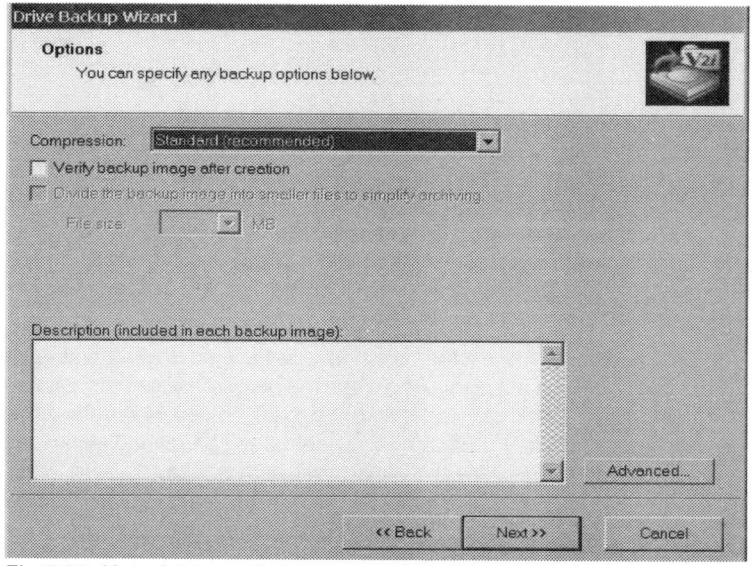

Fig.7.30 Next the type of data compression is selected

Hard disc cloning 7

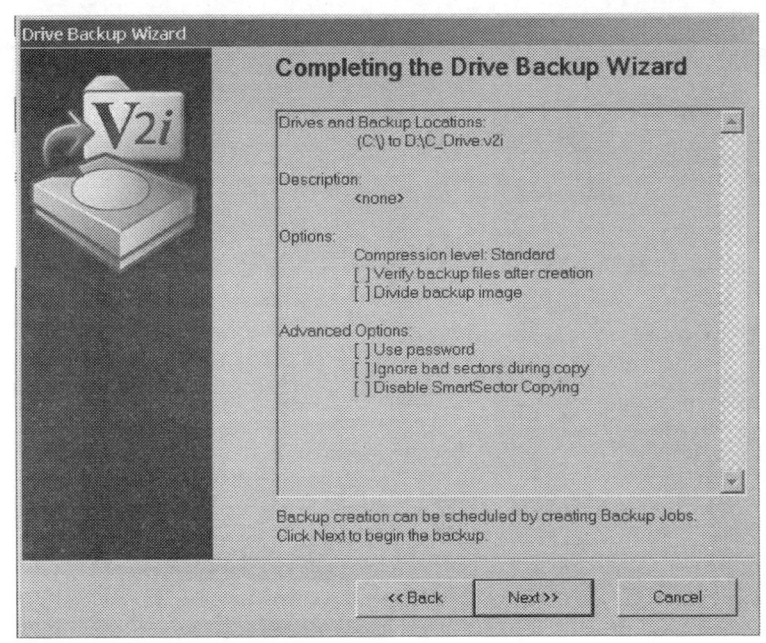

Fig.7.31 This window shows a summary of the selected options

The required type of compression is selected at the next window (Figure 7.30). Compression enables more data to be placed on each disc in the backup set. When making a backup to CD-R or CD-RW discs the compression has the beneficial effect of reducing the number of discs required. With a relatively slow backup device it can also reduce the time take to create and restore a backup. Some types of data compress more readily than others. Some files on the disc may already be in compressed form and will not be amenable to further compression. On the other hand, things like program and simple text files will often compress by a factor of three or more. In practice compression roughly halves the number of discs required. Opt for the Standard method of compression. If required, a description can be added in the textbox in the bottom section of the window (e.g. "Full backup of drive C").

The next window (Figure 7.31) simply provides a summary of the options that have been selected. If necessary, use the Back button in order to return to an earlier window so that a correction can be made. Then use the Next button to return to this window. When the right options have

7 Hard disc cloning

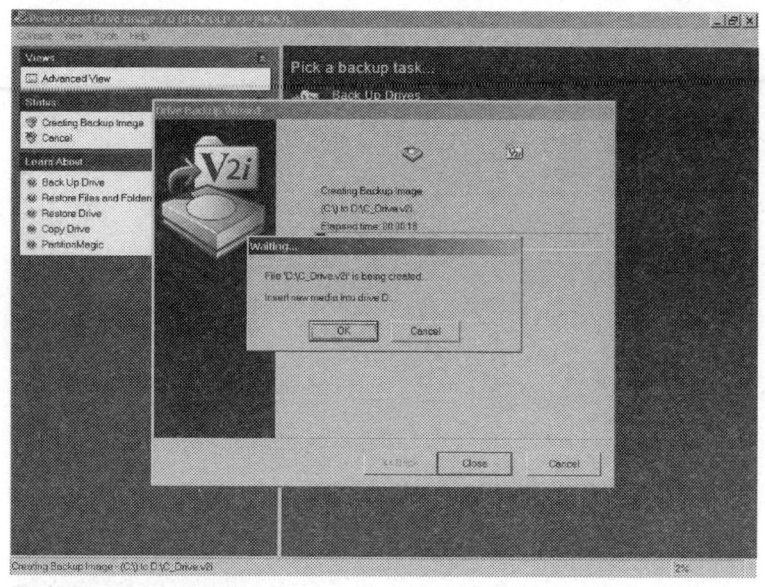

Fig.7.32 Insert the first disc and get the backup under way

been selected, operate the Next button to start making the backup. Eventually a message like the one in Figure 7.32 will appear, and the first disc is then placed in the CD-R drive and the backup process starts.

A full backup is likely to require about six to twelve discs, and could obviously require substantially more than this if a large and almost full disc is being backed up. The program will prompt you each time a change of disc is required. Carefully number each disc because they must be used in the correct order when the backup is used to restore the contents of the hard disc drive. Eventually the program will indicate that the backup has been completed, and you are then returned to the main screen of Drive Image 7.

Restoring

There are facilities in the main Drive Image program for restoring data, and this route is usable provided the destination PC already has Windows and Drive Image installed. In its intended backup application, the system will often be unbootable or the hard disc might be blank. Drive Image

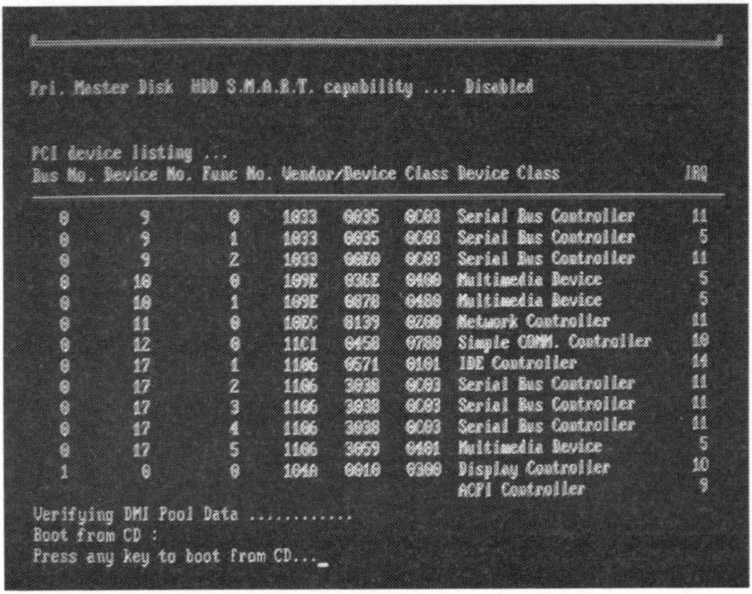

Hard disc cloning 7

Fig.7.33 Press F2 if this message appears

therefore offers the alternative method of booting the computer using either a set of boot discs made using the program or via the Drive Image installation CD. These days practically any PC can be booted from a suitable CD-ROM, and it is probably best to use this method where the option is available. Note that this option is not available with earlier versions of Drive Image and with some other backup programs. With some PCs it might be necessary to alter the BIOS settings in order to boot from a CD-ROM. The computer's operating manual should explain how to do this. Using a set of bootable floppy discs is one way around the problem if you do not feel confident about dealing with the BIOS Setup program.

The computer will usually start booting from the CD-ROM or bootable floppy disc without any preamble. Depending on the BIOS used in your PC, it might instead try to boot into any operating system on the hard disc unless you press a key at the right time. If a message like the one in Figure 7.33 appears at the bottom of the screen, immediately press F2 or whatever key the message indicates. The PC should then boot into the operating system contained on the bootable CD-ROM or floppy disc.

7 Hard disc cloning

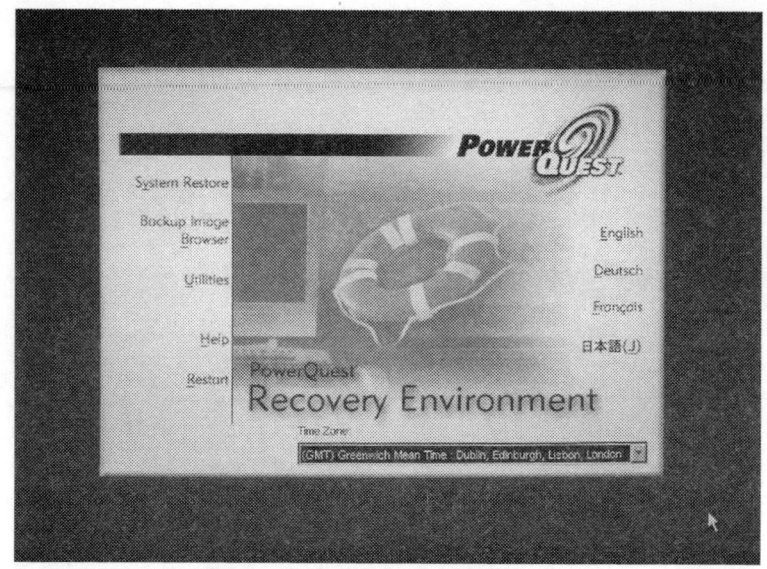

Fig.7.34 The options available from the recovery program

This will usually be MS-DOS or something similar, but the Restore program usually includes a simple Windows style user interface. Some messages will probably appear on the screen giving a brief explanation of what the program is doing. When using the floppy disc method there will usually be a boot disc and one or more program discs. Change discs when prompted. The boot process can be quite long, because the Restore program will probably scan the PC's hardware so that it can operate with the mouse, etc., you are using. Where appropriate, networking might be activated so that the hard disc can be restored from an image file stored on another PC on the network.

Eventually the boot and loading processes should come to an end and a screen like the one of Figure 7.34 will then be obtained. A number of options are available, but it is the System Restore facility that is needed in this case. Selecting this option moves things on to the screen of Figure 7.35 where the radio buttons provide two options. One is used to restore only certain files or folders, and the other is used to restore a complete drive. It is obviously the latter that is required here. The next screen (Figure 7.36) provides the option of restoring one drive or multiple drives. In this example it is only drive C that is being restored, so the single drive option is selected.

Hard disc cloning 7

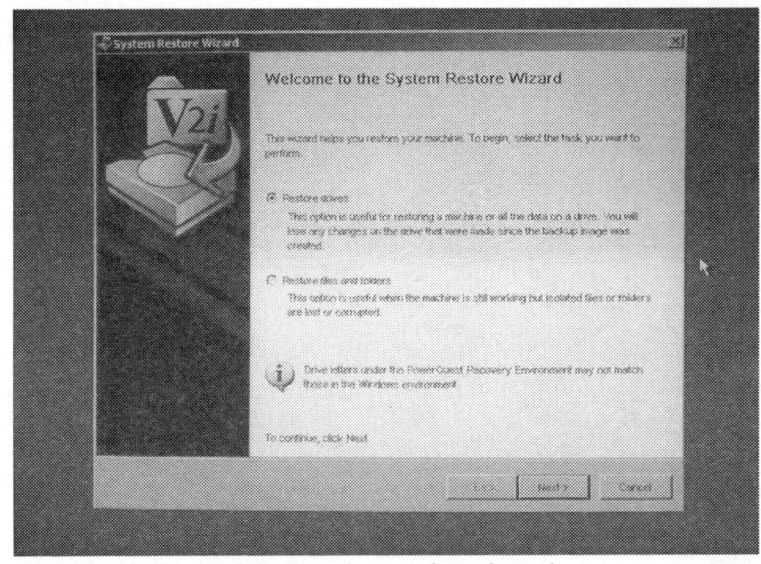

Fig.7.35 A full or partial restoration can be selected

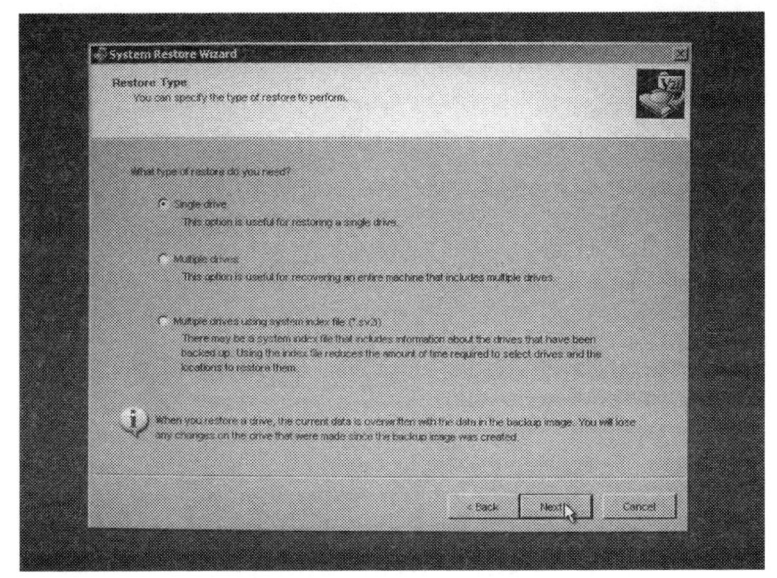

Fig.7.36 One or multiple drives can be restored

7 Hard disc cloning

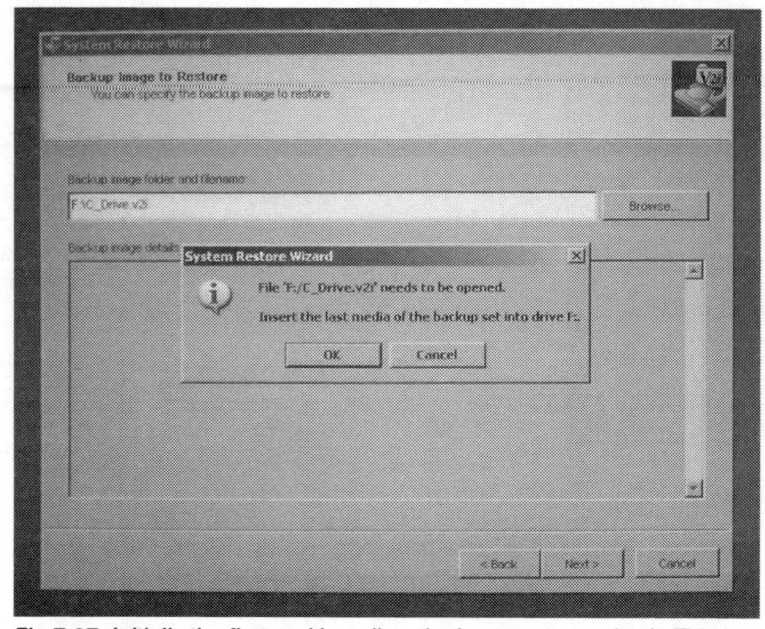

Fig.7.37 Initially the first and last discs in the set are required. This is quite normal for programs that use multi-disc sets

At the next screen the backup file is selected, and a file browser is available via the Browse button. Having pointed the program to the drive containing the first disc in the backup set, a message like the one in Figure 7.37 will appear. It is normal for programs that use multi-disc sets to require the first and last discs in the set before proceeding. After the program has read from the last disc you will be prompted to replace the first disc in the drive. You should then have something like Figure 7.38, with the screen showing the location of the backup file and some basic information for it.

Figure 7.39 shows the next screen, and here you must select the drive to be restored. You must be careful to choose the right disc if there is more than one hard drive or partition. Restoring the image to the wrong drive or partition will destroy all the data contained on that drive or partition. Once the right selection has been made it is just a matter of following the onscreen prompts, and changing discs when necessary. The discs in the backup set must be numbered so that you can provide them in the correct order. The program will detect the error if you should get the

Hard disc cloning 7

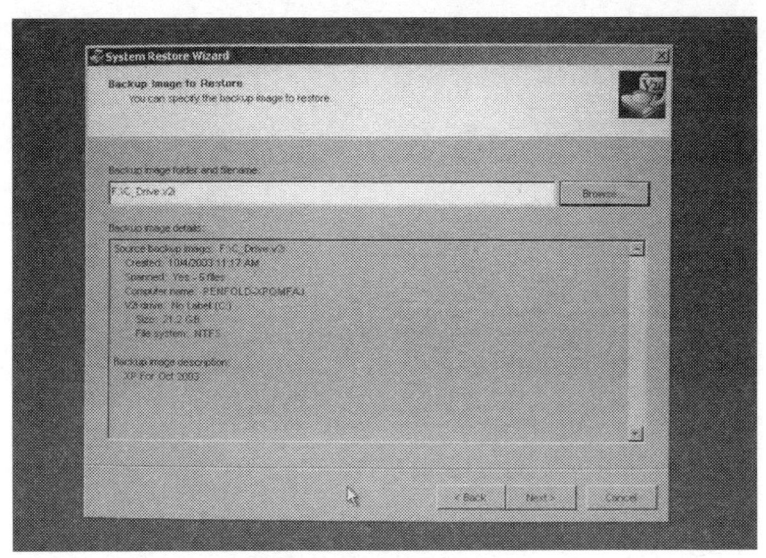

Fig.7.38 This screen shows the backup's location, etc.

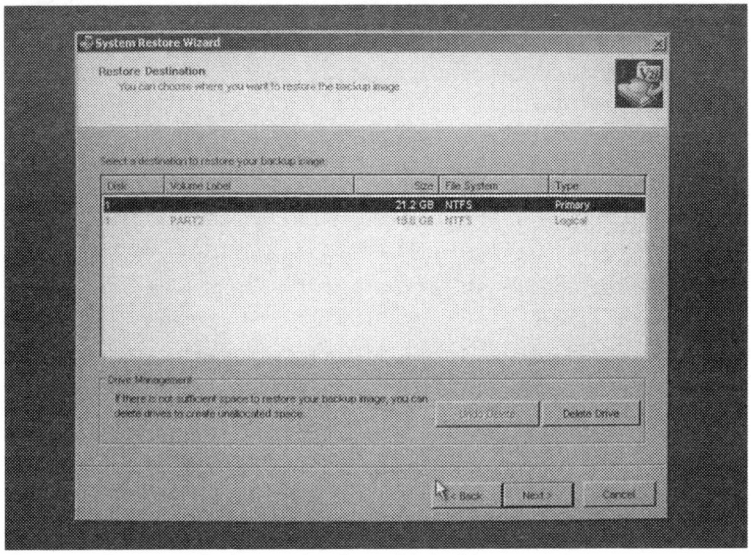

Fig.7.39 Be careful when selecting which drive to restore

7 Hard disc cloning

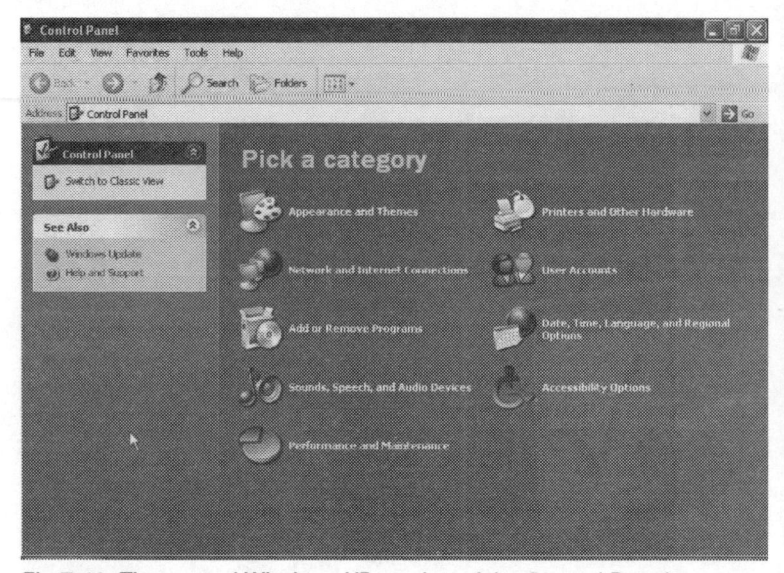

Fig.7.40 The normal Windows XP version of the Control Panel

discs muddled-up, and it will not proceed until the right disc has been placed in the drive.

Once the restoration has been completed, remove the boot CD-ROM or floppy disc from the drive and reset the computer. It should then boot into the newly restored operating system. When restoring a backup to the same PC, everything should operate exactly as it did at the time the backup was made. There can be minor problems such as stored passwords being lost, and automatic login facilities failing to work in consequence, but in general things will operate as they did previously.

This is not the case when using a cloned system on a different PC. Windows will detect the changes in hardware and will try to install the appropriate drivers in place of the existing ones. Some of the changes might be made automatically, but the various driver discs supplied with the PC will be needed in order to install most of the hardware's support software. The Windows installation CD might also be requested at some point in the proceedings. It will not always be clear which of the driver discs is required, but Windows is unlikely to accept the wrong disc. If necessary, you can use trial and error to find the right disc.

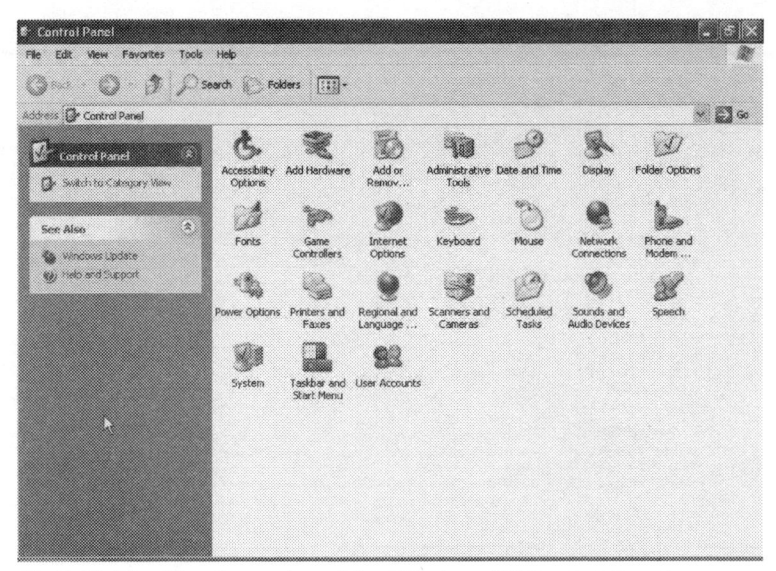

Fig.7.41 The Classic version of the Windows XP Control Panel

Tidying up

Provided you can get the PC to boot into Windows you should be in business. Even at this stage it is likely that not all the drivers will have been installed successfully. In some respects the computer will be much as if Windows had just been installed from scratch. It will be working after a fashion, but a bit more effort will be needed in order to get it functioning at optimum performance. The big difference is that once any final installation work has been completed, you should have a PC that has all the application programs and data installed, and it will be ready for use.

It is virtually certain that proper video drivers will be needed. Even if the graphics card can be set to use high resolutions and colour depths, it is almost certainly using a generic driver rather than one designed specifically for the video card in use. Although high resolutions and colour depths can be used, the video system will probably be very slow in operation. There might be other items of hardware that Windows has missed completely, or has been unable to identify.

The first step is to go into Device Manager to look for any obvious problems with the hardware. First choose Control Panel from the Start

7 Hard disc cloning

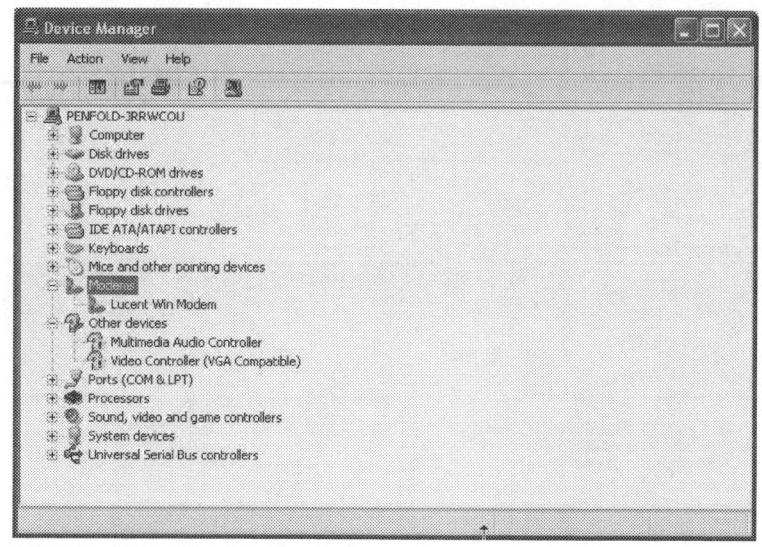

Fig.7.42 Check Device Manager for hardware problems

menu, which in Windows XP will produce a window like the one in Figure 7.40. In Windows XP it is advisable to left-click on the Switch to Classic View link, which will change the window to the familiar Control Panel layout of Figure 7.41. This provides easy access to the hardware settings and other useful facilities. Launch the System Properties window by double-clicking on the System icon and then operate the Hardware tab. Left-click the Device Manager button, and a window similar to the one in Figure 7.42 will appear.

The important thing to look for here is the yellow exclamation marks that indicate problems with the hardware. In this case the hardware appears to be trouble-free apart from the integrated audio system and the video card. It is worthwhile double-clicking some of the other entries to check that the hardware has been identified correctly. Internal modems can sometimes be troublesome, although the modem has been correctly identified and installed in this case.

If there are any problems with the main hardware on the motherboard, it is advisable to install the drivers for this hardware first. The main hardware means things like the IDE controllers and the PCI slots, and not integrated hardware such as audio systems and network adapters. Where

Hard disc cloning 7

appropriate, your PC should have been supplied with a CD-ROM containing the device drivers for the hardware on the motherboard. Next the video drivers should be installed, and then the device drivers for other hardware such as audio systems and modems.

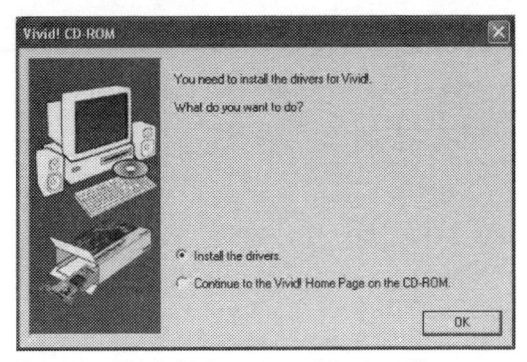

Fig.7.43 The initial screen of the installer program

Driver installation

Windows has built-in facilities for adding device drivers, but few manufacturers seem to make use of these. Most hardware has its own installation program. This copies the device drivers onto the hard disc,

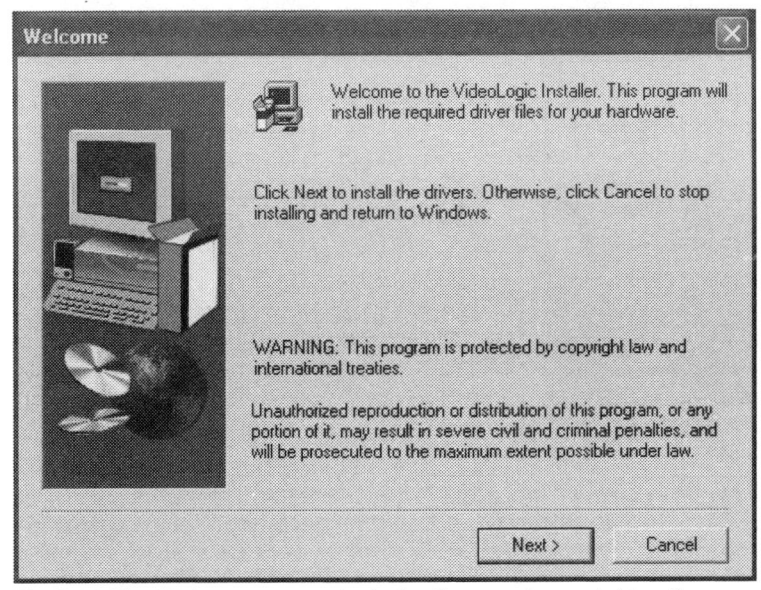

Fig.7.44 The Welcome screen includes the usual copyright notice

7 Hard disc cloning

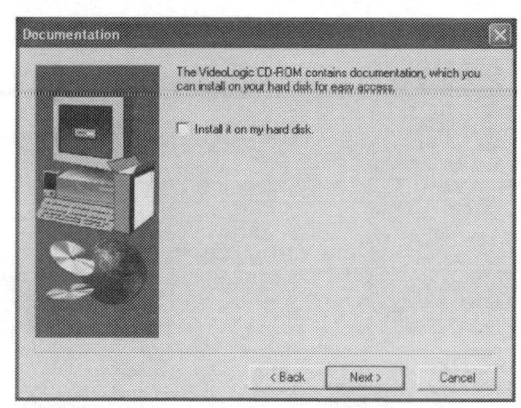

Fig.7.45 It is advisable to load the manual

and then the computer is restarted. The device drivers are installed automatically during the boot process. The instruction manuals for the hardware should give concise information about installing the device drivers, and the installation instructions should be followed "to the letter". Note that the installation process is not always the same for each version of Windows, so make sure that you follow the right instructions and use the correct device drivers. Windows XP will almost certainly display a warning

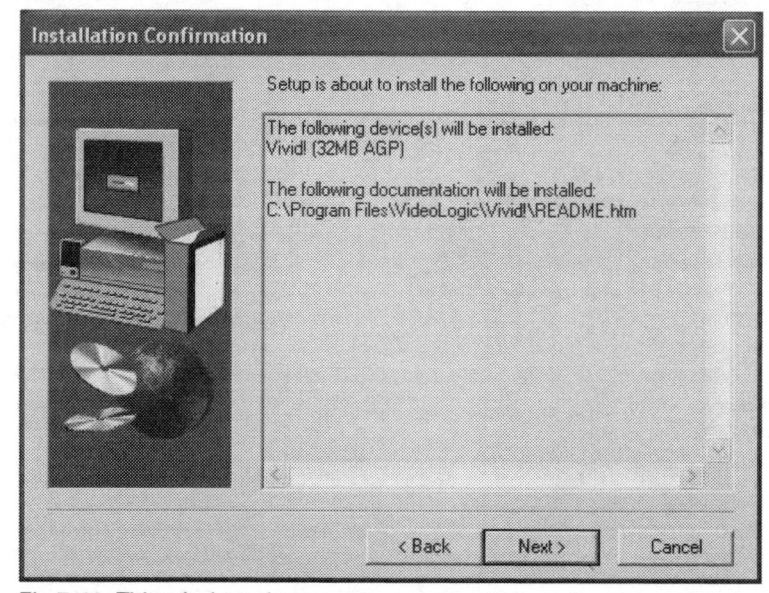

Fig.7.46 This window gives you an opportunity to review the options that have been selected

Hard disc cloning 7

message if you try to install inappropriate device drivers, but this will probably not happen when using an earlier version of Windows.

In this example there is no need to install any additional drivers for the motherboard's system hardware, so the first task is to install the proper video drivers. The installation CD-ROM will usually auto-run, as in this case, and Figure 7.43 shows the initial window. This provides two options, and in this case is clearly the default "Install the drivers" option that is required. The next window (Figure 7.44) has the usual copyright notice, and operating the Next button moves things on to the licence agreement. Left clicking the Yes brings up a further window (Figure 7.45), and this one gives the option of loading the on-disc instruction manual onto the hard disc. Since the manual is unlikely to require much disc space it is a good idea to install the documentation onto the hard disc when this option is available.

The next window (Figure 7.46) simply shows the options that have been selected, and assuming everything is in order it is just a matter of left-clicking

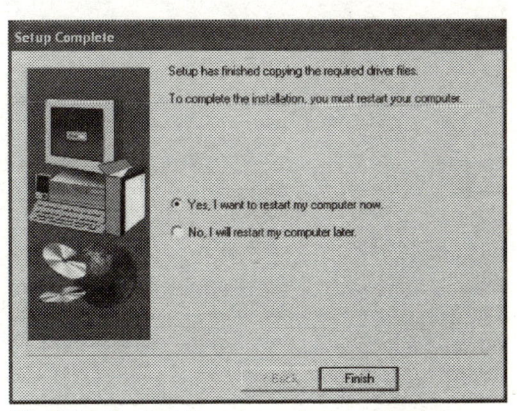

Fig.7.47 Restart the computer to complete the installation

the Next button to start installation. Once the files have been copied to the hard disc, the window of Figure 7.47 appears. It is definitely advisable to restart the computer immediately rather than waiting until later. This finalises the installation of the drivers and gives you an opportunity to check that they are functioning correctly. Installing several sets of device drivers and then restarting the computer might seem to be a more efficient way of doing things, because the computer only has to be restarted once. In practice it is not a good idea and is simply inviting problems.

Video settings

Windows will almost certainly detect that a new video card has been installed, and it will then produce the message window of Figure 7.48

7 Hard disc cloning

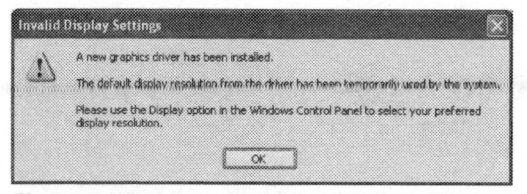

Fig.7.48 Windows will almost certainly detect the newly installed video card

when the reboot has been completed. Operate the OK button and then adjust the video settings using the Display Properties Window (Figure 7.49), which will be

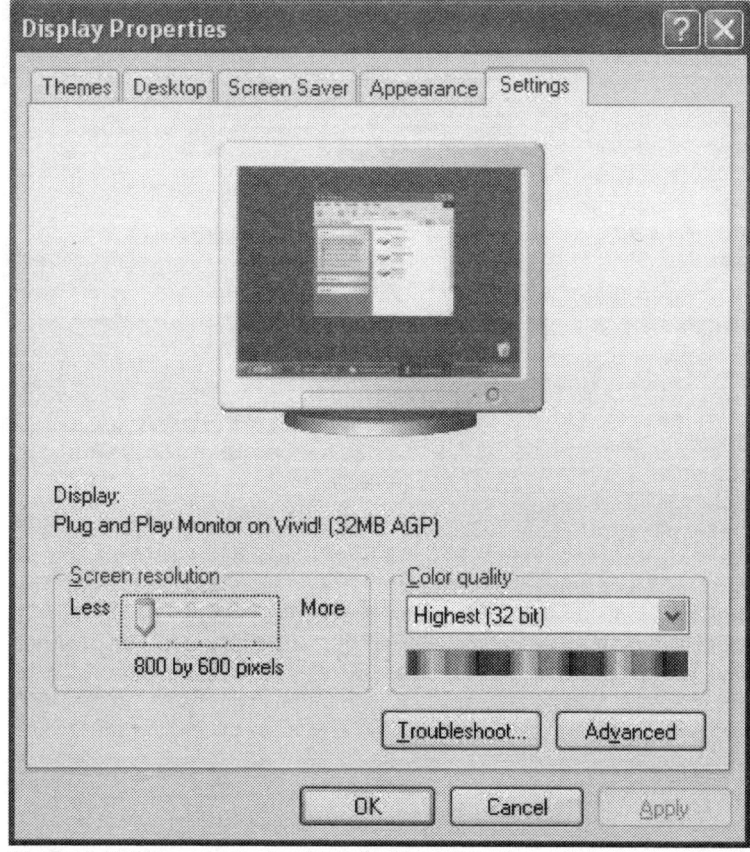

Fig.7.49 Set the required colour depth and screen resolution

Hard disc cloning 7

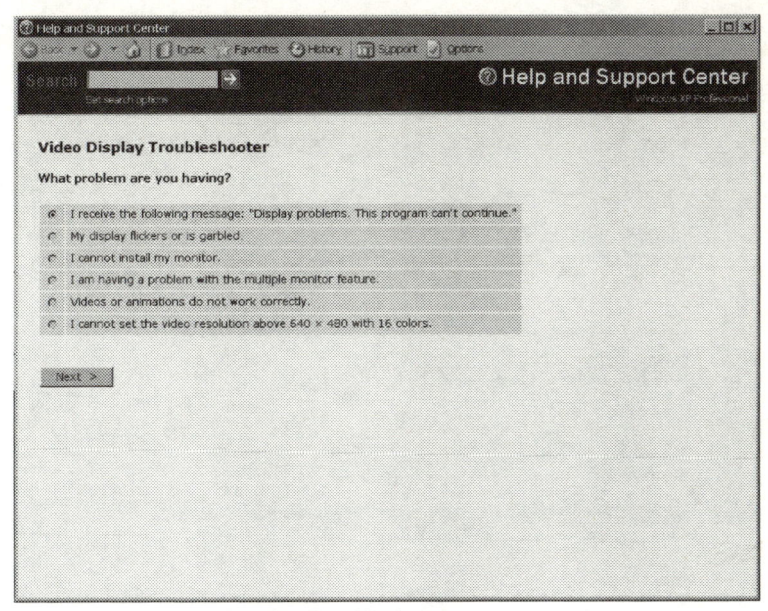

Fig.7.50 The Video Display Troubleshooter

launched automatically. If the newly installed video card is not detected by Windows, the display settings window must be run manually. Launch the Control Panel, double-click the Display icon, and then operate the Settings tab in the window that appears.

Having set the required screen resolution and colour depth, operate the Apply button. It is likely that Windows is overestimating the abilities of the monitor if the screen goes blank or produces an unstable image. The screen should return to normal in a few seconds though. One way of tackling the problem is to operate the Troubleshoot button, which launches the Video Display Troubleshooter (Figure 7.50). By going through the questions and suggested cures it is likely that the problem would soon be solved. However, the most likely cause of the problem is Windows setting a scan rate that is too high for the monitor, and this is easily corrected.

First set the required screen resolution again, and then left-click the Advanced button to bring up a window like the one in Figure 7.51. Next, operate the Monitor tab to switch the window to one like Figure 7.52.

7 Hard disc cloning

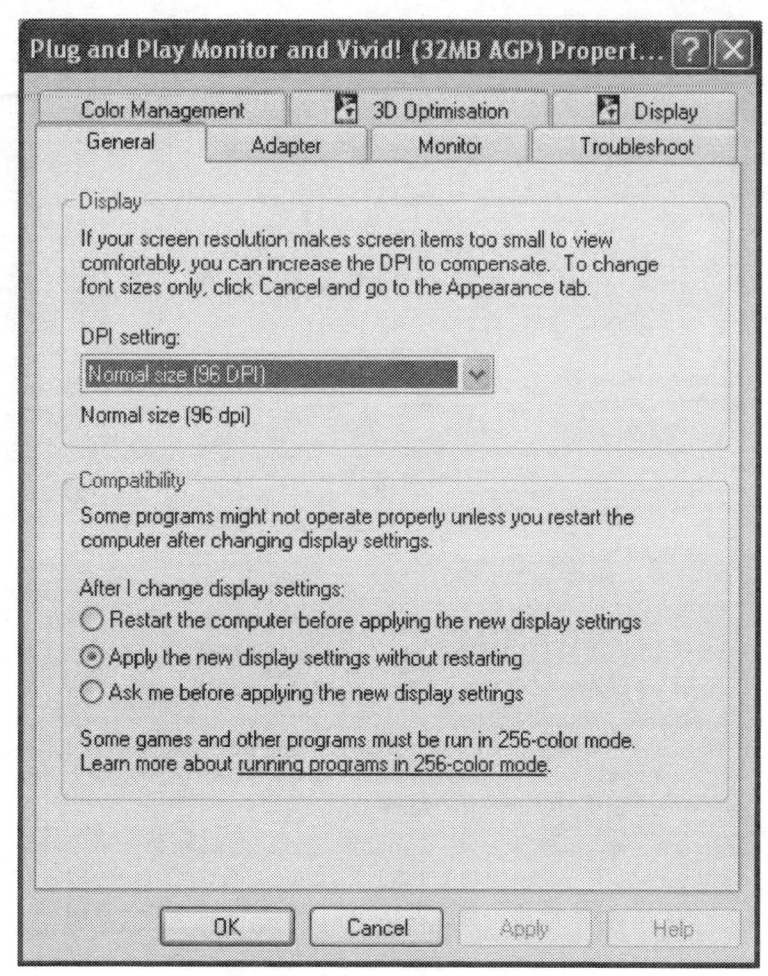

Fig.7.51 The Advanced Settings window

Activate the Screen refresh rate menu, and choose a lower rate than the one currently in use. In this example the rate was reduced from 85 hertz to 75 hertz. Left-click the Apply button and observe the screen. With luck, this time a small window like the one shown in Figure 7.53 will be visible on the screen. If so, operate the Yes button to keep the new scan rate. If not, wait for a proper display to return and then repeat this process

Hard disc cloning 7

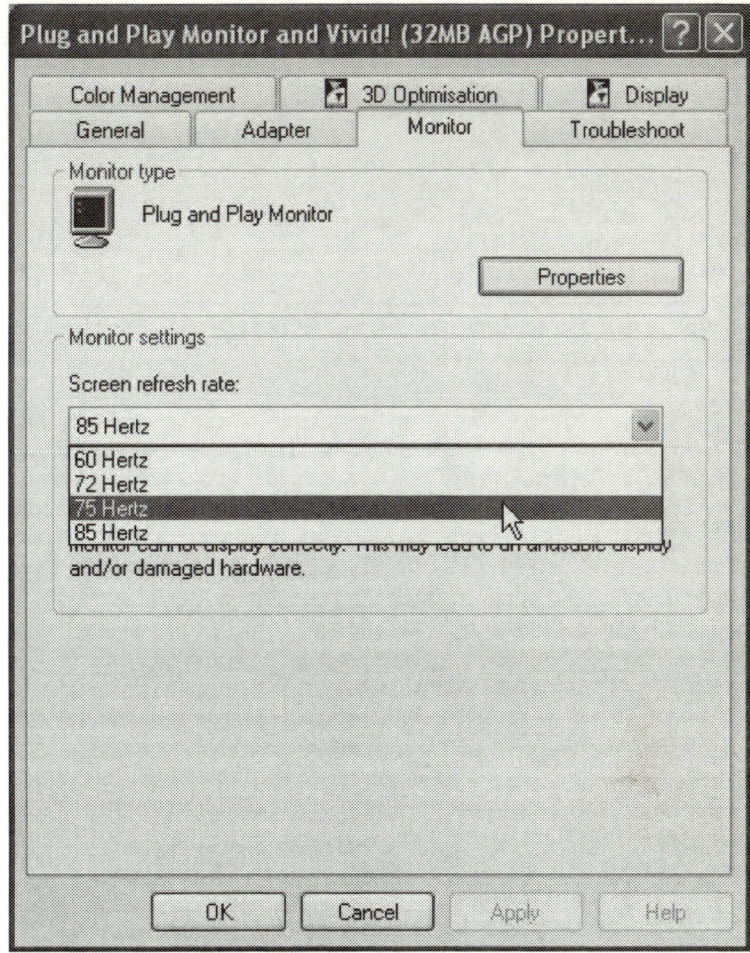

Fig.7.52 A lower scan rate should cure the problem

using an even lower scan rate. Note that the maximum scan rate for a monitor generally reduces as the screen resolution is increased. Consequently, the higher the screen resolution used, the lower the scan rate that will have to be set.

Obviously the installation of the video card will vary slightly from one card to another, but most cards are installed using the general method

7 Hard disc cloning

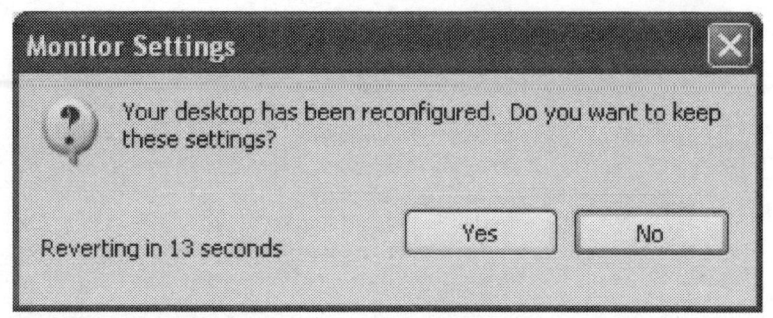

Fig.7.53 If this pop-up appears, operate the Yes button to retain the new settings

outlined here. With the video card installed and set up correctly, any further drivers that are needed can be installed. In this example it was only necessary to install the device drivers for the audio system. Device Manager then showed no problems with any of the hardware (Figure 7.54), indicating that the hardware was all installed successfully. The PC is therefore ready for use again, and all the applications programs should run normally.

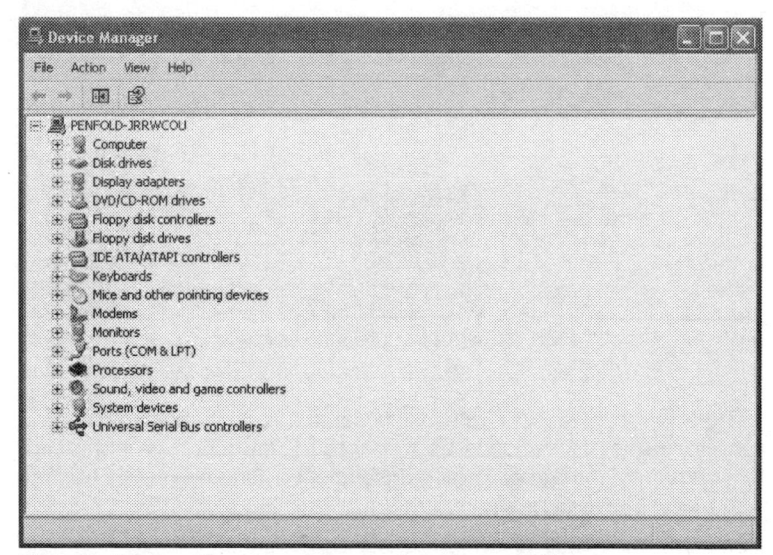

Fig.7.54 Device Manager shows no hardware problems

Direct cloning

Directly copying from one hard disc to another is the quickest way of cloning a hard disc, but it normally requires one hard disc to be removed from its PC and transplanted into the other PC. There is a possible way around this in that it is possible to obtain USB gadgets that enable an ordinary internal IDE hard drive to be used as an external USB type. This offers an easy way of copying the old disc, which still needs to be removed from the old PC, but does not have to be installed inside the new PC. It can simply be fitted into the USB drive cradle and plugged into a USB socket on the new PC. In order to obtain a reasonable reading rate from the old drive it is essential to use a drive cradle that supports USB 2.0, and to use a USB 2.0 port on the new PC.

If the copying is accomplished by temporarily relocating one hard drive to the other PC, it does not matter too much which drive is moved to the other PC and back again. It is probably a little easier to move the new disc into the old PC, clone the old disc onto it, and then move it back to the PC. Whichever disc is temporarily transplanted, it will be necessary to remove the lids or side panels of the PCs. Some delving around inside the computers will then be needed.

The process involved is not particularly difficult, but unless you are reasonably practical and have some experience with computer hardware it would probably be best not to attempt this method. Also, if the new PC has a serial ATA hard disc interface, it is not a good idea to attempt direct cloning unless you have the necessary expertise to handle the task. The two discs will have different interfaces, and direct cloning from one to another is less straightforward than copying from one IDE drive to another.

Assuming you feel confident enough to go ahead with the upgrade yourself, the first task is to open the PCs to determine the current configurations. With older PCs the top and two sides of the case are in one piece, and are released by removing four or six screws at the rear of the unit. Be careful, because there will probably be other screws here that hold other things in place, such as the power supply unit. With the right screws removed, the outer casing should pull away upwards and rearwards, but it will probably take a certain amount of force to pull it free.

More modern cases have removable side panels, and with most types these are again held in place by four or six screws at the rear of the unit. Both panels must be removed in order to give full access to the drive bays. If your PC has one of the more unusual case styles it will be necessary to carefully examine the exterior in order to "crack" it.

7 Hard disc cloning

A modern PC has the hard disc interface on the motherboard rather than provided by an expansion card. In fact, there are two hard disc interfaces on the motherboard, or possibly four on a modern PC. These are known as IDE interfaces, and this simply stands for integrated drive electronics. In other words, most of the electronics for the hard disc drive controller is built into the drive itself. At one time the IDE interfaces were strictly for hard disc drives, but in a modern PC they can be used for other types of drive. These multipurpose interfaces are more accurately called EIDE interfaces, which stands for enhanced integrated drive electronics. In practice they are still often referred to as just plain IDE interfaces, and by other names such as "ATA". Many types of drive can be used with an EIDE interface, including CD-ROM, Zip, and LS120 drives.

In a typical PC the hard disc drive is connected to IDE port 1 and the CD-ROM drive is wired to IDE port 2. However, each IDE interface supports up to two devices, so the hard disc and CD-ROM drive could be connected to IDE port 1 via a single cable. A more common configuration with modern PCs is to have the hard disc on one IDE interface, with a CD-ROM or DVD drive and a CD writer on the other interface. Provided your PC has no more than three internal drives, excluding any floppy drives, it should certainly be able to support another hard drive.

If you look at the cabling inside the PC you should find some wide cables, know as "ribbon" cables, that connect the drives to the motherboard. With some modern PCs these leads are the normal round variety. Either way they should be easy to find as they are the only cables that connect between the hard drives and the main board. With luck, at least one of these cables will have an unused connector that can be used with the drive from the other PC. Note that any spare connector on the drive that connects to the floppy disc drive is of no use with a hard disc drive. The floppy variety uses a completely different interface having a smaller connector. A suitable power supply lead and connector is also needed. The connectors come in two sizes, which are a larger one for 5.25-inch drives and a smaller one for the 3.5-inch variety (Figure 7.55). However, all the hard disc drives I have encountered use the larger connector regardless of whether they fit 3.5-inch or 5.25in bays.

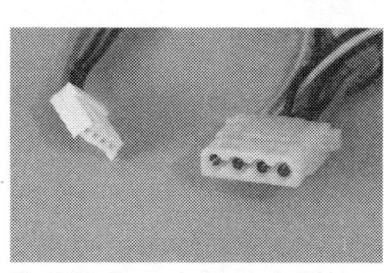

Fig.7.55 The two types of drive power connector

Hard disc cloning 7

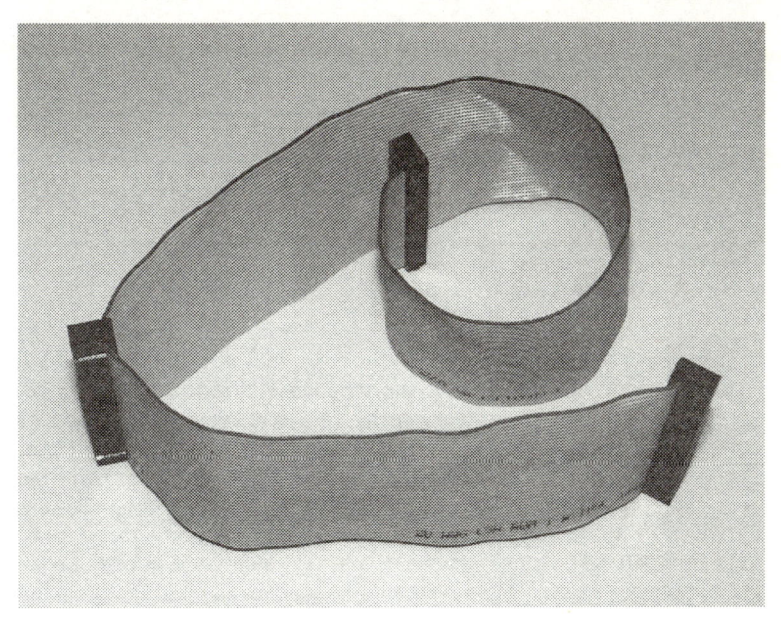

Fig.7.56 A twin IDE drive lead

If you are out of luck, one or other of the required leads and connectors will not be present. If the hard disc and CD-ROM drive share an IDE interface, the other IDE interface will be available for the additional drive, but it will not be fitted with a cable. Another possibility is that the existing drives are connected to separate IDE interfaces using single cables rather than types having two connectors for drives. In either case a standard twin IDE data lead is needed in addition to the drive (Figure 7.56).

It is possible that the PCs will have been supplied complete with an instruction manual for the hard drives, but this is by no means certain. If no manuals are supplied for the drives this should not be a major problem. The web sites of most hard disc manufacturers include downloadable versions of the manuals for most of their hard disc units. Unless one of the drives you are dealing with is very old or unusual, the information you require should be available on the manufacturer's web site. The drives themselves should be clearly marked with the manufacturers' names and the model numbers.

When handling the hard disc drives it is important to bear in mind that they are vulnerable to damage from static charges. Although hard disc

7 Hard disc cloning

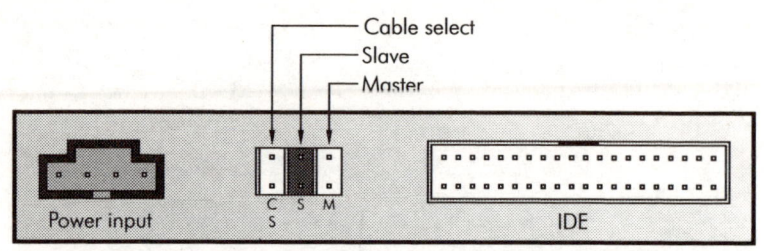

Fig.7.57 Most CD-ROM and hard drives have three sets of terminals for configuration jumpers

drives are not as costly as was once the case, they are still far from being "dirt cheap". Also, if you should happen to "zap" the source drive there will be no easy way of recovering the data and system information it contains. A specialist data recovery company should be able to recover all the contents of the disc, but the cost of such services tends to be quite high. It is a good idea to do a complete backup of a disc before removing it from a PC. However, the discs should come to no harm provided you take the basic antistatic handling precautions detailed earlier in this book.

Jumpers

An IDE device has configuration jumpers that are used to set whether the unit will be used as the master or slave device on its IDE channel. Even if there is only one device on an IDE channel, that device must still be set as the master or slave unit. By convention, a single drive on an IDE channel is set as the master device. Therefore, if you are adding the new disc to an IDE channel that already has one device installed, the new drive must be set to operate as the slave device. If the new drive will be the sole device on its IDE channel, it must be set for master operation.

The rear of most CD-ROM drives and some IDE hard disc drives look something like Figure 7.57. The connector on the left is the power input and the one on the right is for the data cable. In between these are three pairs of terminals that can be bridged electrically by a tiny metal and plastic gadget called a jumper. A jumper can be seen in place in Figure 7.58. The "cable select" option is not used in a PC context, so only two pairs of contacts are relevant here. You simply place the jumper on the master or slave contacts, depending on which option you require. The configuration jumper should be supplied with the drive incidentally, and is normally set at the master option by default on a hard disc drive.

Hard disc cloning 7

Fig.7.58 A jumper can be seen in place here

With hard disc drives matters are not always as simple as the arrangement shown in Figure 7.57. There is often an additional set of terminals, and these are used where the drive will be used as the only device on an IDE channel. Using this setting will allow a lone drive to be correctly identified and used by the PC. If the drive has these additional terminals (or they are fitted in place of the cable select pins), you must use them for a sole IDE drive. It is very unlikely that the drive will be picked up properly by the BIOS if the normal master setting is used. Getting it wrong is not likely to produce any damage, but the drive will be unusable until the mistake has been corrected.

If the transplanted drive is used as the slave device on the primary IDE channel, the other hard drive will presumably be the master device on this channel. The existing drive will need its configuration setting altered if it is set to operate as the sole IDE device on its channel. The transplanted drive will presumably be set as the master device, and it will have to be changed to slave operation. It must be changed back to master operation when it is returned to the new PC. Before searching for instruction manuals for the drives it is worth looking at the top plates of the drives. These often have a small diagram that gives details of the configuration settings.

7　Hard disc cloning

In the unlikely event that there is no spare capacity on the primary IDE channel it will be necessary to use the transplanted device on the secondary IDE channel. Here it will presumably be used as the slave device. The transplanted drive will have to be altered from master to slave operation, but there should be no need to alter the existing drive on the secondary IDE channel. If there is no existing drive on this channel, the transplanted drive should be left with its master or sole master configuration.

Note that it is not essential to bolt the transplanted drive into a spare drive bay of the old PC. On the other hand, it is essential to make sure that any exposed connections on the underside of the drive do not come into electrical contact with the computer's chassis or any electronic parts. Some drives are fully enclosed, but most seem to have at least one circuit board that is not covered. Probably the easiest way of avoiding short-circuits is to fit the drive into a spare bay and secure it with one fixing bolt.

Minimalist cases

If your PC has one of the minimalist cases you may find that there are no spare bays for another hard disc drive. It will then be a matter of improvising, but make quite sure that there is no risk of any exposed connections accidentally touching anything metal. Plenty of newspaper placed under the drive should do the job, but be careful not to disturb he drive and move it off the paper.

The IDE cables use polarised connectors that can not be fitted the wrong way around. There is a protrusion on the lead's connectors and a matching groove in the connectors on the motherboard and drives. Figure 7.59 shows the polarising keys in the two IDE connectors on a motherboard. The connectors on IDE drives are exactly the same. With an ordinary IDE cable it does not matter which connector is used for the master device and which is used for the slave unit. With the drives connected either way round the BIOS and operating system should locate and use them correctly.

A spare power cable is needed for the new drive, and if there is a spare drive bay there should really be a spare power lead as well. However, it might be fitted with the smaller connector for 3.5-inch floppy drives, whereas it is the larger power connector that is required for hard disc drives, whether they are of the 3.5-inch or 5.25-inch variety. A large computer store should be able to provide a 3.5 to 5.25-inch power connector adapter.

Hard disc cloning 7

Fig.7.59 Two IDE connectors on a motherboard

If there is no spare power cable, a splitter adapter is available. This provides two power connectors from a single power lead. Disconnect the power lead from the existing hard disc drive and connect it to the splitter. The two remaining connectors of the splitter are then connected to the hard disc drives. The power connectors are fully polarised and can only be connected the right way around. They are also quite stiff, and often need a certain amount of force in order to get them properly connected or disconnected again.

The transplanted drive will only be usable if the BIOS has appropriate parameters stored for it. With any reasonably modern PC it is not normally necessary to enter the BIOS Setup program and add the appropriate figures manually. The BIOS will automatically detect the new drive and use appropriate settings for it. It is only necessary to use the BIOS Setup program if the automatic detection fails to select suitable parameters, or you are using an older PC that does not use automatic detection by default. In either case it is advisable to obtain the drive's instruction manual and follow the advice it gives regarding the BIOS settings. In the vast majority of cases this is unnecessary, and the drive will be picked up correctly by the BIOS and used by the operating system.

Once the drive has been installed, the old system is copied onto the new drive using the methods described previously. It is then a matter of removing the new drive, returning the configuration jumpers to their original settings if appropriate, and then reinstalling the drive in the new PC. With luck, it should then be possible to get Windows to make the

7 Hard disc cloning

necessary changes to the drivers so that the PC can be booted into Windows. Once any final adjustments have been made, the new computer should operate as a clone of the original. When cloning Windows XP it might be necessary to reactivate the operating system. If no changes have been made to the hardware of the old PC in the last few months, reactivation should not be necessary.

Points to remember

Making a backup of the hard disc on your old PC and restoring it to your new PC is a good way of handling things, but only if it works. In theory it should be possible for Windows to adjust to the different hardware of the new computer. However, in practice there is no guarantee that it will work, even with some manual installation of hardware drivers.

A CD writer, Zip drive, external hard disc, or some other form of mass storage device is required to store the backup. Note that some backup programs (including the Windows XP Backup program) are not compatible with CD writers. The alternative is to copy direct from one hard drive to another, but some experience in dealing with computer hardware is a big advantage when using this method.

The Windows Backup program can be used to backup selected files, or a full backup of the hard disc can be provided. The same is true of practically all backup programs. In this case only a full backup that contains an image of the original hard disc is of any use. This will produce a bootable copy of the original disc.

The Windows XP Backup program can be used without wizards, but for most purposes the wizards provide the easiest and most reliable means of handling backup and restore operations. Where possible, it is probably best to use the wizard approach with other backup programs.

It is necessary to buy a backup program such as Norton Ghost or Drive Image in order to make a full backup copy of a hard disc on CD or DVD discs of some kind. These programs produce an "image" of the hard disc drive, which can be used to produce an exact (and bootable) clone of the disc that is copied.

Programs of this type are useful for making a copy of the system that can be used as a backup if a major disaster results in the contents of the hard disc becoming corrupted. They are also useful when upgrading a hard disc drive, and it is easy to justify the moderate cost of a disc imaging or backup program.

7 Hard disc cloning

It is possible to copy the image straight from the old hard disc to the new one. This method provides a very fast transfer from one disc to the other. However, it requires some meddling with the hardware of both PCs, and it is not something that is suitable for those with little knowledge of a PC's hardware.

8

Internet file swapping

FTP method

If you need to transfer files from your PC to another PC many miles away, one option is to copy them onto removable discs such as CD-Rs and send or take them to the location of the other PC. An increasingly popular alternative is to use the Internet to provide some sort of data link between the two PCs. It is possible to obtain software that enables two PCs to "talk" to each other via the Internet, but this software is not applicable to all types of Internet connection.

Also, some PC users feel that any software of this type poses a security threat. However, it is not really possible to guarantee that any method of swapping data via the Internet will be totally secure. Even taking or sending discs containing the data does not guarantee total security. Discs can be lost or stolen if you send them through the post or deliver them personally. You have to accept a degree of risk when sending data from one location to another.

Most users settle for an indirect method of swapping data when using the Internet. In other words, the data is first uploaded to a server, and then it is downloaded from the server to the other PC. An FTP or HTTP site can be set up for this purpose, but either method can be expensive. You might have some free web space provided by your ISP (Internet service provider), and this could well be suitable for swapping data. Not all types of Internet account include any web space, and where it is included as part of the deal, the amount of space provided might be no more than a few megabytes. However, five or ten megabytes of storage space are sufficient for most data swapping.

Broadband accounts often seem to come complete with about 50 or 100 megabytes of web space, which should be more than adequate for most purposes. There are also companies that provide free web hosting, and some of these provide substantial amounts of free web space. Unfortunately, many of them are not very reliable, and in the past these companies have often been short-lived. It is probably best to choose one of the larger web hosts that are well established.

Up and down

Some web hosts provide software that enables files to be uploaded to and downloaded from your "site". Of course, in reality you do not actually have a web site. The web host will usually put in place a dummy index page for your supposed web site, and normally this would be replaced by your homepage. The latter would have links to other pages and files in the site. In this application you could actually put in a homepage, complete with links to the files that can be downloaded. Apart from the additional work involved, this has the drawback of providing easy access to your files if anyone should happen to stumble across your homepage. Things are probably a little more secure if your files are "in limbo", with no links to them.

It will still be possible for you to access them by way of the software supplied by the web host. In some cases the software is web-based, and you access your files via a browser such as Internet Explorer. A small applet might also be required, but this will be automatically downloaded and installed when it is required. This is the easiest method of uploading and downloading your files, and deleting them when they are no longer required.

FTP program

Probably the most common way of uploading and downloading files is to use an FTP (file transfer protocol) program. Note that this type of program is often used with an ordinary HTTP site, and not just FTP sites. However, not all web hosts provide FTP access these days, so check this point before trying this method of access. There are numerous FTP programs available and they mostly have quite low prices. The one that will be used in these examples is WS_FTP LE, which is free for non-corporate users. It can be downloaded from the usual software sources such as www.download.com.

A configuration window pops up when the program is first run (Figure 8.1). A name for the new configuration is typed into the menu textbox at the top of the window, and this could be the name of the web host for

Internet file swapping 8

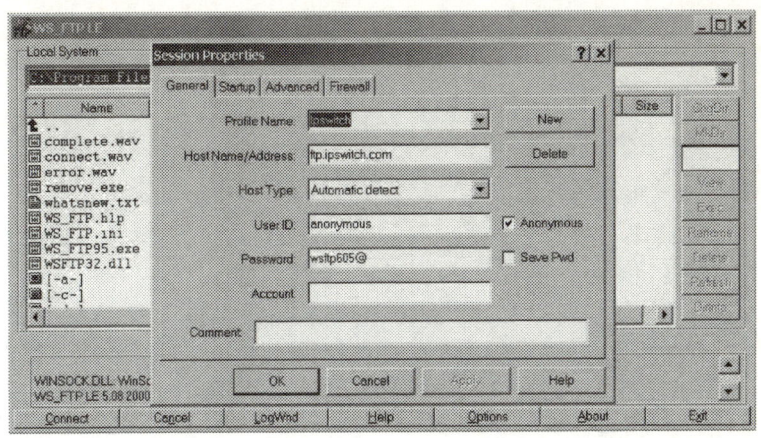

Fig.8.1 A configuration window appears when the program is run

example. You can select the host type from the menu, but the automatic option should work well enough. There is no need to add anything in the Account or Comment textboxes. The other three fields are for the information provided by the web space provider, such as the password. Operate the Apply and OK buttons when all the information has been added.

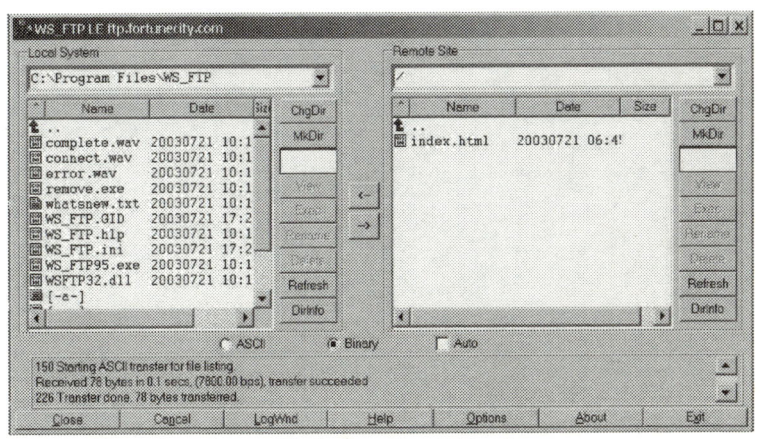

Fig.8.2 There is only one file in the site at this stage

263

8 Internet file swapping

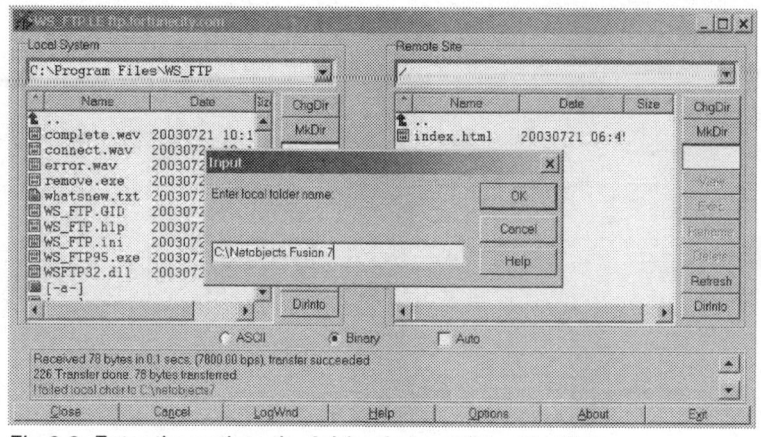

Fig.8.3 Enter the path to the folder that contains the files

The program should then connect to the web host and the right-hand panel will show the files present in the site (Figure 8.2). Initially it will either be empty or there will be an index file supplied by the web host. This is usually a simple page which explains that the site for that address has not been uploaded yet. Of course, in the current context any existing index page can simply be left in place. The left-hand section of the window shows the files and folders in the default directory.

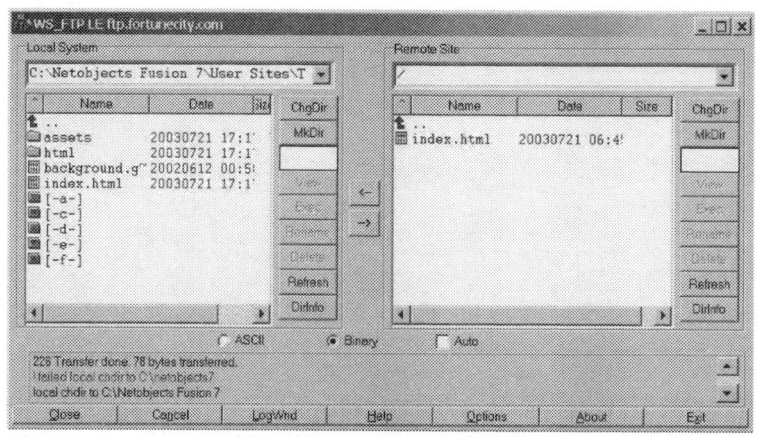

Fig.8.4 The panel on the left shows the files on the hard disc

Internet file swapping 8

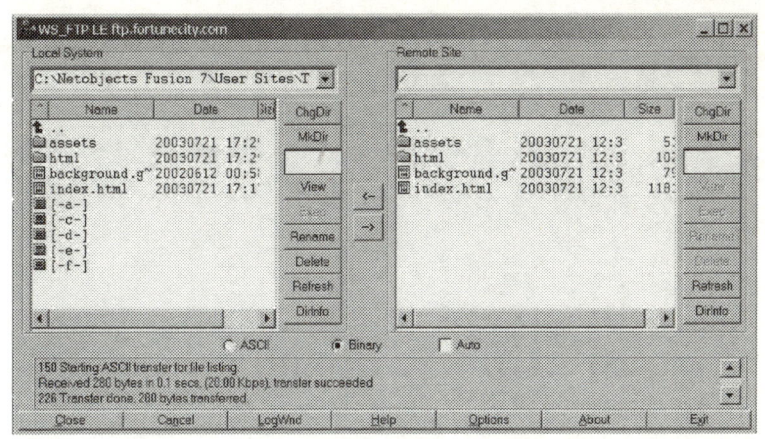

Fig.8.5 The files have been successfully uploaded

Uploading your files is done in exactly the same manner as uploading a real web site. In order to upload the files it is necessary to operate the ChgDir (change directory) button and type the path to the appropriate folder into the textbox that appears (Figure 8.3). The left-hand section of the window will then show the files and folders that must be uploaded (Figure 8.4).

Next it is a matter of selecting the files and folders that are to be uploaded. This can be achieved by pressing the Control key and left-clicking on each entry that you wish to select. The selected files are uploaded by operating the button between the two panels that has the arrow pointing to the right. A window asking if you wish to go ahead and upload the files will probably appear, and the upload will proceed if the Yes button is operated. The left and right panels should show the same files and folders once the uploading has been completed (Figure 8.5).

Downloading

Using an FTP program it is just as easy to download files as it is to upload them. In Figure 8.6 the MkDir (make directory) button has been used to make a new directory on the hard disc, and then the ChgDir button has been used to make this the current directory on the local system. The button with the arrow pointing to the left was then operated, and the files on the remote site were downloaded to the new directory.

8 Internet file swapping

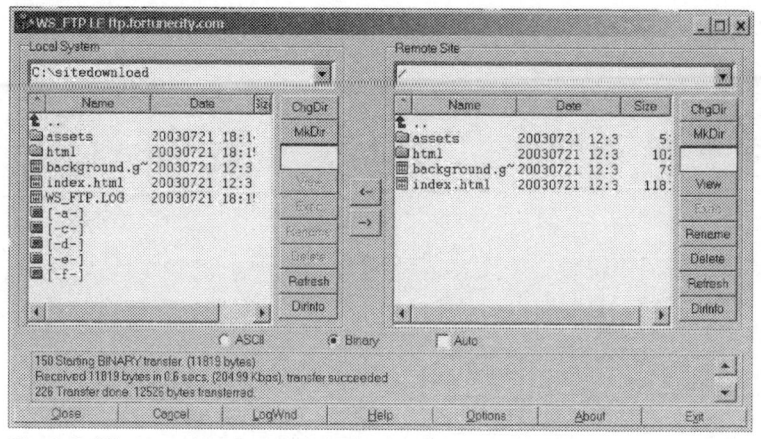

Fig.8.6 Files can be downloaded as well as uploaded

A slight flaw in this method of file swapping is that it will only work if you provide the recipient with the information needed to access your web account using an FTP program. This would not be a good idea unless the recipient is someone you know and trust. An alternative is to provide them with the full web address of each file. It should then be possible to access and download the files using a browser or download manager.

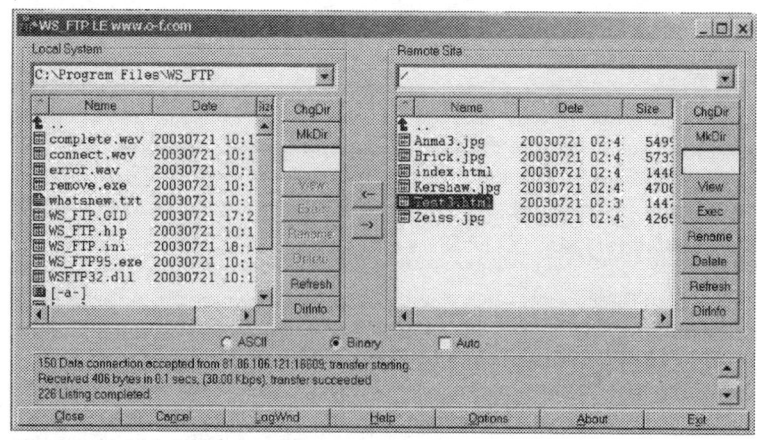

Fig.8.7 The highlighted file is superfluous

Internet file swapping 8

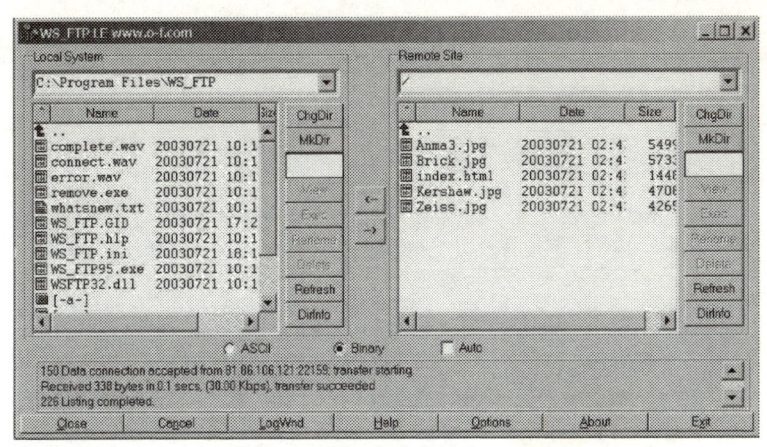

Fig.8.8 The unwanted file has been deleted

Using an FTP program it is possible to make changes to the files on the remote site. In Figure 8.7 the file called Test3.html is no longer needed and must be deleted to free some storage space. The unwanted file is easily deleted, and it is just a matter of selecting it and then operating the Delete button. Figure 8.8 shows that the file was successfully removed. Other changes are possible, but they are probably of limited practical use. For example, a file can be selected and then renamed by operating the Rename button and typing the new name into the pop-up textbox.

An advantage of the dummy site method is that it enables quite large amounts of data to be swapped, with the obvious proviso that you are able obtain a suitably large amount of web space. Actually, it is not essential to have a large amount of web storage available in order to swap substantial amounts of data. It is possible to upload and download some files, delete these files from the remote site, upload and download some more, and so on. In order to keep things manageable it is best to keep this type of thing to a minimum, but it is a useful ploy.

Bear in mind that swapping large amounts of data via the Internet will not be a practical proposition using ordinary dialup connections. In the real-world a 56k modem is unlikely to download data at more than about 46k to 50k. The upload speed is nominally 33.6k, but is likely to be more like 28k in practice. This means that it will take about six minutes to upload each megabyte of data, and more than three minutes per

8 Internet file swapping

megabyte when downloading. Broadband is typically around ten times faster, making it a more practical proposition when swapping many megabytes of data.

Email transfer

Email is becoming a very popular means of swapping data. The Emails themselves are of little use for swapping anything other than simple text files, as explained in detail at the end of this chapter.. However, any Email service should be able handle attachments. These are simply files that are sent with an Email, and they can be opened or downloaded by the recipient. This way of working has obvious attractions, but the main advantage is the ease with which it can be implemented.

Most people already have at least one Email address, making it possible to exchange files over the Internet with a minimum of fuss. There is no need to find any web space or to use any special software. You just use your existing Email account and software. Even if you would prefer not to use your main Email account for file swapping, there is no major problem. There are plenty of free Email services, and signing up to one of these takes very little time.

Of course, there are some drawbacks to using Emails as a means of file swapping. As with any method that involves the Internet, transfer rates are likely to be quite slow when uploading via a dialup connection, and not much better when downloading. A broadband connection is needed in order to obtain good transfer rates. Unfortunately, some Email servers are not particularly fast, especially at times of high demand. This means that transfer rates can occasionally be quite slow even when using a broadband connection.

The restriction on the number and size of attached files used to be a major drawback, but recent competition amongst the providers has resulted in much more generous allowances. In the past, some providers only permitted one or two files to be attached to each Email, with a total file size of only one or two megabytes. Sending multiple Emails seemed to permit larger amounts of data to be sent, but in practice there was a problem with this method. The capacity of many Email inboxes was often in the region of two to five megabytes, and some of this would usually be occupied by stored Emails. It was therefore necessary to download and delete one lot of attachments before the next lot could be received. Doing things this way was possible, but decidedly cumbersome.

Large inboxes

Many Email service providers gave users the option of paying for a larger inbox, but these days it should not be necessary to opt for one of these premium services. Free accounts now seem to come complete with inboxes having capacities of between about 100 megabytes and one gigabyte. Even the lower figure should be adequate for most users, but you can seek out one of the more generous providers if you need to transfer and store large amounts of data online.

When transferring data via Email attachments you have to bear in mind that the number and size of attachments permitted by most providers has not kept pace with the increased sizes of inboxes. In general, it is possible to send more and larger files than in the past, but there is likely to be a limit of something like six files and a total of ten megabytes. The restrictions seem to be different for each service provider, so you have to check on the limits imposed by your particular provider prior to sending large amounts of data. Bear in mind that there might also be restrictions on what can be received by the system used by the recipient. If your Emails fail to meet any restrictions imposed by the receiving system, it is certain that some of the attachments will be filtered. It is possible that all the attachments will be filtered.

A limit on the number of files is not really a major drawback. It is possible to combine a number of files into a single archive file using programs such as WinZip and WinRAR. The recipient can split each archive back into its constituent parts using the same program that was used to create it. The main purpose of programs such as WinZip and WinRAR is to compress the data so that files are made as small as possible. With some types of file this can reduce the amount of data, which makes it easier to keep within the service provider's restrictions. It also helps to speed up the uploading and downloading processes. Unfortunately, many types of file already incorporate data compression. Trying to "squeeze" these files is unlikely to provide a significant reduction in their size.

Filtering

Internet security is now a major issue for users and providers of Internet services. One practical outcome of increased Email security is that some service providers do not permit certain types of file to be included as attachments. At the other end of the system, some providers will not accept attachments containing certain file types. Trying to send a file of

8 Internet file swapping

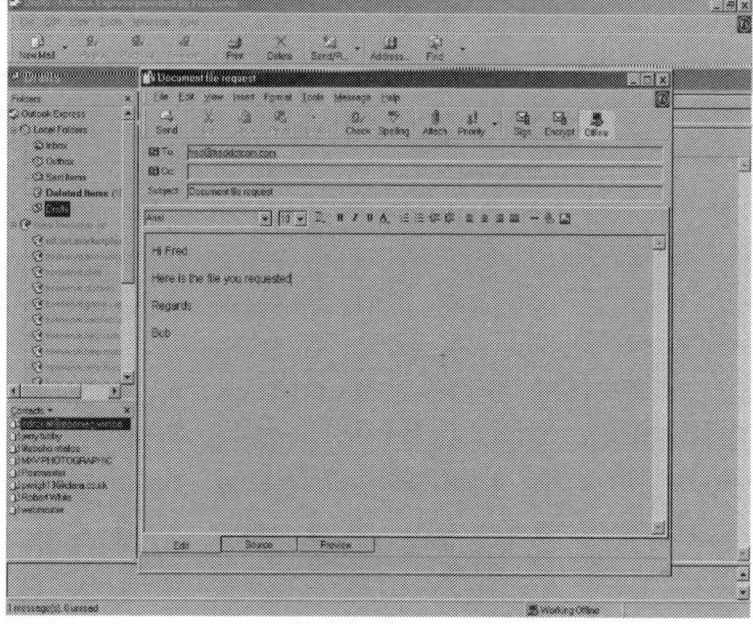

Fig.8.9 Start by composing the Email in the usual way

a proscribed type will usually result in an error message. Sometimes a certain file type might be acceptable to your Email provider, but not to the recipient's provider. This will usually result in the attachment being filtered, and the recipient's service provider will then send you an Email explaining why the attachment has been filtered.

The file types that are most likely to be filtered are executable program files, such as those having EXE and COM extensions. Extensions to program files such as DLL types might also be prohibited. It is quite likely that you will never need to send any of the proscribed file types, but compressed files can sometimes cause problems. Most types of compressed files should be permissible, including those having the common filename extensions such as ZIP and RAR. It is the self-extracting files that are likely to cause problems. This type of file is a program file that usually has an EXE extension.

The file is actually a simple decompression utility plus the compressed data. Running the program results in the data being decompressed, and then it is stored in the folder specified by the user. This type of

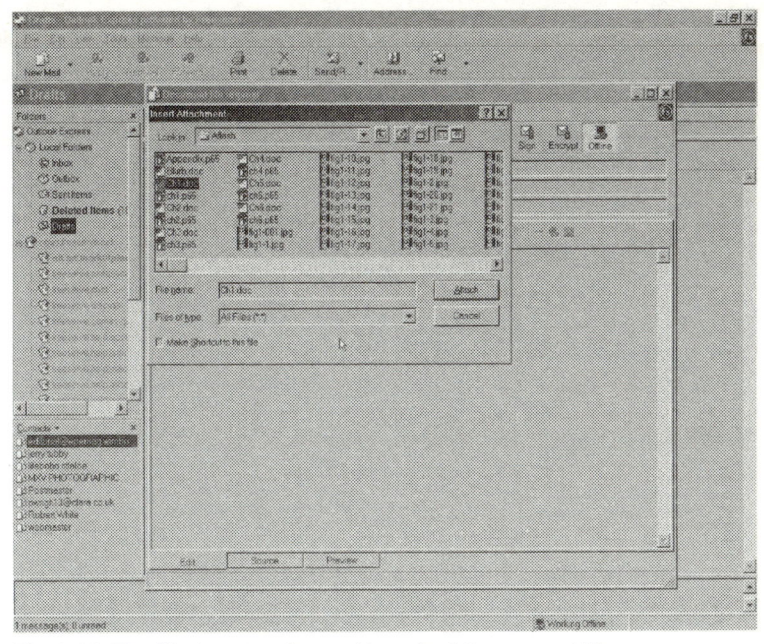

Fig.8.10 The file browser is used to select the correct file

compressed file has the advantage of not requiring the recipient to have a decompression program of the appropriate type. There is a slight drawback in that including the decompression program with the data results in a larger file. When sending compressed files via Email it is better to use an ordinary type that does not include the decompression program. This should avoid problems with the file being filtered, and ensures that the amount of data sent is kept to a minimum.

Sending

Sending an attachment is usually pretty straightforward. In Outlook Express the first step is to compose the Email in the normal way (Figure 8.9). Next operate the Attach button near the top of the window in which the Email has been composed. This produces a standard Windows file browser (Figure 8.10) where you can select the file for attachment to the Email. Operate the Attach button when the correct file has been located and selected.

8　Internet file swapping

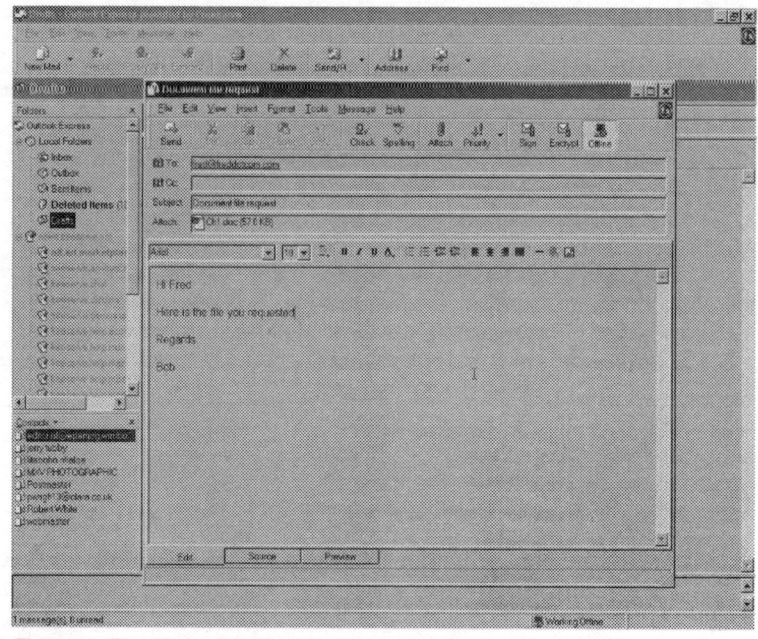

Fig.8.11　The file's details should appear in the Attach field

This takes the program back to the document window where the Attach field near the top should show the name of the attached file and its size (Figure 8.11). To attach more files to the Email just repeat this process as many times as necessary. The Attach field in the document window will show the names and sizes of all the attached files (Figure 8.12). The

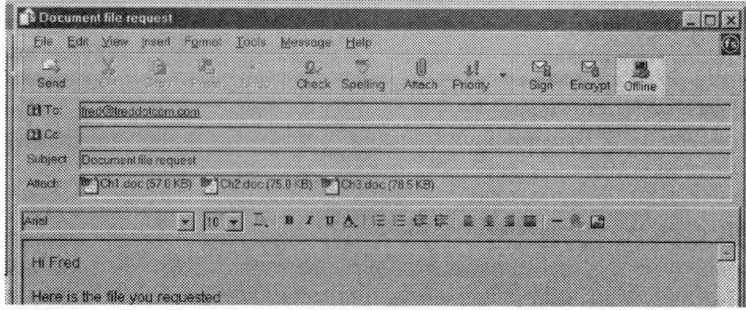

Fig.8.12　A number of files can be attached to each Email

Internet file swapping 8

Email is sent in the normal way once all the files have been attached. Web based Email services such as Yahoo! And Hotmail have similar facilities. Normally it is just a matter of operating the Attachments button when composing the Email, and then using a simple file browser to select the required files.

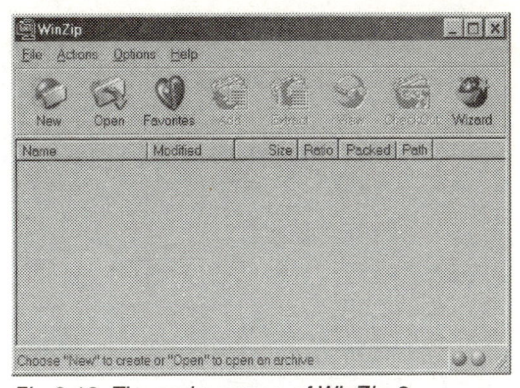

Fig.8.13 The main screen of WinZip 8

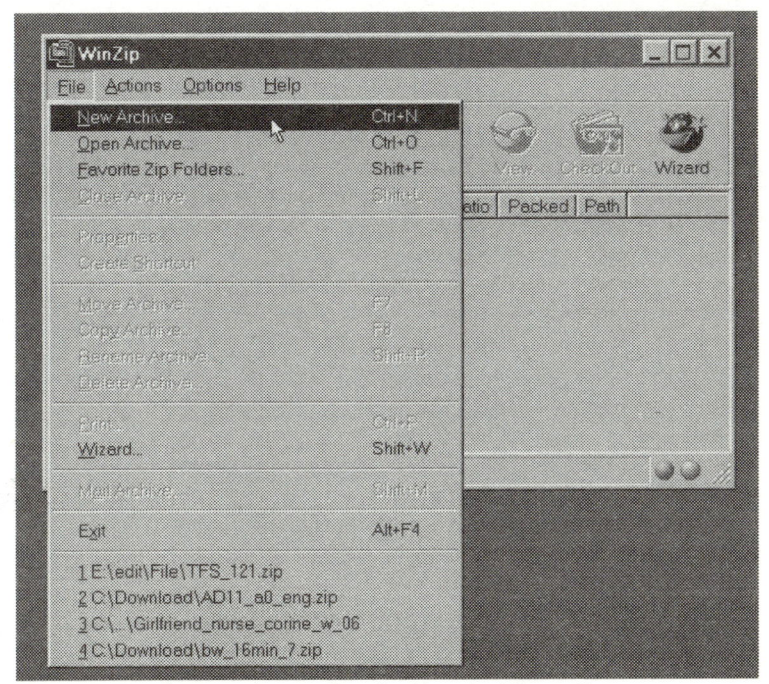

Fig.8.14 The first step is to select the New Archive option

273

8 Internet file swapping

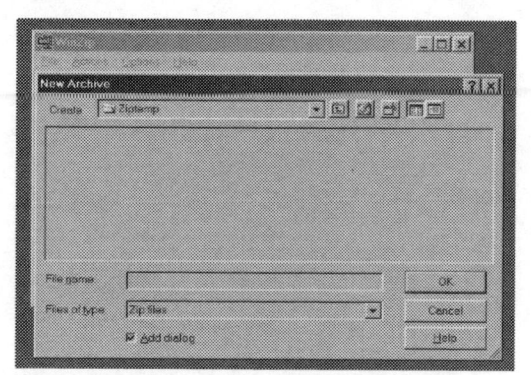

Fig.8.15 Selecting a filename and folder for the new archive file

Archiving

If you need to archive files in order to reduce the number of attachments, using an archiving and compression program such as WinZip is very straightforward. When using an unregistered version of WinZip you must first agree to the

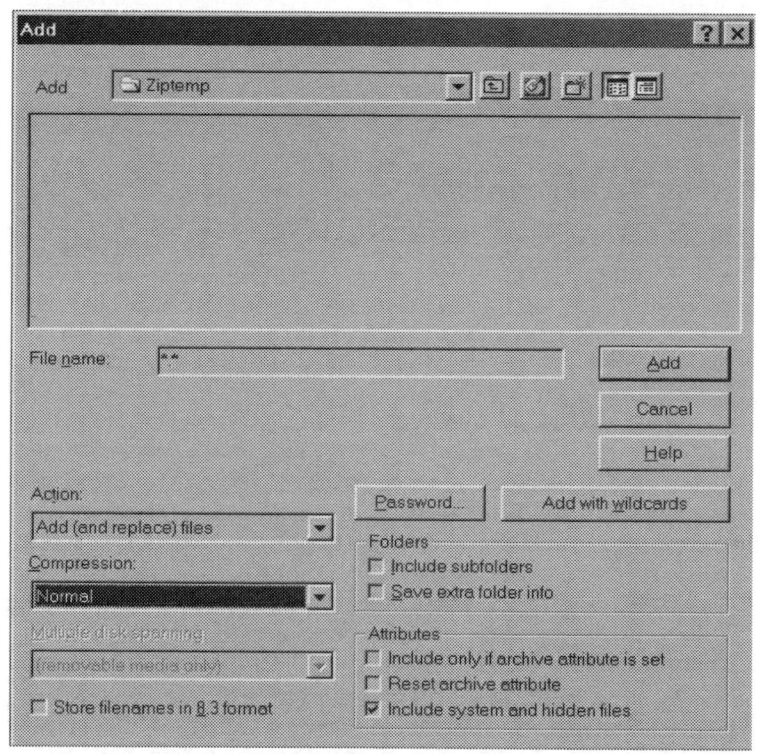

Fig.8.16 Another file browser is used to select the files for the archive

Internet file swapping 8

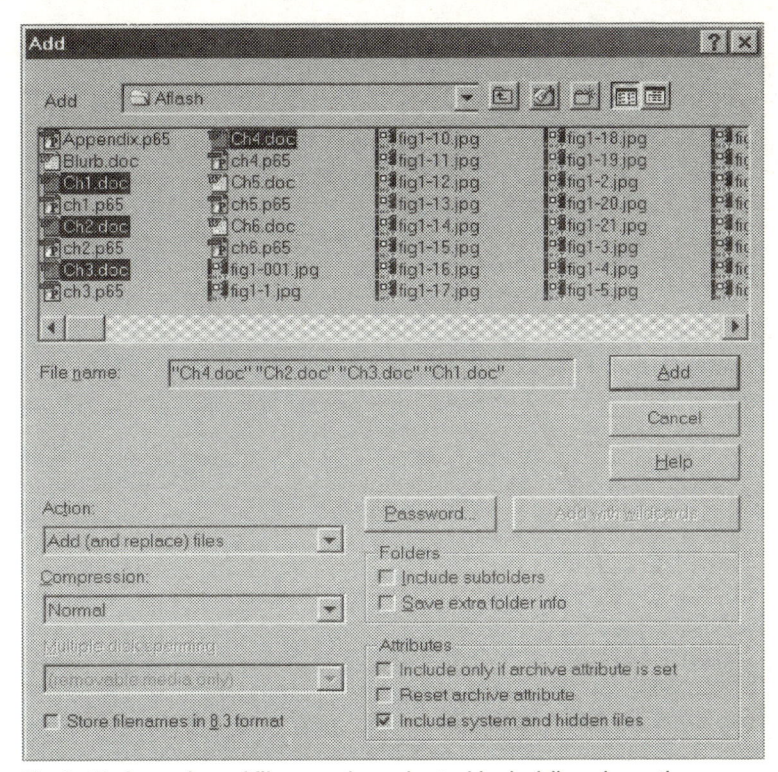

Fig.8.17 A number of files can be selected by holding down the Control key

licensing conditions by operating the appropriate button, and then the main window will appear (Figure 8.13). It is assumed here that the "classic" interface was specified during the installation process. You can opt for the wizard approach if preferred. However, as the standard Winzip "classic" interface is not difficult to use and it is generally quicker than using the wizard, I would recommend using the standard interface.

The first task is to tell WinZip where you wish to deposit the archive file, and to provide a name for the file. Select the New Archive option from the file menu (Figure 8.14) to bring up the usual file browser (figure 8.15). If necessary, use the menu at the top of the window to alter the folder to be used for the archive file. A name for the file is entered in the File Name text box, and there is no need to add the Zip extension. This will be added automatically by the program.

8 Internet file swapping

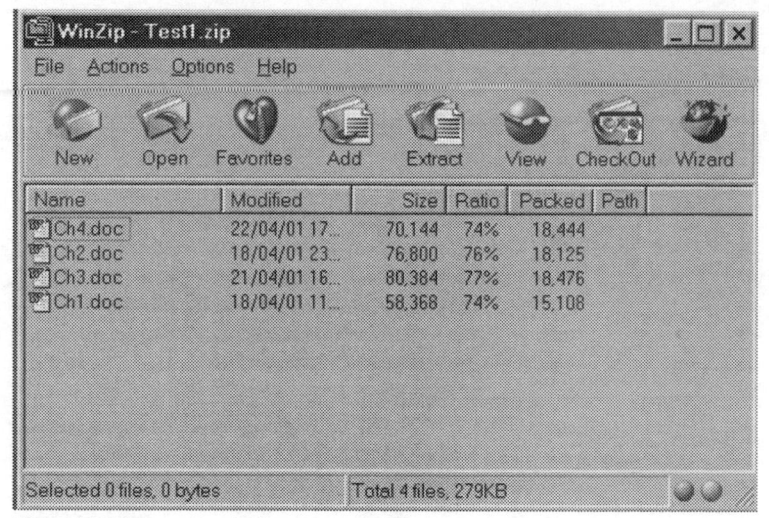

Fig.8.18 The main window shows the contents of the new archive

Operate the OK button to move on to the next window (Figure 8.16), where the files to be archived are selected. This is done using the top section of the window, which is a standard file browser. It is advisable to have all the files for the archive in a single folder as they can then be selected in one operation. Use the browser to locate the right folder and left-click on the first file to select it. Select the other files by holding down the Control key and left-clicking on their entries in the file browser. There are various options available in the bottom section of the window, but for most purposes the defaults will suffice. With all the required files selected (Figure 8.17), operate the Add button to create the archive file.

The main window then returns, and it displays the contents of the newly created archive (Figure 8.18). It shows the original size of each file together with its compressed size and the degree of compression. In this case the Word DOC format files have been compressed by impressive ratios of around 74 to 77 percent. Some 279k of data has been compressed to a mere 69k. This shows the effectiveness of this method with the right types of file. A ten-megabyte limit could effectively be increased to nearly 80 megabytes with suitable files.

Internet file swapping 8

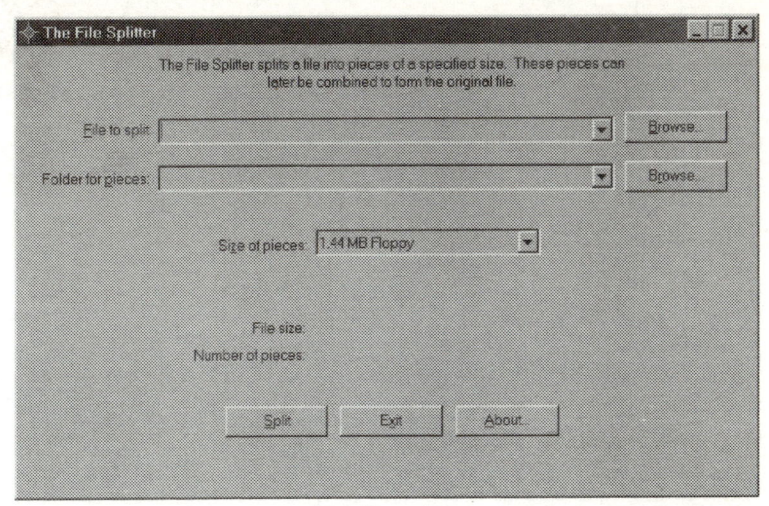

Fig.8.19 The initial screen of the file splitter

Attachment too large

A compression program such as WinZip is a possible solution where a file is only slightly too large for your Email service. As pointed out previously, some types of file compress very well while others remain virtually the same size after compression. The only way to tell how small or otherwise a file will be after compression is to try the "suck it and see" method. Where compression will make a file small enough to pass through the system, this almost certainly represents the best way of handling things.

With some types of file there is no major problem in breaking them into small pieces and reconstructing them again. With something like a large word processor file for example, there should be no difficulty in breaking the document into several chunks and then recombining them again using the word processor. This type of thing is clearly not applicable to all types of file, and it can not be used with a program file for instance. However, there are programs that can take any file, slice it into several pieces, and then combine the pieces again to produce the original file without a byte out of place. In fact the search engine of a major software download site will probably come up with about 50 or more programs of this general type.

8 Internet file swapping

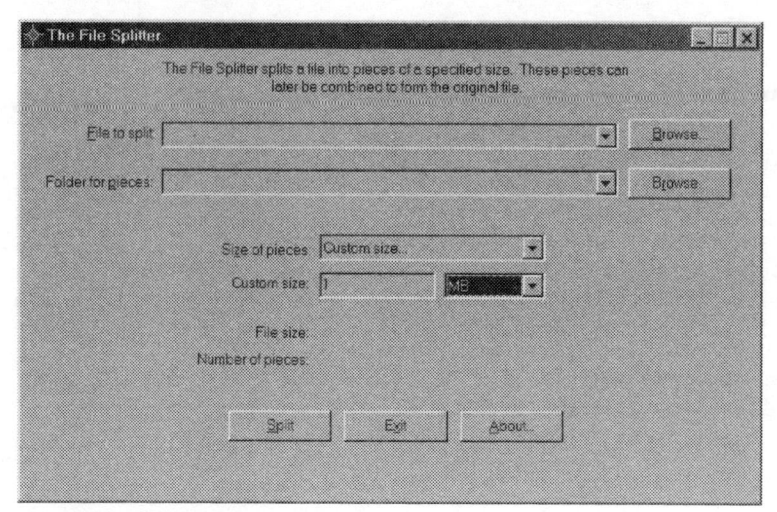

Fig.8.20 A maximum size can be set for the file fragments

A program by Marc Bjorklund called The File Splitter is one that I have found easy to use, and it is available from the big software download sites such as Download.com. It is freeware incidentally, so it offers a zero cost method of splitting and recombining files. Unlike many other file splitting utilities, it does not require the recipient to have the program installed. The recombining of the file fragments is accomplished using a MS-DOS batch file and the standard MS-DOS facilities. Obviously the recipient must have a system that can provide these facilities, but there should be no problem using any PC running Windows 98, ME or XP.

The window of Figure 8.19 appears when the program is run. By default the program breaks the source file into pieces that will fit onto standard 3.5-inch 1.44-megabyte floppy discs. For use in an Email context it will normally be necessary to alter the size setting by selecting the Custom size option from the Size of pieces menu. The size is then entered into the Custom size textbox (Figure 8.20). The little drop-down menu to the right of this enables the size to be specified in bytes, kilobytes, or megabytes.

Size matters

It is advisable to be slightly conservative when selecting the file size. Bear in mind that the maximum size allowed by the Email service provider

Internet file swapping 8

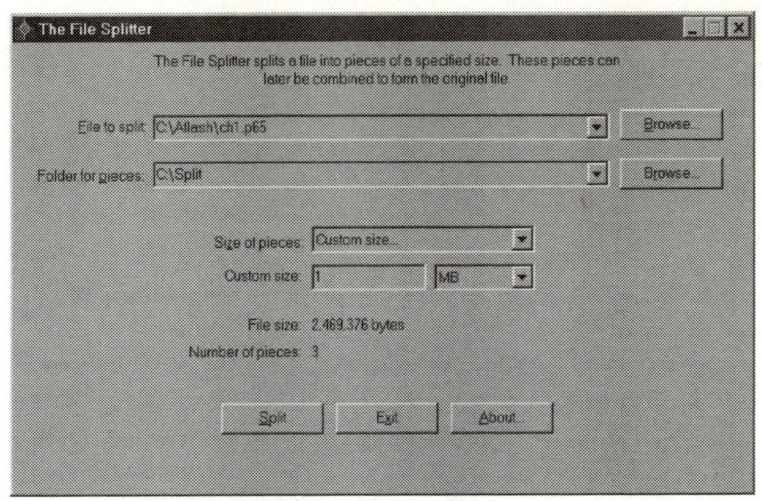

Fig.8.21 The programs gives the size of the source file and the number of pieces it will be broken into

includes the Email itself, which will normally only be about one kilobyte. Another complication is that there are two definitions of a megabyte. Strictly speaking it is 1048576 bytes, but some consider a megabyte to be a straightforward one million bytes. File Splitter seems to work in terms of genuine megabytes. Consequently, it is advisable to make the file size slightly smaller than the stated maximum of your service provider.

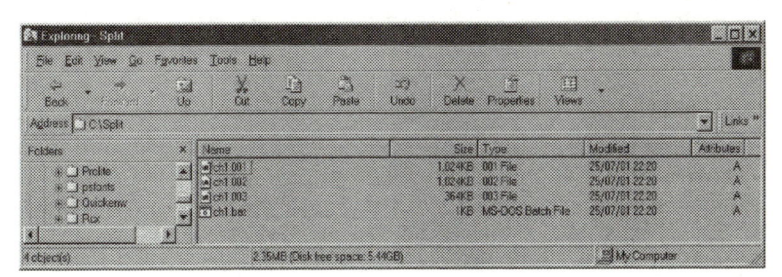

Fig.8.22 You can monitor the progress of the splitting process, which generally takes a few seconds

The two browsers at the top of the window are used to select the file to be split and the folder for the files that are created. Note that File Splitter leaves the original file intact, so there is no need to make a copy for it to

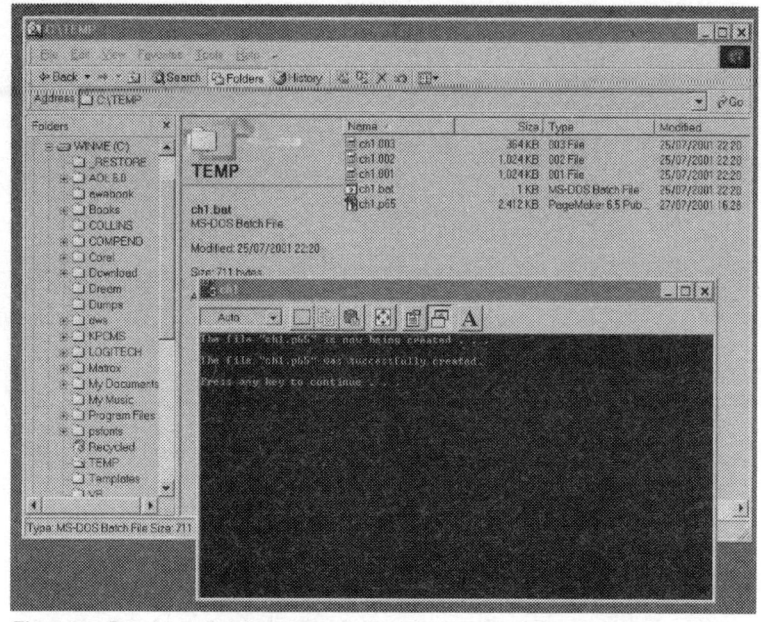

Fig.8.23 Double-clicking the batch file opens a DOS window

operate on. With the source file and destination folder selected, the window with display the size of the source and the number of pieces that it will be broken into (Figure 8.21). In this example the source file is just less than 2.5 megabytes and it will be broken into three pieces. Operating the Split button completes the process. A small window (Figure 8.22) shows the progress of the processing and indicates when it has been completed.

Having completed the splitting process, Windows Explorer can be used to check that the file fragments have been generated. This check will show that an MS/DOS batch file has been created in addition to the three file fragments. It is essential to send this file with the fragments, because it is needed in order to reconstitute the original file from the pieces.

Reconstruction

With most file splitting programs it is necessary to have the program in order to recombine the file fragments. As pointed out previously, this is

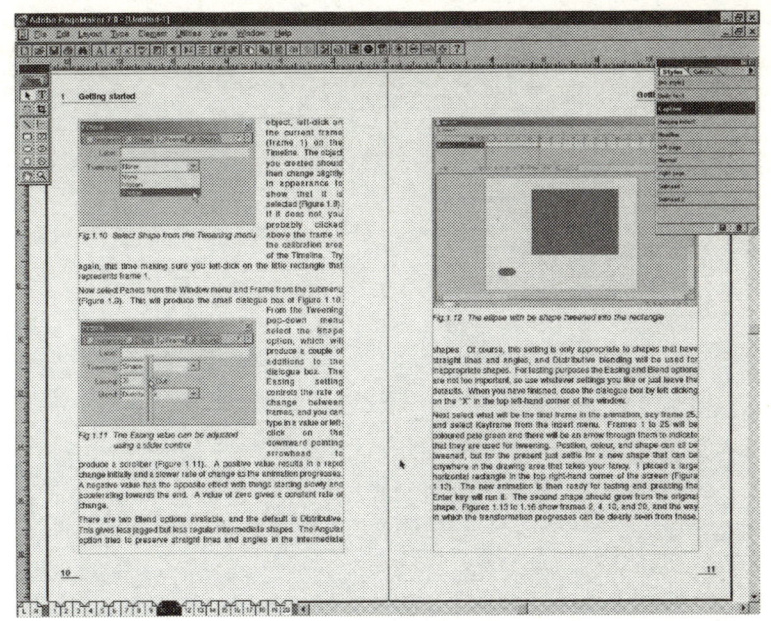

Fig.8.24 The reconstructed file should work perfectly, as in this case

not the case with The File Splitter. All the recipient has to do is place the pieces of the file and the batch file in any convenient folder, locate the batch file (the one with the "bat" extension) using Windows Explorer, and then double-click on it. A MS/DOS window will appear, and should state that the new file has been created successfully (Figure 8.23). The new file will appear at the bottom of the list of files in Windows Explorer. The reconstructed file should be identical to the original. The PageMaker 6.5 file used in this example was certainly free of errors and loaded correctly into PageMaker (Figure 8.24).

Photo albums

In the early days of the Internet there were numerous companies offering free web space, but this type of business went into steep decline when the dotcom bubble burst. One exception to this trend is the number of companies offering free web space for storing digital photographs. The massive upsurge in demand for digital cameras has been matched by an ever increasing number of companies offering online photo album

8 Internet file swapping

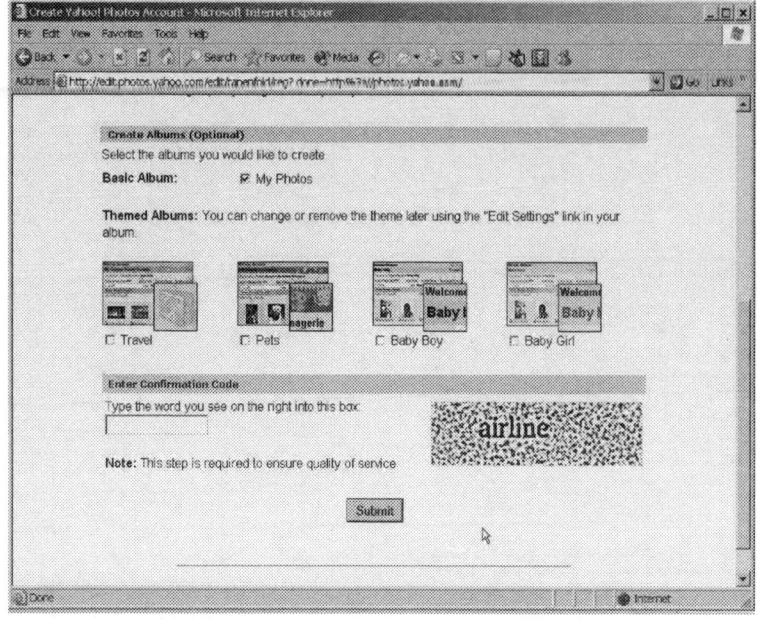

Fig.8.25 Templates for various types of album are available

facilities. Any Internet search engine should be able to produce a large list of sites that provide this service.

It is easy to see why this type of facility has become so popular. An online photo album is an excellent means of sharing photographs with your family and friends. They are also a really good way for those having a common interest to share photographs. Online photo albums can be used for enthusiasts to share wildlife pictures, photographs of steam railways, and so on. Many clubs have an online album, or a web site that includes a similar facility.

Free online photo albums are sometimes provided by photo processing companies. This may seem to be exceptionally generous of them, but the idea is that users of the album can order prints that are paid for online and delivered by post. The provider of the service is hoping to make a profit on the service by way of increased print sales. However, there is usually no obligation to buy a certain number of prints in a given period. Also, it is normally possible to download images, making the service suitable for file swapping.

Internet file swapping 8

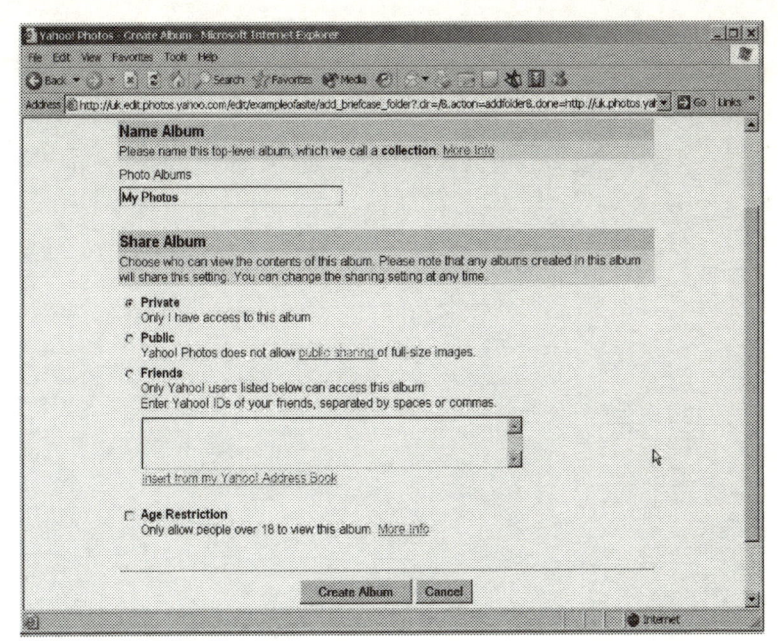

Fig.8.26 From this page the album is named and access is controlled

Of course, before signing up to any service it is important to read the "small print" to make sure that there are no hidden surprises, and that it does actually meet your requirements. Obviously there will be a limit on the amount of storage space provided, but there could also be a limit on the size of each file. This could make it impossible to transfer high resolution images via the album. Note that the majority of free web space is supported via advertising, so your online photo album is likely to have a few banner or pop-up advertisements. Companies operating in this field are sometimes short-lived, so it is probably best to use a well-established service.

Making an album

Yahoo! has a photo album facility that offers a very reasonable limit of 90 photographs and 30 megabytes. In order to make use of the Yahoo! photo album facility it is necessary to register with Yahoo! if you are not already a Yahoo! or Geocities member. The online album facility can be accessed via the Photos link in the Organise section of the

8 Internet file swapping

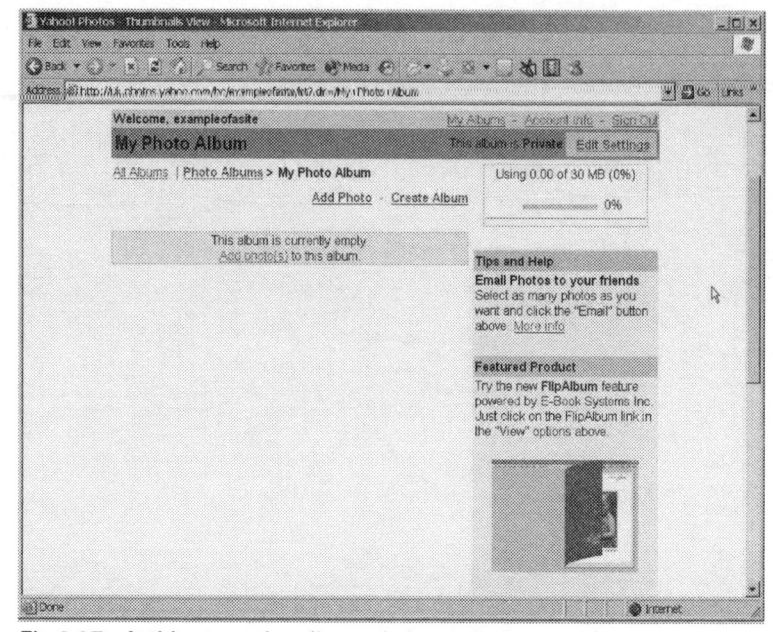

Fig.8.27 At this stage the album obviously lacks any pictures

www.yahoo.com homepage. During the initial stages of setting up the album you may be offered the choice of producing special types of album (Figure 8.25), but here we will produce the standard type.

You will probably have to type the "hidden" word into the textbox in order to continue with the process. This is rapidly becoming a standard feature when obtaining any form of free web space. It is designed to stop automated systems from setting up numerous false accounts for use by those looking for free storage space for their porno sites, pirated software, etc. You should be able to decipher the word quite easily, but it is very difficult for automated systems to do so.

The first task when you start creating the album is to name the album and choose the amount of access there will be to the site (Figure 8.26). In the case of the Yahoo! album facility you can have the site for you own use only, for use by the listed Yahoo! members, or there can be general access. With general access the photographs might not be available at full resolution. This is presumably done to deter illegitimate use of the photo album facility. There is also a facility to block those under 18 years of age from viewing the album.

Internet file swapping 8

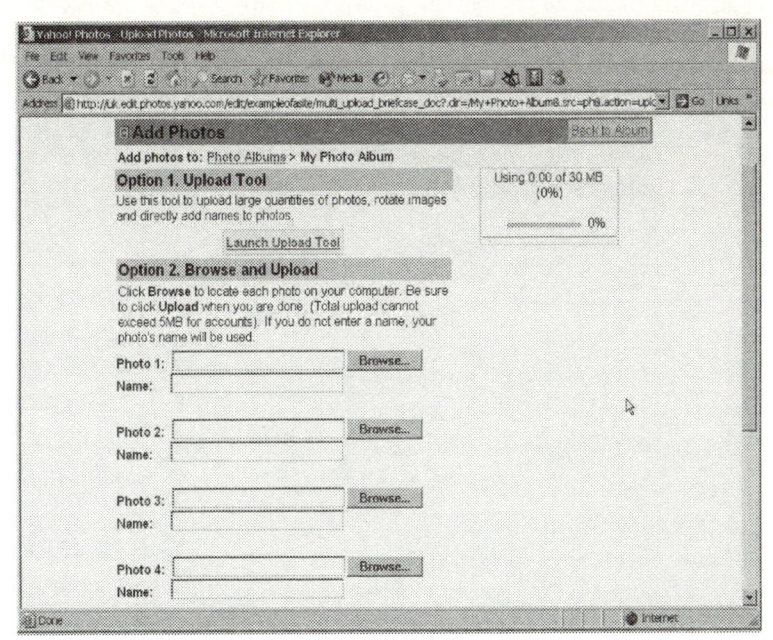

Fig.8.28 This page is used to select and upload the photographs

At the next page your new album is displayed, but obviously it is empty at this stage (Figure 8.27). In order to start adding photographs it is merely necessary to left-click the Start Adding Photographs link, which will bring up the page shown in Figure 8.28. Here the filenames of the photographs, complete with the full path, can be added into the textboxes. Alternatively, operate the Browse button and use the file browser to select each image file. The photographs should be in a standard web format, and Jpeg is probably the best option. Scroll down to the bottom of the page and operate the Upload button to go ahead and upload the images, or operate the Cancel button if you wish to abort the operation.

Resolution

If all goes well a confirmation screen like the one shown in Figure 8.29 will appear. This lists the photographs that have been successfully uploaded. By operating the appropriate link it is possible to add more photographs to the album or return to the album page. Figure 8.30 shows the album page with some more pictures added. In order to view

8 Internet file swapping

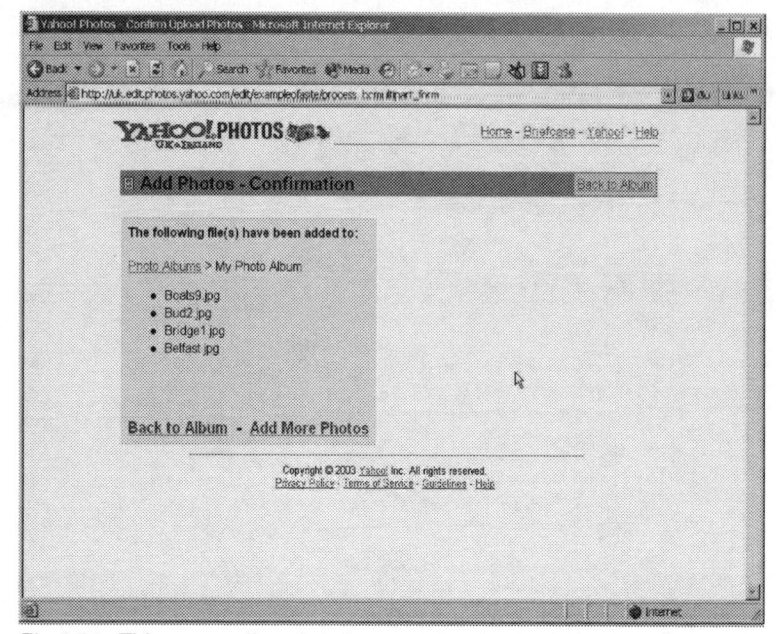

Fig.8.29 This screen lists the photographs that have been uploaded

one of the pictures larger it is merely necessary to left-click on its thumbnail view on the album page (Figure 8.31). With high resolution pictures this will not produce a full-size view of the image.

A low resolution thumbnail image is automatically generated when each photograph is uploaded, and so is a medium resolution version. It is the medium resolution image that is displayed when the thumbnail version is left-clicked. This has a much smaller image file that will download much more quickly than the full-size version. The image can be viewed at maximum resolution by left-clicking the Full Size link that is above and to the right of the medium resolution version. Note though, that a high resolution image will be too large to fit the screen even if a fairly high screen resolution is used (Figure 8.32). The entire image is still accessible, but only with the aid of the scrollbars. Of course, there will only be higher resolution version if the resolution of the original image was high enough to make this possible.

There are various facilities available from the album page and when an individual image is viewed. The Rename facility enables the name of the

Internet file swapping 8

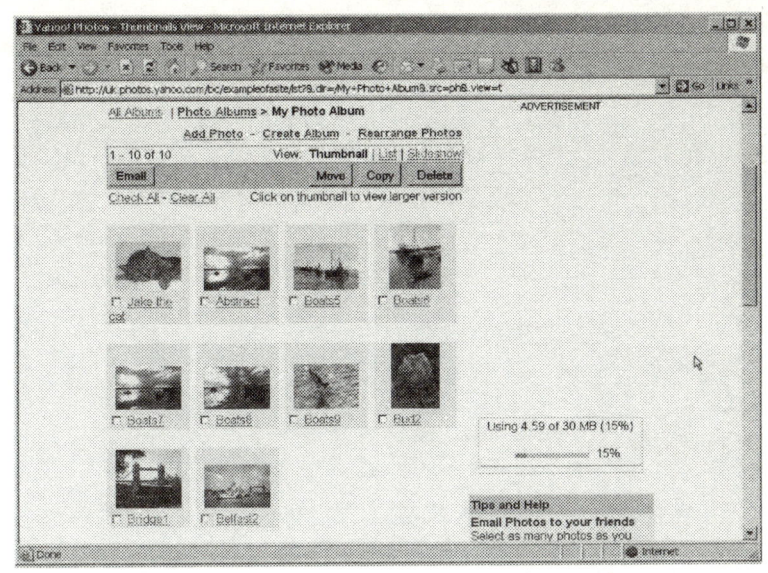

Fig.8.30 The album with ten photographs uploaded

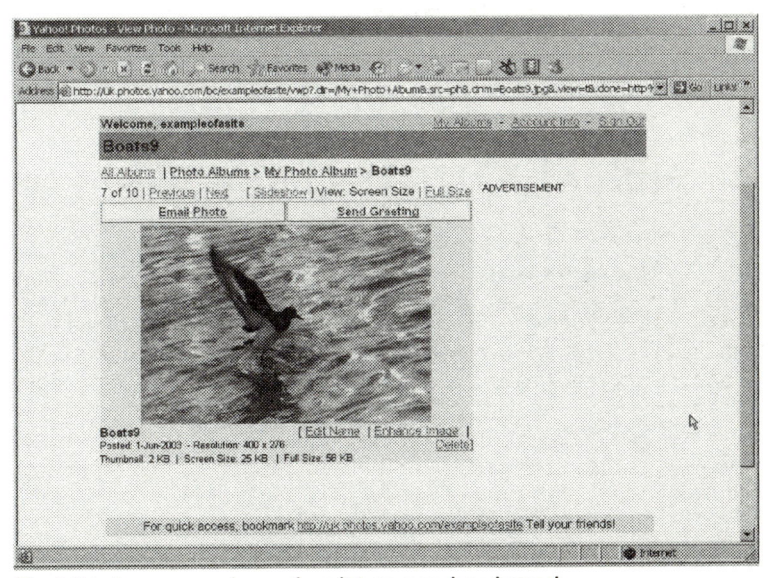

Fig.8.31 Larger versions of a picture can be viewed

8 Internet file swapping

Fig.8.32 Scrolling might be necessary to view all of a large image

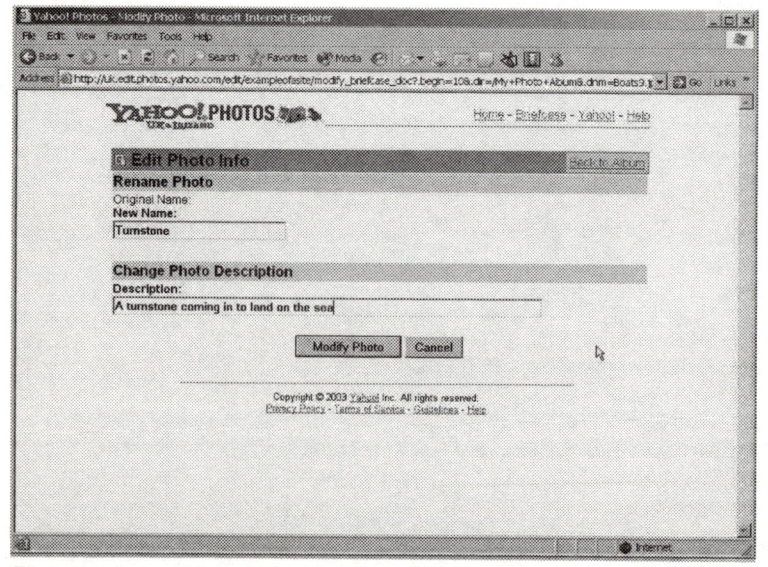

Fig.8.33 A short description can be added to a picture

Internet file swapping 8

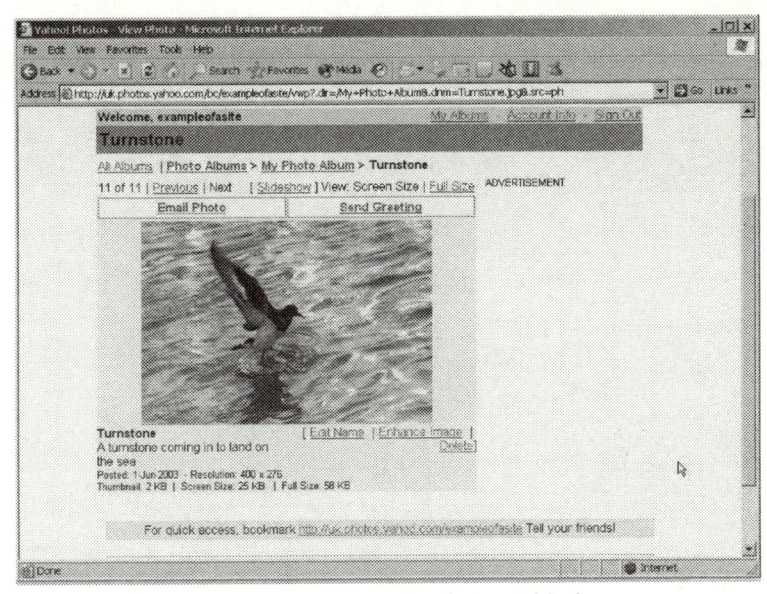

Fig.8.34 One of the pictures with a description added

Fig.8.35 Some basic image editing facilities are available

8 Internet file swapping

Fig.8.36 The cropped version of the image shown in Figure 8.35. In general it is better to process images prior to uploading them

image to be changed, but it also permits a short description to be added (Figures 8.33 and 8.34). The Enhance Image facility produces a window that provides some basic image editing facilities (Figure 8.35). While these facilities are by no means unique, not all online albums have anything comparable.

As a couple of examples of what can be achieved, Figure 8.36 shows an image that has been cropped, and Figure 8.37 shows an image that has been filtered and saved as a separate image, leaving the original intact. Clearly facilities such as these are potentially useful. However, in general it is better to undertake this type of thing using image editing software prior to uploading images. Image editing software is faster and offers a more comprehensive range of features. I suppose that online editing could be useful for last-minute changes, where it would avoid the need to upload the image again. This method is obviously worth a try if you do not have access to suitable software.

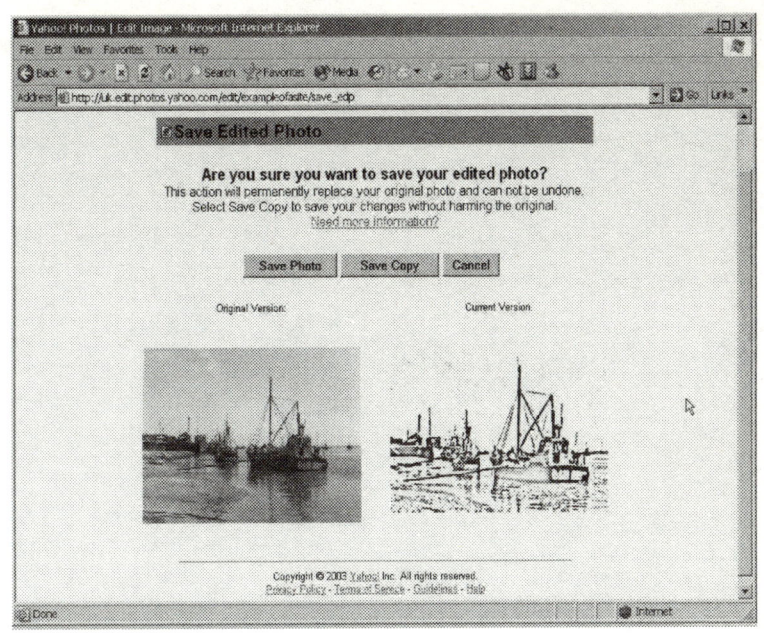

Fig.8.37 The filtered version has been saved as a separate file

Encryption

Many people are unhappy about sending personal or any form of sensitive information via Emails because this method of communication is something less than totally secure. In fact any form of file swapping via the Internet has to be regarded as something less than totally secure, and some methods lack any form of built-in security measures. There is a way around this problem in the form of encryption. However, with any personal or otherwise sensitive information it might be better to use a different method of transferring the data. Being realistic about matters though, there is probably no method of transferring data that can be guaranteed 100 percent secure.

Most web users have probably used secure web sites, and essentially the same technology can be used to scramble an Email before it is sent. In order to descramble the Email its recipient must have the same program that was used to encrypt it, together with the correct password. Most programs of this type are not only suitable for sending Emails, and can

8 Internet file swapping

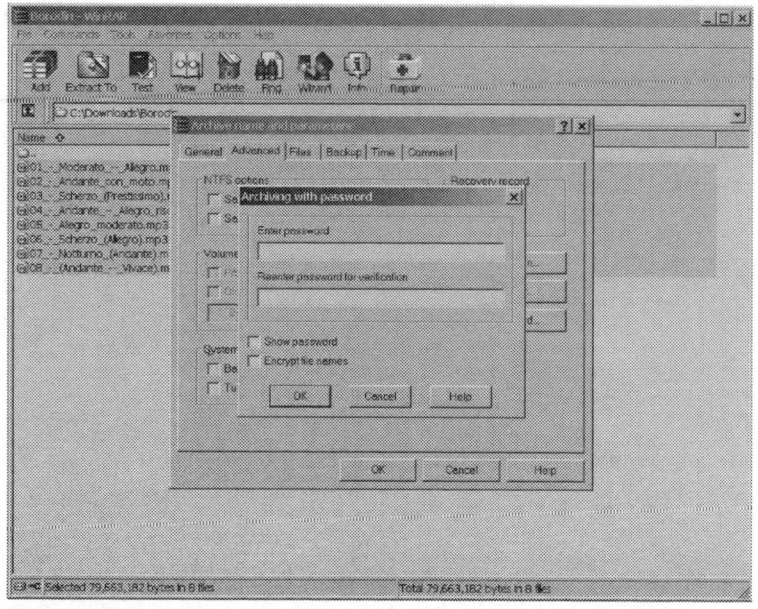

Fig.8.38 The password must be set before the files are encrypted

also be used to encrypt any form of data file. You can, for example, encrypt word processor files so that anyone gaining access to your PC will not be able to read them.

In fact this is doing things the hard way, because many word processors now have some form of built-in encryption facility. With Microsoft Word for instance, documents can be password protected. This operates at two levels, and at the highest level it is not possible to open a document without giving the correct password first. At a lower level of security it is possible for anyone to open the document and look at its contents, but only authorised users can make any changes to it.

Before using any form of password protection for data it is important to realise that modern encryption techniques are extremely powerful. Should you manage to forget the password it is unlikely that you will ever see your data in readable form again. Writing down passwords is not normally considered to be a good practice, but the reduction in security it provides is probably better than finding yourself locked out of your own documents. Those with poor memories would be well advised

Internet file swapping 8

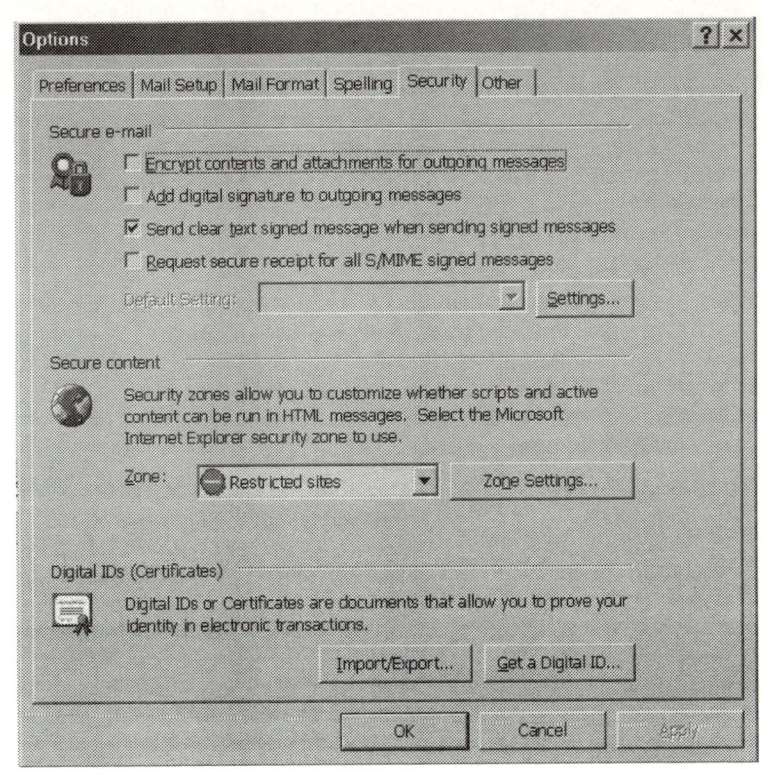

Fig.8.39 There is a built-in encryption facility, of sorts, in Outlook and Outlook Express

to write down the password and hide it away in the bottom of a drawer where no one can find it easily. Many passwords are case sensitive, so it is as well to work on the assumption that they are all case sensitive. That way you should never be caught out by using any letters of the wrong case.

There are alternatives to using special encryption programs when sending information via Emails. Many data compression programs can provide password protection, so it is possible to use one of these to compress and encrypt a file which can then be sent as an Email attachment. Unfortunately, the free versions of these programs often lack the ability to password protect files, so it might be necessary to buy the full version in order to use this facility.

8 Internet file swapping

Note that it is usually necessary to set the password before any files are placed in an archive. With WinRAR for example, you select the files in the normal way, but go to the Advanced section before adding them to the archive. Operating the Set Password button produces a small window where the password is entered in both textboxes (Figure 8.38). It is normal for a password to be entered twice when it is being set. This is a simple form of error trapping, and the password will not be accepted unless it is the same in both textboxes. Having set the password, the archive is completed in the normal way.

When extracting files from the archive, a small pop-up window prompts the user to enter the password. The program proceeds in the normal fashion provided the correct password entered. Things may seem to progress normally if the wrong password is used. However, at the end of the process an error message will be produced, and no files will have been extracted from the archive.

Users of Outlook and Outlook Express have a built-in encryption facility, but it is of no real use to most users. In order to encrypt a file, select Options from the Tools menu and then operate the Security tab in the new window that appears (Figure 8.39). Tick the top checkbox in order to use encryption on your Emails and any attachments. Unfortunately, this method is only usable if you purchase a digital certificate from a company such as VeriSign. The cost is not that great, but probably few private users are prepared to go to the trouble and expense of obtaining one and keeping it up to date.

Simple text

It is worth making the point that it is not essential to bother with attachments when you need to swap a simple text file. Of course, if you prefer to do things that way, the file can be saved as a text type or a word processor file that the recipient's PC can handle, and then used as an attachment. With a very large amount of text this might be the most practical approach. It is probably the only practical approach if the text is something that needs to be encrypted. Where security is not an issue, an alternative method is to produce the text in the normal way using a word processor, and then use the normal Windows Copy and Paste facilities to place the text in an Email. Note though, that any formatting of the text is likely to be lost. The Email system is unlikely to support Windows fonts, text sizes, etc.

Internet file swapping 8

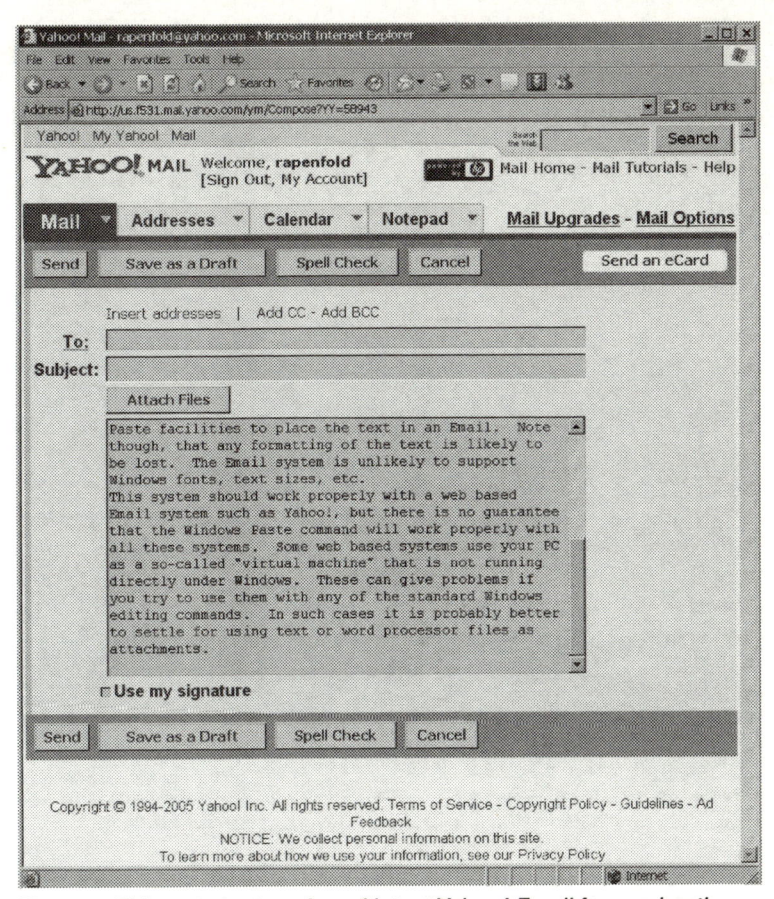

Fig.8.38 This text was transferred into a Yahoo! Email form using the standard Windows Paste command

This system should work properly with a web based Email system such as Yahoo!, but there is no guarantee that the Windows Paste command will work properly with all these systems. Some web based systems use your PC as a so-called "virtual machine" that is not running directly under Windows. These can give problems if you try to use them with any of the standard Windows editing commands. In such cases it is probably better to settle for using text or word processor files as attachments.

295

8 Internet file swapping

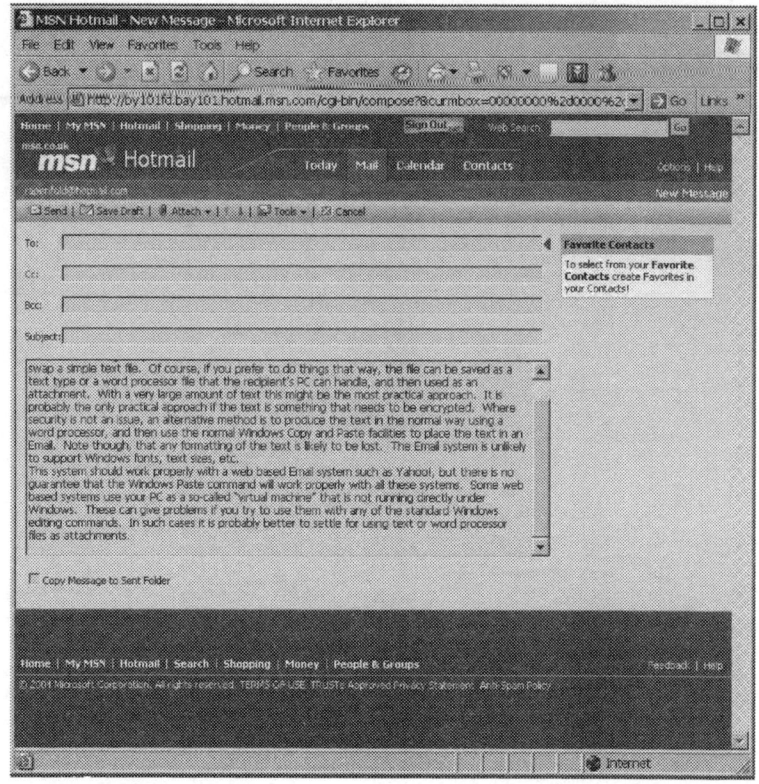

Fig.8.39 The Paste method also worked with a Hotmail Email form

As an experiment I tried copying some text into blank Email forms when using the services of Yahoo! and Hotmail. As can be seen from Figure 8.38 (Yahoo!) and Figure 8.39 (Hotmail), both accepted the "pasted" text without any problems. It is possible that some email services place a limit on the amount of text that can be sent via the body of an Email, but it seems to be possible to send several thousand words. I tried sending this chapter (about 6700 words) in the body of an Email, and it did make it through the system.

However, the received Email (Figure 8.40) demonstrates a potential problem with this system. The sending system has introduced line breaks that do not match up with the line lengths of the receiving system. Some manual editing is therefore needed in order to get the text formatted

Internet file swapping

```
Note that it is usually necessary to set the password before any files
are
placed in an archive. With WinRAR for example, you select the files in
the
normal way, but go to the Advanced section before adding them to the
archive. Operating the Set Password button produces a small window
where
the password is entered in both textboxes (Figure 8.36). It is normal
for a
password to be entered twice when it is being set. This is a simple
form of
error trapping, and the password will not be accepted unless it is the
same
in both textboxes. Having set the password, the archive is completed
in the
normal way.
When extracting files from the archive, a small pop-up window prompts
the
user to enter the password. The program proceeds in the normal fashion
provided the correct password entered. Things may seem to progress
normally
if the wrong password is used. However, at the end of the process an
error
message will be produced, and no files will have been extracted from
the
archive.
Users of Outlook and Outlook Express have a built-in encryption
facility,
but it is of no real use to most users. In order to encrypt a file,
select
Options from the Tools menu and then operate the Security tab in the
new
window that appears (Figure 8.37). Tick the top checkbox in order to
use
encryption on your Emails and any attachments. Unfortunately, this
method
is only usable if you purchase a digital certificate from a company
such as
VeriSign. The cost is not that great, but probably few private users
are
```

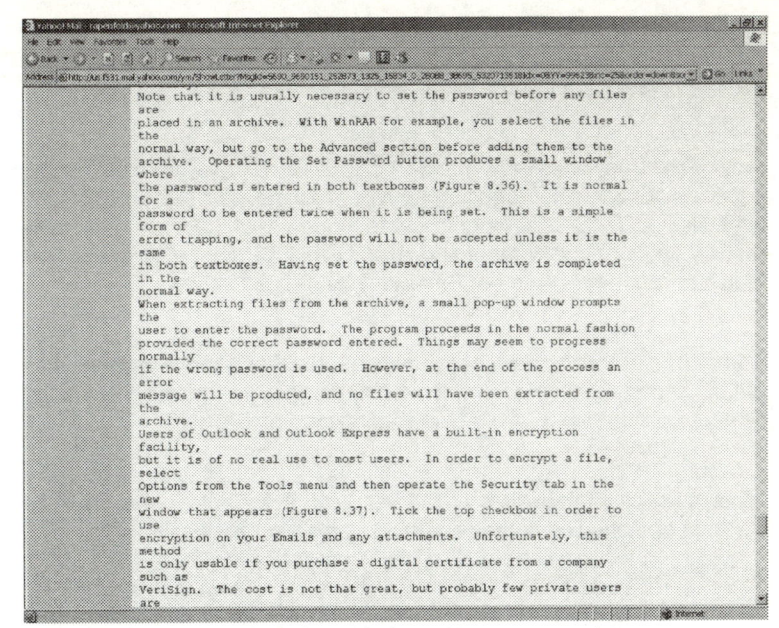

Fig.8.40 The text made it through the system, more or less

more sensibly. This method could still be worthwhile if you need to send text to someone who is unwilling to accept or open an attachment, even if it is something as basic as a text file. Some work might be required on the received text, but at least it would get through the system.

Points to remember

It is probably worthwhile obtaining some web space if you need to regularly exchange large amounts of data via the Internet. Using this method to exchange large amounts of data is not very practical unless you have some form of broadband connection at both ends of the system.

Some web space providers have their own utilities for uploading files, but it should be possible to download files in the normal way using nothing

8 Internet file swapping

more than a browser. Uploading and downloading files using an FTP program is not always supported, but is likely to be the best option where this method is permitted.

Most Email services now provide users with large inboxes having capacities of a few hundred megabytes. This makes it easier to transfer large files as Email attachments. Note though, that there are often fairly modest limits on the number and size of Email attachments. A size limit of five or ten megabytes per Email is typical.

Some Email services have security measures that remove certain types of file. In particular, any form of executable (program) file is likely to be filtered, so it is best to avoid using self-extracting archives.

When swapping image files via the web, an online photo album could be the best choice. There are web publishing sites specifically for this type of thing. In fact there seems to be an ever growing number of album sites. In most cases the albums can be for your own viewing only, for viewing by selected friends and members of your family, or by the general public.

Some album sites have additional facilities, such as simple photo-editing capabilities (cropping, filtering, red-eye reduction, etc.). These are useful if you do not have any image editing software, but it is worth obtaining a good but inexpensive photo-editing program if you produce more than the occasional digital image.

There is probably no 100 percent secure method of swapping computer files, and using the Internet is definitely not a totally secure method. It might be better to use a different method when dealing with sensitive information. At the very least, use some form of encryption or password protection when exchanging important information over the Internet.

Simple text can be sent in the body of an Email, and there should be no problem in transferring large amounts of text in this way. However, any formatting will be lost and some manual editing might be needed in order to make the received text usable.

Index

Symbols

1.2 megabytes	1
1.44 megabytes	1
10/100	65
128-bit encryption	131
2.4GHz	99
2.88 megabyte	2
3.5-inch (drive)	252
360 kilobytes	1
3Com	104
480 kilobits	12
5.25-inch drive	252
56k modem	81
5GHz	99
720 kilobytes	1
802.11a	101
802.11b	101, 129
802.11g	101, 129
802.11i	134

A

absorption	116
accelerators	117
Access	183
access point	103, 113, 124
Ad Hoc	138
ad hoc	113
adapter	105, 136
Adaptive Frequency Hopping	106
Add button	276
Add Printer Wizard	166
adding ports	67
Additional Drivers	163
address backup	198
address book	199
ADSL	81, 96, 148
Advanced mode	226
Advanced Settings	248
advertisements	283
aerial	110
AFH	106
album	283
alignment	71
allocation table	32
amps	12
anti-static packaging	73
antivirus program	88
application program	16, 183, 207
applications program	171
approval	103
archiving	274
ASCII	133
ASR	219
ATA	14, 251
Attach button	271
attachments	269, 295
audio	250
automated system	284
Automated System Recovery	218
automatic	124, 230, 263
automatic detection	257

B

backup	14, 23, 28, 203
backup copies	14
backup disc	212
backup drive	226
backup file	215, 238
Backup Progress	218
Backup Wizard	212
badge of approval	103
band	104
banner	283
bargraph	23, 138, 193
basic network	76
batch file	278
baud	44, 55
bays	251
Belkin	104
BIN	30

299

Index

BIOS 58, 209, 218, 235, 255, 256
bits 44
blanking plate 68
blind spot 107
block 18, 89, 136, 284, 297
Bluetooth 100, 104, 121
boot 218
boot discs 235
boot drive 231
bracket 69
broadband 67, 81, 261
Browse button 189
browser 155
browsers 7
bug 124
built-in security 103
Burn Compilation 33
burning 30
button 23

C

cable 5, 41, 42, 253
cable select 254
cables 68
capacity 1
card 6, 110, 194, 249
card reader 6
case sensitive 293
casing 251
CD burning 30
CD drive 13
CD Writing Wizard 28
CD-ROM 9, 252
CD-RW 13, 24
CDR disc 14
certification 103
CF 8
channel 100, 129, 254
channels 102, 106
ChgDir 265
chip 209
Classic version 46
clean installation 207
cloning 207, 251
colour depth 241, 247
COM 270
COM1 50, 57
Compact Flash 6, 188
compatibility 86, 101, 103
compatible 10
compressed 217
compression 2, 233, 269
configuration 78, 125
configuration jumper 254
configuration software 176
configuration window 262
Connection Status 127
connectors 62
Control key 18, 265
Control Panel 46, 92, 151
control program 137
cookies 183
Copy 294
Copy and Paste 22
copying files 17
copying methods 209
cropped 290
crossed cable 77
CUE 30
cursor key 60
custom cables 96
Custom size 278
customisation 207
Cut option 22
cyber crime 98

D

data 1, 14
data cable 254
data compression 2, 269
data link 261

Index

data packets	127	Drive Image	208, 230
data recovery	254	drive lead	253
deactivation	5	drive letter	11
decompress	270	drive letters	4
decryption	130	driver	208
default	191	driver installation	243
default printer	169	drivers	122, 166, 172, 229, 245
Del key	59	drop	16
delete	32	duplex	44
Delete button	267	DVD drive	13
Delete temporary files	30	DVD-RW	15, 24
deselecting	18		
desktop computer	5		
desktop PC	107		
destination drive	23		

E

Device Manager	125, 241, 250	earthed	74
diagram	255	ECP	61
dialling	54	Edit menu	17
dialup connection	84, 267	editing	290, 295
digital camera	8, 281	EIDE	252
direct cloning	251	Email	183
direct network connection	47	Email attachments	269
directional	116	Email service	268
directory	31	Email transfer	268
disable sharing	149	embedded data	175
disc	217	encryption	130, 291
disc sharing	144	EPP	61
disc space	245	error message	171, 204
disc storage	11	Esc key	59
Display Troubleshooter	247	Escape key	62
disposable wristband	74	estimate	23
DLL	270	Ethernet	41, 65
DOC format	276	Ethernet port	52, 79
Done button	35	Excel	183
download	38, 124	exceptions	91
download manager	266	EXE	270
download.com	262	Exit Setup	62
downloading	265	expansion card	110
drag and drop	16	expansion cards	71
drive	2	expansion slot	68
drive bays	251	Explorer	15
		export	200
		exposed connections	256
		extending range	115

301

Index

extension cable	5, 107
extensions	270
external CD-RW	14
external drives	11
external storage	215

F

F2	219, 235
FAT16	7
FAT32	7
faxes	85
fields	201, 263
file browser	7, 17, 276
File Splitter	278
file swapping	261
files	16, 142
Files Transfer Wizard	182
filtered	290
filtering	269
Finish button	193
firewall	88
firewall settings	135
Firewire	13, 15
firmware	123, 174
firmware upgrades	172
firmware version	138
Flash	188
Flash drives	3
Flash memory	2
floppy disc	1, 182, 217
folder	212
folders	17, 22, 142
format	7
formatted	219
free accounts	269
free web space	281
front-end	37
FTP	261
FTP program	262
full-duplex	44

G

General page	55
generic devices	104
generic hardware	123
getting connected	107
gigabytes	14
graph	138
Guest option	49
GUI	16

H

hackers	88, 98
hard disc	207
hard drives	13
hardware	123, 236
Harold Bluetooth Gormson	107
hertz	248
hidden word	284
high resolution	286
highlight	60
highlighted	17
Home Edition	211
home network	182
homepage	182, 197, 262
host	264
Host option	49
Hotmail	273
HTTP	261
hub	110

I

icon	46
IDE	251, 253
IDE channel	254
IDE controller	242
IDE drive	208
IEEE	101
image	21, 209
image editing	290
Import button	203
importing	202

inbox	268	Local File	231
InCD	26	local printer	164
incompatible	102	logging on	54
index page	264	logo	103
Infrastructure mode	114	LPT1	50
Ins key	59	LS120	252
installation	121, 136, 164		
installation CD	235, 240		

M

installation disc	187
installation instructions	122
instruction manual	124
integrated audio	242
integrated hardware	242
interface	12, 275
interference	99
Internet	85, 135, 261
Internet Explorer	182, 262
Internet sharing	81
Invert Selection	18
invisible files	225
IrDA	105
ISO	30
ISP	126

mains plug	74
manual	122, 235
manufacturer	123
mass storage	210
master	42, 106, 254
ME	4
megabits	65
megabyte	2
megabytes	65, 279
memory	2, 209
memory card	6
menu	17
microcontroller	125
microfilter	83
Microsoft Office	197
MkDir	265
mode	114
modem	55, 242
modes	61
motherboard	70, 209, 243, 256
MP3 players	6

J

Jpeg	21, 285
jumpers	254

K

key	141

L

label	217
LAN	41, 65, 231
laptop	5, 15
lead	253
left-clicking	17
licence	245
link	42, 126, 129, 181, 261
List option	21

MS-DOS	16, 45, 229, 236, 278
multi-disc	238
multiple selection	22
multisession	32
My Computer	46
My Document	212
My Network Places	143

N

name	129
naming	50, 145

Index

Nero	25	partition	219, 238
Netgear	104	passive hub	110
network	41, 98, 181	passphrase	141
Network Connections	47, 52	password	52, 126, 263
network drive	182	password protection	293
network key	141	Paste	22, 294
network name	50	PCI	68, 107, 141
Network Places	154	PCI adapter	111
network risks	88	PCI slot	242
Network Setup Wizard	146	PDF	177
networking	65	pen drive	2
New Archive	275	peripherals	42
New Computer	187	Pg Dn key	60
new connection	47	Pg Up key	60
New Connection Wizard	47	photo album	32
non-volatile	3	photo albums	281
Norton's Ghost	208	photographs	282
notebook	5, 15, 162	Photoshop	159
null-modem	44	piconet	105
numbered	238	Plain Text	200
NV memory	3	players	6

O

Old Compute	189	plug	5
omnidirectional	116	Plug and Play	4, 121
onscreen prompt	61	pop-up	28, 283
operating range	99	pop-up menu	17
operating system	7, 15, 45, 163, 166, 229	port	45
Outlook	294	port cluster	57
Outlook Express	183, 199	port settings	60
overwrite	23	portable PC	5

P

packet readers	38	ports	43, 57
packets	127	power	12
PageMaker	281	power cable	256
palmtop PC	105	power connector	252
parallel	45	power management	58
parallel port	12	power supply	68, 251
		precautions	75
		preinstalled	207, 212
		Press F2	219
		printer	80, 115, 163, 196
		printer installation	164
		printer server	80
		printer sharing	151, 161

Index

printers	5
Printers and Faxes	162
prints	282
processor	209
profiles	141
program disc	188
properties	53
Properties window	153
PS/2	67

Q

Quick Start	122

R

radio button	31
radio buttons	194
range	99, 105
RAR	270
rating	9
reactivate	258
reader	6, 36
Real Player	184
reboot	196, 222
recipient	266
reconstruct	2
reconstruction	280
Recorder menu	33
Recovery disc	222
reformat	34
Registry	204
reliability	1
Removable Disk	4, 6
Rename	286
reprogrammed	123
resolution	247, 285
resolutions	241
resources	79
Restore program	228
restored	208
restoring	217, 234
restrictions	269

rewritable	34
rewritable disc	14
right-clicking	22
risk	261
RJ-45	68
Roll Back Driver	172
router	55, 85, 126
RS232C	44
rules	136

S

Save	62
scan rate	247
scanners	5
scans	137
screen colours	182
scrollbars	286
scrolling	21
SD	8
Secure Digital	8
security	98, 121, 128, 137, 261, 269
Security Center	92
security measures	103
Select All	17, 33
selection	22
self-extracting	270
sending	271
serial port	45
serial transfer	44
server	80
service provider	126
setting up	124
settings	126, 181
Settings Only	193
Setup menu	128
Setup program	58, 257
shared resources	79
sharing	97, 142
sharing folders	149
Sharing tab	152
Shift key	17

Index

shortcut	52
Show Statistics	127
side panel	67
side panels	251
signal absorption	116
signal level	97
signal strength	97
simple file sharing	151
slave	42, 106, 254
SmartStart	37
software	43, 176
software control	12
SP2	90
speech profiles	203
speed	9, 109, 267
speed rating	9
SPP	61
standalone	125
standards	100
Start menu	146
Start Restore	228
static	73
statutory rights	104
storage device	11
storage media	210
straight cable	77
string	136
super-floppies	1
supply	12
System Properties	242
System Recovery Wizard	222
System Restore	198, 236
System Tools	184

T

table	32
tape	2
tape backup	213
telephone socket	67, 84
temporary directory	31
temporary files	30
terminals	255
text	294
text file	200
text string	136
The File Splitter	278
Thumbnails option	21
tied	209
too large	277
tower case	68
traffic light	92
transfer rate	12, 97
transfer speed	105
Transfer Wizard	182
transferring settings	181
transfers	1
Trojans	88
Troubleshooter	247
Type 1 Compact Flash	8

U

UDF reader	36
Unblock button	187
unbootable	91, 234
unreadable	34
updated drivers	137
upgrade	123, 174
upload	265
upload speed	267
US Robotics	104
USB	42, 251
USB 1.1	10
USB 2.0	10, 251
USB cable	42
USB connector	2
USB drives	12
USB hub	111
USB interface	3
USB port	5
username	52, 126

Index

V

video card	249
Video Display Troubleshooter	247
video settings	245
video system	241
View menu	21
virtual machine	295
viruses	88

W

wallpaper	183
warning message	23
watts	12
web address	125
web format	285
web host	264
web site	122, 137, 253
web space	261, 281
web-based configuration	125
web-based Email	183
Welcome screen	48
WEP	130
WEP key	132
wi-fi	95
wi-fi adapter	124
Wi-fi Alliance	103
wi-fi certification	103
wi-fi link	129
Windows	4
Windows 2000	8
Windows 95	208
Windows Backup	211
Windows Control Panel	46
Windows Explorer	15, 143
Windows ME	4, 8, 110, 187
Windows Registry	204
Windows Security Center	92
WinRAR	269
WinZip	177, 269
wired network	124
wireless adapter	107
wireless connection	96
Wireless Options	128
wizard	35, 125, 275
Word	183, 276, 292
word processor	292
workgroup	145
workload	81
WPA	132
WPA-PSK	133
wristbands	74
writing speed	34
WS_FTP LE	262

X

XP	4, 8, 25, 182, 217, 242

Y

Yahoo!	273
Yes to All	23

Z

ZIP	270
Zip	252
Zip discs	213
ZIP drives	11

Index

PRODUCT KEY –
- FOR IBM COMPUTOR

K6PGT-R96ZJ-WCQBR-38SGX-
-JT7JY